Strategies for Human Development

Contents

First Published, 2017

Published by

Kalpaz Publications
C-30, Satyawati Nagar,
Delhi – 110052
E-mail: kalpaz@hotmail.com
Ph.: 9212142040
Printed at: G. Print Process, Delhi

Cataloging in Publication Data—DK
Courtesy: D.K. Agencies (P) Ltd. <docinfo@dkagencies.com>

Deb, Samar, 1963- **author.**
    Strategies for human development / Dr Samar Deb.
    volumes cm
    Includes bibliographical references and index.
    ISBN 9789386397140 (set)
    ISBN 9789386397157 (vol. 1)

    1. Quality of life. 2. Social policy. 3. Social justice.
    4. Sustainable development.   I. Title.

HN25.D43 2017   DDC 306   23

Strategies for Human Development

Volume - 1

Dr Samar Deb

DEDICATED TO:

ALL SOCIAL THINKERS WHO HAVE BEEN
WORKING TIRELESSLY

FOR

SOCIAL RECONSTRUCTION THROUGH HUMAN
DEVELOPMENT PROCESS

Preface

Human development is an interdisciplinary subject, which requires scientific understanding regarding conditions of human living parameters worldwide and philosophic perspective for developing human beings in bringing world peace. As a matter of fact, it is expected that there are certain important strategies required for the purposive study of this global subject. Accordingly, we have analyzed five Chapters in knowing exactly – how to bring in human development world around us, for meaningful interaction between nations as well as resourceful discussion on various strategies that give birth to human understanding level, for innovating ideas in reinventing civil societies; so that world peace emanates from human foundational pyramid of civic living rights and existential freedom of life bringing possibilities. In Chapter 1, we have analyzed "Introduction to Human Development" as recourse to creative thought for developing human beings in universal manner. The approach of universality of development is strategized through nurturing of the social integrity concept, for which, Vedic values and ideals are stressfully emphasized in emancipation of human life from severe kind of social sufferings. In this Chapter, human development initiatives are narrated in sparkling manner, to arrive at environmental sustainability in restoration of social balance, and to pave the way for human civil rights as well as free existential autonomy. However, Chapter 2 deals with "Science and Technology for Human Development", wherein; global empowerment of people, irrespective of caste, creed, color, sex, nationality, religion, race, etc. has been voiced with different confidence building measures to motivate people to adjust with 'path-goal' relational approach as the scientific strategy for human living practices. In this connection, development strategy formulation with scientific temper has been assessed with human up-gradation techniques. In Chapter 3, we have discussed "Religious Perspective for Human Development", which narrates the concept of humanity through religiosity in understanding well common responsibility of religious organizations for the sake of application of religion for scientific nature of human development, in reinventing the major causes to establish world peace by way of Vedic management system. In consequence of this thought, religious paths are rediscovered for organizational work behaviour in bringing human excellence building process for global dynamism, social integrity and peaceful business relationships.

All these areas are interrelated with religious ideology for the foundation of global sustainability, in creative endeavour of human beings for empowering people through religious policies in directing civil social order with the scientific resource match techniques. Again, in Chapter 4, "Philosophical Foundation for Human Development" has been analytically discussed for the realization of development-related dynamics of human behavioural prudence. In this Chapter, anti-humanity ideals are reflected through philosophical perspective in initiating world peace in terms of justified norms of development. As a whole, common barriers for human development are analyzed in synthetic manner in strategizing human empowerment philosophy, to understand global philosophical entity, which is inherent in human excellence building process. Thus, this Chapter has been made relative towards the boon for global peace in interrelating issues of human upliftment conditions with the Vedic thought provoking ideals in scientific approach. Lastly, Chapter 5 has been considered to discuss "International Cooperative Environment for Human Development", where to international regulatory mechanism depicts the process for cooperative human development as the challenge of change. Further, this Chapter briefly provides the way of human development effectiveness in terms of environmental scanning and innovative guidelines for environmental match, in rejuvenating social justice and equity as instruments of human cooperative business undertaking as well as world trade relationships. It is suggested through this Chapter that integrated process of human development will reflect cooperative endeavours towards reaching at world peace, by way of social transformation. To arrive at transcendental social order, Vedic work philosophy has been narrated in vibrated manner through environmental reformative paths, in which, human cooperation has been found as the exposit requirement for increasing international understanding towards bringing human unity, social integrity and worldwide effectiveness in carrying out people to the enlightenment of civil living goal. Thus, balanced measures for environmental control mechanism are denoted by means of human cooperative behavioural prudence, and adequate policy resolutions in this area. As a whole, this Chapter illuminates the picture of universal peace by way of discussing international brotherhood concept in scientific nature, and thereby, integrated approach of human development potentials has been revisited for attaining objectives of human civic living foundational structure.

In concluding about human development, it is highly noteworthy to mention that the strategies which are propounded for making guidelines regarding human existential freedom of living pursuits, have been analyzed in relativity concept of 'path-goal' initiatives, for the innovative reformations and creative human foundations to attain the objective of world peace, by way of cementing human organizational relationships, group behavioural pro-foundation and civil living possibilities with the scientific temper of thought.

In a nutshell, it is expected that this volume will guide to policy-makers and social thinkers, besides those who have been working tirelessly for the pious cause of human development purposes for long in unstinted and painstaking manner. Moreover, students of management, social sciences, and also professionals and administrators from varied fields, social architects, and all those who have been dedicating to the social cause of humanization, in order to attain scientific solutions of human fundamental problems of life bringing conceptualities will be benefitted from these new innovative techniques of thought provoking work. It is, therefore, humbly submitted that this volume will be immensely helpful for social re-engineering process in bringing world peace.

Dr Samar Deb

Chapter 1

Introduction to Human Development

Understanding Human Development

Human Development is an inter-disciplinary subject in modern time. It concerns sociology, social anthropology, economics, public administration, political science and many other subjects studied under the disciplines, like – humanities, and other branches of social sciences. The world order has been changing fast, and so, importance of human development in every facets of human civilization[1] has been reflected towards bringing adequate social change in positive direction. It is because of the fact that, enormous growth rate of world population created by abnormal crisis situation consistently have endowed with conflicting nature of restlessness in societal parameters[2], in which modern sovereign governments are working with stressful conditions, have been supplemented for initiating social responsibilities, on the part of respective elected governments, public body corporate and private agencies. In this way, it is observed that human beings who are suffering a lot due to social crises could be well managed for enlarging benefits in demographic potential of the democratic demand for ameliorating conditions of mankind. This is the reason, for which modern administrative thinkers and social experts are in a perplex situation to resolve adequate policies for initiating social change in environmental sustenance, governance efficiency and social balance restoration; otherwise, there will come emergent situation in this world of living which would be out of hands of the global administrators to control effectively in coming future. After observing all such pertinent issues, it is expected that human development paradigms of social changing reasons are to be analyzed in encountering problems of mankind, and giving thereby solutions – how to resolve disputes between nation-states in regard to initiate social peace and global tranquil atmosphere. To substantiate this view, it is expected that framework of policy issues concerning human development could be well addressed for liberal business practices and efficient nature of human economic activities, rendered towards bringing adequate level of social change in terms of globalizing industrial and trading sectors, which would ultimately lead to the path of social peace in the overall world order of the historical background of human civilization.

From the past incidences, it is scientifically observed that due to lack of human indignation, social crisis for relevant nature of subsistence and global distressful situations are all together playing dominant role in areas of human living with free social environment. Consequently, the world agencies which are concerned about social transparent rolling for global balance and administrative liberal practices for initiating social change in positive direction, have enlarged responsibilities in making plans and programmes to implement ideas of human integrated development initiatives[3], which would be viable for advancing human life to illuminate social picture on the screen of global environment. In this matter, empirical researches are carried on for rectifying social situations in which people have been living in pathetic conditions, for surviving civic life from all sorts of benefits like, education, health-care activities, transportation and electricity services, infrastructural development, besides their basic necessities of life bringing elements. However, the followed path has yet to be made more and more strengthened for the purpose of initiating social growth potentialities in realistic nature, and development of people in right direction[4] to accumulate human progress by way of supplying all the necessities, comforts and luxuries of happy and peaceful living ideals. Here comes actual requirement of the study on strategic human development purposes, which has become an international challenge as well as national issue for respective democratic governments. These obligatory functions are studied under the subject public administration, to which liberalism, equity and justice principles are voiced from time-to-time. In working with modern tools and techniques of governance model, there comes naturally question in mind of judicious people and experts – what is the nature of human development should be undertaken for social transformation, global balance restoration and managerial communication system for encouraging the synergistic path, in attaining peaceful social environment through scientific temper of resources match between different regions of the world. In reply to all such pertinent problems, we have dealt with the ancient Vedic techniques in this volume[5]; so that modern world is enlightened through scientific discoveries and man-made inventions to search for real avenues in this era of liberalization, privatization and globalization (LPG).

Keeping in mind all such complexities and justified reasons, some strategies are analyzed in Chapters ahead to pave the way for human economic behaviour, commercial relationships and industrial activities, pertaining to human up-gradation, social transformation and for liberal practices of living existentialism; which go to make human life easy, simple and straight forward in marching for peaceful goal of human civilization for survival, stability and vitality of life bringing order. To connote such principles, the Vedanta order of the thought: "Vasudhaiva Kutumbakam" has been enshrined in ancient times, which are immensely reflected in the Hindu scriptural order as well as the Sanatana practices of life in ancient Bharat Bhumi, that can be followed for scientific nature of human development and systematizing social growth potentials in economic order of managing things and business activities. The potential role of the Vedas are therefore the foundation stone of the progressive path of modern civilization, which can be well tested, verified and experimented for the sake of human up-gradation, social transformation and transcendental global order[6]. As and when, we will be interested to resolve such policies for modern organizational planning purposes; the social imbalances would also be rectified by means of integrated human development approaches, in confining tasks and responsibilities towards dynamic nature of social change. It is therefore suggested that the techniques of equanimity and nature of equipoise thinking should be followed by modern corporate entities in their work culture, to find-out means and ways for solving human poverty from the present order of the world environment. Ifs and buts are to be eradicated from the part of implementing agencies, to correlate functions of the organizational constituencies, so as to get exact result by means of scientific experimentation while implementing schemes of social development, for the purpose of initiating human integrated approach of leading role. It thus, becomes clear that an understanding on the part of all kinds of experts will require free decision-making capacities for eradicating social poverty as the challenge of modern societies. So, it comes true about the fact of human development process, that modern world has to follow the path of equanimity[7], for the greater interest of human welfare, in which ingrained natural elements of human behavioural prudence for considering economic backgrounds as the basic reason for social imbalances. This is the vibrating cause of human development perspective, to nurture social growth, transform global society and re-orient the life-style of mankind to station themselves in the path of actual realization, on the basics of public administration and social psychological clinical experimentation of human activities, for the greater advantage of mankind in missionary way of dealing with the things, for organizational effectiveness in time and space.

To uproot the case of human development, it is permeably to be noted that social backwardness in mankind has been like a severe disease, which the modern thinkers are observing for its in-depth study to know the fundamental causes behind it. From empirical research findings, it has come now, clearly that the picture of human deprivation has been continued shamefully, and is also reflected in mass media as well as electronic print media as the subject of theoretical debates and discussions, so far made for analyzing human demographic situations, social imbalances. One most important conclusion drawn out of all these discussions that the fundamental reasons, among which politics and educational backgrounds play dominant role in the mystery of human underdevelopment as well as social backwardness. Due to some political advantages taken out of the social environment, in which people are kept ignorant about educational facilities, and also thereby created social consciousness about camouflaging governance activities, by dint of non-performance of the elected government from time-to-time. It is rather reflected in mischievous form to widespread chief popularity, to get people in confusing stage of information and knowledge regarding realistic consequences of, in making them concerned about the corrupt leaders. They use ignorance of humankind by keeping themselves in darkness, and take opportunities in vote banking system of winning by unfair means in the name of castes, secularism, which they provoke unnecessarily for their personal benefit in corruptive means of propagating their own self made explanatory ideas about people's development agenda. So, the society has been ruined day-by-day and years-after-years by cheating people to capture their democratic voting rights by means of bribes, money laundering, and distribution of cash in times of voting periods. Many other unfair activities have cropped up as the social burden, which ultimately degrades people in societal structure to make themselves in coming out successfully to the path of progress. Again, our leaders are sometimes remaining busy in deciding about subsidy norms and announcing for some kind of packages before election, which have altogether paralyzed the present society in making effective development. All these are consequent advantage of social corruption by net-working of the overall system of management in nexus between politicians, bureaucrats, business and corporate houses, legal machinery and other segments of social forces. Besides, the ultra-modern concept of terrorism in the name of jihad and underdevelopment are all to be taken into consideration for resolving an understanding about the realities in development programmes. Accordingly, there should be think-tank group in every society, and in every political system as well as governance procedure consisting of people who are having sacrificing mentality, should concern about the twenty-first century periods of human poverty and backwardness. Similarly, it is observed that some social groups are also fighting out a lot to come-out of these vicious and severe problems. They have been working day-and-night in silence mode to protect the society from the catastrophic destruction, to which the modern governments are to be very much conscious about involving those people from various facets of social life, to participate in the system of democratic nature of dealing with the liberal concept of human development paradigms. Their decisions could be taken as the agenda for improving onslaught of suffered human beings. Again, it is essential that these groups of people should be apolitical, who are to be involved in the planning process of deciding things for making strategic partnership with the modern body corporate, government agencies and, thereby activities of human development programmes are to be carried through liberal policy initiatives, with a view to guide entire social fabric. People from all fields having expertise like – religion, politics, economics, sociology, law, psychology and all other branches of social science, humanities, technology and, legal and natural science practices are to be involved in initiating discussion on development paradigms for social change mechanism. In this way of thinking about the process of dynamics of development model, it will become highly scientific for forecasting things where decision variables are to be concentrated for selecting right path in making policies for adequate level of social change, by way of dealing with practical problems of human social life, based on realities of management. To perpetuate this idea, development strategies are to be reformulated by means of flexible decision-making approach[8] for due delivery of the policies in practice, in terms of scientific implementation of programmes for creating innovative nature of social change through actual development of human beings, who are otherwise remaining in distressful conditions without getting adequate facilities from the elected government and body corporate.

From the above discussions, it is worthwhile to note that human development requires positive mindset on the part of planners, who run the system and also, on the part of implementing agencies for their responding nature of role model in realizing things, by way of adequate delivery mechanism in time-bound fixation of responsibility for the purpose of attaining result in effectuating things, and thus; empowerment of people should be made for initiating social change in proactive manner, to which radical adjustment of situations for undertaking responsibility in delivery system could also be made flexible. This is the backdrop of understanding human development strategies for dealing with things in equity, fraternity and honesty. Liberal practices of socio-economic behaviour have to be made efficient towards attaining social equilibrium tendencies, by means of mitigating human needs in time and space, for making dynamic nature of human development initiatives[9], to uproot social value system, organizational abilities and good governance ethics of social building norms. It is therefore, pertinently essential that social resources are to be exploited in diversified means for "input-output" relationship, in dealing with human crises, social imbalances and world-wide gaps between haves and have-nots. To verify all such possibilities, strategies of the Vedic concept of equanimity principles are to be adopted in organizational policy-making issues, governmental decision-making affairs and legal justice for establishment of guidelines, giving thereby a scope for universal idea of the programme implementation opportunities, for solving social problems and human poverty at an speedy rate to bring in human welfare with the realistic norms of growth potentials. Thus, human development should be understood from holistic perspective, so as to correlate practical problems of human beings with the social changing norms and techniques. Considering such kind of strategy, it would lead to the goal of global peace, social stability and human cooperation in international level; for the purpose of realizing overall spectrum of life process in transcendental order. Hence, it is expected to deal with all such issues of human development agenda to the dynamics of social balance[10] restoration, under the Chapters narrated for this pious purpose in vibrated and sparkling manner. In concluding about the human development concept in an absolute principle, it is said that development is a dynamic concept of social continuity, for which we require pragmatic approach in initiating social responsibility, on the part of modern sovereign governments; who run the machinery of the state authority as the powerful agency. It is therefore essential to note that human development should be perpetuated in existential form with the diversity of addressing issues contained under it, and solving problems of modern societies for global peace initiation.

Human Development for Global Change

Human development is the alternative solution for making global level change in the style of living in human beings. Today, there are conflicting situations found in the world environment, for which, necessary elements of surviving like – educational facilities, health-care activities, infrastructural amenities of life bringing sources for better living, healthy going and peaceful sustaining of mankind and their living potentials have been observed as the instrumental weapon for reforming the pattern of the present problems of the global atmosphere[11]. In this context, it is undoubtedly to be mentioned that many countries – developing, developed and underdeveloped nations are now facing problems of human needs required for right way of leading life processes. Consequently, there have been tremendous conflicting situations arising out of such crying need of the world societies. It is therefore, my dare note to the world sovereign governments, irrespective of socialist, communist and capitalist, and also democratic, military nations that they should concentrate for civic living elements of their respective national goal, for increasing facilities in regard to their citizens with a view to enlarge ideas of motivating work culture and enlighten thereby to their national entities' cause for rejuvenating educational path; so as to attain the goal of human survival in peaceful manner. To perpetuate such objective, it requires that the leaders in the national framework should have a mind to serve people with all kinds of facilities required to optimizing life order in new dimensional way, by means of participating in the decision-making process, and involving people to join hands for the reconstruction of national entities. Thus, it becomes clear that global change in positive direction should be made through democratic nature of delivery system for its relevancy with that of human development perspective, in undertaking for responsibility on the part of national governments in this century. Accordingly, all kinds of governments throughout the world should come-out to deal with the common agenda for human development dimensions, in increasing human efficiency, speeding social rolling in cohesive nature of dealing with the problems of people and encouraging people to participate in respective nation building activities, by way of liberal practices of business and socio-economic activities for all-round social prosperity, human free existential autonomy and maintenance of global peace and tranquil order. In confining tasks to organizational system of efficient management, leadership will force should be enlarged for motivating people by way of effective coordination as well as trustworthy cooperation between people and various social groups, which will help in proactive nature of social change in terms of poverty alleviation programmes, educational and literacy mission, health-care schemes for vital life bringing; and besides, there should also be universal approach of human socialization process by way of good governance paradigms for increasing social balance[12], global transformation and human integrated approach of development objectives. In this way, efficiency and effectiveness for flexible nature of social change should be incorporated for practical solution of human burning problems of leading life in happy as well as peaceful manner.

From all such explanations, we would like to cite examples of social restlessness like – law and order situations and failure of the respective governments, failure of administrative justice for restoration of social equity in living objective, world-wide conflicts in the name of jihad, militancy activities, and castes related conflicts undertaken through political compulsion, religions related issues concerning people and governments to de-motivating nature of social disputes and discrepancies, and also many other issues having political nexus for corrupt human behavioural situations could well be addressed through right dimensional studies on human development vision, for which global unity, human integrity and social diversity would be balanced in terms of efficient delivery mechanism, to reduce human poverty, social distressful conditions and regional imbalances. It is my suggestion therefore, that integral nature of humanism should find place in all operational fields for initiating human development purposes, to move the society in right direction by way of environmental sustainable means of national progress as well as international prosperity. Thus, adequate amount of change will come forward with the specific nature of job concerning human upliftment agenda, in these days of crying social need for advancing life-style of deprived population. If this is to be accumulated in society, it should be resolved through government policy initiatives for the purpose of attainment of the task, with the framework of good governance guidelines and justice and equity principles, related to delivery mechanism in every facets of organizational activities, administrative system of management, and building-up of human competencies through training facilities and skill building provisions. All these are to be made vibrant for changing life-style of mankind; so that people feel for sacrificing with the self will for providing services towards minimizing social problems and human disguised situations. As a whole, integral concept of humanity should be incorporated in corporate human responsibility and accountability chapter, for dealing with social crisis and human poverty related issues, which are fundamental tasks for re-orienting the world order[13] in making dynamic change through initiating nature of human upliftment programmes. It is therefore, suggested that universal education to rectify severe problems in modern days society would be enriched, by making law and implementing goal of the government programmes in time-bound schedules, managing targets and fulfilling quotas for measurable kind of development scope and opportunities. In doing so, leadership strategies are to be remodeled through the Vedic work culture concept of human development issues. In Vedic age, it was prevalent that liberation of mankind should be made as compulsory by way of human emancipation from darkness. Thus, modern governance policy should adopt rules for people's enlightening programme, to make compulsory education for all citizens' emancipation. This order of making good to the society will lead to the path of positive social change, which requires reformation on the part of modern governments. Accordingly, global level cooperation should be required by government agencies to unify social problems – the UNO as the nodal implementing agency of different social oriented programmes and human upliftment packages should follow up strict rules, and will also give some adequate guidelines as the measure for social welfare and, to the maximization of benefit for the deprived classes, for their emancipation from the pathetic stage of uncivilized living norms, as found over the world at large.

In correlating issues of human development for the purpose of building nations of the world, there is the urgent need of increasing responsibility towards social orientation through changing technology of the time, for which responding nature of job should be performed to eliminate corrupt administrative system, and to replace government policies by keeping human resource accounting system in job performance; so that each human being is made conscious about social development goal, for making policies and implementing practices with the kind of service oriented system, backed by the philosophical nature of sacrifice. Because, it is human sacrifice can only help in making relevant changes to the social orientation process, without which only corrupt practices will ruin this civilization of human beings and, at the same time, environmental stressors will be increasing day-by-day and years-after-years in coming future. To rectify all such mismatches, participation and involvement of people in nation building activities would relate to strengthen organizational guiding forces, in terms of delivery mechanism; especially, in areas of social basic needs of human up-gradation through managerial effective dealing, to establish human relationship, group coordination and social prosperity. In coagulation of these circumstances, modern policies regarding human developmental norms are requiring continuous nature of planning for utilization of the resources of the environment, for the sake of profitable as well as beneficial employment and diversification of activities; which go to enlarge ideas in making positive social change by way of human motivational programmes and clinical counselling, to effectuate global transformation and bringing in adequate level of change in increasing standard of life for all kinds of population[14], who are always deprived from means and against opportunities to develop their self. This is the simple technique of right kind of social change should be inculcated through 'teaching-learning' philosophy of management, for which, organizational transformational leadership will find its place in the cooperative way of dealing with trusteeship principles that the Vedanta advocates for measuring human performance goal. As and when objective guidelines are to be framed taking importance of our civilization rolling towards right direction, there will come global change in proactive nature to encourage people for shouldering responsibility in initiating social change through qualitative performance model, quantitative techniques of productivity rationality and optimum level of welfare in each modern society, to establish relativity between 'input-output cost' for the greater interest of human progress, social diversity in strengthening resources mobilization and transparent behavioural prudence on the part of each organizational entity, for result-oriented growth and respective social change. It is therefore human empowerment must be taken care of, for balancing our environment sustainable impact on human happy and peaceful living goal, to idealization of the purpose of managerial tasks by means of proper administrative guidelines and objectives. To simplify this practice, scientific temper of social building notion should be caused for making resultant social change in all means of productive journey in life of human solvency, social stability and vitality towards the changing techniques of the harmonized world environmental scanning through organizational coordinated approach for leading with change mechanism. The systematic effort so suggested to be made for enrichment of human life in nurturing the world environment, for the preservation purpose of our natural habitation and ecological balance maintenance with a view to understand the nature of scientific envisagement process. Here lies the importance of utilizing resources for capacity building and skillful application of organizational tasks and managerial responsibilities, for communicating things in regard to right movement of social wheel; so that all organizations will be able to find freedom for working with zeal and maximum opportunities. These are necessarily to be observed and implemented by means of free operational system, where corruption should be totally stopped for bringing radical social change[15] in realization of human welfare goal, with the maximum social advantage norms for efficient transactional dealings and effective organizational matching mechanism.

After assessing the above noted facts, it is observed that the whole world, as it is coined as "global village" should be followed this theoretical assumption, based on the Vedic principle of unified human rolling goal for forwarding people in progressive way, to the path of salvation of life as the process of relevant nature of global change in human perfectionism, organizational balance theory for human integrated performance goal and the world-wide change for socialization objective of managerial role model practices. In doing so effectively, leadership theories as advocated in the Hindu scriptural order like – (i) optimization of welfare through natural balance; (ii) strengthening human civilization by means of cooperative group effort; (iii) transparency in leading and directing by value-based practices and sacrificial nature of job performances; (iv) unity and integrity between mankind and the other aspects of the social pyramid like – animal kingdom, plant life and overall emergent elements of the natural balance subsistence procedural mechanism; (v) all kinds of ecological-environmental forces of the nature like – rivers, seas, oceans, forests, hills, mountains; and besides, Plautus and Himalayan ranges which are prima facie relevant to human civilization balance restoration and preservation of precious life of mankind and animals. Under all circumstances, we should conserve natural habitation process for harmonious living, transparent moving and tranquil feeling of mind to set free our great environment, to help to manage ourselves with certain kind of visionary goal of life. Here, all should be treated equally, irrespective of any kind of discrimination, so as to keep our environment clean from social hazards[16]. Another factor important for changing global society in right dimensional way is the serious call of the jihad groups, terrorists and various kind of nexus between political groups with these social destructive forces, are all to be considered with due attention for managing social peace world-wide; which has positive impact in transforming the world scenario. At present, throughout the world there is severe threat on the part of sovereign governments given from time-to-time and going against safety and security of people, which has bad repercussion on the overall social structure; because, citizens are de-motivated by such provocative remarks and activities. These are very much detrimental reasons against adequate development of people, and therefore, there should be global level forum or plate-form to remedy such aspect of social imbalances; so that correct mode of managing things will lead to the process of restoration of global peace and tranquility, by means of equanimity thinking to preserve social entity through development related issues and implementing right packages, for solving problems of life to the world mankind. In this way, equipoise nature of doing for eliminating social crises would streamline social balance and reduce regional imbalances, and the consequence of all such organized nature of activities and group efforts would lead to human civilization to the path of global integrity, human unity in action oriented concept of social upliftment programmes, and also equity in living parameters will come to safeguard the whole pattern of scientific moving of civilization, diversified and cohesive social rolling and transcendental order of establishment for human free living existentialism.

In concluding about global change, it is worthwhile to note that scientists are now awakening people by means of their alarming call for global warming, which is a great challenge in front of global community, and it should be remedied by matching environmental resources for efficient utilization in production purpose; as and when it is observed that everywhere in the world there has been rampant corruption in utilizing and exploitation of natural resources for the purpose of speedy production activities, large market oriented demand and supply chain management system, and pertinently, gigantic character of organization operational entity without caring about our precious environment. In this field, legal instruments are to be made more flexible for implementing strict rules in regard to safeguard of our whole environment in holistic approach. The bad impacts of global warning as have been given by scientists are found to create problems of severe and sudden flood as well as natural calamities, cloud blast in Himalayan ranges causing for environmental destructive incidences which are making modern governments perplexed in managing all such natural devastations. These are highly reciprocating due to imbalances caused by unnecessary and unscientific exploitation of our natural resources, which should be curbed; if the humanity as a whole has to be preserved by means of right kind[17] of natural habitation and rational productive norms. It is therefore suggested that the Preksha meditation is one such policy should relate to such irrelevant things and issues, to contain positive result on environmental safeguard for balanced nature of human development paradigms. Hence, scientific temper of managerial guidance could well be adjusted with integral organizational functioning for the purpose of human competencies, organizational credibility and social creativity. All these are to be attributed in Chapters ahead for analyzing various postulates of socio-economic growth and human progress, in directive and transformational leadership initiatives as expected to deal with the relevant issues. It is highly important now, to change global order by means of effective and proactive management goal, so as to make our Earth tolerable for human potential development by way of supplying more and more ingredients for producing in correct industrialization purposes, and maintaining sustainable order for free living objective of mankind. This is the Vedic thought for scientific global change mechanism, in order to develop mankind for world-wide unity, integrity and social transparency to establish peace in diversified way of living.

Human Development in Making Environmental Sustainability

Clean environment is essential for peaceful human life that needs sustainable nature of utilization of material resources, which are exploited for speedy industrialization and productive purposes in this age of population explosion over the world at large. So, it is very much important to match a real balance between 'input-output' harmonization, for the purpose of effective development of human beings. When there will be balanced development of the society, our environmental pressure in sustainable way of living will be minimized by means of rationality in industrial productivity. Hence, it is immensely important to frame environmental policies for the efficient utilization of natural resources, which will require scientific scanning on environmental sustenance, social dynamism and world-wide transparency in cocoordinating human socio-economic activities, for effective organizational task analysis, government objectives in implementing rules and practices for nurturing overall environmental structure, and to the establishment of ecological balance with a view to preserve precious characteristic attributes of human civilization foundation. In this way of looking, it is observed that human development, if made in challenging manner to the right directional path can lead to progressive goal of global society[18], to increasing social welfare with the right kind of managerial guidance and correct administrative order of dealing with the issues of environmental sustainability, in terms of human creativity and skill building approaches to systematize organizational activities, for the purpose of optimum nature of human upliftment from the pathetic stage of the present inhuman conditions of living scenario. Thus, there should be holistic approach while organizational tasks are related to strengthen human capacity building, so as to attain the goal of human rolling towards unifying process of advancement in forward looking tendencies, with the tools and techniques of industrialization mission as well as global level transformational vision for attaining sustainable environmental creativity, with the kind of required leadership and communication process for increasing human betterment to rejuvenate social dynamicity as well as organizational innovative competencies. From this standpoint, it is permeably to be noted that human potential development commensurate with the ideas of initiating responsibility on the part of both modern organizational constituencies and administrative crises handling mechanisms, are required adequate policy framework, to build-up infrastructural facilities like – road transportation, railway net-work of communication system, rail-road coordination in connecting people of backward areas and zones, electricity facilities, provisions for water supply for the purpose of urban-rural demographic match between people in the way of better living; and besides, there are some other conditions for healthy living practices to be provided by creating amenities of health and educational facilities for poor as well as deprived people, sanitation facilities for those having no such means at home and in schools, colleges, etc. Further, it is also important to realize that standard of living is guided by the facilities of modern survival benefits like – marketing and distribution facilities, creation of financial bodies and institutions, banking industries, insurance companies for the purpose of financial solvency, transparency and efficiency in conducting all kinds of commercial and trading activities, social safety and security measures in terms of equitable and judicious management of police administrative functions, village level agricultural reformative measures like – supply of quality seeds, pesticides and manures for agricultural productivity increase, tools and implements for carrying out harvesting jobs, electricity and water supply to agricultural fields in time, and many other facilities in the form of land reformative activities, agricultural credit services to free our poor and small agriculturists from the clutches of village money lenders, who charges exorbitant rate of interest which the farmers are unable to pay due to higher production cost and lower rate of income (return on investment), equitable price mechanism for strengthening poor and marginal village agriculturists, etc. have positive impact on supplying goods to the society at reasonable time, in administered prices; which go to handle corruptive means of organizing business activities, against black-marketing and hoarding by big entrepreneurs and corporate houses. All these are to be attributed by means of human equity in living parameters for the sake of balanced environmental subsistence, that have positive repercussions in increasing potential nature of human growth with the adequate level of developmental programmes, for greater efficiency of organizational activities in strengthening socio-economic base of the weak social structure and demographic diversification, in terms of scientific work relationship as well as human up-gradation from miserable conditions, to chalk-out the plan for total human quality (THQ) enhancement in time and space.

When the quality of life[19] in societal fabric of survival will come to increase human potential nature of working with the principles of environmental balance, there would be possibilities for emancipation of mankind from severe stages of social backwardness, and consequently, human consciousness for optimizing environmental scanning system will control things for profitable as well as sustainable nature of global transformation in dynamic way. To incorporate such policy in organizational social growing tendencies, adequate training facilities are to be provided for making provisions in healthy environmental relationship, towards bringing people to realize for the necessity of environmental creativity, organizational transformation and innovative leadership guidance. However, it is suggested for correlating development planned approach to that of increasing socialization, in terms of humanization of organizational programmed way of decision-making as well as government initiatives for implementing policies pertaining to environmental nurturing mechanism, by way of curbing pollution in land, water and air to strengthen supply-chain management system through human competencies, organizational efficient utilization of resources required for production purposes, and social existential free environment in regard to increasing ecological balance as well as reinforcing checks against all kinds of man-made disasters and lapses, to eliminate human unjust and corruptive behaviour in distressing environmental situational adjustments. Therefore, making of environmental sustainability requires consciousness on the part of civil society, non-government organizations (NGOs), legal experts, social thinkers, good political thinkers and leaders of industries, etc. Thus, entrepreneurial excellence building will help in the process of preserving good condition for work environment, natural habitation tools and techniques by way of reducing emission in air with the help of maintaining industrial hygienic conditions, minimizing toxic effluents in land and water, harmonizing a system of autonomous character of waste recycle by means of utilization of degradation and waste materials to create new bye-products and so on, for the sake of transparent human behavioural prudence. Another way of looking about problems of environmental safeguard is to plant more and more trees, by means of a forestation policy resolutions and programme implementation in time-bound schedules for taking measures against solution of burning problems of deforestation, social erosion, flood, earth-quake, etc. All these are required technological innovation and scientific investigation for healthy social survival and environmental subsistence. Accordingly, it is further to be noted that global level consortium should be established for increasing good health of the overall environmental richness[20], in matching through entrepreneurial abilities with that of environmental degradation and required tendencies of quality production, for efficient coordination purposes. Hence, the developing, underdeveloped and developed nations are to be made more responsible oriented towards confining things of production for effective human development purposes, to illuminate global environment in sparkling nature to the societal screen, the flesh of light should reflect for motivating people to free the entire environment from the clutches of human corruptive behaviour, and nurture of social pyramid in strengthening human life for inculcating habit of free living, along with reducing social poverty by means of establishment of social balance in between different backward regions of the world order. This is the most important part of socio-economic growth will be made possible through eliminating all kinds of social hazards, by increasing managerial effectiveness to organizational working strategies in conjoining humanitarian aspects to that of social transparency, human upliftment from pathetic nature of living qualities and social rolling towards solvency of human life in indiscriminating way. This can be done by harnessing environmental situational changing mechanism, to embrace issues of human upliftment, social cohesive dynamism for equitable nature of livelihood among man, animal and plant life.

The Vedanta version of equipoise nature[21] of organizational performance behaviour can help to lead to the path of social balance, in advancing people towards confining modern organizational tasks and activities for attaining goal of integral humanity by means of relativity between work and welfare concept. In this regard, the Vedic thought for working with welfare condition is imposed in character of human knowledge about bondage and freedom for liberation. It is here suggested by scriptural order of directions given in the Hindu philosophic order of life-cycle process. The notion had been reflected in scriptures by the Rishis, Sages and Seers long back in ancient 'Bharat'. It is therefore, said that the work which is the cause of bondage, the same work can also be a cause for human freedom for liberation. This technique is called as 'disinterested way of working'. When there will be knowledge about this process of work motivation, people will learn for increasing real social welfare by means of optimum sacrifice for working in the greater interest of whole mankind. The fruitlessness and disciplined nature of work will provide actual result in making people uplifted for progressive development of life order, along with safeguarding the whole environment. Such type of holistic approach is the sustainable concept of environmental balance – the 'Vasudhaiva Kutumbakam' ideology ingrained in such philosophic order of doing things[22] for the purpose of global balance restoration. Hence, we would also like to suggest for its implementation in practice by following 'triguna techniques' narrated in the scriptural order of the Vedic values of work culture. In the triguna concept – sattva, rajas and tamas, there are philosophical explanations made scientifically for environmental balance as well as sustainable character for transforming human life bringing process, by way of motivating people for understanding technology behind such kind of science that leads to the path of human salvation in life for overcoming problems of the gunas by means of working with the philosophy of human disinterestedness, in getting fuller realization of life process. In accordance with this principle, organizational leadership should be working for the purpose of objective environmental balance. The techniques of its effective role model will encourage people to sacrifice for the greater interest of mankind for their common welfare, and thus; people will realize – how to free life, even involved in work and gaining maximum satisfaction by optimizing social welfare for human integrated nature of development. In this order of working with the organizational value system, managerial ethical guidelines and philosophical principles for matching resources, environment beauty, human truth for growing with realities and social goodness will commensurate forever.

In modern times, scientists are experimenting things for unifying forces of the environment. This sort of unification is concealed in human core idea of life, where it should be observed that coordination is the real principle of natural association; in which attributes of evolutionary tendencies merged for mingling nature of molding character of life with integrity – this is the magnified nature of environmental subsistence engineered in social sustainability, for encouraging human integrity towards social transformation and global balance restoration. Such concept of social engineering philosophy in managerial destiny of coordinating things can help in rebuilding social fabric with the kind of transparent social behaviour, enumerated and incorporated in the Vedic nature of universal ideology for human development with environmental dynamism, and now; at this moment, we would like to rejuvenate this type of systematic and synergistic approach in our 'path-goal relativity' between human development and environmental sustainability for the greater cause of preserving the entire humanity[23], along with environmental dynamic rolling for welfare of mankind. In regulating such principles, there is the necessity of environmental balance can be restored by organizational work culture and human consciousness for increasing global peace, with the kind of discriminative policy resolution that should be entangled with leadership innovative character of dealing with the conditions of socio-economic behaviour, where there is enormous crises would supplement human integrated nature of social transformation with the infrastructural development facilities, needed for social emancipation in enlarging tasks for renovated way of establishment for human skill building operational ideas, narrated through modern concept of integral human subsistence conditions backed by the policy of total human quality enhancement and organizational creativity. Thus, human development as the core idea of social rolling should require modern amenities and creating provisions for providing all the facilities required in healthy socialization process. Consequently, scientific approach of dealing with the norms of skill building operations would be stimulated to produce goods and provide services for the greater interest of mankind, in re-engineering social reconstructive path for human up-gradation, social balance measures in initiating global transparency and peaceful living environment for whole mankind. To sustain, create and nurture environmental subsistence, it is highly important to measure performances of organizational guiding techniques in changing social diversification norms for equitable human upliftment process, and narrating principles thereto for the purposive cause of social transparency in balancing human working relationship to that of progressive development[24], to which reinforcing of the systematic supplemental production goal must commensurate human growth initiative process for social transformation; where humankind should be given ample opportunities for growing with the nature of free environmental dynamism.

In concluding about the fact of developmental strategy to occupy importance in managerial effective guidance, there is the tendency for organizational active cooperation should be built in human growing demand for analyzing entrepreneurial abilities, to measure-up organizational techniques of sound coordination, which has to be incorporated in managerial foundation for enterprising goal of modern social rolling, confining tasks for qualitative nature of social development perspective. To emulate this principle in work theory of organizational changing mechanism, we must realize that there is the optimum need for human solvency in life bringing potential, so as to make environmental balancing idea of scientific scanning in resourceful means, to lead the goal of human up-gradation, social transformation and global level dynamism. Thus, human development guided by the philosophy of social progress will reflect environmental sustainable balance through human capacity building, by means of organizational training facilities to be provided for human competencies, social up-gradation and global nature of innovative practice in dealing with incorporated ideas for increasing organizational value system contained in productive elements. It is therefore, free environmental atmosphere requiring leadership guidance in organizational control mechanism to utilize resources in beneficial exploitative tendencies, to reciprocate goal of integral humanity in relation to social balance restoration for the purpose of organizational creativity, human integrity and social dynamicity in cohesive approach for global environmental sustainable means of operational ideas. To formulate this principle in work-related ideologies of organizational guiding mechanism, there is the need for global transparent behaviour which should be made prudence towards social capacity building assumptions; so that human oriented aspects of environmental schemes are readjusted for global sustainable means of productive technology, where there is the resource match could be entertained for global level up-gradation of humankind, in relating developmental activities by means of cooperative organizational guidance and managerial counselling system. It must bring in human equity through organizational control mechanism for enriching ideas of global human integration philosophy, in augmenting corporate values towards finding opportunities for global mankind, which could be stimulated for encouraging people in participating for universal human quality assessment; by way of reducing social imbalances and poverty eradication programmes, meant for human change and organizational balanced way of adjustment for social transparency. In doing all such things, there is the urgent need for human development criterion supplemental towards environmental dynamic relational approach to human living peace and happiness, for strategic nature of social up-gradation of mankind[25].

Strategic Nature of Human Development

The strategy regarding human development perspective is surrounded by the concept of socialization of organizational activities, in which communication of things regarding social uplifting nature of regional imbalances should be incorporated in removing human incapacities towards social advancement, in the way of dealing with those activities which cause human creative process of matching things for holistic nature of integrated development, confined with the tasks of organizational leading role that binds people to shoulder responsibilities towards enhancing goal of human orientation purposes. In it, there is the tendency of human relationship towards enrichment of social balance by rectifying working elements, incorporating human behavioural prudence for optimizing organizational undertaking in the nature of dealing with maximum possible change regarding elementary issues of human creativity, where tasks are required to be emulated for encouraging people to participate the decision-making areas concerning human developmental conditionality, to embrace the goal of universal social diversification; containing thereby global transparency, human solvency of life bringing elements to relate organizational delivery mechanism to integrate the relative aspects of growth initiatives for global balance restoration, and equitable principle of human participation for encouraging organizational leading practices to the path of global transparency. It is the strategic nature of dealing with organizational reformative tasks[26], which go to enlarge modernization concepts for increasing human capacities in resulting towards attaining goal of human substantial nature of developmental conditions, which enlarge benefit for advancing human challenges for incorporating group initiative for the purpose of effective measures that strengthen human efficient nature of dealing with social existentialism. In this way of working with the principles of organizational leading role, and modeling for policies of total quality consciousness, there should come human creative nature of development for encouraging change in relation to social dynamicity, which increases human acumen and leadership training experiences for purposive social orientation and global balance restoration, in correlating results of organizational guiding mechanism towards confining things for human upgradation and social progress, for innovating things in achieving goal of integrated development. In this connection, it is immensely required human experience and training qualities for uplifting social transparency, which go to enlarge organizational effectiveness for embracing idealistic measures for correlating things in potential human development objectives. Thus, the strategic idea of dealing with human development perspective rests on the nature of organizational consistency for delivery mechanism, human upgradation and social balance restoration for rejuvenating global transparent tendencies in advancing human welfare, by way of establishment of the relative concept of 'input-output' balance as well as modern corporate group relational approaches for increasing human betterment, social subsistence and worldwide solvency[27] of living parameters.

The noted facts are essential factors in making strategies for human equitable nature of upliftment from pathetic conditions of sufferings, for which integrity between corporate entities are required to be established in the nature of increasing performance goal; so that sectors of societal backward areas can be coordinated through modern technological tools and implements, where communication system has to be evolved for encountering issues of human poverty, social deprivation and distressful conditions for peaceful living as well as increasing happiness to all mankind. Thus, gaps between poor and rich have to be reduced very urgently, in rectification of government policies regarding human upliftment programme implementation, and packages application by way of utilization of schemes and government benefits, which should reach at the grass-root level for scientific operational objective to attain the goal of universal development dimension. Here, it is very much necessary to mention that esoteric way of dealing with the problems of social crises could be assessed on the basis of competitive strategic role in organizational foundation of work culture and government system of delivery mechanism. This requires clean administrative policies and strict legal instrumentation regarding package implementation procedures and schemes advancement targets, to reach at the right place where there is the severity of co-operating such elements in need-based as well as value analysis assumptions of things and activities. All these are to be supplemented in time-bound programmes to meet targets in reducing social improvement imbalances, so as to make provisions for efficient nature of human training facilities to incorporate habit of regularization programmes for social innovation in nurturing human welfare ideals; which must be followed by means of clean administrative guidelines and corrupt-free supervision means, conditioned with sacrificial means of quotas to be created in terms of implementing measures, to reduce social poverty and enhance human motivational techniques for the purpose of effective leading as well as transformational directive path[28]. In this way of working in team building approach, 'private-public partnership' (PPP) consortium agency function should be created by putting role model practice of technical ombudsman to respond situations, which require urgent social elimination of the factors of irrational productivity. Consequently, organizational guiding forces are required flexible mechanism for increasing social welfare in indiscriminative way of dealing with human poverty, social backwardness and global level advancement of mankind. It is therefore permeably to be resolved that universal human welfare should be needed, for which social infrastructural means are necessarily to be emulated for holistic nature of change, confining things of organizational performance analysis to be attributed for the sake of value judgment and goal initiative in process of making social proactive change instrumentalities. So, the strategy regarding human up-gradation should be adopted by government machinery, taking into consideration of the base-line of choice method for effectiveness in guiding people, to come-out successfully from the clutches of severe poverty and chronic distressful conditions, as have been found in social screen that has been increasing day-by-day and years-after-years. An important strategy that can be applied in practical exposition of things for social betterment purposes is the 'Preksha meditational' method as teaching-learning concept of modern social transformation goal. The actual methodical modifying idea of such measure is to deal with human talents and experience in organizing things for the highest good of people, which has relevancy in the field of scientific investigation of the problems and seriousness of the issues concerning human welfare. As a matter of fact, it is suggested that this type of balancing nature of work should be experimented by means of institutionalization of planned programmes, which can be useful for strengthening social means and ways to reach at the end result in revitalizing social pyramid. For such things to be operated in practice, patriotic nature of sacrificial services will come to light human motivational path for adopting agenda of development in organizational competencies, human creativities and social transparencies to mould growth character in new dimensional order, with the techniques of overall development programmes and organic system of employable capacities, like – provisions for health and education, safety and social security measures, basic necessities for healthy living means, transport and electricity provisions, communication facilities, games and sports for recreational life building approach, all means of social services needed for human advancement in progressive manner for forward looking tendencies[29].

We should think about development from global perspective and so, the Vedic philosophical foundation of global socialism policy captioned in the core approach of "Vasudhaiva Kutumbakam" theory, for human integrated development culture as the way of life in organizational directive mechanism should be strategically adopted in the plan of action, for unifying human civilization progress through principles of equanimity and equipoise nature of job performance. To emphasize this practice in modern organizational directive path, leadership role model has to be initiated for enlarging social improvement ideas through human-face of organizational entity concept for guiding people; to substantiate human innovativeness in the way of social transformation, human upliftment in a stage of civility from the present condition of living in slavery and global unity and integrity in mankind for realization of the scientific fabric of life bringing process. Accordingly, accountability measures are to be adopted for enrichment of organizational work culture and empowerment of people, by way of judicious decision-making approach to be incorporated through participative techniques in leading people for their welfare goal. Thus, management by objectives (MBO) should be viewed as the corporate mission, and in accordance with this method of work organizational vision document must have to be prepared, for realization of the entire road-map of social transformation reformations. To strategize all these performing ideas, leadership creativity and directive sensitivity will have to be taken into consideration, from the view point of social rolling in dimensional way of dealing with the burning problems of human poverty related measures and guidelines. As and when, organizational policies are adopted to respond such severe issues, there will be social enlightenment through poverty alleviation programmes and package implementation policies requiring disinterestedness in the working goal of both the government and private counterparts, which will further percolate to channelize social resources for the greater advantage of human welfare conditions, to realize fundamental growth initiative policies in correct implementation of schemes and organizational activities from time-to-time. However, it is immensely important for integrated nature of development that humanity should be given the highest priority in administrative and authoritative functional relationship of modern organizational entities, and from all counts, there should be transparency to correlate developmental activities[30] for the purpose of social stability, human free existentialism and global level unity and integrity between man and man. So, it is asserted that strategic policy of human qualitative nature of development requires quantitative techniques of supply-chain management system for delivery mechanism, for initiating responsibility in the field of human demand for uplifting corporate veil, to nurture social welfare measures in necessitating fundamental truth for advancing backward people, by way of facilitation services; and thus, regional imbalances have to be curbed through implementing welfare schemes for the purpose of universal order of development. This is the urgent call of the modern civilization progressive rolling, which should be confined through human indignation policy, social betterment measures and integrated development tools and techniques from different organizational constituencies, and also from power-centre and goal concept behavioural prudence, on the part of managerial challenges to bring-forth adequate level of social change relevant to human advancement process in areas of social transformational needs and ideas.

In synthesizing about the strategic way of dealing with modern organizational activities, it is hopefully asserted that universal understanding in between nations has to be strengthened for cooperative work environment, with a view to analyze various causes of human deprivation and accordingly, policies for increasing human quality of life bringing possibilities are to be measurably adopted in organizational guiding paths, for attaining result on human self-sufficiency. This should be made through administrative guidelines, which go to supply human necessary factors for peaceful social living conditions, taking due attention towards those responsible factors without which happiness in society will not come to advance people, who have been living in distressful conditions as well as uncivilized way of leading life. As a result of all these consequent incidences, we should require consciousness about increasing social good by means of creating provisions for social balance restoration with all types of modern amenities of human survival needs. Hence, strategic organization mission for upliftment of the backward classes of the society should come as the framework of development potential. This requires modernization of industrial activities through the global environment set-up in speedy pace, as per the growing needs of increasing population. Again, agrarian set-up of societal base has to be strengthened, particularly in underdeveloped and developing countries which are based on agricultural productivity. To increase such productivity, modern innovated technology should be applied for effective and rational production of agricultural output, which can also help for supplying raw-materials to industrial advancement purposes, to supply various kinds of consumer products as well as industrial commodities for speedy socio-economic growth. It is thus, essential that a strategy which strengthens both industrial and agricultural sectors could be allowed in making plan for human adequate nature of social development initiative. For doing all such activities, government policies are to be framed in a way which can rebuild social infrastructural sectors in new dimensional order, along with the changing need of the time. Hence, social upliftment of people should require actual coordination between work and welfare in holistic approach, in re-engineering human qualitative nature of development prospective, where entrepreneurial abilities are required to be enhanced for human capacity building through skill development programmes, and scientific nature[31] of social welfare practices. To realize this method of dynamic social development orientation, corporate activities are to be carried through scientific investigation, for which financial fund management diversification and channelization of social resources are to be made for integrated nature of human development approach. In substituting development related objective, there should be adequate work culture and efficient team building approach for measuring organizational performances; so that human upliftment becomes easy and consistent with dynamics of social rolling in positive direction, to unify human core idea of living potential by means of judicious effort for bringing social change, along with the establishment of world peace through reducing social imbalances and disparities between man and man. In this way of managing organizational activities, there will come human cooperation for effective industrial relationships in between nation states, to which, technological innovative character of scientific social development would commensurate in realizing human potential development goal in universal nature, through democratic principles of organizational management, in value judgment objective for initiating dynamic social growth potentials. All these are to be discussed in Chapters ahead through Vedic nature of human upliftment policies, for which various strategies are taken in hand in permeable nature to deal with human indignation, social backwardness and solution of life problems in equipoise way of analyzing organizational tasks, for the purposive social transformational goal in transcendental order of human living parameters, in unifying human understanding with a view to restore social peace and tranquility. Thus, integral humanity has been given due stress for making development strategies, to illuminate social pyramid on the screen of human betterment and universal existential system[32], as propounded in the Vedic scriptural guidelines and policies.

Human Emancipation through Human Development Initiatives

Emancipation of mankind from the pathetic stage of living in societal structure has become quite important part of the study under human development programme and initiatives, in modern world of social transformation which has relevance to social peace and tranquility. When we come-across about socio-economic empirical studies made in social sciences, it is observed that conditions of living of mankind in different parts of the world are guided by the politicized nature of socio-economic activities, for which people are suffering a lot, due to lack of adequate facilities necessary for healthy living practices as well as peaceful survival goal of social orientation process. Accordingly, there have been many type of crisis felt by human beings, like–food, clothing, shelter, health and education; besides, many other social living facilities, which have not been possible to be provided for lack of transparency in human life bringing with adequate means and ways[33], from the side of both government as well as corporate entities. As a result of this situation, social responsibility that should be shouldered by the government, and also by those who are in the planning process for reducing social gaps have not been played with responding nature of role model, to incorporate human development agenda in socialization of things and activities for the purpose of effective rolling of the societal goal of life, in objective social orientation purposes. Thus, dynamics of organizational behavioural prudence in making people efficient towards utilizing social resources will comprehensively advance fundamental roots of human indignation, narrating thereby – how should we complement things for the betterment of people, either by sociological means in working with the policies of human development parameters, or by means of religious activities, confining thereto scientific understanding for increasing means of human welfare conditions; so that equity in living is being made persistent to coagulate integrated approach of human upliftment through social diversity as well as human upliftment programmes, in terms of developmental activities, to commensurate cohesive path of nurture for universalizing human existential freedom for the sake of peaceful and healthy living potential.

In regard to human up-gradation, it is highly important to follow those principles as depicted in the Vedic order of living ideals. Here, it is imperative to say that the Vedas are the original sources of human foundation of civilization. The humanity as a whole should follow the path of the Vedic truths, where it is said that the core of humankind is ingrained in basic values of life, which should be realized through work philosophy. Accordingly, it is asserted that there are trigunas in creation – sattva, rajas and tamas, prevail in human society. Hence, human karmic cycle is operated through all these gunas, called as the life-cycle process of salvation, in realization of the scientific notion of karma (duty). When organizational activities are performed in disinterested nature of dealing with tasks and activities, two (dual) aspects of human life bringing processes are completed together with an end of realization of life. One is the *moksha* (liberation), and the other aspect is the welfare of society. For doing these practices by means of artistic play of things in games of organizational mechanism, there is the absolute necessity of surrendering attitude that can lead to the path of human salvation through general welfare of mankind. Again, it is suggested that equanimity principle[34] should be followed for the purpose of globalizing organizational system of management, which will result in human up-gradation by way of promotion of life order from lower to higher species. In this way of working with the scientific nature of social building norms, there will come human integrity to safeguard dignity of life, to incorporate social responsibility in organizational leading procedure in terms of contingency approach. It is therefore essential that human behavioural school of thought should be articulated for optimum development, in terms of Vedanta order of administrative guidelines and truths. This will produce social balance in the long-run for increasing human welfare through socio-economic diversities of living goal, along with performing in disinterested way of doing for the services of humanity. It is the real emancipation programme should be felt and chalked out in planning process, to rejuvenate social pyramid through all kinds of human activities for the highest good of mankind. Such an emancipation programme should follow the path of equipoise approach, while working in free leadership by efficient communication system for the purpose of achievement of effective organizational result, with a view to attain the goal of global peace, human cooperation and social transformation in unified way of developing the foundation of human civilization for integral humanity. This kind of initiative, when incorporated in corporate mission, managerial vision and organizational strategies will lead to progress mankind, by way of mutual cooperation and group effort to all endeavours of organizational guiding forces and techniques of dealing with man-power resources. We should therefore believe that the Vedic thought which has envisaged the idea of "Vasudhaiva Kutumbakam" as the philosophy for holistic nature of development[35], will come to light for enlightening entire humankind towards reaching at optimum level of emancipation, from the unscientific dangers of working without following the principles of truth, beauty and goodness as enshrined in Vedic philosophical order of doing things. Hence, it will open the door of spirituality for socialization of modern technological foundation, to accumulate resources match for the purpose of oblation of light in social screen through development agenda as the most important slogan as the need of the time.

It should thus, mutually corroborate for encompassing human development with that of human emancipation, in so far as the philosophical foundation of social reconstruction by way of Vedic reformative guidelines has been followed, for purposive establishment of global peace and human liberation. In considering emancipation for human up-gradation to hierarchy of life, organizational activities are to be carried through cooperative endeavours and systematic order of scientific working balance, so as to increase human welfare in terms of maximizing output delivery mechanism and minimizing cost maintenance policy in organizational leading strategies, for the purpose of human efficiency as well as capacity building initiatives. To embrace such goal in realities of life, management of resources are to be made diversified by means of international cooperation and human understanding level, to optimize goal of human universal rolling towards the path of dynamic social transformation in relation to industrial rationalization and democratic participation. Thus, human empowerment policy should be resolved for developing social foundation of growth and sustainability, in nurturing people to upgrade from sufferings, who have been leading life in pathetic inhuman conditions[36], in this age of technological reformations and scientific development worldwide. Accordingly, it is immensely important to note that human emancipation requires true nature of performance, based on scientific investigation for innovative effort on the part of modern organizational entities. Thus, human competencies will require a good focus for strategic nature of balanced development goal, to occupy vital position in making people to realize development as the mantra of global peace and sustainability. In this regard, we should remember that bilateral trade negotiations, multi-dimensional level of industrial relationship between different nations and government initiatives for cultural transformation with a view to social orientation purposes will go a long way, to bridge the gap in societal order of human living disparities and reducing conditions of regional imbalances from socio-economic perspective. In today's world of fast change, technology should be made development oriented for increasing human educational and health-care activities, rural communication system, network of infrastructural facilities to be provided for inception of human qualities to the level of global competition, etc. These are attributing factors responsible for adequate emancipation programmes, which have relevance in corporate social responsibility and good governance paradigm of human capacity building measures for initiating social growth, by way of human upliftment that requires scientific temper of effective leadership for enrooting the directive of the societal order, in relation to adopting policies for measurable condition of development issues, which has become redundant in present situation of strategic social rolling to the path of pragmatic humanization approach in managing things and activities. As a result of all these repercussions on human development goal for effective emancipation programmes and targets of work culture, there is urgent need of international understanding for global cooperation to the fact that development is the alternative, and the only alternative for social peace and minimization of human conflicts between nation states. To uproot this value, corporate legal obligation for utilizing national natural resources on the part of each country should be fundamental tool for initiating development, to emulate perspective of human up-gradation from severe sufferings as observed worldwide. As and when, modern governments are made more and more responsible towards incorporating all such issues in administrative guidelines, for narrating things in advancing people to participate in democratic nature, decision variables will require flexible coordinating strategy to commensurate adequate level of growth, in initiating social transformation by way of human resource accounting responsiveness[37].

The above discussions are made for analyzing areas of social discrepancies, for which humankind over the world have been observed living in distressful conditions of misery and pitiable situations of survival; where corruptive system of government and bureaucratic guidelines have resulted for social value erosion, to which so long years bad management was treated to be prescriptive measures for such kind of social imbalances, as we have dealt in this study.

According to the need of the hour, urgency in adopting standing organizational plan for immediate development of suffered people, and also long-term plan for radical transformation of the social foundation requires organizational challenge for changing social veil, as per tools and techniques of human emancipation role model, to embrace the goal of human existential freedom, social effective transformation and integral concept of humanity for addressing development as the rejoinder to all fields of modern business and commercial activities, in systematizing social orientation programmes through procedural mechanism in rebuilding industrial leadership towards human upliftment initiative, by means of entrepreneurial professionalism, managerial benevolence thought for human side of the enterprising attitude and narrating fundamental causes to solve burning problems of human backwardness in time and space. To make system of human development consistent towards dynamic social journey, it is highly important to resolve policies for international trade, by mutual cooperative agenda in between sovereign nations, in inculcating a vibrant growth model by all international agencies; which will come to light development on the screen of social functional relationship, for the purpose of betterment of conditions to the fate of suffered human beings. Here, it is suggested for such visionary type of management that corporate culture of international human familiarity incorporating brotherhood as the policy for universal up-gradation should be encompassed for profitable nature[38] of social dignity of mankind, where all should feel for concerted efforts in sacrificing for the holistic nature of social development, human equal up-gradation through positive as well as realistic emancipation, and in the long-run, international cooperation will exist for making this world a place of human legacy to restore peace in continuous manner, through transcendental order of doing things in initiating welfare to whole mankind. It is thus, *ipso facto* necessary in undertaking activities by all sovereign nation states to accumulate financial resources by means of bilateral trade agreements, international finance pooling cell and industrial relationship, technology transfer and up-gradation programme for strengthening human skills as well as training man-power resources for the sake of global unity, human integrity and business transparency, so as to bind people in united bond of mutual human relationships; particularly, for making development in all-round spheres of societal upliftment which will enlarge human competencies for increasing welfare of people, towards the pattern of diversified nature of investment potential that can rebuild social structure on the frame of human healthy existentialism. The techniques of leadership should follow therefore, principles of equanimity in carrying out business for common benefit of the world population; who have been deprived off, from all means of justified opportunities required for peaceful social living condition, in integrating human core idea of behavioural dynamism for the purposive balance in socio-economic activities[39], pertaining to human emancipation programme in regard to initiation of goodwill and international brotherhood, for understanding in qualitative improvement of people to the cause of social harmony as well as global peaceful atmosphere.

Narrating thus all elements of human development issues, there should be democratic decision-making attitude on the part of government agencies and planners in all countries of the world, for approaching towards maximization of human living comfort and minimization of prevailing conflicts as found everywhere in the world atmosphere of business. Accordingly, transactional analysis should be made from the view point of strategic global relational approach of total human quality (THQ) enhancement, and achievement of the objective for self-reliance perspective on the part of national identities and organizational entities, to establish international relationship regarding encouragement of human participation level for the safeguard of the humanity. As a result of all these beneficial interaction, there will come global unity in diversifying human upliftment opportunities by creating employment provisions, and innovative social need for reforming business activities to the path of broad socialization programme in humanizing entrepreneurial abilities, to shoulder risks and initiatives in making social foundation sound for re-engineering modern business activities, based on equitable nature of social growth and upliftment of mankind worldwide. It will pave the way for effective social transformation to nurture human justice for living in dignity, thinking in commonality instead of diversity in human race, and above all, global order of human capacity building should empower people to initiate social responsibility of development through reducing human inequalities, by means of efficient work culture from the side of corporate entities. In concluding about the strategic nature of development model for social transformation by way of human emancipation issues, we must keep in mind for actualizing norms of effective social building initiative which will go to preserve human dignity and social balance. In restoration of an integral system, in confining tasks for the purpose of effective social balance, in challenging organizational marketing activities to competitive environment of business, realization of the goal of human up-gradation as well as social transformation, in this age of technological change and global balance will be made positive towards possible nature of human group efforts. Thus, innovativeness in managerial abilities[40] will come to light human emancipation from all sorts of social deprivation and sufferings of people. So, it is suggested that human resources will require to be developed from the view point of global cohesiveness, in reducing social gaps between rich and poor; where input-output relationship between development and human up-gradation should be mutually inclusive, for profitable nature of human advancement and social rolling in dynamic way through objective means of human corporate initiatives. In this way of doing organizational activities, good programmes of human emancipation are to be taken at hand by corporate work cultural mission and government vision of administrative policies and guidelines.

Human Development for Social Balance

In modern times, everywhere in human society there has been growing conflicts between man and man. The reasons behind such conflicting situations are varied in nature. Some conflicts are due to ethnic problems; whereas, others are prevailing for sociological problems, pertaining to human imbalances in living standard which go to dissatisfy people regarding pattern of government activities, organizational planning for exploiting resources to monopolistic tendency in earning income by suppressing legitimate rights of the people, and so on. It is therefore prevalent to say that social imbalances are caused due to lack of adopting adequate policies which are helpful for developing people, who are not getting proper facilities of healthy living necessities of life, in peaceful as well as comfortable means of social survival towards realizing value of civic life bringing attitude. Thus, developmental strategies are required now[41], to fulfill human crisis in regard to dynamic social orientation purposes. So, it can be attributed by saying that human development perspective is the real directive path of society, which can rebuild social structure in innovating things for reformative activities and confining people to participate for decision-making approach of growth initiatives. By doing so, a balanced stage in societal living pattern could be followed for reducing gaps between people, who have been suffering a lot due to all essential means required for civic living tendencies, in orientation of healthy as well as potential survival goal to co-existential purposes; which should be propagated for human living justice by way of restoring equitable nature of social balance, in terms of finding out scope and opportunities for reducing regional imbalances. From this view point, it can be said that social distrust among various groups in regard to living objective has been increasing day-by-day, which has relationship for optimizing social restlessness, as followed from the present picture of the world order. Connoting such ideas in balanced social developmental goal, our strategic objective of human upliftment will be fulfilled through creative planning system, in which government policies are to be redrafted for the purpose of optimum nature of human performances by way of democratic participation of people in organized character of managerial guidance. Hence, it is highly important on the part of both government authorities as well as social organizations to systematize things for efficient utilization of resources, which can serve in better way for reducing human poverty and social distressful conditions to increase quality of life, with the objective of attaining human equality in living parameters, along with maintaining justice for reducing gaps between rich and poor.

By all such means, which are applicable for eliminating social poverty we would be able to solve human conflicting nature from this world, and therefore, it is expected that proper implementation of schemes relevant to emancipation of suffered human beings to a stage of civic living potential, will go a long way for strengthening societal structure in new dimensional order for revitalizing human core ideas of living[42]. To advance such goal of living in social demographic situation, there is the emergent need for adopting strategies, on the part of modern government administration to make urgent provisions for the betterment of the life of suffered human beings, who are unable to attaining prosperity due to lack of timely reach of adequate facilities needed for civic living opportunities of life bringing possibilities. We should therefore suggest that proper social re-engineering is a must for comprehensive human development objective[43], in scientific reformation of the societal structure to the path of dynamic social rolling as well as human cooperation for understanding the concept of integrated approach of development through real growth initiatives. This will be working as the fillip to bridge gap up to the point, where human crisis situation prevails in spheres of the societal structure. Understanding thus, human development pattern for balanced social order of life bringing perspective, socio-economic activities are to be carried for increasing human welfare in holistic approach of doing things; so that conflicting situations prevailing in different parts of the global society could well be managed, by means of planning things in strategic way as well as directing organizational functions through innovative leadership guidelines. This type of policy should be framed in organizational work related statements, which are immensely helpful for mitigating social crisis, like – human poverty, restlessness and many sorts of social imbalances, as observed to be prevailing in world order. Consequently, it is better to know that social diversifications in terms of socio-economic progress could reach at people, in realization of the goal of free social existentialism, for the purpose of emulating things in nature of dealing with the conditions for attaining human transcendental order of living[44], by means of cohesive human relationship, in betterment of the pillars of social orientation where integral humanity should be given highest priority, for effective analysis of developmental objectives pertaining to project out the purpose of social balance restoration. It is therefore undoubtedly to be assessed that human development, if carried through propagation of the principles of equity, will lead to mankind for attaining goal of social peace and tranquility; where, it is possible to enhance international brotherhood condition by different objective functions of global organizations – this can be a new mission of human undertaking through scientific social framework of industrial rationalization, along with agricultural comprehensive part of productive orientation for social building objective, to be nurtured for the sake of visionary zeal in mankind, in restoration of social balance in terms of working principles like 'truth, beauty and goodness' for amplification of the condition of human integrity[45].

In doing so, it should be observed that the four types of fundamental truth as expressed in the Vedic philosophical order of balancing human life bringing attitude, like – 'dharma, artha, kama and moksha' have been maintained through principles of work in containing issues of social development perspective, by means of organizational policy for enhancement of human qualitative value of life. So, it is permeably to be noted that the disinterested nature as required for working to advance social people in realization of their goal will be reflected in organizational functioning, whereby we would be able to increase human welfare for holistic development purposes. Such kind of work culture will further require human sacrificial nature of performance at the work place, that would lead to achieve goal for equipoise nature of doing things in regard to fulfillment of human satisfaction with view to increase human quality of life in indiscriminating way, for purposive upliftment of suffered people to a stage of developed condition, for establishment of social balance, human cooperation and global level existential free atmosphere to unify character of the diversified nature of socio-economic activities of mankind. It is therefore essentially to be noted herein that modern organizational framework of policy resolution should be guided by the principles of integral humanity concept of performing things and activities; wherefrom, illumination of the light of development will glee for understanding happy as well as prosperous relationship in solving burning problems of human life worldwide – this is the pervasive character of development related agenda, which will go to bring in societal peace by way of creative human development objective, for the realization of life order in rolling towards global unity and international human survival integrity. As a whole, human development initiative when made for encompassing ideas of justice, liberty and equity will find-out the new vista for accommodating adjustable features of life value, instead of multi-faced diversities in living parameters; which are fundamental assumptions of social equality can be experimented through innovative practices of inclusive model of development goal. From this, it is clear that development of mankind should be considered from the view point of reducing social imbalances between poor and rich, by way of serving people in providing through all amenities and provisions for surviving in comfortable manner, to enhance mutual growth in societal order of human upliftment for the sake of unity and integrity. Accordingly, modern organizations are to be guided by the philosophy of 'Preksha meditation', which has already been discussed in the work of the author entitled – "Unified Thought on Management". It is here, cited once again, to illustrate the view of social transformation by way of diversified nature of development related to human upliftment from uncivilized nature of living, to a stage of civility; in this age of technological reformation and scientific investigation of things and activities for developing social structure. Thus, conditions for social equality will prevail when organizational activities are performed in uplifting people, to harmonize a social balance in regard to human sufferings and oppression of life, which require effective nature of guidance through proactive leadership approach, as observed for experimenting ideas of integrated development as to the kind of sustainable impact on human free living existentialism. To confine development with strategic social balance restoration, we are needed urgent social reformative policies as well as organizational procedure of working relationship, to implement things and activities for speedy solution of human crisis felt in regard to make life transparent towards realization of peace, and bringing order of society dynamic for attaining 'path-goal relativity' between human development and positive social mobility. Optimization of this objective idea will provide for human fraternity[46] of doing things, and thus; human motivation will come in producing things for common welfare of mankind, to overcome problems of all-round sufferings of poor and distressed human beings. Hence, it will lead to strengthen international understanding for increasing human cooperative endeavours to reduce social imbalances and improve condition of life in mankind, by way of living goals and objectives for global human unity and integrity.

Despite analyzing above reformative factors of social development initiatives, it is worthwhile to note that corruptive political system, backed by discriminative policies of castes, communalism and religions, etc. have been found in some countries of the world; which are essentially detrimental towards social building process by way of increasing problems of human sufferings and social deprivation, in kind of their living standard, whereby, as it were, democratic system of people's participation in nurturing social harmony through welfare goals could not be attained in directing modern societies to right path. In this way of working, government agencies are observed to be failure for accountability towards social building norms of human upliftment and emancipation, from their pathetic stage of survival for the purpose of optimizing the fate of human beings in living towards healthy conditions, in regard to social mobility and strategic development for realizing fundamental assumptions of life bringing possibilities, for undertaking things of production and services in sacrificial manner. Taking advantage of all these consequences, separatists and terrorists have been playing their dominant role to divide people, either in the name of underdevelopment and human backwardness, or even in the name of jihad; which when put to due attention by the suffered people comes in the nature of social conflicts and human restlessness. Here, again, it is observed that corruptive nature of political thinkers time-and-again raise hands and shake hands with those, both the anti-social elements as well as depressed and suppressed people to win for their election games. In this way, universal development of human beings, irrespective of caste, creed, colour, sex, language, religion, etc. and also, other attributing means could not eliminate social poverty for long; which we have addressed by means of analyzing different issues in Chapters ahead, in scientific temper of mind, to strategize government policies in right direction, and to help in implementing issues of good governance paradigms for the reconstruction of social structure in new dimensional way, where restoration of social balance by means of socio-economic activities would be possible for the purpose of effective development of all human beings in holistic approach. From such perspective analysis, it goes to say that 'teaching-learning' system should be modified through practice of patriotic nature of leading the overall economy of any nation, so as to find-out means and ways – how to eradicate social poverty[47]; which has been increasing years-after-years and considered to be a chronic problem for socio-economic betterment of life and emancipation goal of mankind. It is therefore time now, to adopt policies for positive human development mission in organizational system of guiding societies, by modern tools and techniques in regard to dynamic social rolling, and to identify by the international agencies all those who are acting against destructive path of human civilization, by means of putting wrong signal through propaganda on different subjects, like – separatism, religions, castes, communalism, etc. for their group interest in exploiting people towards the path of negativism. Hence, it is suggested that the Vedic thought on global development and social equality as enshrined in ancient Vedic scriptures in Bharat Bhumi (land), and also in Upanisadic order of human familiarity for realizing life aspects, entitled through "Vasudhaiva Kutumbakam" philosophy should be propounded as the core idea of social building optimal objective, for orderly confining things of modern organizations in directing human society towards complex to simple, hard to soft and misery to happiness. Thus, it should also be advocated for adopting total human quality (THQ) development programmes by all modern sovereign governments of the world, to establish social balance by means of initiating works for peaceful and healthy living practices, where humanity should be given special priority as the rejoinder of social upliftment goal, to integrate nature of human development process for enlarging ideas of social unity as well as international cooperative environmental order of assimilating life of mankind towards enriching pillars of the modern society.

In concluding about social balance restoration by way of universal human development initiatives, creative mode of organizational guidance and counselling should conform human skill development perspective for undertaking things of production and services, with challenging nature of professionalism in making positive social change, by means of radical ideas of good governance which go to help in increasing human competencies level, organizational credibility and governmental transparency for attaining human self sufficiency in regard to life orientation purposes. One such important aspect of integrated social development objective is to strategize technological idea for increasing human knowledge and holistic nature of social development, with all equitable means of scientific social rolling, where mankind will find optimum opportunities for their fuller personality spurt and all-round development by means of cooperative work culture and integrated living conditionality, ensuring for their peaceful survival goal and right direction towards realizing meaning of value-based management vision, organizational mission of work and worldwide social reformation in cohesive nature of dealing with growth potential, and initiating model for scientific human development[48] perspective. Thus, there should be policy initiative in the framework of development related guidelines, which must also incorporate human participation for optimizing organizational activities by matching harmonious order of resources efficient utilization process, for enlarging human creativity and innovative approach of social transformation; where unification of social pyramid will be made through liberal practices of trade and business potentials in enumerating objective of universal social rolling, for encountering problems of human sufferings and social distressful conditions of living. To attain all such objective ideas through performance goal, organizational coordinating elements are to be made flexible for increasing human efficiency through effective managerial guidance and control mechanism, for advancing people who are lying in backwardness, to the path of general welfare in mass estimation of the standard of living potential in nature of their progressive goal; whereto, dignity of work should be made liberal with the adoption of the principles of equity, justice and human fraternity. Thus, human existential freedom should be assimilated in indiscriminative ideas of social sustainable means of operational mission, so as to confining things for the betterment of life bringing initiatives by way of reducing human conflicts and establishing social justice for deprived human beings. In this order of developing the societal structure, we should try to harmonize social balance between different economies, for the sake of human understanding towards the process of human integrity, social unity and global harmony. In doing so, government system will require wide policy change for reformulating planned objectives in the changing order of the present world situation. It is therefore expected that positive social change through human participation level, and organizational decision-making approach for implementing things and packages in making people to uplift from severe sufferings, will come to light societal structure towards the process of transcendental order of human living goal; whereby, social equality and human dignity of living will be reflected toward initiating responsibility, for encompassing realistic growth in terms of social balance restoration and human orientation purposes[49].

Creative Human Development Thought

We have already seen that human development is the core idea of human civilization, which guides people to the path of universal unity for the establishment of world peace and social tranquility. It is therefore relevant to say that optimization of human welfare would be made through creative process of human development[50], required for reducing social imbalances between people in different nation states; otherwise, human conflicts are prone to subject the state of social restlessness in between different groups of people. Thanking from such angle, it is permeably to be considered that creativity in doing things for managing resources by means of entrepreneurial abilities will result in balanced as well as sustainable nature of social development, for which scientific tools and techniques are required to be applied in analyzing human performance at organizational level – this is now, felt as the aim of social diversification in regard to socio-economic activities which are required to be carried by means of efficient skills, and therefore, creative endeavours made on the part of organizational entities should correlate issues of human development for correct social building measures, which will enhance human capacity for effective growth of social people, by way of increasing human betterment and dynamic social movement towards uplifting principles of integrated nature of social development, along with survival of mass population in happy and peaceful societal relationship to life in comfortable manner. Thus, scientific creativity with professional leadership aided by means of efficient productivity will help in performing things for the greater interest of humankind, who have been suffering in society due to lack of adequate facilities of living for free existentialism. It is thus creative thought on human development perspective can guide modern societies for attaining human welfare, taking into consideration all attributes of human backwardness which have resulted for societal imbalances and human unjust conditions towards living goal. From this standpoint, it comes true to all judicious persons who are quite attentive to concentrate for social mobility, along with diversities of organizational activities and government guiding forces that human dissatisfaction in regard to living standard will be reduced, as and when organizational planning process becomes vibrant towards changing the fate of suffered people, in correlating socio-economic activities by means of creative assumptions for dynamic human relationships and group behaviour, which should be made unique towards attaining goal of universal development.

Assessing all such strategies required for increasing human creativity to optimize quality of work, there should be organizational effective communication as the net-work of managerial guiding tools, whereby group efforts will be made more and more challenging in unifying tasks of organizational system for the efficient utilization of resources as well as channelization of organization's fund towards social building objectives[51]. Thus, creativity should be seen from sensitivity approach in getting proper fed-back towards effective monitoring of the overall system which guides people in right directional path for attaining goal of social welfare. Hence, it is mentioned without any doubt in mind that solution of human problems for leading life in comfortable manner is dependent on scientific creativity in analyzing organizational activities, which are immensely responsible for social sustainability and holistic nature of growth. If the plans are made effective in modern organizations, by means of creativity in decision-making approach of organizational management system, there will be positive social change in directing people to the progressive means of social upliftment through all kinds of managerial undertaking, in responding towards solution of many problems of human sufferings and social distress, caused due to mismanagement of things which are not addressed properly in time. Pertinently, it becomes highly important to assess organizational activities based on creative nature of dealings, in shouldering managerial responsibility in reducing social poverty, by way of supplying goods to areas of human needs most urgently.

According as to this principle, consistency and relevancy of organizational duties and responsibilities should be made more creative oriented for the functional relationships[52], which have the features, like – (1) unity in action for diversity in developing people; (2) transparency in human behavioural prudence for undertaking things in developing social backwardness; (3) reducing social poverty through effective correlation between work and welfare; (4) advancing people by way of efficient training and developmental measures; (5) nurturing social harmony in terms of good governance philosophy for effective social orientation purposes; and so on. By following all these principles in organizational working model for human development in objective manner of utilizing resources, creative endeavors for capacity building could be enlarged for all kinds of mankind, who are; otherwise, suffering from crisis of malnourishment, decaying stage of living due to lack of adequate facilities, like – education, health-care, basic needs of food, clothing and shelter, electricity, road transport, railway services and other means of communication facilities required for healthy and peaceful living opportunities, and besides; many other essential provisions requiring for survival, say, fresh drinking water supply, sanitation and sewerage provisions, games and sports, cultural and amusement facilities, facilities related to free atmosphere of living or living in pollution free environment, facilities to curb natural calamities, like – flood, which have been observed to be prone for agricultural production purposes, timely water supply to agricultural fields, land reformative activities, electricity provisions for agricultural production management, drainage to paddy fields for supplying measurable quantity of water required in harvesting season, town and country planning, and municipal services required for hygienic life bringing potential, facilities to village agriculturists in terms of provisions for quality seeds, manures and necessary pesticides, tools and implements required for harvesting in the field, etc. Besides, creative endeavors of human development process in shaping human civilization in new dimensional path should be further concentrated from the view point of scientific aspects, like – space research programmes for various objectives of peaceful as well as dynamic social orientation, weather forecasting measures, water-shed management proposals to utilize natural water for many purposes of human comfortable living potential, creation of scientific network between 'river-sea-ocean' for boosting up of social productivity in multi-dimensional order, military research activities, spacecraft building innovative facilities, police services and security measures by way of supporting latest surveillance facilities, and maintenance of social safety, industrial and agricultural research activities pertaining to rationalization through effective production and measures for efficient distribution system, information technology related research activities for increasing sound system of communication network required in trade and business areas, etc. All these are attributing factors of human efficiency level for producing things with a view to social transparency, and human integrated nature of creative development potential[53].

From the above analysis, it is undoubtedly to be noted that creativity should be encountered from all fields, which are helping in the process of social building by means of reformative nature of tasks carried through modern organizational entities and government agencies. It is not true to say that creativity is the property of particular class in society; but rather, it should emanate from multi-dimensional players and groups who are devoted to the process and notion of social reconstruction activities. Hence, it is permeably said that the steady-state way of social development requires spurt of human creativity from different aspects, like – creative writing, creative scientific temper of thought, creative intellectual property of humankind, creative art and so on. All these are essential nature of socio-economic growth contained in organized endeavors of human beings, and therefore, creativity should be reinforced in leadership guidelines and managerial practices for establishing social justice and equity for proper value measurement purposes; so that human poverty and social sufferings could be eliminated altogether in this age of technological reformation and dynamic progress of civilization in rolling towards human integrated way of development. Thus, we should believe in scientific creativity for human personality development, which could be utilized in an endeavor towards building human society on the foundation of eternal peace, transparent survival objective and overall global transformation to achieve the goal of integral humanity, for qualifying the nature of social stability, human initiatives and modern reformative activities of different organizations. In doing so, creative idea should be propagated through transformational leadership policies in guiding society to the path of optimum welfare, in equipoise nature of dealing with the things and activities, as prescribed in the Vedic thought for human integrated approach of social reconstruction[54]. To apply tools and techniques for increasing social creativity, free atmosphere of work environment should prevail, so as to find-out objectives of social transformation and increase human value system to consider potential elements of all mankind. Accordingly, creative sensitivity should be applied, when organizational plans are adopted for social change in diversification of resources match, for the sake of balanced development and speedy human upliftment from the uncivilized nature of living situations, as observed to be creating much social problems in regard to social imbalances and human differences in living order. So, it is suggested that effective nature of dealing with environmental resources and financial efficient fund management capabilities will render human creativity for developing social structure, based on equity, justice and liberal human behavioural relationship as well as group efforts, in confining things for the accommodation of human skills and talents which will go to enlarge social unity, human integrity and rational productivity for the pursuit of balanced human development objective and cohesive social reformative activities. Thus, creative thinking should be given special priority in making human beings free to find-out such resourceful elements to work culture related atmosphere, where all should find adequate opportunities for development of human personality in diversified nature of doing things for the greater interest of mankind. Ensuring creative environment at the work place will render as profitable means of human understanding level to uproot social value system, conjoining the nature of organizational directive mechanism and reformative change, for the purpose of developing human interpersonal relationships and for establishment of sound coordination at organizational level, which are immensely helpful for potential nature of human development[55] thought envisaged to the scriptural ideas in ancient Vedic civilization. From this standpoint, it is asserted in pragmatic nature of thinking that creative talent and human scientific consciousness about the reformative path should be propagated by way of dealing with the subjective view in flexible manner, so as to reorient human civilization on the foundation of effective social reconstruction, by means of equitable human development in all-round spheres of the societal pyramid. To incorporate such kind of development notion, government policies are to be revitalized by changing legal instrumentalities to rectify all kinds of ills and maladies creating problems for balanced human development strategies. Hence, it is evident that the scope and opportunities in identifying creative talents of human beings are to be decided in terms of human competencies, organizational credibility and social transparency; which are fundamental aspects of global transformation towards bringing integrated nature of human development through all kinds of sustainable means, as incorporated for organizational effectiveness by way of sound coordination in the system of work. Under this system, human capacity will be rebuild for unifying functional relationships and managerial control mechanism to objectify resources' diversification in the field of efficient social transformation, by taking corrective decision towards human right kind of action-oriented principles for optimum level of social development. In this way of working with the nature of imbalances, measures for eliminating social poverty and indignity in mankind could be adopted for undertaking social responsibility purposes, in planning through government initiatives and for strengthening pillars of social structure, to modify rules of organizational guidance in systematic order of social diversification through growth potentials. Hence, creative organizational measures for objectifying human development perspective should be made transparent and dynamic by all means of group efforts, where unity and integrity regarding spelling needs of human orientation would commensurate result of human upliftment possibilities in convergent manner, to the underlying reasons for human divergent social conflicts that are requiring harmonious balance towards efficient nature of social transformation. In a nutshell, creativity when enlarged in work related policies by radical adjustment of things in nurturing human talents, will illuminate social welfare goal from all counts to recount every aspect of responding nature of group behaviour expounded for human existential free atmosphere in social environment[56]. Such an idea will help in resourceful human upliftment condition by creativity of organizational matching mechanism for utilizing resources in efficient diversification process, to the growing needs of human demand for reducing social imbalances.

In coagulating about the nature of creative human development potential, we are required to follow principles of coordination in managing organizational activities, and thus; it is suggested that human training facilities are to be enriched for developing entrepreneurial skills, so as to produce for effective supply-chain management system and for maintaining customer relationships, to increase human welfare through all types of measures as adopted in organizational good governance plans and strategies. We are therefore, to be conscious about human motivational background in enthusing group relationships at organizational level, which requires creative endeavour towards confining things and activities based on interpersonal relationship as well as intra-personal relationship, to actualize functional relationships in organizing things effectively. Thus, plan of action should be incorporated in deciding about the aspects of human creative development, where organizational control mechanism and its feedback are required to be adopted from the view point of creative value assessment in directing things for effective social change by way of people's involvement as well as organizational initiatives. From such idea of creativity, it is imperative to say that creative foundation of modern organizations will replace obsolete things in terms of implementing new ideas for increasing organizational performance criterion, on which depends social diversification in managing funds of organization and putting due attention in increasing human welfare condition, to nurture ideas of social transformation in goal related functional responsibility on the part of management. To incorporate such aim in managerial guiding[57] forces and administrative practices, goodwill and cooperation between employees of organizations will require correct synthesis for advancing people through elementary needs of living pursuit; whereto, application of tools and techniques of organizational decision-making approach will have to be made human oriented in all spheres of working environment. In this way, projection of human skills through rational creative endeavour could well be judged for actualization process in initiating responsibility towards maintaining social balance, by objectifying activities of modern organizations in upliftment of poor people to stabilize their living necessities for the purpose of increasing standard of living parameters. From this idea, it is asserted that creative innovation in the field of rational industrialization as well as agricultural diversified nature of productivity could also be enhanced through scientific investigation of things, in which planned development approach should be reformed for 'path-goal' relativity between human welfare and social sustainability.

From the thought provoking nature of creativity and its importance for social transformation, we should predict in mind that creativity is uncompromising towards bringing human efficiency level at the work atmosphere, in nurturing human element in organizational set-up. Hence, effectiveness of social upliftment of suffered people will be made through potential skill development programme and managerial guidance and counselling. For doing all these things, leadership traits will require democratic nature of human participation and involvement in organizational work at free atmosphere, to strengthen human capacities in increasing societal good in terms of public utility services and responding nature of work culture. So, it is permeably to be said that scientific creativity requires efficient order of human sensitivity as well as effective organizational guidance, for increasing resources' utility by way of cost-benefit analysis, which will help in accumulating social welfare in directing global order towards unifying the system of human work elements, in search of ideas which will encourage people to eliminate social poverty and establish a balanced order in economic functions. To implement ideas of human creativity in industrial undertaking, communication system should be developed by means of information technology utilization, to commensurate healthy growth of the societal environment. Again, creativity should also be seen from environmental point of view, as it relates to work atmosphere, and therefore, it is suggestible that creative endeavour of modern organizations will be guided by the philosophy of ecological balance and environmental sustainability, in nurturing the foundation of human civilization. So, pollution free environment in holistic approach should be taken into consideration for harmonious human living goal, in which creative assessment regarding environmental balance scanning will work as guiding mechanism for increasing social good and human peaceful living condition[58].

Human Development in Nurturing Social Integrity

Human development is a subject concerns everyone, who has been devoted to pious endeavour for the social reconstruction activities, in confining things for the betterment of life of mankind in this real world of living. So, it is viewed from integrated approach for the holistic idea of social building process and its nurturing elements, which are more important for result-oriented approach of human upliftment programmes to incorporate the subject of social transformation, global equity of living parameters for unifying organizational tasks in the midst of diversity of operational ideas, human integrated behavioural approach in reinforcing organizational system of productive activities in reducing social disparities. Thus, all kinds of activities pursued for enlarging knowledge base and enriching learning attitude at work relationship of organizational setting, could well be adjusted for modification of human behavioural pursuit to the endeavour of overall development objective in compounding manner, to attain the goal of maximum social advantage for suffered classes of humankind with the minimization of production cost, maintaining quality concern concept in establishment of the relationship of 'path-goal' sensitivity. In this manner, integrated part of the programme as carried throughout the journey of organizational life in enumerating things for envisagement of societal harmony, should be placed in nurturing ideas of human betterment policies to encompass behavioural prudence in dealing with activities, for the optimum necessity of human upliftment mission, organizational guiding vision for social reconstruction through effective reformation, and diversity of resources match in balancing towards profitable nature of productive goal for increasing human welfare[59], etc. It is therefore true to say that strategic idea of human development initiative is predicted for long-term benefit of social transformation, keeping due attention to the norms of human upliftment policy for the purpose of social orientation goal, in dynamic growth perspective and leadership command of organizational responsibility to effectuate human up-gradation from severe sufferings, with a view to understand the meaning of social emancipation objective. To correlate organizational activities with that of human dignity of living, it is highly important to follow the path of integrated management system, as it employs resources for efficient dealing with the tools and techniques of managerial prudence in optimizing 'input-output' relationship, with a view to achieve goal of human integrity by means of developmental identity for the purposive nature of socio-economic growth; which would come to enlighten social picture on the screen of human behavioural relationships. As per this rule, it can be assessed that social development is the agenda for holistic nature of human development requiring healthy organizational practice, for enriching work related atmosphere to nurture human element of entrepreneurial professionalism based on human integrity; as it were, in the very nature of social existence where people will find-out their opportunities for personality development, in initiating dynamic nature of social growth by means of cooperative work atmosphere and harmonious human interrelationships[60], in reducing social gaps between rich and poor.

From this standpoint, we are in a position to arrive at a decision level that human development has no other alternative; but to follow strategic idea of social development in holistic perspective for the overall spurt of human personality, by way of providing scope and ample opportunities for developing the standard of living, in which social equality and human justice for complementing value system have been found to be real order of social integrity–this is the kind of living atmosphere requiring scientific temper of thinking for upliftment of mankind from pathetic stage of sufferings to a comfortable stage of survival, and is required to be maintained through integrated development objective by means of organizational entities and government machineries. So, the predicted goal of social transformation will come from real diversification of resources and efficient utilization of the financial system, making thereby human upliftment for the effective nurture of human resource potential, in managing things and activities for all-round social development; where humankind will be seen as the central point of organizational accountability towards performing tasks, in embracing the eternal goal to the foundation of human civilization for peace and social tranquility. Thus, integrated idea of development is related to sustainable social dynamicity in reorienting human superstructure on the path of learning culture[61] and organizational work atmosphere. As and when, efficient diversification of resources are made for potential human development objective, there will come human integrity in work related atmosphere at organizational setting, which should require effective communication system for commanding height of organizational performance criteria, depending on which social re-engineering will be made architectural for the larger benefit of distressed classes of mankind living in ill-fed and ill-clad situation. Responding such social situation, modern technological innovative ideas and scientific research activities are to be utilized for increasing organizational activities, which are fundamentally assumed to be optimizing human beneficial mode of living, if the policies are incorporated in organizational planned approach for unifying the nature of human development related goals and objectives. To increase human performance related idea for social building objective and human up-gradation mission, there is the need for integrated approach in dealing with organizational functional aspects, which are corroborated to all means of efficient managerial guiding system for creating provisions necessary in making social welfare. Accordingly, leadership accountability and managerial transparency should be made more and more responsive oriented towards confining things and activities of modern organizations for the greater interest of speedy human upliftment programmes; because, this is the urgent call of modern human civilization which will be made open to survival aspect of mankind in free atmosphere, for existential autonomy, human integrated nature of development and dynamic social rolling for effective global transformation.

An understanding on the plate-form of global business set-up to open the door of mutual collaboration and strategic partnership between nations can help building relationship, to uproot value system for all in merging towards global level convergence in areas of public and private activities, by means of inclusive growth initiative and talk for peaceful healthy relationship will strengthen international cooperation, to nurture industrial and manufacturing productive paths on current issues of global employment problems and correcting standard of living for global mankind. In this pattern of thinking for encouraging business players by dominant democracies of the world[62] can build-up the superstructure of the society in regard to human capacity increase to deal with the problems of social imbalances, by developing human beings to respective sovereign national entities, which will increase social health by way of uplifting people from the lower level layers of the social pyramid. Thus, social sustainability will be made possible through human upliftment in terms of up-gradation and reformation of business potentials, for the sake of suffered classes of humankind who are needed, at least, two handful meals a day; along with peaceful living environment in societal structure. Accordingly, government goodwill gestures and international level tie-ups in increasing trade relationships will commensurate socio-economic growth, for the purpose of creating employable conditions needed to safeguard the poor stage of the economies of scale in production function and manufacture related activities, to the horizons of social integrity based on international cooperation and fruitful understanding in carrying out business activities for the common benefit of all nations who are required to change the picture of social status of their citizens. Thus, foreign policies of the nations are to be redrafted on the flexibilities of operational skills, investment diversification norms and organizational quality leadership guided by the philosophy of strategic social orientation and business diversification, in underlying issues of global social integrity, human behavioural prudence and social development objectives. This way of doing with decision-making models for planning the size of the economic order of organizational functions, can be immensely helpful for re-orienting social structure for purposive human upliftment programmes, by taking national investment strategies and adopting policies for enhancement of human qualities in all-round areas, which will go to increase human talents for creative reformation of social building norms to the path of equitable living potential and justified order of doing businesses; so that human emancipation from the grass-root level to higher stages could be made possible through global business initiatives and human integrated nature of social upliftment, for reducing regional imbalances and increasing purchasing power by means of export stabilization and import substitution. Thus, balance of trade will be maintained in positive direction to move the entire economy for growing in a steady-state manner. To accentuate such kind of business paradigm shift in nature, there should be industrial nurture along with agricultural productivity boost-up; which will commensurate adequate human development for reducing different types of social conflict, and integrating the path of integral humanity by means of combined effort on the strategic functional model of 'private-public partnership' (PPP) in global level sustainability and human existential benefit towards social transformation[63].

From the discussions made so far, we would like to suggest that by benevolence leadership approach conditioned with patriotic nature of doing things, there will come social diversification in undertaking responsibilities and shouldering duties for increasing human skills, organizational competencies and social transparency to eliminate poverty from the present world order and to establish the concept of human fraternity in living goals and objectives. To accommodate such kind of social scenario, organizational intervention policies are to be reinvented with the new kind of road-map for assuming development as the call of the present century. As a matter of fact, strategic programmes for initiating partnership alliances in business areas by organizational entities will pave the way of speedy social development perspective, in this age of population increase and growing challenge for changing socialization scheme for balanced human development ideology. Naturally, it is urgent time now, to settle disputes between nation states for the greater interest of mankind who have been suffering a lot due to many crises in their way of leading life comfortably. We are to strategize our interest in concentrating on investment potentials to boost-up economic activities for quick development of the national economy by accelerating socio-economic activities and industrial reformative progress[64], in nurturing human resource potential to augment social sustainability as well as global convergence towards the path of integrated human upliftment programme. It can therefore be predicted that integration line with social inclusion of deprived people will be made through development oriented schemes and plan of action, on the part of modern sovereign governments; which should have coverage for containing elements of decisive areas concerning social elimination of deprivation that marginal classes of humankind have been suffering for long. In the context of doing things by the elected governments for planning social reconstruction as well as reformative activities, there should be mutual collaboration in co-operating at international level by way of human participation agenda in relation to art, science and composite cultural activities, confining people for their excellence building possibilities and confidence measures that are being emergently needed for emancipation of people, for the healthy reflection of social unity and universal integrity. So, it is imperatively conceived that the fact of inclusive development compounded with welfare measures would strengthen social convergence, in making people realize the thought of justice for peaceful living goal through augmentation of social harmony, in nurturing international peace and global tranquility – finding such goal for rejuvenating social restructuring method in calculating human value system and comfortable living parameters, it is needed that universal integrity for shaping culture of the world unity should accommodate human fellow-feeling nature of thought, in view of the enormous responsibility for developing social structure[65]. Consequently, human face of entrepreneurial professionalism should be inculcated for leading and guiding people, in organized system of management to communicate those measures that go to enhance social health in terms of corrective measures and collective efforts, perpetuated for encouraging backward people in taking things in challenging manner; so as to develop their conditions in incrementing benefits out of liberal practices of trade and business relationships. To address all such things in proactive manner, human participation level has to be remodeled by initiating responsibility on the part of the elected governments; which would further be made correlative of statistical analysis of things and activities in capacity building issues pertaining to human up-gradation programmes. This is the real technique of integrity where social rolling will become dynamic oriented for carrying out tasks of modern organizations, in nurturing human element at industrial psychological dimensions where development should be placed as the highest priority, among other things prevailing at social environmental phenomena with a view to understanding the need for human radical emancipation[66] from all types of social sufferings and deprivation.

The above prospective ideas are required to be nurtured effectively in benevolence leadership practice to democratize human participation level of undertaking, in realization of the goal of social welfare by means of holistic approach of considering growth initiation process for social reconstruction purposes, in which all should find adequate opportunities to develop at the maximum level for their upliftment objective, that can be immensely helpful for coordinating socialization through integrated nature of inclusion in reducing regional imbalances and human conflicts. Hence, it is essentially to be suggested that ifs and buts, in regard to develop social structure will be overthrown and instead, positive strategies and reform policies are required to be reformulated on the basis of human integrity and organizational dynamic communication system, to encourage people in making society vibrant by way of individual as well as group efforts, for which government policies requiring social strength should be revisited by accounting measures for human poverty eliminated issues and guidelines. Inculcation of comprehensiveness in areas of human challenges for initiating social responsibilities, in equality of status in living situation will commensurate from the practice of sustainable thought, which are required adequate government attention in planning for developing the societal stage in time, to the extent of bringing people for their enlightenment about sacrificing at the fullest level with a view to understand inclusive nature of development concept. Thus, integration of organizational entities and government agencies[67], both at the national as well as international level will be made very urgently, in repairing the irreparable situations in societal way of upbringing human qualities, with quantitative measures to rectify human uncivilized conditions of living by means of potential services norms, in making effective social change through work culture as the mantra of human development formula plan. In reconciling social balance in all-round areas, human development objective should be given extra-ordinary priority than any other conflicting nature of doing things, and therefore, international understanding should be strengthened among the nations, for the purpose of global human existentialism in bringing peaceful social environment; which requires social integrity for inclusive nature of development and transparent ideas for social growing tendencies[68].

Objective Functions of Human Development

Modern world has become multi-polarity plate-form to consider various aspects of life in human race. Accordingly, it is believed that human development has now become not only a challenge for the world community; but also, it is a strategic part of human peaceful living atmosphere to stabilize international cooperation, in enriching pillars of the global society. Thus, there are various objectivity related to social sustainability as well as global free existentialism, for which human development functions are to be carried in optimizing human capacity building to increase human competencies, social creativities and international capabilities, in regard to reducing regional imbalances with a view to solve problems of living and elimination of poverty and hungriness of global mankind. We should therefore assess those glaring important functions of overall human development process in objective manner, so as to encounter problems of healthy and comfortable living purposes, in encouraging people to mutually carry forward things in integrated approach for the sake of inclusive nature of growth potentials, along with the safeguard of the global environmental situations. As a matter of fact, it is highly believed that coordination in societal counterparts, as and when made by the national entities as well as international agencies could help build-up of the world society in dynamic manner, by way of modification of social elements that have repercussions to the sustainable nature of growth, in bringing people to the path of social emancipation for creating human value system in unified level of the world rolling[69], instead of having multi-diversities among the sovereign nations. From this standpoint, the objective functions of human development programmes can be discussed through under noted points, having relevancy in changing the societal picture for the welfare of mankind.

(1) Adequate functions pertaining to human development for inclusive nature of social growth are, naturally required by creating urgent provisions for providing fresh drinking water, electricity facilities, sanitation programmes, health and educational activities, among others; which are measurably important for people who have been suffering for long in the present society, as observed from the real situations of human living conditions in different parts of the world order.

(2) Human empowerment by way of inclusion in their rights for justified living potential and equitable nature of growth through inculcation of the human resource asset management policy[70], for global behavioural prudence and optimizing social peace and tranquility to upgrade human qualities of living and standard of life bringing possibilities. Thus, this functional aspect will stabilize social transparency in moving people towards sacrificing for nation building activities, by way of performing socio-economic functions for integrated human development objectives. Here, organizational entities are to be considered as the instrument of social changing element for creating group efforts, in innovating pattern of living through sensitizing human development

activities on ground realities of taking challenges, by initiating responsibilities for social development in equitable manner.

(3) Government policies requiring change, both at national and international level should be redrafted connoting therein the principles of work ethics, socialization with demarcation of the problems of modern societies, unity in action which will go to reduce social poverty and rampant corruptive activities, integrated as well as sustainable means of production, distribution and marketing activities, coordinating organizational functional relationship between tasks and responsibilities for performing to eliminate human deprivation from all sorts of living, creating social imbalances and regional disparities. Thus, policies should be adopted for mechanization of technological revamp in speeding human activities confined to those works having exigencies and urgencies to harmonize human relationships, in shaping the world order towards the path of universal development notion by way of people's movement for enlightening social welfare through effective growth potentials.

(4) Unilateral, bilateral and multilateral approaches are to be adopted for trade, industrial and business diversification, modernization of organizational activities in terms of 'private-public' cooperative work relationships and tie-ups, functional supremacy towards the tendencies of social cohesiveness for making dynamic programmes, narrating goals in procedural framework of government intervention for organizational development and social inclusion, in areas of people's need, human distress and social self-sufficiency. Thus, the objective functions related to human up-gradation are necessarily to be carried through effective management of resources pool, in pushing for long-term development as the agenda of modern social rolling, in the midst of optimum diversifications to correlate all elements of human asset management goal in efficient nurturing of the social resources, for elaborated nature of organizational innovative thought in creating and recreating human resource potential to accumulate the holistic growth of the society, by expansion of measures and techniques of human existential objective for steady-state development of the world order.

(5) Human dissatisfaction conforming social conflicts and regional threats are also to be balanced by way of objective analysis of the causes of such repercussions, and their enlarging affect on socio-economic behavioural prudence distorting the fabric of the modern societies against the equanimity of operational goal, which are required timely planning[71] through statistical formulation of strategies, considering human up-gradation, social emancipation of mankind and integral order of peaceful social living, incorporating therein the philosophy of social science and natural science for the envisagement of the objective of global human participatory performance, for the optimum utilization of natural resources to benefit for causing universal level of human development perspective.

Having regard to the above mentioned functional objectives in strategizing goal of human development for social balance, there is the need of governmental reformations in areas of laws concerning destabilization impact on human society, for creating imbalances throughout the socio-economic parameters, which could be seen from the present stage of human sufferings worldwide and the nature of nation building activities, particularly, in underdeveloped and developing countries where living potential of mankind has yet to be reformulated through scientific selection of projects, emanating mission for human substantial growth and dignified order of living objective, in fulfillment of the conditions of global transparency as well as social dynamicity. To illustrate the picture of human participative opportunities, we should follow the principles of organizational convergence in utilizing technological improvements to the ramification of social diversification, by means and ways which are optimally important to reduce social poverty for rejoicing justice for living in equitable pattern of dealing with the resources match. It is therefore proactive nature of reinforcement should be aided through organizational working behaviour, and dynamic group behaviour in building effective team in approaching towards conformity to reduce conflicting tendencies, by new methods of doing business and performing socio-economic activities for the greater interest of deprived mankind[72], who have been suffering from all essential needs required for civic living goal in societal environment.

Thus, management of work requires perseverance on the part of authorities to respond all the fields of social backwardness, in addressing towards changing human fate by implementing all important packages and schemes of operations, to inculcate habit for human positive relationship in organizational reformative movements for the purposive social orientation goal of living. The dynamics of behavioural analysis in agricultural fields by means of technological up-gradation and improvization of the types of production will reflect development, to attain the goal of maximum social advantage which should have modernization methods in increasing output to eliminate social poverty and human starvation death. Again, rationalization of industrial activities by reconciliation of crafts and guilds in removing bottlenecks will be made imperative towards socialization programmes, in rejuvenating human skills and creative potentials for the purpose of diversification, modernization and innovation; so as to balance 'input-output' relationship to upgrade standard of living in societal objectification of reorientation, in all issues pertaining to domestic as well as external business potentials should require a pattern of dynamic moving, in rolling towards human mission for capacity building assurances would be nurtured in vibrated and sparkling manner. Accordingly, comprehensive measures are to be taken in adopting ideas of social transparency, by way of technological vision for which technical 'Ombudsman' should be created with adequate functional responsibility, for accountability in areas of social delivery needed for reducing imbalances in kind of living pattern in a spirit of equity, justice and human solvency in life related elements of social dynamicity. In optimizing production goal for effective management of resources and efficient handling of social backwardness, there is the urgent need of structural adjustment[73], and therefore, coordination for sound organizational directive functions has immense impact on social building goal; where innovative research and empirical studies made in line with human integrated planning for reformative social goal should require international understanding, in complementing independent nature of working through human skilful techniques of production.

The directive functions of human development should be merged with the weaker sections of the society, in eliminating social inequalities to pave the way for human dignity in living potential, for inclusive nature of social growth which requires decentralizing all norms of human specialization order towards building society, in healthy human relationship to the attainment of goal of integral humanity. In helping to orientation of social people, there is the need of austerity measures which should be conceive as the framework of social rolling in dynamic way, to the continuation of human emancipation programmes and policies resolution of global integrity for motivating people to encourage healthy growth with trusteeship relational approach. Hence, it is undoubtedly to be noted that organizational mission should incorporate delivery mechanism with challenging attitude, which could be affordable to modernize industrial activities in regard to suggesting efforts toward the optimization of human welfare initiative. The logo of services in this context should be engraved with the sacrificing norms of social building goal, in regulating people to upgrade ideas of innovative paths for social reformation, where every individual being should be empowered in realizing the objective of self-reliance programme to stabilize social harmony, universal integrity and the world peace. The undone aspects of social challenges creating human imbalances in order of living should be regenerated through new innovative methods of performance criterion, so as to reassure social inclusiveness in growth patterns to all those who are needed special treatment in supplying necessaries of leading healthy and civic life. It is thus, prima facie need to incorporate legal balance with justified norms of social transparency, which could be seen as the rejoinder[74] towards making people to take oath for public good by means of public services, in all fields of social reconstruction means of productive activities. To inculcate measures of human up-gradation in organizational guiding system, tools and techniques of human competencies are to be related with that of leadership initiatives; if development has to be seen from proactive as well as holistic approach where deprived human beings will get involved with the functional ideas of social inclusiveness, in radicalization of those programmes that are important for human emancipation to a stage of social reconstruction. Thus, objective functions in claiming human up-gradation should be resulted from organizational top level initiative, in percolating towards the down level-via-middle level executive functional responsibility for implementing schemes of development in time. In harmonizing things for better human relationship and profitable employment of resources, propaganda for publicity will immensely destroy the objective utility of human efficiency, and so; there should be encouraging zeal and motivating spirit to the patriotic needs of services, which are to be corroborated in all functional areas of social reconstruction programmes, where people to people interaction is highly important for speedy development of the social structure. It is further to be justified in suggesting that human development is a matter of continuous activities to be carried through ongoing experience[75], in dealing with the system of work culture in objective fulfillment towards building social pyramid in healthy human relationships, to optimize the order of living in harmonious manner with all inclusiveness ideologies, where social transformation should be made objective oriented towards guiding people in matters of overall improvement. So, it is a functional dynamicity comprehensively objectified for human capacity building approach, in growing modern societies to the path of human existentialism for embracing the goal of common welfare of people.

In a nutshell, objective functions of human development should accommodate principles of association, attributing the growing consciousness policy in organizational strategies for social change in timeframe schedule, with all constituents of modern organizations and its counterparts occupying parity towards nation building norms of human emancipation goal, compounding for human capacities with the optimizing nature of skills and experience initiatives, in rejuvenating modern social pyramid[76]. Thus, the approach of creative human development function will interrelate things and activities for the dynamic rolling of all national entities, with their independent character of familiarity in upgrading people by means of maximum social benefit, in unifying the objective of social diversification for human living autonomy complementary towards attaining the goal of human dignity, social integrity and global transcendental order of transformation. To pave the way for social justice, peace and tranquility, there is the urgent need of holistic reformations having human interface in all-round spheres of social structure, which go to enlarge human integrity and brotherhood for universal understanding in mankind. As per this role model, leadership techniques are to be reformulated for initiating social growth in dynamic movement where humanity should be given the highest priority, to the ramification of the objective functions for social reconstruction in dignified order of human living goal. From such perspective we should guide our organizational entities in removing social poverty, human distressful conditions of living and reducing social imbalances; so that the conflicting nature in society caused by human restlessness will be eradicated for establishment of global peace. Hence, the comprehensive model for social inclusiveness of the marginal classes will be integrated towards nation building approach of human cooperative living endeavor[77], in dignifying human living potential with the trusteeship principle of work culture, emulating all for realizing the spirit in living order with the norms of free existentialism. To upgrade human beings from the pathetic stage of social living, necessary steps with legal measures are required in rebuilding modern societies, to reorient human life bringing objectives toward the functional role of social changing in positive direction. It is therefore human face of social reformation that could be enhanced through unity in operative functions of organizations, in fulfilling conditions of solvency in life, integrity in living goal and objectivity in optimizing social peace.

Methodology for Universal Human Development Approach

Human development is the key issue in shaping modern world to pave the way for global peace and international understanding between human races. It is therefore essential that total human quality (THQ) in the context of living parameters has to be assessed, on the basis of human requirements like – health, education, electricity, water supply, infrastructure, communication and so on. These are the primary as well as fundamental aspects of human civilization progress, where modern sovereign governments, multinational and international corporate houses, non-governmental organizations (NGOs), religious and philanthropic institutions, charitable institutions, etc. have all their participatory role model in rejuvenating the world society; for efficient human resource management potential to enlarge social unity and human integrity. Hence, it is also important to deal with the subject of human development effectively by the United Nations Organization (UNO), which is the backbone to erect world civilization on the foundation of common human benefit for living in peaceful manner. Today, the UNO has a great potential role to modernize civilization activities as the watchdog in recreating human skilful potentials to the path of social reconstruction, eliminate unsocial as well as anti-social activities from the world platform, curb all kinds of terrorism in the interest of fabricating peaceful social atmosphere worldwide, establish mutual collaboration in between important economic forums and international agencies for developing world masses in line with equality of living in dignity, justice for thinking towards human unity, and fraternity for enjoying life by all legitimate human rights[78] in living peacefully. Thus, human development with the methodical operation of things and activities can be applicable for global unity, international brotherhood and human integrity, to pave the way for world class citizenship and unified pattern of living goal. Having regard to the possibilities of human personality development to the fullest level, there is the requirement of economic equality which must be strategized for forward looking tendencies, on the part of each sovereign nation; otherwise, the recent development that has been taking place worldwide, like – terrorism, regionalism, separatism, communalism, chauvinism, racialism, etc. could have a destructive repercussion on the world platform, which might result in destructive impact to destabilize harmony and social unity. Thus, connecting humankind to the path of global level problems, like – castes, religions, communalism, regionalism, terrorism, racialism and many other similar situations, there has been created a restless tendency throughout the world environment in between people, which are to be curbed by taking remedial measures on performing various economic activities and bringing thereby, human self-sufficiency in establishment of free social existentialism. Therefore, it is suggested that international methodology for human development programme should be reformulated on grounds of human equity and unity in living backgrounds.

For universal human development, speedy social reformative activities are needed, so as to eliminate problems of human distress, misery and hungriness. As a matter of fact, it is highly essential that banking sector reforms, insurance sector reforms, industrial rationalization policy, agricultural productivity increasing packages and research activities are all should be integrated towards socialization of schemes, and removing difficulties for human peaceful living tendencies[79]. To eliminate social backwardness, modern marketing facilities are to be reconstructed through cooperative dealing models and practices. Again, land reformative activities are to be taken at hand by resolving new policy guidelines to safeguard interest of landless poor agriculturists, marginal farmers, etc.; where government level control mechanism should be reformulated[80] for reinforcing agricultural productivity to reshape the onslaught of poor village agriculturists. All modern amenities, like – high quality seeds, biotic manures, and pesticides having less affect on human and animal life should be made available to the farmers by government distribution measures. Further, tools and implements, tractors and other machineries required for timely harvesting in seasons should also be provided by the respective government agencies. Irrigational facilities and rain water preservation for seasonal harvesting, construction of canals and dams, drainage facilities for carrying water to agricultural fields to the destination of plough, etc. should be provided with making provisions for reaching all such schemes to the realities of need by modern government functionaries. Scientific weather forecasting by means of satellite communication system should be made for knowing adequate kind of weather conducive for plough; so that harvesting loses are minimized to the lowest level possible by government machinery with adequate administrative guidelines. Thus, agriculture should be made more and more scientific oriented in approaching towards productivity perfectionism[81], for enlarging agricultural produce; which could help in minimizing rural poverty. Moreover, administered agricultural prices should be made compulsory to secure benefit to rural poor farmers. Thus, by means of providing them minimum support prices, government will help themselves to earn legitimate amount of profits, at least, to safeguard their interest of livelihood, along with continuing activities for the purpose of regular production, and also to curb monopolistic as well as restrictive tendencies that have been found prevailing in society; for which farmers are suffering severely from their legitimate rights of getting minimum rate of income. Agricultural insurance should further be made compulsory by the government agencies in reducing harvesting losses against flood, famine, draught, etc. In this way of working, total agricultural reformations (TARs) are to be made by government authorities for human upliftment and reducing social poverty, which has been observed as the greatest curse of human civilization.

The long-run perspective for human emancipation from severe sufferings in respect of living situations has to be remedied with the skilful employment provisions, in terms of industrial reformative activities, like – new industry relocation system for eradicating regional imbalances, innovative technological research to the field of sick industrial concerns for renovation purposes, modernization of industrial guilds and crafts management system for increasing productivity, scientific research on industrial rehabilitation programmes, technological know-how and collaboration between nations by means of industrial consortium in government level bilateral agreements, corporate level trade negotiations, etc. are to be guiding pattern of industrial reformative processes and programme implementation purposes[82]. Hence, it is imperative that creation of employment opportunities are not only guided by industrial reformations; but also, there should be infrastructural projects to be taken at hand for speedy development of human society, which will be augmenting marketing facilities for selling industrial products at low cost. In this way, market competition will be made scientific towards maintaining equilibrium rate of demand based productivity and supply-chain distribution potentials, to eradicate all ills in socio-economic pattern of human living parameters. Again, electricity and power supply has been a great problem for industrial relocation in many parts of the underdeveloped and developing nations, which should be planned according as to the need of the local problems. As a matter of fact, it becomes now obligatory on the part of the sovereign governments, both in underdeveloped and developing countries that there should be appropriate strategies for increasing power supply to revamp industrial activities; which should be done by means of creating and innovating new small river dams, instead of big dams, keeping in mind the concept of holistic welfare measures to all social citizens, to safeguard their local interest as well as harvesting and living facilities. As of now, we have assessed on agricultural and industrial activities for approaching towards methodological foundation of human social rebuilding measures, in new kinds of reformative paths for eradicating problems of human sufferings, and for creating employment opportunities in areas of such kind of priority sectors that have social value addition[83], in rejuvenating human living potentials to the reoriented pattern of social ramifications, in augmenting 'demand-supply' equilibrium realities of managing socio-economic activities. Moreover, we are to suggest that human society, now, at this time of global competition requires the latest technological foundation for communicating all types of information, which are having importance towards changing sociological progress in unified nature of dealing with the crisis driven areas of human needs and aspirations. It is therefore, human communication system can lead to the goal of welfare measures in challenging against poverty and hungriness. Furthermore, it is expected that government measures in initiating provisions for supplying fresh drinking water to both urban and rural areas could help in minimizing human sufferings. Hence, public water resource management system has to be coordinated with the private body corporate, for which, there should be local level tie-ups between public-private partnerships (PPPs) in carrying out all such programmes needed for mitigating social crisis. In this line of thinking, government policy should be changed for eradicating problems of fresh drinking water supply system; so that rural people are served with such essential amenities, along with urban water supply provisions and schemes which go to reduce water supply service crisis that has been found for long in towns and city areas.

Another aspect of human development is the educational facilities requiring universal and compulsory education up to the level of tenth standard, giving human potential to develop for increasing social good, on the part of the government initiatives. However, multinational corporate houses are also to join hands with the local government[84] officials and agencies to widespread educational facilities in remote village areas, where children are not having such facilities, and for which, they remain illiterate during their course of living in poverty and misfortunes for survival. To accelerate educational activities, there is the necessity of providing sanitation facilities, due to lack of which rural girl child remains uneducated. Because, they do not get urinal and latrine facilities in remote villages, which should be provided by corporate houses to upgrade living standard[85] of village people, and to make themselves educated for understanding socio-economic parameters of healthy living potential. For compulsory education up to high school level, there is the urgent necessity of government policy resolution at appropriate measures which could be found increasing rural literacy for healthy social building norms, and initiating skills[86] in regard to employment provisions; so that rural population suffering from poverty[87] could get their legitimate rights of employment. Again, the government should adopt appropriate measures for strengthening higher education related activities and research related need based programmes; so that educated youths are easily absorbed in big industries and corporate houses. Nevertheless, it is important to note that science education should be given special priority for speedy industrial development. Accordingly, technology[88] related programmes are also to be enhanced for increasing standard of living, by means of social reformation through industrial parks and factory rationalization measures[89]. To accelerate industrial estates, entrepreneurship development programmes have been found to be the need of the hour, for which modern governments must be conscious in managing educational activities[90], keeping regard to the innovative research and creative educational opportunities for needy and talented students. For social health, and for reducing human diseases, there is the necessity of increasing health education, for which many more new medical institutions are yet to be established, so as to increase doctors in society to serve not only urban people; but also village population who are surviving without such facilities, and dying untimely due to lack of medical services. Government should be conscious in planning for all such activities[91], to increase life span of citizens to healthy norms of living parameters. Latest medicines reducing severe diseases could also be found through innovative research practices. Hence, in line with international standard of living, there should be propagation of science education in creating new medicines, for which government should increase resource outlets to the field of laboratory experiments. Strict abidance of the principles of fund utilization and laboratory production at the same time would result in increasing health of mankind; along with wide spreading education in this field. This kind of policy will help to correlate fund management along with innovative research practice and production potential, for standardization of human health related initiatives in increasing life span and stabilizing social health. Thus, health and education has both social impact and economic incidences for healthy social transformation[92], in making people to revitalize socio-economic parameters of peaceful living goal.

In concluding about the process of human development and its role for increasing social goodness, it can be well predicted that service sector reforms are necessary ingredient part of social development, on which stands social stability, human peace and tranquility in world environment. Hence, the methodical approach for developing humankind should be conceived through reorientation of service sectors, where social mobility will be made dynamic towards cohesive nature of human up-gradation, social transformation and world class prosperity of all kinds of human beings, irrespective of caste, creed, colour, race, sex, religion, etc. This kind of policy will rebuild social structure based on human foundation, and therefore, ecological balance has to be restored by means of environmental planning, which is the major area of human survival, social growth and worldwide integrity between people in connoting growth perspective towards the existential freedom of mankind[93]. From all such measurable facts, it comes true to mention that human dignity in living potential should be guided by the philosophy of social orientation in creative path of development, for nurturing deprived humankind and, to place themselves in a position to upgrade their living situations through conceivable nature of growth, finding which social peace and stability could be equally set-up to restore human integrity, worldwide cooperation and transcendental order of living in the midst of coherent human relationship[94]. Hence, human competencies are to be increased for human capacity building initiatives, in reconciling social imbalances and reducing regional disparities between people. It will serve the whole mankind to address against terrorism, which is the severe problem in front of the world community and a great challenge for the survival of the foundation of human civilization. Consequently, internationalization of development mantra as the core idea of human living together as well as national agenda for human upliftment programmes, from all sorts of healthy living[95] parameters could only help in safeguarding the entire world against all types of anti-social activities and destructive elements. Here, it is also relevant to say that defence research programmes and all kinds of warfare instruments as well as missile technology should be developed not to make any warfare activities, but to safeguard the humankind against terrorism, by means of mutual collaboration and trust between nations; otherwise, human development in steady-state manner would become quite impossible, along with safeguarding timely the precious human civilization for the purpose of restoring world peace and social tranquility. The global community should all come forward together in the interest of all mankind for establishing an international level forum to fight against terrorism, and to destroy totally all kinds of terror activities from this world; if the world community along with national sovereignty has to be developed in permanent nature. In short, human development has to be made with the holistic approach of social reformative activities[96] as suggested so far, for which universal methodology in initiating social peace is the prerequisite to equity in living and to upkeep human fraternity, in harmonious existential reformative pattern of dealing with the case of global dynamism, at par with human familiarity.

Notes and References

1. The first point to note is that the "carrying capacity" of the world was enormously different in the Stone Age than in the era of agriculture, and considerably lower than it is now. – Ray, Debraj: "Development Economics", Oxford University Press, New Delhi, 2013, p. 302.

2. Like economic growth, population growth is a modern phenomenon. Indeed, even if we were to know very little about the world, we could deduce this very quickly by regression in time. If we assume the world population today, say, at around six billion. Let's go backward and decrease this number by two per cent year. This exercise would yield a population of 250,000 around 500 years ago, or a population of 10 around 1,000 years! This is obviously ludicrous. As late as in the eighteenth century Malthus (1798) wrote of God's checks and balances to the sexual energies of women and men. A spontaneously high rate of reproduction was countered with all manner of disasters, such as regular outbreaks of plague, pestilence, and famine. So, although birth rates were high, death rates were sufficiently high to keep growth rates down to a crawl. We may think of this as the first phase of demographic history.

3. It is here predicted undoubtedly that political issues seem to shape the social or economic activities of the structures of the international system. – Ghosh, Peu:

"International Relations", PHI Learning Private Limited, New Delhi, 2011, p. 208. In regard to such initiatives, Kegley and Wittkopf point out: "The reality is that technical cooperation is often more severely impacted by political considerations than the other way around ......" – Kegley, Charles W., Jr. and Wittkopf, Eugene R.: "World Politics – Trends and Transformation", St. Martin's Press, New York, 1981, p. 454.

4. Right-wing social scientists and policy-makers never tire of insisting that government intervention in economic activities is harmful for growth. – Sikdar, Soumyen: "Principles of Macroeconomics", Oxford University Press, New Delhi, 2012, p. 173. According to the supply-side economists, the sharp downturn of the U.S. economy during the 1980s was due in large part to the proliferation of government regulations of business. The blame for the lackluster performance of the European economies over the last decade (i.e., 1990s) has likewise been laid at the door of excessive government interference.

5. As a reasonable background of such selective process, it is said like: "The religion of the Hindus is divided into two parts: the ceremonial and the spiritual. The spiritual portion is specially studied by the monks. In that, there is no caste. A man from the highest caste and a man from the lowest may become a monk in India, and the two castes become equal ......Caste is simply a social institution." – Chaudhuri, Asim: "Swami Vivekananda in Chicago – New Findings", Advaita Ashrama, Kolkata, 2012, p. 228. This is obviously scientific in looking about the ancient Vedic techniques, where methods of social reconstruction were prevailing for global thought, in liberal practices of human living existentialism for growth of individuals and to the salvation of life.

6. All these are possible, when we would be able to think scientifically about the goal. Accordingly, Sri Ramakrishna's mission on earth–so far as our human understanding goes and as his disciples have, time and again, declared – was to demonstrate that all religions lead to the same goal and that, through right practice, this goal is realizable. – Bodhasarananda, Swami: "Vivekananda the Great Spiritual Teacher", Advaita Ashrama, Kolkata, 2012, p. 147. Having regard to such spiritual riches, it is asserted that global order is the real goal of all human activities.

7. It is because of the fact, that: "The Lord is all blissfulness. He is the reality behind all that exists; He is the goodness, the truth in everything. You are His incarnations." – Bodhasarananda, Swami: "Swami Vivekananda on Himself", Advaita Ashrama, Kolkata, 2012, p. 233. This is the actual idea, for which, equanimity concept should be infused in mind of all for poverty eradication programmes by way of different agency functions as well as government initiatives. Thus, general human welfare will be made through unity in work and living in equity.

8. Our approach should be to have comprehensive economic and social planning as a means to promote economic and social development in respective nations, particularly, in countries of South-East Asia. However, there is also the need for modernization and expansion of existing industries for selling their products at home and in other countries of the world. New industries are to be started for matching new demands, as per population growth rate. In underdeveloped and developing countries, we are needed to provide for basic infrastructures such as approach roads, safe and adequate water supplies to villages and cities, opening

of schools in villages and primary health centres within easy reach and increasing agricultural output by modernization of techniques to meet the food needs of people and fibre needs of industries. Veterinary hospitals and dispensaries were to be built in order to provide facilities to farmers for their livestock, among others. Again, the flexibility in decision approach should relate to the process of planning of land use that is determination of locations for housing, industries and commercial and other service activities, of transportation routes and of various physical and social infrastructure, etc. Because, these are altogether form the core of a development plan. – Also see, Nath, Dr V.: "Economic Development and Planning in India", Concept Publishing Company Pvt. Ltd., New Delhi, 2010, pp. 102-107.

9. As an example, it is worthwhile to note that in the past there were relations between England and India, which originated mainly in commerce. The Indian products then, created a lucrative trade with Egypt, Greece and Rome – the markets which met the needs of whole of Europe. – Raychoudhary, S. C.: "Social, Cultural and Economic History of India (Earliest Times to Present Times)", Surjeet Publications, Delhi, 1989, p. 242.

10. In pursuant of dynamics study in economic science, it is believed that the orthodox view in economic theory is that the real interest rate cannot be less than the growth rate of real GDP over a long period. – Joshi, Vijay and Little, I.M.D.: "India's Economic Reforms 1991–2001", Oxford University Press, New Delhi, 1996, p. 31. But the case of social balance, while studied with reference to an empirical fact, it is observed that some East Asian countries have for long periods grown faster than the real rate of interest, but it is also notable fact that most of them have had significantly lower public deposits than India. – See Chapter 2 of Chopra et al. (1995). Again, as a measure of policy reformation, the Indian representative at GATT's trade policy review (GATT, 1993, Vol. II) asserted that developing countries need an escalating tariff structure......the Ministry of Commerce suggests that this Ministry is still imbued with erroneous protectionist ideas that diverge from the main thrust of policy reform. – *Ibid.*, p. 75. It is very confused and confusing. We therefore require responsible governance policy to lift the veil of bottlenecks in entire economic front from the overall socio-economic background of people.

11. To substantiate this view, we must keep in mind that the technology strategy, particularly, for rural development in case of India, along with other countries of the world, which have been found to be remaining as more backward in this age of scientific revolution should require a perspective appraisal of all these issues. Kumud Nath Jha has rightly said: "Technology is as much necessary for physical and material well being of the rural people as they are for their economic emancipation." – Jha, Kumud Nath: "Economics and Impact of Technology Transfer to Rural Areas", Deep & Deep Publications, New Delhi, 1994. It is now well recognized view that technology has played a dominant role in rural development in various countries of the world. Thus, we are not only needed suitable technology in the field of agriculture, animal husbandry and in industry for strengthening the economy of the villages, but we also require, as Jha opines: "Appropriate technologies for housing, health and hygiene, transport and communication, recreation, education and energy needs for the rural people for their survival without agony." – *Ibid.*, p. 25.

12. To employ a customary expression, we can say that money thus far represents only the cloak of economic things and nothing essential is overlooked in abstracting from it. However, this conception is to be found as early as Berkeley. It has never been lost, and J. S. Mill more recently gave it currency. In contemporary German literature it is found chiefly in Bendixen. It contradicts neither the quantity theory, nor the cost of production nor the "balancing" theory. – Schumpeter, Joseph A. and Opie, Redvers: "The Theory of Economic Development", Harvard University Press, Cambridge, 1955, p. 51. Again, Avadhani asserts that: "The total of credits and debits in current and capital accounts may not always balance. There can be a surplus or deficit which is made good by a corresponding balancing entry, namely, official financing items. These items may be gold, use of IMF assistance or drawl on the country's foreign assets......" – Avadhani, V. A.: "International Finance: Theory and Practice", Himalaya Publishing House, Bombay, 1987. In this way, the perspective idea of good governance is guided by the philosophy of development, which requires scientific balance in restoration of economic growth with human developmental issues from sociological standpoint as well as global human integrity.

13. The wide disparity in income distribution was a common feature of the less developed countries (which are fully developed today) in their initial stages of development. – Mankar, V. G.: "Economic Policy and Planning", New Age International (P) Limited, Publishers formerly Wiley Eastern Limited, New Delhi, 1995, p. 211. So, the realistic norms of growth potentials would be assessed from the development of 18th century England, 19th century Western Europe and early 20th century Japan. All these, reveal this stage in the history of their development. Our programme implementations are to be measured therefore, through employment targets too, which are very far from reality to cause for abnormal growth rate in making economy vibrant. To suggest as remedial measure, it can be said that human poverty should be reduced for economic growth potentials. Probably, this is the reason why the American system of government has placed due emphasis on liberty of the individual and stability and strength in institutions. – Griffith, Ernest S.: "The American System of Government", Frederick A. Praeger, Inc., New York, 1961 (Revised edition), p. 15.

14. Here, it is observed that the discrimination in favour of import substitution and against exports did not permit the development of manufactured exports in countries engaging in second-stage import substitution behind high protection. This has resulted for imbalanced order of global development. But, Meier and Rauch predict that there were also adverse developments in primary exports, because low prices for producers and consumers reduced the exportable surplus by discouraging production and encouraging consumption. – Meier, Gerald M. and Rauch, James E.: "Leading Issues in Economic Development", Oxford University Press, New York, 2004 (Reprinted), p. 183. In going through all such cases, it is evident that inadequate level of export and import functions in the arena of world trade has caused for destabilizing human standard of living in many countries of the world. Therefore, it is required proper strategy for improving export and import situations to stimulate the process of human development in bringing global transformation and human fraternity for liberal trade practices.

15. In this context, Jibendra writes: "When civilization flourishes under the garb of increasing commercialism and politics becomes a power hunt for men and nations disregarding all the cherished moral and spiritual values of the past, it only indicates the extent and enormity of the degeneration. We have probably touched the bed-rock of moral and spiritual degradation. Now a powerful lever is needed to raise humanity from the level of beasts to which it has sunk (except in a few rare cases) to the level of the gods." – Jibendra, Sri: "Sri Aurobindo's Philosophy and Yoga", Sahityasree, Calcutta, 1983, p. 48. Thus, radical nature of social change will be brought forth by means of scientific plans for human development issues.

16. To substantiate all such views, it is undoubtedly to be said that the history of political economy is instructive. At a time when capitalist production, in the first stage of its evolution, had not yet transformed the mass of the bourgeois into parasites, the Physiocrats, Adam Smith, Ricardo, etc., could make an impartial study of economic phenomena, and search out the general laws of production. But since the machine-tool and steam require the cooperative efforts of wage-workers alone in the creation of wealth, the economists confine themselves to the collection of facts and statistical figures, valuable for the speculations of commerce and the Stock Exchange, without endeavoring to group and classify them, so as to draw theoretical conclusions, since these could only be dangerous to the dominance of the possessing class. Instead of building up science they are fighting socialism; they have even wished to refute the Ricardian theory of value because socialist criticism had taken possession of it. – See also, Lafargue, Paul: "Social and Philosophical Studies", Naya Prokash, Calcutta, 1981, pp. 31-32 (Foot note).

17. About this right kind of thinking, it is observed that by a parallel progress there has been established that right of free speech on political questions, which in early days was denied. Herbert Spencer says in this regard: "Among the Athenians in Solon's time, death was inflicted for opposition to a certain established policy; and among the Romans the utterance of proscribed opinions was punished as treason. So, too, in England centuries ago, political criticism, even of a moderate kind, brought severe penalties......" – Spencer, H.: "The Principles of Ethics", Liberty Classics, Indianapolis, 1978, p. 161. Later times have witnessed now greater liberty of speech and now greater control: the noticeable fact being that during the war period brought on by the French revolution; there was a retrograde movement in respect of this right as in respect of other rights.

18. This right directional path should have the idea that the highest form of life, individual and social, is not achievable under a reign of justice only; but that there must be joined with a reign of beneficence. In this way, our goal can lead to the process of human emancipation.

19. In understanding about the concept of quality of life in sociological perspective, Sinha predicts: "The contradiction between 'being' and 'non-being' is resolved in the notion of 'becoming'. A new contradiction appears in this concept, which is reconciled by a new synthesis, and so on, until the most comprehensive concept of the 'Absolute Idea' is reached which reconciles all oppositions and contradictions". – Sinha, J. N.: "Introduction to Philosophy", New Central Book Agency (P) Ltd., Kolkata, 2009 (Reprinted), p. 53. The fabric of survival issue is concerned with environment parlance in the sense that: Nature is self-development of thought; thought is nature becoming conscious of itself, predicts

thus Sinha further, to clear the views of Hegel who was directly an advocate of 'Dialectical Idealism'. Again, for welfare of mankind, Karl Marx who is follower of Hegel has said about 'Dialectical Materialism' as the method for analysis and it dominates the radical thought of the present day.

20. To pronounce rich conditions on environmental balance for human sustainable impact on life, we should not seek our own personal good apart from that of others. But we should realize a rational universe. Jadunath Sinha again, predicts that "We should realize the most perfect type of human existence......" –Sinha, J.: "A Manual of Ethics", New Central Book Agency (P) Ltd., Kolkata, 2009, p. 163. So, our match abilities are to be enriched for entering into subject of healthy survival, which requires it content from value as the standard health, physical exercise, recreation, happiness, knowledge, culture, virtue, beauty, love, comradeship, social service – contribute to self-realization; because, without these contents self-realization is a vague ideal. In this way of work with organizational activities, human beings will make upliftment from the clutches of corruptive behaviour, and thus, habit of free living will be inculcated for existential freedom to reflect the illuminative idea of environmental balance.

21. Accordingly, Bhagavad Gita has said: "Man must endeavor to understand that this mundane world and its uses are of no use and transient". – Kuppuswami, A.: "Bhagavad Gita", Chaukhambha Orientalia, Delhi, 2005 (Second edn.), p. 244. The Vedanta version of equipoise thinking is therefore related to endeavour of human beings to aim at attaining 'moksha'. It is the only permanent abode of peace. This can be done by working as the greatest happiness of the greatest number as the highest good. – *Op. cit.,* p. 162. Altruistic Hedonism calls it as the general happiness.

22. This order is called by Sri Aurobindo's Yoga as the integral and it is the aim of Sri Aurobindo's Yoga. – See also, Lal, Basant Kumar: "Contemporary Indian Philosophy", Motilal Banarsidass, Delhi, 1992, p. 222. This is the reason, why the Vedanta concept holds good to the unity among all religions; otherwise, the idea of human development will be marred by illusion and maya, because passions mislead a man. It involves a struggle within, a fight against oneself – a very difficult indeed. Radhakrishnan says: "It is easy to fight non-human nature, forests, floods and wild beasts, but it is difficult to fight the passions in our heart, the illusions that we embrace". – See Radhakrishnan's Occasional Speeches and Writings (1952-59), pp. 361-62. Thus, Kutumbakam philosophy is ingrained with the affirmation of the ultimate of 'Religious Experience'. – *Op. cit.,* p. 292. In getting things done through, therefore, we must have such philosophical order in our mind; if we want to bring in human welfare in society and restore peace in humanity.

23. To preserve humanity, a good example is enough. Jibendra says, in the words of Aurobindo: "When a man comes to you to bestow some favor, you can tell him to go and bestow it on some beggar". – Jibendra, Sri: "Aphorisms on Life and Yoga", Sahityasree, Calcutta, p. 47. Hence, to preserve humanity our business instincts are required to give up, which is very hard. Because, one always computes in terms of profit and loss even when one ceases to engage in active business. Probably, this is the reason that Jibendra cites: "The world would be an ideal place to live in if only we attended to our own business and ceased to

poke our nose in others' affairs". – *Ibid.,* p. 48. The 'path-goal relativity' will therefore be adjusted through our spiritual life, if we really, are busy with finding out some means and ways for ultimate development of human beings in this world of living. Because, it is not the number of years spent in sadhana that counts but the humility, patience and energy developed for self-giving and surrender to the Divine. In this way, the entire humanity can be well safeguarded against catastrophic destruction.

24. If this is so, then for normal human beings one's life may be better or worse in itself because it includes morally right or wrong action. – Frankena, William K.: "Ethics", PHI Learning Private Limited, New Delhi, 2011, p. 94. Organizational guiding techniques should therefore be felt as Alyosha exclaims at one point in The Brothers Karamazov, "How good it is to do something good!" – *Op. cit.,* p. 94. Morally right action is one kind of activity that satisfies a standard of excellence, and so being morally right is a kind of excellence...... See also, Dewey, John: "Theory of the Moral Life", ed. Arnold Isenberg, New York: Holt, Rinehart and Winston, Inc., 1960. It is an important book in its own right. So, our guided techniques should be followed from moral grounds of doing right to others for human emancipation purposes.

25. Up-gradation of mankind requires a creed of services to the humanity. In this context, Tapash Sankar Dutta writes: "This creed of service to humanity through disciplined action, right conduct, right thought and right association – produced huge upsurge in the vast ocean – like expanse of Swamiji's soul". – Dutta, T. S.: "A Study of the Philosophy of Vivekananda", Sribhumi Publishing Company, Calcutta, 1982, p. 93. Towards rational approach in making senses good to the wellbeing of mankind Aristotle said of each man in particular: "There is nothing in the intellect unless it has first been in the senses". – Carritt, E. F. (Ed.): "Philosophies of Beauty", Oxford University Press, London, 1931, p. 74. Living peace should be made through conduct of human behaviour for realizing happiness. This is the truth and beauty of work might be expressed in goodness for human beings, to upgrade themselves in a stage of living fraternity.

26. In strategic nature of dealing with reformative tasks, we must remember that the things in the world would behave in their own manners according to their specific nature. – Dasgupta, S.: "A History of Indian Philosophy", Cambridge University Press, London, 1955, p. 115. We are to understand that the individual souls are naturally full of impurities, and it is for that reason that they pass through the cycle of birth and rebirth......He can be the real agent for the motivation for the development of the animate and inanimate world. – *Ibid.,* p. 115. Thus, it is admitted that there is the permanent will of God, that things would evolve in particular directions in accordance with the karma of the individuals. In dealing with the tasks of human organizations, we should follow the principles of karma as well as natural will of the God.

27. It is asserted by the orthodox claim that the Veda is the repository of absolute wisdom, so also its full knowledge will make human beings enlightened about the concept of sociological betterment with human perfection of works in life. All living parameters should therefore be anticipated to Vedic idealism, in bringing mankind to the door of success in life. – See also, Chattopadhyaya, D.: "Indian Philosophy", People's Publishing House Private Limited, New Delhi,

1964, for further understanding on Vedic principles to arrive at a conclusion – what should be transparent tendencies for establishment of our 'input-output' balance theory in regard to deal with human development perspective.

28. This path requires everything should be done on people's initiative. Thus, democratic government is to be based not on mere passive consent but on active participation of individuals. Vivekananda made it clear thus: "Being always governed by the kings of God-like nature, to whom is left the whole duty of protecting and providing for the people, they can never get any occasion for understanding the principles of self-government. Such a nation, being entirely dependent on the king for everything and never caring to exert itself for the common good or for self-defence becomes gradually destitute of inherent energy and strength. When this state of dependence and protection continues long, it becomes the cause of the destruction of the nation, and its ruin is not far to seek". – Vivekananda, Swami: "The Complete Works of Swami Vivekananda", Vol. IV, Advaita Ashrama, Calcutta, 1962, p. 441. Thus, he laid emphasis on self-help and not a governmental assistance in the building up of man-making process. – Reddy, A. V. Rathna: "Political Philosophy of Swami Vivekananda", Sterling Publishers Private Limited, New Delhi, 1984, p. 131. It is undoubtedly to be noted that society or government can only help the individual but real growth must come from people themselves.

29. It should be done through controlling human ego, because Radhakrishnan utters thus: "Good and evil presuppose the basis of egoism". – Radhakrishnan, S.: "Eastern Religions and Western Thought", Oxford University Press, Delhi, 1989, p. 103. So, forward looking tendencies for progressing human beings will come from good acts. The justification is good acts aim at the well-being of oneself and others. To the contrary, evil acts are those which interfere with the well-being of oneself and others.

30. Stability comes when we leave bad things or bad works having bad impact not for the self only, but for the humanity as a whole. Thus, Thurber says rightly that man will be better off if he quits monkeying with his mind and just lets it alone. – Thurber, James: "Let Your Mind Alone", Harper & Brothers, New York, 1937, p. 5. Transparency in leading with human development process must be carefully adopted against our psychological tendency for knowledge about beings. Because, Dr K. P. Sinha predicts that the self liberation is endowed with knowledge. – Sinha, Dr K. P.: "Reflexions on Indian Philosophy", Chaukhambha Orientalia, Varanasi, 1984, p. 187.

31. About scientific nature, Moritz Schlick explains: "I believe science should be defined as the 'pursuit of truth', and my opinion is that the future of science hinges on this idea of the discovery of truth". – Schlick, M.: "The Future of Philosophy", in the College of the Pacific Publications in Philosophy, 1932, p. 54. Hence, welfare practices in scientific temper would be, according to Beck, "Formulated in a conceptual scheme that would be a theory about ultimate reality". – Beck, Lewis White: "Philosophic Inquiry", Prentice-Hall, Inc., New York, 1952, p. 239. Our plan of action should be supported by scientific scheme of works for adequate human development purposes, for dynamic social orientation by means of corporate activities; so that channelization and diversification of resources are made in right direction to reduce social poverty, enhance human productivity and rationalize industrial activities.

32. While saying about existential system, it is remarkable that: "Those who believe that individual freedom is a fundamental right can admit that the familial system may have affected fewer dysfunctions against intelligent and satisfying match-makings than other social organizations". – Hindery, Roderick: "Comparative Ethics in Hindu and Buddhist Traditions", Motilal Banarsidass, Delhi, 1978, p. 265. We are, therefore, to adopt scriptural guidelines in making policies, otherwise, we may even grant that some systems might confuse our free choice with blind choice or confound to the lack of a single programming factor, such as the family with an alleged or consequent absence of all other societal determinants, economic, conventional, etc.

33. All these consequences in socio-economic behaviour of human beings can be related to wishes, conflicts, guilt feelings, and impulses that are a source of disturbance to the individual are projected outside the self. – See also, Page, James D.: "Abnormal Psychology", Tata McGraw-Hill Publishing Company Ltd., New Delhi, 1988 (14th Reprint), p. 54. Governments as well as corporations will be suggested to make transparent system in supplying necessaries for better human life, for bringing social peace through human personality aspects and social relationships in living pursuit.

34. For this, there should be love and affection, tolerance and obedience, kindness and sympathy in beings. Probably, Gandhiji wanted such kind of equanimity in man and man, for which he suggested: "Every individual to imbibe the spirit of love, tolerance, kindness, fearlessness, non-violence, etc. – Mishra, Anil Datta: "Fundamentals of Gandhism", Mittal Publications, New Delhi, 1995, p. 15. Hence, the equanimity principle can only lead to the goal of human salvation in life by bringing perfection at the work place, in disinterested manner of doing things for general welfare of mass people.

35. M. Todaro, a social scientist in his book 'Economics for a Developing World' has mentioned three components of development corresponding to three universal core-values of good life, namely, (1) Life-sustenance, (2) Self-esteem and (3) Freedom. However, the philosophy of the approach of holistic development means that development is conceived as a multi-dimensional process involving re-organization and re-orientation of the entire economic social system. – Roy, J. and Roy, D. (Eds.): "Rediscovering Swami Vivekananda in the 21st Century Discourse", Towards Freedom, Kolkata, 2013, p. 102.

36. It is remarked, backward countries are poor because they are poor. Backward countries suffer from various vicious circles both on the supply side and demand side. – Mankar, V. G., Kulkarni, C. Y. and Sadasivan, C. R.: "Foreign Trade and Development", Himalaya Publishing House, Bombay, 1981, p. 244. Thus, the pathetic inhuman conditions are created by these vicious circles which throw light on the obstacles to development which are both a cause and consequence of backwardness and poverty.

37. The real cause of the trouble is the immobility of resources. – Also see, Lewis, W. Arthur: "The Principles of Economic Planning", George Allen & Unwin Ltd., London, 1969, p. 21. About the responsiveness in accounting human resources for commensuration of growth initiatives, it is to be suggested that if everyone in the community had the same sort of opportunities of becoming an entrepreneur, businessmen would not earn more than anyone else. As a flexible measure to

coordinate the strategy, it is undoubtedly to be remarked that we are still at the stage of experiment, and the best contribution that a government can make is to experiment in its own nationalized undertakings and so try to give a lead to private industry. – *Ibid.,* p. 91.

38. It may nevertheless be helpful when analyzing developments in the whole economy to regard the pricing behaviour of manufacturing as a norm for the whole economy. – Neild, R. R.: "Pricing and Employment in the Trade Cycle", Cambridge University Press, London, 1963, p. 54. Thus, the prices of a public enterprise should be such as to enable it to raise adequate resources for re-investments in the same way as capital formation takes place in the private sector. – Srivastava, S. K., Nigam, R. S., Sahai, Bishamber and Banerjee, Mrityunjoy: "Industrial Economics", S. Chand & Co., New Delhi, 1967, p. 394. For profitable nature, it should be recognized as an index of efficiency and not inconsistent with the socialistic pattern of society.

39. As an example, it can be predicted that irrigation has most vital and significant role to play in the regional agricultural development. – Bhargava, Archana: "Resources and Planning for Economic Development", Northern Book Centre, New Delhi, 1991, p. 78. In Indian context, it is observed that in spite of innumerable strides in agricultural development technology, it is heavily dependent on natural conditions; and provides livelihood for majority of humanity. Thus, our socio-economic behaviour requires balancing phase in strengthening the progress by way of industrial development, by increasing food production capacity, capital formation, and providing market for industrial output of consumer's goods and lastly, by utilizing agricultural inputs originated in industrial sector (T. W. Schultz, 1968, pp. 3 and 6). For further study, also refer to Schultz, T. W.: "Connection between Natural Resources and Economic Growth", 1961, pp. 1-9, in J. J. Spengler, ed. Natural Resources and Economic Growth, Washington, R. F. F. Inc.

40. Such abilities will be earned when the whole mind should flow towards the goal aimed at. – Yatiswarananda, Swami: "Meditation and Spiritual Life", Advaita Ashrama, Kolkata, 2011, p. 428. In innovating so our mind, transformational idea should be provided for human upliftment, and therefore, also global balance will be restored for realization of the goal of human social emancipation.

41. In order to achieve this goal Swamiji emphasized the great need for rapid economic growth through modernization of industrial and agricultural technology. – Roy, J. and Roy, D.: "Rediscovering Swami Vivekananda in the 21st Century Discourse", Towards Freedom, Kolkata, 2013, p. 102.

42. Looking at the present socio-political and economic scenario of India and world at large we really need to take recourse to Swami Vivekananda's Religio-social philosophy which taught us that the ideal of unity or universality is at the root of human existence. – *Op. cit.,* p. 103.

43. In realizing about this kind of social re-engineering process, Sister Nivedita predicts, "undoubtedly this power comes nearer, with depth of education and intensity of experience......" – Nivedita, Sister: "The Master As I Saw Him", Udbodhan Office, Kolkata, 2012, p. 312. This is not only a beautiful and philosophical logic for secularism, but also the most pragmatic way to adopt it socially. – Shukla, Ajay: "The Philosophy of Shri Bhagavad Gita", Gyan

Publishing House, New Delhi, 2001, p. 107. This kind of secular thought maintains samabhava, i.e., sameness of attitude towards all situations and to all beings. It will help in rejuvenating the process of equanimity thinking, and therefore, human objective development will be made for salvation of life.

44. As in the case of linear polarization, for which polarization vectors can be taken to be real, and the polarization density matrix and number density matrices are real and symmetric, which Weinberg writes in his analysis on cosmology (See Weinberg, Steven: "Cosmology", Oxford University Press, Indian Edition, New Delhi, 2008, p. 555), so also, the transcendental order of living is related to the fact of liberation, which is realization, and predicted thereby to explain this: "The Upanisad tells that Brahma is really known when it is known with each state of consciousness, because thereby one gets immortality". – Aggarwal, D. D.: "Upanishadas the Real Truth", Kalpaz Publications, Delhi, 2003, p. 199. Hence, transcendental order relates to human social existence in free atmosphere, to emulate things for the purpose of human welfare and social reconstruction; so that development becomes the mantra of human cohesive order of living goal.

45. This can be said like: "It is sheer ego to think that we can become rulers of the universe". – Rao, T. N. Achyuta (ed.): "Vedanta the Knowledge of Supreme", Kalpaz Publications, Delhi, 2004, p. 198. What we can do is to integrate among things for the purpose of understanding that 'One' Absolute appears as 'Many'. So, our development thinking is like worshiping through our mind in sacrificing towards the goodness of all, in which ingrained way for the realization of the Self, the Brahman, the Absolute, the "Truth". It is thus, suggested that the real truth is experiencing with experimentation for working in the holistic nature of development for growth of beings, in which, Ishvara, or God can be realized.

46. Human fraternity will come, when: "It is freed from all states of cause and effect and exists merely as the substratum of all, as Existence-Knowledge-Bliss. – See also, for understanding – how to optimize our objective function, in an idea of fraternity thinking, Gambhirananda, Swami: "Eight Upanish ads", Advaita Ashrama, Kolkata, Translated form, 2012.

47. To eradicate poverty for ever from the society, we should have bliss for total development of all beings, as like Swami Bhajanananda writes: "The ancient Vedic Rishis saw the whole world permeated by consciousness and bliss". – Bhajanananda, Swami: "The Light of the Modern World", Advaita Ashrama, Kolkata, 2012, p. 95. In this way, we can think about dynamic social rolling for co-existence of beings and to restore world peace, doing good to others who have been suffering a lot, in the process of betterment of life of mankind.

48. Scientific human development is possible: "When religion as an open-ended system of universal ethics must provide moral basis on which people can nurture their capacity of living together in harmony". – SVD, K. Jose, Bera, Gautam K., Medhi, Birinchi K. and Athparia, R. P. (eds.): "Concept of God and Religion", Abhijeet Publications, New Delhi, 2012, p. 175. Because, this will help to frame our policies and implement those for the all-round development without any interruption, while organizational activities are performed in effective utilization of resources.

49. To serve as an ideal for countries of varying religious experience, secularism must be reformulated from a Western to a universal ideal. – Bhargava, Rajeev

(ed.): "Secularism and Its Critics", Oxford University Press, New Delhi, 1998, p. 267. Hence, to reflect the path of human orientation, secularism which has been observed as the great debate, now, in this world, requires that there be greater specificity and differentiation so that we have ways of talking about the varieties as well as degrees of freedom, of equality (indifference), of separation. These are all the facets of encompassing nature of growth should be interrelated on issues of human development purposes.

50. Under this notion, Indian order of development process is said to be more creative in nature, while it is observed that Swami Vivekananda proclaims to every person – 'Arise, awake, and stop not till the goal is reached'. – See also, Aleaz, K. P.: "Harmony of Religions: The Relevance of Swami Vivekananda", Punthi-Pustak, Calcutta, 1993, p. 100. Thus, development means, expressing the divinity within us, instead of our differences in beliefs, thoughts, way of putting up with our customary activities, or rules and practices, etc.

51. Social building objectives will be fulfilled, when we would be able to utilize our infinite power for existence. So, manifestation of our consciousness for dignity of life will help everyone to help others, and thus, social reconstruction will be made on the foundation of human spiritual character, which is inherent and most of the time remaining as dormant. This type of human behavioural prudence will last for long in binding people together with the fraternity of thought for development.

52. Thus, our functional relationships are to be established in relation to God, because, Aurobindoo remarks while writing in his "Essays on the Gita": "We have to look courageously in the face of the reality and see that it is God and none else who has made this world in his being and that so he has made it", p. 181. So, our functional relationship in organizational duties should be performed as the bhakta (devotee) – like a devotee who surrenders everything to God for welfare of mankind. Then, and then only, we would be able to reduce social poverty by way of working in equality to eradicate inequalities from this world of living.

53. It is transcendental in nature, and therefore, Mahendra Nath Sircar predicts: "Transcendence and creativeness are blended in the life of spirit......" – Sircar, M. N.: "Hindu Mysticism", Bhârati Mahâvidyâlaya, Calcutta, 1951, p. 24. Transparent behaviour is indeed an art of human work ethics, which helps in the making of our creative expression for integrating to the original nature of development. It is interesting because it discovers truth through the direct reading of the life-forces, through their finer modulations and activity and through the acquaintance with the unconscious. – *Ibid.*, p. 108.

54. The Vedic thought in integrating our approach is needed for social reconstruction purposes because, as Swami Bhajanananda writes: "Industrialization, unfavourably living conditions, break down of family life, cut-throat competition, demanding jobs, hectic work schedules, financial uncertainties and several other factors have made the lives of modern people very stressful". – Bhajanananda, Swami: "The Light of the Modern World", Advaita Ashrama, Kolkata, 2012, p. 160. So, by integrating in organizational activities, we can find out unity in action. This is the cause of: "Every action of our lives the most material, the grossest as well as the finest, the highest, the most spiritual – is alike tending towards this one ideal, the finding of unity". – The Complete Works of Swami Vivekananda,

Vol. VI, pp. 4-5. Therefore, optimum welfare of mankind requires the Vedanta version of spiritual thought, along with modern technological tools, to be applied for coherent nature of human development process.

55. Here, it is worthwhile to note that our development perspective should be holistic in nature. In this context, Aleaz remarks rightly: "We must have our platform broad enough to embrace all mankind". – Aleaz, K. P.: "Harmony of Religions: The Relevance of Swami Vivekananda", Punthi-Pustak, Calcutta, 1993, p. 47. It is because, every religion and every creed recognizes man a divine, and you should do him no harm...... – See also, The Complete Works of Swami Vivekananda, Vol. VIII, p. 199. Development is to be understood from eternality concept, for which, Swami Vivekananda in his paper on Hinduism utterly mentioned that the Vedas are eternal in the sense the spiritual laws they convey are eternal. He further remarks: "Human person is really a spirit living in a body. Human soul is eternal and immortal, perfect and infinite, and death means only a change of centre from one body to another as per its past actions". – The Complete Works of Swami Vivekananda, Vol. I, pp. 7-10. Under all such circumstances, the potential nature of human beings can in no way be stopped for developing furthermore, towards realizing the concept of soul by way of working in disinterested nature of doing things.

56. In group behavioural aspect, we are also to understand our free inner stage and work accordingly. Because, we have free existential inner divisions like – "Suddha-Suddha". The Vedas explain the inner divisions of Suddha-Suddha state are: Suddha-Kevala, Suddha-Sakala and Suddha-Thuriya. Suddha-Kevala is the state of Upasantha; Suddha-Sakala is the state of expensive Thuriya-Suddha. Suddha or Suddha-Thuriya is the state of Shiva-becoming. These three stages belong to the Suddha-Suddha state of Jeeva. – Eraianban, H. H. Swamiji: "Vedas: An Extract of the Universal Values", Gyan Publishing House, New Delhi, 2001, p. 341. It appears thus, exponential behavioural module for human free existential norm could achieve the harmonious balance between beings in living order, and therefore, cohesive nature of dealings with the things will bring in organizational order to reduce human conflicts, and to establish social peace for overall transformation.

57. Managerial guidelines are required to incorporate ideas of truth. Truth can only lead people in achieving goal of human – (i) prosperity here and hereafter, and (ii) salvation. – Gambhirananda, Swami: "Eight Upanisads", Vol. One (Translated), Advaita Ashrama, Kolkata, 2012, p. 132. Thus, due attention must have to be given while organizational administrative functions are performed. It requires scientific analysis of human noble practices for the synthesis of advancing people, in order to live peacefully in social atmosphere, and to co-operate with the dynamic system of working conditions to set-up human dignity in societal order.

58. This condition should be recognized because, Swami Ashokananda writes: "All agree that infinite power and blessedness are potential in the individual soul and that these must be manifested if the Divine is to be realized." – Ashokananda, Swami: "A Call to the Eternal", Advaita Ashrama, Kolkata, 2007, p. 42. It makes us broadening our standing on the understanding of development of beings, for which we should sacrifice for others, and accordingly, for spiritual realization

our environment has to be regarded as the essential element of progress of human civilization, which requires scientific scanning mechanism for harmony of living order.

59. Reinforcing welfare can only guide for realization of life. It is a character, a life, a centre, a God-man that must lead the way, that must be the centre round which all other elements will gather themselves and then fall like a tidal wave upon the society, carrying all before it, washing away all impurities... ... – Bhajanananda, Swami: "The Light of the Modern World", Advaita Ashrama, Kolkata, 2012, p. 181. This welfare of people should be our ideal, path and goal, and so on. It is the reason probably, for which Swami Vivekananda spoke of Sri Ramakrishna as the ideal of India and of the modern world, and by "ideal" he meant both subjective and objective ideals. – *Ibid.,* p. 181. This kind of welfare concept can bring in human development in real perspective to the fields, namely, - morality, spirituality, education, science, etc.

60. It calls for, as Taussig remarks: "Better ways and traditions than are commonly found in modern industry would mean much for human happiness". – Taussig, F. W.: "Principles of Economics", Vol. II, Fourth Edition, The Macmillan Company, New York, 1947, p. 515. And therefore, he further opines that we can see our way ... ... which the coming generations will establish. – *Op. cit.,* p. 566. Thus, its original idea was democracy carried into business. To reduce gaps between rich and poor, we are to see that a democracy carried into industrial life is the dominating principle of every political body that can hope for success. – Salvadori, Massimo: "The American Economic System", Compiled Work, The Bobbs-Merrill Company, Inc., New York, 1963, pp. 123-24. Again, in narrating on the "Program of the People's Party" (1892), Hacker asserts that our purposes to be identical with the purposes of the national Constitution. – See also, Hacker, Louis M.: "The Shaping of the American Tradition", Columbia University Press, New York, 1947. In this way, it is predicted that cooperative work atmosphere will come "to form a more perfect union and establish justice, insure domestic tranquility, provide for the common defense, promote the general welfare, and secure the blessings of liberty for ourselves and our prosperity". – Salvadori, M.: "The American Economic System", The Bobbs-Merrill Company, Inc., New York, 1963, pp. 244-45. Hence, people's agenda of development strategy requires its spirit may enter into all hearts for the salvation of the national entities, and the uplifting of mankind from sufferings.

61. In this context, K. E. Boulding has indicated like: "...... a perfectly fluid or homogeneous class structure may not be the most conducive to economic progress". – Boulding, K. E.: "Religious Foundations of Economic Progress", Harvard Business Review, May-June, 1952, pp. 35-36. Now, in reorienting human superstructure on the path of good learning culture should be to find out problems, which are affecting economic progress. We are therefore, to encourage people to become 'innovators', because this ability has been lacking in society years-after-years; and so, equal opportunity for all to enter the easier-going will be reflected through free learning culture in assessing human personality in organized way of leading life. However, S. K. Mangal writes: "There is an innate creative spark in every individual the basis of which also lies in the unconscious depths of his mind". – Mangal, S. K.: "Advanced Educational Psychology", 2nd Edn., PHI Learning Private Limited, New Delhi, 2012, p. 73. Our path should recognize in

this way, that one has a strong inner urge or motive to express one's talents or abilities or to make self-actualization the ultimate goal of one's life. Thus, life urge or life energy responsible for every type of human constructive activity should manifest itself, to spurt personality in so many ways, like turning man into – a writer, scientist, artist, mathematician as needed by him in his struggle for self-actualization. This is the sustainable concept of social dynamicity can be reflected through free atmosphere in our learning system.

62. In this regard, by analyzing economic system "reforms" in the Soviet Union, China, Japan and many other European countries dominating the world economy, besides, the American Economic system, we would be able to know that their economic problems are concentrated to piece-meal system of radical reformative activities done through problem-solving initiatives. Accordingly, we can refer to, for instance, to see Nove Alec: "An Economic History of the USSR", Pelican Books, London, 1982. Zaleski, Eugene: "Planning for Economic Growth in the Soviet Union, 1918-1932", Translated from the French and edited by Marie-Christine Mac Andrew and G. Warren Nutter, University of North Carolina Press, Chapel Hill, N. C., 1971 and also Bergson, Abram: "Soviet Post-War Economic Development", Almqvist & Wiksell International, Stockholm, 1974. Similarly, other nation's reformative activities are required to be followed for understanding well – how to encourage people for business in setting out developmental activities, to objectify goal of human emancipation. Here, it is suggested that Indian Vedic system had entered into the depth of human problems long back in human civilization, and therefore, ours is the philosophy like – "Vasudhaiva Kutumbakam" can be accepted as the most universal strategy for human development perspective.

63. "... ... this argument – assuming that it is legitimate to let the State appropriate the bulk the rural surplus – only proves the necessity for State control of the marketing of produce and not of production. As a strategic function, for this purpose, if the warehousing and marketing programme is effectively implemented, with State partnership in the agencies established, the Government should be able to acquire a large proportion of the commissions and profits of marketing". – Krishna, Raj: "Cooperative Farming", Indian Cooperative Union, p. 34, cited in Mehta, S. B.: "Cooperative Farming and Agrarian Development in India", S. Chand & Co., Delhi, 1961, pp. 71-72.

64. In boosting up socio-economic activities, we are therefore to assess on the model as propounded by the Cobb-Douglas production functions with allowance for technical progress. Further, as it resembles, Smithies' growth model can also be referred to, in case of industrial reformative progress in diversifying investment potentials for profitable amount of relevancy. – Smithies, A.: "Productivity, Real Wages, and Economic Growth", The Quarterly Journal of Economics, LXXIV, May (1960), pp. 189-205. Therefore, socio-economic activities concerned with human development is the art in scientific thinking, just as a physicist uses different assumptions when studying falling marbles and falling beach-balls. – See also, Mankiw, N. Gregory: "Principles of Macroeconomics", Fourth Edition, Cengage Learning India Private Limited, Delhi, 2006, p. 21. However, various fiscal-policy models of growth have been constructed since Keynes's seminal and powerful suggestions about the State exercising 'a guiding influence and acting as balancing factor'. – For guiding influence the reader can also refer

to General Theory of Keynes, p. 378, where they will find "a somewhat comprehensive socialization of investment" and elsewhere (p. 376) to "commercial saving through the agency of the State". Also, readers are suggested to study General Theory, p. 220 as a recall to Keynes's reference to "loan expenditure ... ... whether on capital account or to meet a budgetary deficit" (p. 129). In submitting thus all economic models, we can propose for dynamic nature of growth for nurturing human elements in regard to quick development of respective national economies, because, it will help in world peace, by way of solving human social crisis.

65. Our responsibility should be counted to see that we intend to do something for the greater interest of society. Here, Adam Smith says: "Every individual endeavors to employ his capital, so that its produce may be of the greatest value......He frequently promotes that of society more effectually than when he really intends to promote it". – Smith, Adam: "The Wealth of Nations", 1776. The fact to emphasize is that miracles are going on all round us all the time – if only we look around and alert ourselves to the everyday functioning of the market. – Samuelson, Paul A.: "Economics", Eleventh Edn., McGraw-Hill International Book Co., New Delhi, 1980, p. 38. But then, my admission is that social structure should be developed in consonance with the view of the Gita. Accordingly, Raychoudhary cites the line from the Gita that Lord Krishna declares: "All paths lead to me". – Raychoudhary, S. C.: "Social, Cultural and Economic History of India", Surjeet Publications, Delhi, 1989, p. 186. As a man of society we should therefore work like selfless and also to be completely free from all taint of attachment. In this way, we can shoulder our responsibility to build-up social structure.

66. The need for understanding in radicalization of the programmes of human emancipation can be felt from the picture of trade unions activities in England. In England, such organizations extend their activities beyond the organization of strikes. They provide benefits and amenities to their members, run the labor colleges and libraries, endeavor to train up the prospective leadership of trade unions. – Shaikh, A. J. and Mannur, H. G.: "A Short Economic History of UK, USA, USSR and Japan", S. Chand & Co., Delhi, 1971, p. 32. Thus, social sufferings of deprived people have to be remedied through activities of actors, teachers, doctors, bank-men, journalists, civil servants, etc. as could be found in England, where trade unionism has been working as a living and a dynamic force, full of life and vigor with their workers. In doing so, we can look at upon emancipation of human beings from severe sufferings for their material progress and prosperity.

67. Depending upon the socio-political and economic objectives, government organizations are recommended that they should adopt legitimate pricing policies for the purpose of making units or enterprises effective towards social building norms and models of activities. Thus, some important pricing policies, like – (1) No Profit, No Loss Concept; (2) Marginal Cost Pricing Principle; (3) Principle of Average Cost Pricing; (4) Principle or Policy of Making Maximum Profits; (5) Policy of Charging Discriminating Prices; (6) Cost Plus Pricing; (7) Import-based Pricing; among others, should be made practical oriented for the sake of socio-economic convergence in dealing with the problems of human living potential, and thereby, to integrate organizational entities in competitive market structure, in this age of technological reformations and human resource upliftment

programmes. – See also, Desai, S. S. M.: "Economic Systems", Himalaya Publishing House, Bombay, 1982, pp. 243-331 and pp. 410-15. But the fact remains that whatever the objectives and circumstances under which public sector enterprises are working, they must aim at making the best use of their resources and show maximum efficiency.

68. All these are possible, when we will be able to increase national income at a moderate rate, achieve self-sufficiency in food grains, and to increase agricultural production to meet requirements in industry and export, to bring about rapid industrialization of the country with special emphasis on heavy and basic industries, to expand basic industries, like – steel, chemical industries, fuel and power, and establish machine building capacity; so that the requirements of further industrialization of the country can be met within a specified period of time. Our transparent ideas in social growing tendencies will include, like – bringing about large expansion of employment opportunities for the people, establishment of progressively greater equalities of opportunities and to bring about reduction in disparities of income and wealth, and a more even distribution of economic power, reformation of administrative structure to carry out various programmes of people's development, checking inflationary pressures on economy during the process of development, etc. Besides, we could also suggest for social integrity – to attain economic stability, self-reliance and to bring about balanced regional development. As a whole, peaceful social environment will prevail when we would be able to implement a 'National Program of Minimum Needs' for the poorer sections of the community by providing facilities, like – elementary education, fresh drinking water, medical as well as health-care facilities, housing, sanitation and rural electrification, slum improvement and development to landless agricultural workers, backward classes, tribal people, and to help the poorest sections of the whole community.

69. Human value system should be made a growth oriented concept, confining corporate responsibility towards carrying people to the path of self-sufficiency, for which, industrial development is a must. Therefore, Jaiswal rightly remarks: "The process of economic development of the countries all over the world shows that by and large industrial development is a pre-requisite for economic development and the growth of corporate sector a necessary concomitant of industrial development". – Jaiswal, G. C. R.: "Bank Finance to Corporate Sector in India", Deep & Deep Publications, New Delhi, 1989. Further, human value system is to be created through work of the developed pattern of banking activities, for economic prudence in making people self-sufficient towards rolling in unified nature of doing things for human social emancipation, which results in special responsibility as well as attention towards making sick industries vibrant that can fulfill the needs and aspirations of people.

70. This is very much important in case of Assam, because in India, Assam has been lagging behind in socio-economic development, instead of abundance of its potential amount of natural resources. Accordingly, people have not been empowered properly since Independence, which makes regional imbalances severely, particularly, to this important place of Indian province. We are to redraft new industrial policy for developing this place very quickly, in making people realize to be at par with other developed provinces of the country. Again,

agricultural sector, land reformations, housing, transport and communication, especially, railway net-work, warehousing, banking and financial services; besides, education, health and social sector services, Assam requires special attention to provide for its people all types of basic infrastructure facilities and to provide also incentives for industrial development. Also refer to, Goswami, P. C.: "The Economic Development of Assam", Kalyani Publishers, New Delhi, 1988.

71. It is surprising to note that in the construction of our planning models for application to Indian conditions such definite emphasis on productivity gains and the organizational methods for securing economies is scarcely to be found. – Sengupta, Jati Kumar and Sen, Amitabha: "India's Economic Growth", The Post-graduate Book Mart, Calcutta, 1961, p. 110. Thus, the objective vision in the emerging world of crises, which Samar Deb opines: "Will open up the opportunity of living through the resurgent policy measures of machine related activities, to be founded with the social development character through organizational behavioural planning , to the crest of human upliftment in aesthetic manner of productive goal-orientation; wherefrom, the managerial values and guiding principles will lead to all to the successful orientation of human zeal for spiritual work practices, connoting the idea of socialistic pattern of humanistic values and ethics, and also managerial effective nature of dealing with mechanical foundations for the purpose of human existentialism with the dynamicity of life". – Deb, Samar: "Global Principles on Management", Dominant Publishers & Distributors Pvt. Ltd., New Delhi, 2014, pp. 165-66. He further comments, in this way: "Every human being will get a scope to actualize the self for understanding the real value of life, if such vision of machine-related production activity is guided for the universal way of living, through managing the self for the greater interest of the whole humankind, in equanimity principles of management practices". – *Ibid.*, p. 166. This the integrated system of planning to be incorporated in organizational activities with the scientific temper of thought for philosophizing the perspective of human development goal, with all-comprehensive nature of human activities to the envisagement of social upliftment objective through human participatory performances of modern organizations.

72. In reducing deprivation of mankind, it should be suggested that our agricultural sector needs now, a relative stability in the wage-share of total agricultural income. – *Ibid.*, p. 250. Moreover, marginal agricultural labourers are to be helped with radical government measures of scientific planning, which will also help in reducing migrant agricultural labour. It is evident from the works of Jati Kumar Sengupta and Amitabha Sen (1961), which have cited that: "A UNESCO study on floating or migrant agricultural labour has revealed that landless or casual agrarian labour tends to move away to the urban sector, particularly when the wage rate becomes most depressed in the agrarian sector". – *Op. cit.,* p. 250. Again, an example of people living in the North Eastern province of India shows that this region still now, continues to be one of the lesser developed areas of the country. Though a small dent has been made in removing infrastructural deficiencies, the region has still to go a long way before the inadequacies of road, railway network. Similarly, only a beginning has been made in development of the vast water, power, forest, and mineral resources of the region. – Ahluwalia, Shashi (Ed.): "Social and Economic Development in North-East India", Gian

Publishing House, Delhi, 1986, p. 20. Similarly, for the greater interest of mankind, we will require to address itself to newer areas, adopting our programmes to the fast changing development of the world order – such as human resource development and introduction of new and appropriate technologies; so that socio-economic development of the sovereign nations are made in accelerated pace. As a whole, we require, particularly, in case of Indian economy people's participation for its overall development, to speed up entire spheres of human progress.

73. It may, therefore, be optimal to reduce the public deficit to zero or even to negative levels. – Joshi, Vijay and Little, I. M. D.: "India's Economic Reforms 1991-2001", Oxford University Press, New Delhi, 1996, p. 31. However, as an adjustment to structural reforms policy, it is imperative to note that less developed nations are to select factors of reforming overall economy, concentrating mainly fiscal consequences, as and when introducing a near free trade regime with almost no restrictions, and with a uniform pattern of protective tariff to a level of determined percentage, as per needs of their socio-economic activities. Further, that in case of India, it is observed that Independent India inherited a structure of corporate management which was dominated organizationally by the managing agency system, and entrepreneurially by some particular business communities. – Sengupta, N. K.: "Government and Business", 6th Rev. Edn., Vikas Publishing House Pvt. Ltd., New Delhi, 1987, p. 126. During the second phase: 1956-1969, in the history of corporate management in India, it is observed that at that time, board of companies could also be managed indirectly through any one from among the categories of corporate managers, such as – (1) Managing Agents, (2) Secretaries and Treasurers, (3) Managing Director, and (4) Manager. – *Ibid.,* p. 127. Thus, sound organizational directive functions were hampered at that time. Now, that twenty-first century demands for wholesale human development process, we need more radical structural adjustments, unlike found in the past.

74. We require justified norms in this context to function as the process of reformations, as this case may be referred to as a rejoinder, e. g., in Independent India, a group of "Panel of Economists" met three times between January and April 1955, wherein eminent thinkers like – Professors C. N. Vakil and P. R. Brahmananda, along with other members prepared a series of papers, and several of them containing important insights on investment patterns in the Second Plan. Again, by the Gokhale Institute, on employment situation and economic policy fundamental insights were noted for recommendation to the government of India. – Sinha, R. K. (Ed.): "Economic Planning in India", Deep & Deep Publications, New Delhi, 1989, p. 126. After an observation of all these incidences, it is noteworthy to mention that it limited itself essentially to comments on the size and structure of the Second Plan and the Policy, and also the institutional implications of the proposed plan-frame. Again, the Panel did not, however, pierce into the flows of logic and substance in the draft plan-frame. It is observed further that it did not insist that the Second and subsequent Plans should face up to the implications of the place of agricultural and the structural features of the Indian economy. Thus, Sinha remarks: "... ... it limited itself unduly to the conditions to be met in the specific context of a 'bolder' Second Plan. – *Op. cit.,* p. 127. In coming to realize people for public services, it is alarmingly to be said that our economy today, has made a disparity between incomes and wealth, and

also disparity in the availability of social amenities in the rural and urban sectors. All these require immense sacrificial nature of job to be performed for eradicating social deprivation of suffered human beings. In a nutshell, the organization space through the hierarchical system of settlements continues to be essentially dysfunctional with respect to productive process. This is the rejoinder to be filled-up with social inclusiveness for tremendous nature of human development, in this age of global competition as well as technological reformations.

75. As an experience, we would like to cite Korean crisis, during the periods of 1951 onwards, whereto; it is observed – that the speaker of the largest opposition party of the German Federal Parliament put forward some important hypotheses on economic reforms ... ... In the meantime, the sovereignty of the consumer in West Germany, and the free formation of prices in almost all sectors of the economy, have become a reality. – See also, Erhard, Ludwig: "Prosperity through Competition", Asia Publishing House, New Delhi, 1959, Chapter V, pp. 79-96. From all these consequences, it becomes evident to all of us that development should be made not only once for all, but also we would be able to contain its continuity in regard to 'push and pull' method, as per our situational change of the societal phenomenon; so that every country proceeds to the goal of attaining human self-sufficiency in living peaceful social environment. It is observed by Samar Deb that the foundation of our social pyramid should be made through all inclusiveness, and so, he asserts to: "Establish a good human relationship to an attitude for the development and growth of society by organizing abilities, capabilities, and effectiveness of people". – Deb, Samar: "Unified Thought on Management", Kalpaz Publications, Delhi, 2004, p. 92. It is, therefore, suggested that in organization, there should be a universal approach bringing men in unity, instead of multi-facets diversity; because, by this process each organization will be able to guide the social being for a unified theory that man needs for the harmonious cause-effect relationship in behavioural pursuits for optimum development and growth of society, by collective development and growth of each individual in organizing different activities of their everyday efforts toward the attainment of result for crossing the barrier of life, in matchless beauty of the nature of management – to synthesize this aspect of development, both from within and without ... ... through relentless efforts in an unflinching manner. – Op. cit., p. 93. Thus, human development at the fullest possible level requires human capacity building approach through human skills, experiences and efficiencies for the purpose of enhancement of overall excellence, and all these will come in practice, by means of free atmosphere at the work place, which should be provided through industrial democracy as well as business acumen.

76. The social pyramid of this world has a good historical record regarding demographic transition. Accordingly, Michael P. Todaro has remarked that: "The theory of demographic transition attempts to explain why all contemporary developed nations have more or less passed through three 'stages' of modern population history." – Todaro, Michael P.: "Economic Development in the Third World", Orient Longman Limited, Hyderabad, 1991, p. 214. If we try to overcome all these stages, modernization is a must for creative endeavors of human beings, which will help in rejuvenating our social order, based on skills and experience, for the ultimate destiny of life – human solvency as well salvation of life. So, we are to adopt an approach of economic integration, for greater "collective

self-reliance". It must be fostered in looking forward with experience of outward and inward activities throughout the world set-up of human living tendencies. Then only, our initiatives will be made possible to render social convergence, in terms of organizational diversification and human potential amount of development functional relationships. Samar Deb therefore, rightly remarks: "To it again, the social architects should confine themselves for a common simile between the aspects of social development and the upliftment of the mass people in realistic manner". – Deb, Samar: "Global Principles on Management", Dominant Publishers and Distributors Pvt. Ltd., New Delhi, 2014, p. 163. Hence, it requires involvement of social technocrats to the value-oriented aspects of social cause, so that all governmental policy implications are learnt by doing things for effectively utilizing the resources through proper delivery system, for providing common benefit that should reap at the grass-root level to the needy class of social population

77. We can go to the past for looking as to how, once in India, as for example, Jute manufacturing industries helped in our economy tremendously in creating employment opportunities as well as to earn foreign dollars, which resulted in strengthening socio-economic life of our people. In this context, the survey report of a team goes like: "The importance of Jute Manufacturing industry in our economic life ... ... underlines the impact of jute goods as an earner of scarce dollars. But still we cannot escape from the fact that the process of disintegration has set in and we have to stem the rot". – Datta, Bhabatosh, Chakravarti, Santi Kumar, Bhattacharya, Manoranjan and Ghosh, Gouri: "Economic Development and Exports", The World Press Pvt. Ltd., Calcutta, 1962, pp. 55-58. Thus, it seems that human cooperation as an approach of nation building is essential in any country. Accordingly, we must be careful to weed out the evils that had beset the industrial activities in the past. We are therefore required rationalization of the industries, replacement of the old worn-out and out-mode machineries and adoption of more advanced technologies. In dignifying human potential order of living, and to establish global peace, modernization along with transformation is a must now, which will reduce human restlessness over the world at large.

78. For legitimate account of human rights, it has been observed that Marx, Lenin, Mao Tse-tung, etc. have fought to bring in economic self-sufficiency in human beings. Therefore, it would be totally at variance with the essentially concrete and historical approach of Marxism-Leninism to attempt to assess the role of Mao in the 1935-1957 periods simplistically in terms of his role from 1958 onwards. – Gupta, N. L. (Ed.): "Transition from Capitalism to Socialism and Other Essays", Kalamkar Prakashan Pvt. Limited, New Delhi, 1975, pp. 52-53. So, in the development of personalities, ideologies no less than in the case of society and nature as a whole there are leaps and breaks in continuity as well as regression and degeneration. Pertinently, in Indian experience also we see that, once a large section of the leadership, being influenced by the Gandhian teachings and its own class-character, believed in class harmony, but still our fate has not changed yet now. In this regard, Gupta rightly remarks: "No unity of the poor peasants, the landless labourers and the share-croppers could be brought about on the basis of their socio-economic demands. The leadership always largely remained in the hands of the well-to-do-peasants ... ... Since the leadership was

more interested in securing gains for itself, it did not allow the movement to become radical". – *Ibid.*, p. 171-72. Peaceful social orientation requiring human dignity of living should confine to tasks of social equality as well as all-inclusiveness policy in legitimizing human beings toward the line of living in unity through equanimity of work relationships. Then, and then only rights of living through justified norms of doing things will be made fraternal towards social building exposition of human endeavors. Bolin Hazarika nicely opines: "The justifications for the existence of the state is for intervention in case of violation of rights. But if the state is owned and controlled by the privileged sections of the society as has been the case in most of the liberal democratic states, state-intervention will be for securing and maintaining the privileges of the privileged few of the society and not for the deprived, oppressed and the marginalized lot. If this be the case, this cannot be a sound theory of human rights". – Hazarika, B. (Ed.): "Human Rights in India", J. B. College Human Rights Study Cell, Jorhat, 2003, p. 65. If we want to do more towards better world, we need to undo the conditions of dominance and restrain powerful man and states; so that people throughout the world can realize their diverse potentialities and live in peace with one another. We are, therefore, to work in reconciling diverse interests in the society for our existential freedom of living.

79. In this context, it is worthwhile to note that the static comparative advantage theory developed by the classical and the neo-classical economists of the Western world does not provide for resource creation, it is preoccupied solely with question of resource allocation. – Mannur, H. G.: "International Economics", Vikas Publishing House Pvt. Ltd., New Delhi, 1995 (2nd Rev. Edn.), p. 190. Social backwardness will be eradicated thus, through reforming all sectors and segments of the overall economy in terms of transfer of consumers' surplus, protective measures; tariffs control mechanism, macro-effects on general equilibrium tendency, by means of labor surplus, income redistribution policy, labour-intensive method of production reconciliation with the capital-intensive method of production, technological development and human up-gradation, etc. Again, we should be careful about inflexibility of wages and prices for remedial measures against social injustice, being prevailing from time-to-time in competitive market structure. In areas of agricultural activities, we are to reduce difficulties in terms of applying agricultural science to identify, describe, and classify all the economic problems and thus, to come to a solution that we can end all such problems for producing effectively. – See also, Forster, G. W. and Leoger, Marc C.: "Elements of Agricultural Economics", Prentice Hall, New York, 1951, p. 9. Market structure reformations are also necessary in the field of agricultural productivity boost-up, marketing and distribution functions by means of agricultural industry status, among others. Cohen says that we are to reduce distributive costs which seem to be a far heavier burden than society will permanently consent to bear. – Cohen, R. L.: "The Economics of Agriculture", Cambridge University Press, London, 1965.

80. Here, it is sincerely followed: "If politics, as one keen observer has remarked, is the art of choosing the path of least resistance ... ..." – David, Felix: "International Development Review", October, 1960. In this context, again, David Cushman Coyle remarks: "It is politically advisable to note that industry will rouse less resistance from the landowners than proposals for land reform".

– Coyle, David C.: "National Development and How It Works", The New American Library of World Literature, Inc., New York, 1963, p. 78. Our control mechanism to be reformulated by sound development programme which requires progress in industry as well as agriculture balanced as well as may be possible. The expanding population cannot be employed in agriculture, except in the rare countries with large tracts of empty land fit for settlement. As a rule, now employment has to be sought in industry and in the service occupations.

81. About perfectionism in areas of overall social productivity, also banking system should be made sound in working with financial derivative system. In this regard, financial market expansion should be done through security market analysis and portfolio management, increasing value for investment potentials, and thereby, government should try to adjust with unemployment situations of the country. Erik remarks thus, some economists believe that a stronger banking system and less volatile security markets, downward inflexibility in wages and prices, and confidence that the government will step in if unemployment rises significantly, make a future collapse of business confidence virtually impossible. – Lundberg, Erik (Ed.): "The Business Cycle in the Post-War World", Macmillan & Co. Ltd., New York, 1957, pp. 287-88. Productivity perfection can also be observed from the view point of making the optimum use of resources for the good of the economy as a whole. – Hicks, Ursula K.: "Development Finance Planning and Control", Oxford University Press, London, 1965, p. 12. In scientific orientation of our approach, it is suggested that productivity can be enhanced through review of resources available for development expenditure in the light of the resources needed for the operation of existing services and the maintenance of existing works. Our decision in production should therefore be guided by the fact that we are to select also the social opportunity cost, as and when going to produce for economic gain. Dams are examples of long construction projects whose benefits for the most part accrue quickly after completion. Again, another alternative view could further be followed, like – a dam erected primarily to provide power can probably also be used to extend irrigation and so increase the productivity of agriculture. This can also be linked with land settlement and reforestation. What is more important, is to see that there is overspill arising in ways like – 1a telephone system put in for government purposes can be of great assistance to the tourist, trade, etc. Hence, in productivity analysis complementary investment potentials should be given emphasis, though it may never come along. – *Ibid.,* p. 21.

82. These are essential because, it is possible to finance a specific project by inflationary methods, but it is not possible to finance the whole economic development through inflation. It may work well with countries which have unlimited excess capacity and immense untapped resources. Here, monetary expansion may increase output, reduce unemployment and raise the level of income. But, as Nandwani points out: "Developing countries are not placed in so comfortable a situation. Production in such countries is inhibited not by the insufficiency of monetary demand but by the lack of factors such as: technical know-how, skill, some strategic raw material, capital and social overhead development". – Nandwani, S. C.: "Trade Dilemma of Developing Countries", Cosmopolitan Publishing House, New Delhi, 1968, p. 59. Thus, there is lopsided development generally observed in most of the developing countries, for which,

these countries must remain within the limitations imposed its resources and a given pattern of investment corresponds to a given set of capital goods. To bring in a striking balance between developed and developing countries, we therefore require that developing countries which are not capable of manufacturing at the present level to supply those quality products as required by the developed countries at the competitive prices, will require to think about reformative measures, along with developing their own people by means of equilibrium position of demand and supply side management. For all these reasonable grounds, industrial reformative process has to be augmented with the speedy implementation of projects, rehabilitation in industrial activities and improvement of technological paths, for reducing regional imbalances, increasing human capacity building and transforming society with the scientific research and technological innovations.

83. A stationary economic system can never exist. Therefore, Morris Bornstein puts ideas in this regard like: "Things are continually changing, and the stationary state, although necessary as an aid to speculation, is a theoretical assumption to which there is no counterpart in reality". – Bornstein, M. (Ed.): "Comparative Economic Systems: Models and Cases", Surjeet Publications, Delhi, 1987, p. 113. That is why; the economic administration may indeed know exactly what commodities are needed most urgently. But this is only half the problem. The other half, the valuation of the means of production, it cannot solve. It cannot assimilate them to a common price denominator, as can be under a system of economic freedom and money prices. We must think about priority and accordingly, all sectors are to be emphasized for equilibrium rate of development. For managing economic activities, today, we are simply, to put attention towards echoes the influential technology. In this context, the reader may also consult the work of Hugh Clegg for further broader aspect of understanding on 'demand-supply' relations, so as to find-out solutions for eradicating problems of poverty with creating adequate social value system. – Clegg, Hugh: "A New Approach to Industrial Democracy", Blackwell, Oxford, 1960. We can also refer to Lionel Robbins's "An Essay on the Nature and Significance of Economic Science", to observe about the shadow fight between 'universality' and 'historic-relativism', and it has the character of inevitability. So, we must admit the reality for social value orientation. – Robbins, Lionel: "An Essay on the Nature and Significance of Economic Science", Macmillan, New Delhi, Second Edition, 1940, p. 127.

84. Briggs and Jordon in their combined work assessed this fact: "This was done, no doubt, to the decline of individualism before the growing sense of the organic unity of society, and the consequence was that the problem of industrial health and safety began to be considered in relation to the welfare of the society as a whole. – For more, see also Briggs and Jordon: "Economic History of England", University Tutorial Press Ltd., Cambridge, Eleventh Edn., 1964. The choice is hard, but yet a system has to be evolved in which mankind will be able to fulfill the twin objectives of earning a living and also find opportunities for the fulfillment of the deeper human values, opines thus K. N. Bhattacharyya. – Bhattacharyya, K. N.: "Planning: Economics and Economy", The World Press Private Ltd., Calcutta, 1971, p. 129. Moreover, the burden of implementing the various plan programmes requires diversity. If economic development becomes

the preoccupation only of the Government, then no plan can ever succeed. So, we are to initiate cooperation in our process of giving benefit to the people. Mangal has said that truly speaking, if one needs to achieve the required objectives in a reasonable time, one must learn to pay sustained attention. – Mangal, S. K.: "Advanced Educational Psychology", PHI Learning Private Limited, New Delhi, 2012, p. 166. So, joining hands in this way the government can enhance educational facilities with a speedy mode to overcome problems of social inequalities, in variety of means.

85. Upgrading our living standard requires rolling adjustments in industry, and therefore, it should be done through consumer's choice. In this context, a report of the Committee on Economic Policy of the U. S. Chamber of Commerce on 'Can We Depression-Proof Our Economy?' is laudable. – See, Wright, D. M., "Economy of Disturbance", quoted in the above report, p. 21. However, provided with certain policy guidelines could be useful in this regard, which might also be drawn from break-even analysis as to the effect of changing conditions, like – on a company's operations, policies and actions. – Vershney, R. L. and Maheshwari, K. Z.: "Managerial Economics", Sultan Chand & Sons, New Delhi, 1994, p. 341. But as soon as possible, and with increasing emphasis as time goes on, there is a second primary duty laid upon it [the proposed World Bank], namely, to develop the resources and productive capacity of the world, with special attention to the less developed countries, to raising the standard of life and the conditions of labor everywhere, to make the resources of the world more fully available to all mankind. (Keynes's Opening Remarks at the First Meeting of the Second Commission on the World Bank, 3 July 1944, contained in Harris, The New Economics, *Op. cit.,* p. 397). Also see, for example, A. H. Hansen, "We Must Grow – Or We Sink", New York Times Magazine (18 March 1962); American Bankers Association, A Symposium on Economic Growth (1963).

86. We take as given the existing skill and quantity of available labour, the existing quality and quantity of available equipment, the existing technique … … (General Theory, p. 245). In this way Keynes advocated for technological progress which is found to be building human skills for initiating social development.

87. In citing about poverty, it is highly necessary that a consumption-based poverty line can be thought of as comprising two elements: the expenditure necessary to buy a minimum standard of nutrition and other basic necessities and a further amount that varies from country to country, reflecting the cost of participating in the everyday life of society. – Meier, Gerald M. and Rauch, James E.: "Leading Issues in Economic Development", Oxford University Press, New York, 2004, p. 18. Thus, living standard is related to employment structure which could easily reduce human poverty. In coming over to education, it is highly important to follow the evidence on the economic impact of education. For further reference of this fact, see Psacharopoulos, George: "The Economic Impact of Education: Lessons for Policymakers", ICS Press, San Francisco, 1991, pp. 8-15. This evidence will help us to know – how to build up social structure for increasing educational potentials in human beings, for the sake of human capital formation in every nation. The appropriate measures are therefore likely to be adopted for social up-gradation of people in initiating regular employment opportunities through skill building operational activities and human knowledge-base activities.

88. For adequate level of human development modern technologies are required to be related to programmes like – rural infrastructure, social infrastructure, physical infrastructure, besides; educational activities, health services, agricultural activities, industrial activities, Integrated Rural Development Programmes (IRDPs) connecting District Rural Development Agencies, rural employment connecting Employment Assurance Schemes, Integrated Child Development Services (ICDS) and many other Rural Development and Poverty alleviation programmes. In all these sectors, centre-state cooperation building elements are to be conjoined with technological reformative services to reduce human poverty, increase skills and initiate scientific growth potentials. Thus, Mukherjea remarks as to the appropriation in our system: "While on the subject of grants and major heads included in one grant, it would be profitable to discuss the principles of appropriation or expenditure of money for any particular purpose". – Mukherjea, A. R.: "Parliamentary Procedure in India", Third Edn., Oxford University Press, Calcutta, 1983, p. 309. In this way, human standard of living will be enhanced through practices of the fundamental principles of legislative control. This control is meant for the finances of State, and it is predicted that thus: "No money may be spent for any service or purpose other than that for which the money is granted... ... money appropriated under one grant may not be appropriated to the another grant". – Ibid., pp. 309-10.

89. Nevertheless, a very general statement can perhaps be made that in course of industrialization in India, the real function of already concentrated cities like Bombay, now called as Mumbai and Calcutta, also now called as Kolkata may be not to attract the location of units in established lines of industries, that can be territorially dispersed elsewhere (e.g., industries having low or medium coefficient of localization), but to stimulate the growth of difficult and newer lines of production, requiring specialized skills of organization, investment and risks. It is because of the fact, that Jati Kumar Sengupta and Amitabha Sen remarked long back in their combined work in terms of growth of industrial productivity. However, this kind of picture is reflected through assumptions like: "The production function study over size-specific or time series data puts its main emphasis not on the average productivity or output-creating effect of one input, like labour; but on the quantitative response of change in output caused by changes in levels of different factors utilized like labour, capital, raw materials, fuel, power, etc.", Sengupta, J. K. and Sen, A.: "India's Economic Growth – Process, Problems and Policies", The Post-Graduate Book Mart, Calcutta, 1961, p. 99. A healthy outlook in this line is yet to be developed in India, so far as rationalization measures are concerned to social reformative initiatives. Sengupta and Sen further asserts reasonably: "It may thus be apparent why economic appraisal of the scope, methods are consequences of rationalization, in the context of major industrial enterprises in India may be necessary". – Op. cit., p. 163. It follows that in underdeveloped economies, the setting of the rationalization process has to keep pace the pattern of skill formation.

90. Such kind of suggestion is important to recognize the difference between luxuries that can be sacrificed and pleasant investment such as health and education that should not be sacrificed. – Coyle, David Cushman: "National Development and How It Works", The New American Library, Inc., New York, 1963, p. 42. We are therefore, to make a good estimate of our future will of the people and also to

determine what uses of available resources will meet with the people's approval. We can make provisions through adequate innovative research-based policies for action-oriented and goal-oriented administrative approach, which will help our budding talents to grow and spurt. While commenting on 'Development Administration', Fred Riggs opines that "The problems related to governmental tasks connected with agricultural, industrial, educational, and medical progress......", cited in S. P. Naidu: "Public Administration: Concepts and Theories", New Age International Publishers, New Delhi, 1996, p. 149. Indian objective for creativity in education in finding out opportunities could well be fit to inhabit that world in which universal peace and brotherhood is a reality and in which all the aspirations and activities of life are harmonized into a shining whole. – Ashokananda, Swami: "A Call to the Eternal", Advaita Ashrama, Kolkata, 2007, p. 116. Thus it, as he remarks, however, if accepted and practiced, will do great good to humanity which is now torn into factions by warring creeds. – Op. cit., p. 117.

91. Also, plans are to be adopted from time-to-time to open public or privately operated school systems, for the gifted, for the mentally retarded, for the deaf and the hard-of-hearing, for the blind and the partially sighted, for other handicapped children. Mahapatra writes: "One of the major goals of special education (beyond developing skills and imparting information) is the ultimate adjustment of the handicapped to the general society of non-handicapped individuals". – Mahapatra, B. C.: "Education in Cybernetic Age", Sarup & Sons, New Delhi, 2006, p. 132. Government plan should further include awareness programme, which will result in social peace through involvement of people, in changing social scenarios. So, Rao and Reddy rightly asserts: "Awareness refers to a combination of identifying and providing accurate information and the fostering of situations in which women and men can begin to believe that change is possible". – Rao, V. K. and Reddy, R. S. (Eds.): "Contemporary Conceptions of Education", Commonwealth Publishers, New Delhi, 2008, p. 131. To bring in healthy norms for living in a hygienic condition, it is suggested that toilets are to be provided in all schools, both in urban as well as rural areas; due to lack of which children not only suffers from education, but also their medical expenses increase which the poor or moderate income group parents cannot afford to bear. Again, social cost of health-care activities increases for all such problems.

92. Pandey has given an exemplary way of thought in this work, which could be useful for social transformation. He remarks: "Global campaign for education suggests that if all children received a complete primary education, the economic impact of HIV/AIDS could be greatly reduced and around 700,000 lakhs of HIV in young adults could be prevented each year – 7 million in a decade. HIV/AIDS is spreading fastest among young women (ages 15-24), not only because their physiology puts them at risk, but also because they have little access to knowledge, economic resources and decision-making power". – Pandey, V. C. (Ed.): "Globalising Professional Education in India", ISHA Books, Delhi, 2006, p. 232. Thus, it is said that universal primary education is not a substitute for expanded HIV/AIDS treatment and prevention. But rather, it is complementary and therefore, urgently necessary if we are to win the fight against the disease. In consequence, we can refer to Sharma and Bakshi thus: "An empowerment process must involve individual awareness, and collective action is fundamental

to the aim of attaining social transformation". – Sharma, S. C. and Bakshi, Sweta: "Education, Employment and Empowerment of Women", A. K. Publications, Delhi, 2009, p. 5.

93. To enhance all such things, it is observed that over the course of a century, interest in protected areas has grown from the dream of a few far-seeing individuals and politicians to a commitment by governments and the international community, and increasingly also by civil society. – Kumar, Sandeep: "Biodiversity Environment and Sustainable Management", A. K. Publications, Delhi, 2009, p. 159. Hence, our social activities are likely to strongly driven by the results of a project 'Environmental and Social Impact Assessment' (ESIA) and any identified value associated with actions that go beyond mitigation to benefit valuable and threatened ecological resources. Thus, a number of different options for investments can benefit biodiversity conservation in a given area. In fact, much of the current concern about resource exhaustion involves renewable resources (Fisher, 1981). The size of the population, in turn, determines the availability of resources for future. As the flow of these resources over time is not purely a natural phenomenon, a crucial issue is the optimum (efficient) rate of resource use over time and over generations. – Bhattacharya, Rabindra N. (Ed.): "Environment Economics: An Indian Perspective", Oxford University Press, New Delhi, 2013, p. 62.

94. This kind of human relationship will bring in a social order, which is fundamental to overcome problems of exploitations – economic, social or even religious. It therefore requires equality of opportunity for all guided by social justice, love, service, sacrifice and to withdraw the self from hatred, jealousy and personal aggrandizement. About cooperation, which causes positive human relationships, Gandhiji also proposes to build the economic and social structure of society on decentralized industry and agriculture with a scope for cooperative enterprise in both the fields. – Patel, M. S.: "The Educational Philosophy of Mahatma Gandhi", Navajivan Publishing House, Ahmedabad, 1953, pp. 107-108. Our cooperative efforts should also protect banking services for healthy growth of the economy – it requires arrangements to provide quick service to their customers. Batra and Dangwal remarks: "In the context of globalization and liberalization of economy cooperative banks should ensure that their business is run on healthy lines by having professionalization, manpower training and infusing a sense of competition". – Batra, G. S. and Dangwal, R. C.: "Globalization and Marketing Management", Deep & Deep Publications Pvt. Ltd., New Delhi, 2006, p. 275. Altogether, we are required innovative ideas and commitments to overcome problems of human development as well as bringing potential growth perspective.

95. For healthy living purposes, we are to assess the art of doing things, as we could find in case of hedging, which Parameswaran opines regarding financial markets and futures services like: "It refers to the art of taking a position in the futures market that is opposite to the position which one has assumed for the spot market. – Parameswaran, Sunil K.: "Futures Markets", Tata McGraw-Hill Publishing Company Limited, New Delhi, 2003, p. 112. Thus, we have observed that a hedger will simultaneously take positions in the spot as well as the futures market. Similarly, safeguarding against all types of development should conform to the rules of seasonal adjustment, whereby it is followed that to analyze all these proposals as suggested, we need to address a simple but subtle question in

rationalistic way. Because, Mankiw utters while commenting in this regard, like: "Rational people systematically and purposefully do the best they can to achieve their objectives, given the opportunities they have". – Mankiw, N. Gregory: "Principles of Macroeconomics", Fourth Edn., Cengage Learning, New Delhi, 2007, p. 6. Hence, we are to work like – a seat belt law affects auto safety, because when a person wears a seat belt, the probability of surviving a major auto accident rises. We are therefore, to uplift people to reduce social gaps between haves and have-nots, who will increase peace and stability in complementing towards healthy living practices.

96. Of all these activities, again, international finance is the Chapter which should be attentively dealt with in making transaction with free atmosphere, considering global concern for attaining effectiveness in our global financial system; because, every firm in today's world is exposed to market fluctuations, as observed from financial market operations, in this age of competitive games of business. Thus, with increasing opportunities has come a quantum leap in financial risks. – Apte, Prakash G.: "International Finance: A Business Perspective", Tata McGraw-Hill Publishing Company Limited, New Delhi, 2013, p. 2. In the social reformative activities, our finance functions should be corrected and modified from global context, to enhance economic growth prospects, social stability and global transparency to develop social structure. So, in reforming social activities, it is to be safely noted that governments produce many of the important things of life, such as education, law and order, and pollution control. – Lipsey & Chrystal: "Economics", Oxford University Press Inc., New York, 2011, p. 344. In doing so, the overall impact of national development will be found to correlate things for international transformation, to advance our ideologies for progressive growth by means of 'just-in-time' methods. Therefore, Debraj Ray suggests: "To raise the income, well-being, and economic capabilities of peoples... ...the most crucial social task facing us today... ...This means, in particular, that development is also the removal of poverty and under nutrition: it is an increase in life expectancy; it is access to sanitation, clean drinking water, and health services; it is the reduction of infant mortality; it is increased access to knowledge and schooling, and literacy in particular". – Ray, Debraj: "Development Economics", Oxford University Press, New Delhi, 2012, pp. 7-8. In nutshell, the issue of development is not easy to resolve. We must have therefore, tremendously intuitive notions for holistic nature of social reformative services, which could bring in equity in living parameters to solve problems of human sufferings and social suppression, to restore an all-inclusive agenda, in making society radical towards changing the fates of peoples' life.

Chapter 2

Science and Technology for Human Development

Global Development

The development of the world order is dependent on the issues pertaining to the process of human development, which requires an understanding regarding scientific investigations on various activities of human organizations[1] that lead to the upliftment of human beings for civic living order, in the stage of societal plate-form. In this regard, it is essential to mention that enormous growth rate of population in the world, and their living necessities can be balanced through adequate implementation of technological ideas; wherein, we find that those things required for civil living would be supplemented by way of matching resources in optimal way, in which technology has a dominant role to play for the sake of mitigating the needs of the growing population over the world at large. Hence, science and technology contributes towards the aspects of developmental areas where human needs are satisfied enormously in the way of advancing life of the world population, which has been growing at galloping rate day-by-day and also year-after-year. Coming over to such a situational aspect of human living practices, it is paramount important to see that human up-gradation from the present stage of worldwide deprivation reaches to the path of global empowerment as well as emancipation, towards the field of making a right journey in the process of adequate salvation in never-ending manner[2].

Thus, the technological field which has been strengthened in this century due to advancement of scientific envisagement in the field of all types of human activities in societal pattern of living could be made more and more dynamic, in so far as the philosophy of work is concerned to upgrade people in a new dimensional way for finding out goal of actual living, in the midst of enormous opportunities and challenges that the various social organizations are now facing in an world of dynamic change. It is therefore necessary that human work behaviour has to be made more and more development oriented, towards enlarging the path of social orientation in regard to global upliftment of the people, who are otherwise; living in misery and thus, the potential in human resource capabilities are decaying for further progress which has caused for societal imbalance in nook and corner of the world[3]. So, the strategies regarding human development aspects are to be related to the process of dynamic nature of global development, which would be helpful for strengthening the world atmosphere that is being found also entangled with the nature of social restlessness situations in many parts of the world environment. To the contrary, our political atmosphere has been immeasurably going out of hands that cause human frustration as well as social value erosion in creating backwardness in different segments of the world society. Resultantly, separatism tendencies throughout the world have also been increasing day-by-day. The separatists who are following the path of regionalism are creating further more problems in the world environment, for which political consensus could not be reached at through the practice and ideals of a sovereign governing system. Ultimately, this has deprived to the political system in the way of developing a new pattern of management in mitigating needs of people by way of coalition politics, which is again, a barrier to the process of adequate development of people through empowering in terms of social sustainability. All such causes have been attributed to the field of science and technology, which we would like to enlarge in our discourses[4] in various Chapters, dealt with herein this volume.

From the above noted facts, we are now in a position to figure out the needs and importance of global development, which is the issue pertaining to the world political system and organizational behaviour in man-power development techniques for the envisagement of global outlook towards the path of human civic living, in matters of encouraging work behaviour through human sensitivity and creativity, in empowering social people towards the ultimate cause of salvation in life by way of doing tasks and activities for global level development. Organizational pattern of matching the resources of the world are observed to be implemented in profitable manner for the sake of its own entity, without caring for balanced and sustainable development[5], which is fully against the law of conservation, and thus befitting the concept of human empowerment due to lack of correct and fair world development strategies or strictures, mapping only for milestone of its own growth potentials ignoring the vicious problems creating impending nature of social backwardness of the world population. This is, among others, sought to be further analyzed in matters of religious perspective with the relativity of the application of scientific parlance to the correct nature of global sustainability in terms of managerial behavioural thought through various organizational norms and practices, necessitated for the purpose of social growth and human development potentials. The philosophical backgrounds of all these aspects are further related to the process of global development, so that advancement of the world society is made by means of organizational dynamics to the caricature of human development potentials. Hence, nurturing of the ideologies regarding the matching concept of resources for up-gradation of human beings towards the path of global level forward looking tendencies are narrated by means of philosophical foundation of human development perspectives, and therefore it is made imperative to the aspects of human growth and social balance for creating religious consciousness among the people of the world. All these are aided through passive norms of socialization, on the ground realities of human emancipation from the pathetic impoverished nature of living to the civilities of life bringing aspects, in relation to human development concept in new way of visualizing life aspects towards the process of salvation by way of doing things in creative management thought. To emulate such ideas in mind of the planners, we should frame adequate policy strategies in the organization of modern political system and, those norms of developmental ideologies required for human skill building are to be assimilated with the techniques of work potentialities; so that each and every aspect that are commonly related to the goal of development would have been judged from the view point of global creativity for enhancing human sensitivity, with certain model formulation[6] to propagate things in relation to optimum growth as well as measurable norms of social up-gradation. Thus, there will be human encouragement in work behaviour to excel more and more for the betterment of the society. It requires again, willful zeal for delivery mechanism towards the suffered class of humanity on the part of respective management system, which is concerned to the business affairs, the games people play at the organizational environment with the condition of immeasurable love and affection for the sake of vulnerable population. All these must be reconciled through strategic view of the mind encountered in passionate thinking behaviour to correlate things and activities, in terms of path-goal relational approach in organization structure for synchronizing a harmonious interrelationships between tasks and people, which go to lead for the kind of development relationship narrated to the process of enormous potentiality of organizational establishment to the grass-roots of the problems of emancipation. It is nevertheless, political agenda must be confirmed with techniques of human upliftment to a stage of global level empowerment, where religious agencies could play proactive role to eradicate poverty by means of an understanding between politics and religion for entertaining business pursuits, to voice things for the betterment agenda of the world population[7].

The above discussions require Indian core values of the Vedic concept which have become now, an important area of study to the standpoint of human sacrificial nature of job, for the lack of which world level politics as well as body corporate are getting no such guidelines that would be helpful for reasonable human development practices. Hence, the term 'Sanatana' practice is quite illuminating for the purpose of enlightenment on the issues of social framework of human development. The philosophic nature of business and entrepreneurial objectives could be matched with the ideologies of such practices, to assimilate goals and objectives of human life with the nature of doing things for the beautification, which is the core value of human management process in the arena of socialization through adequate realization of the self in working behaviour at organizational relationships, where politics would be supplemented to uproot social values for human emancipation, instead of the present system of worldwide mismanagement as prevailing to the organizational atmosphere and its work culture. Not only this, the Sanatana practice would supplement fundamental assumption regarding the value of judgement, comparability, assessment, and also right way[8] of dealing with the things, as it were; so as to find-out the causes of measurable notions regarding the perspective of life, which go to make the norms of civilization to confine goal of every human organization – be it private or public, national or international sectors of business enterprise or organizations, or even political, religious, charitable, philanthropic, or any other type of human organization. It is thus, pertinently true that the new pattern of management through Sanatana practice will accelerate the things to achieve the goal of development in terms of Preksha meditation, which is again, discussed in the Jaina philosophy for human perfection in realities of life. The world societies are therefore to be guided for global level reconciliation in strategic view of the term 'equanimity' thought, that which is possible only through human belief and sacrifice in all the areas of management. It would create things for bringing beauties in work principles to substantiate a thought provoking idea on integral humanity, where religion, politics and business will come to common ground for human development perspective. In this way, global emancipation of deprived masses would be possible in strategic manner to commensurate the goal of human upliftment[9] through realization of the self. Management of the resources of organization will be made for sustainability, conservation and harmoniousness to the aspects of human growth, social advancement and global integration in terms of doing business activities through the Sanatana practices, when games managers, leaders and other social people will play to guide the social wheel by means of various organizational agencies in this world of living. The reorientation of the global society will be made by such norms of the Vedic thoughts and concepts, which we would like to analyze in different Chapters in this volume under various topics dedicated for this specific purpose. The Vedic strategies are therefore taken at hand to suggest measures – how to use science and technology for human resource development purposes in terms of religious thought as well as philosophical foundation for human growth and social development, to come up with the notion of global development in regard to human up-gradation from the present stage of impoverish nature of pathetic condition, to a stage of civil living in the realization of life for optimum possibility of human emancipation in adequate managerial guidelines as well as organizational behavioural pursuits.

Global development which we have attempted to deal with in relation to organizational work culture has to be seen from the view point of 'teaching-learning' atmosphere[10] that should be inculcated by means of proactive leadership training, for which religion plays a vital role because sermons, if propagated for the humanitarian aspects of growth and harmony with organizational work relationship will relate to view things from global perspective of human integrity concept, and thus; the foundational base of human spiritualization would be strengthened, which is a must in the present day backward tendencies of the world order for enhancing forward looking tendencies in all sorts of organizational goal, whereto again, religious notion with the scientific temper of mind could be a correct philosophy for doing human all types of business activities in organizational transformational leadership goal confining towards the realities of management in integral humanity. It is therefore essential on the part of the world governments that they should follow the norms of dynamic behavioural pursuits of organizational ethics for the sake of nurturing the concept of integral humanity, by means of which, order of development would be supplemented towards the aspects of realizing human dignity of work as well as living relationship to integrate the base of global civilization. So, the techniques of reinventing[11] organizational value system with the code of conduct should be formulated in the planning process of working with the system of value judgment, for bringing optimality in human creativity of work in providing environment of fair developmental opportunities. The strategy required to be maintained to such type of work ethics is confined to the goal realization with the realities of managing things and activities, to be operated in the areas of practicalities of organizational delivery system to that of situation of backwardness prevailing world over. It is for this reason, said in the Sanatana practice that we are ultimately all in one unified nature of living, where as the philosophy behind our living goal is the performing idea of bringing people in one area – development through the concept of 'Vasudhaiva Kutumbakam'; because, our life is meant for understanding eternal value which is ingrained with the nature of job. Hence, sacrifice is the only way can be applied in the field of human advancement towards the path of upliftment, from the uncivilized nature of living as prevailing elsewhere and everywhere in this world to a stage of confining things into the ultimate truth, i. e., attaining the goal of salvation in life[12].

In this way, looking from the perspective idea of human emancipation, global level development of people can be concerned with the fundamental values of human life, which we observe only present in the religious philosophy of the past Vedic concept of universal humanity. By means of such dignity being provided in the core idea of this philosophy, human beings would lead to their life for the realization of eternality, which the modern civilization is lagging behind due to such goal of life in guiding their organizational activities with different types of strategy formulation, and consequently, a historical judgment on the phenomenal episode of ups and downs in human organizations from the long past will be evident, that causes human sufferings due to various unknowing reasons to the organizational managerial counterparts, to the constituencies of primary development as well as human emancipation ideology in terms of philosophy of the work ethics; which could not yet be codified the laws of human nature of real base of development with an understanding on the postulates of the eternality in way of guiding organizations, for the existential freedom of men. It is never been made specific on grounds of doing business, except the field of religious institutional ideologies that guide the world civilization norms of human development process. Hence, the science behind the issues of global development is related to the specific problems of human backwardness due to many reasons, which will be discussed elsewhere in this volume. In brief, global development is now a burning issue which can never be ignored at any cost, and which the world governments are to resolve things by planning issues concerned with human sufferings in pathetic nature of uncivilized living as observed worldwide. All the ideals against humanity can be rectified by means of Indian Vedic concept of management strategy being required to be reformulated for the purpose of global level change in proactive manner, so as to attain the goal of integral humanity with the notion of organizational work behaviour for encompassing problems of human growth with required level of development, as is expected from the present status of human backwardness[13]. It is therefore, science and technology can pave the way for attaining the goal of world peace through transformational leadership ideologies, which is the necessary background for human advancement towards salvation in life in terms of performing activities for organizational innovative nature of balancing with the ideology of rolling human civilization, to the correct order of the world societal foundation. In such order, there should be every possibility of development of deprived masses by way of looking life problems inherent in the scientific base of understanding about the organizational aspect of correlating things and activities for human liberation process[14], to the existential freedom of men.

Human Up-gradation

Human development is the core area of study in human civilization in modern times, which is observed to be lagging behind some sort of up-gradation concerning the living style of people around this world. This can be felt and imagined[15] from the societal condition of living of different people, who are at least not getting two-handful of meals a day, better educational and health care facilities, facilities of personality development like games and sports, amusement and recreation, and many other civic living conditions required for healthy living in societal stage of survival, like – sanitation, infrastructural opportunities of road transportation, railway connectivity, and communicational activities, etc. – all these are treated to be essential elements for the well-nourishment as well as survival of adequate living norms in peaceful manner. Thus, one area of up-gradation is concerned with the survival needs of human beings. But Maslow, in his 'Need Hierarchy' theory has given five important types of human needs categorically, while defining the ladder of needs. He says the needs are like ladder because of human safety and security, belongingness, love and affection and self-actualization; besides, the survival needs which human beings are required in sustaining life towards some kind of perfection. Again, Aristotle says that human beings are rational in nature, and the aspect of that rationality is dependent on the up-gradation of men from the savage stage to a stage of world class citizenship, that we talk about now in modern classical way of thinking about the humanity which is further dependent on the upliftment of people from all sorts of social sufferings, concerning the dignity of living in the way of leading life towards the confluence of thought of harmony. For this purpose, we require absolute love, absolute beauty and the reasoning ground of absolute truth in doing everything in the excellence building pattern of modern management thought. The present set-up of organizational activities has thus been made on this concept of human existentialism, but yet there is lack of freedom on the understanding of the philosophical foundation of human development parameters, which have caused for societal imbalance[16] everywhere in regard to distribution function necessary to be reconciled in the process of managing with the matching of resource potentials. This has resulted for a wide gap in the social structure[17], and consequently, regional imbalances are created; that give birth to regional disparity. The repercussion of this type of imbalanced notion has also enhanced social immobility among various people, due to sectarian feeling in mind of human beings. Besides, there are many types of chauvinistic attitude being played by means of present governance. Also, religious disparity have been fashioned in a way that has been provided with the fair-play of things in the name and style of development in corruptive behaviour of people, who either merge their views in depoliticizing all human activities, or misguiding some groups of people in the society who form certain other plate-form in terrorizing the overall system of the modern managing concept with all sorts of negativities. All these functional behavioural conditionality are to be curbed by means of balanced development thought on the workings of the modern organizational counterpart[18], which are to be made more and more prudence to uproot a social value system, standing on which humanity should be mould in a character assimilating factor for social sustainability. The sustainable concept of such an idea would supplement real growth in human beings, optimize their behavioural tendencies by means of specific delivery functions to advance social wheel in a new dimensional pattern of living. This is 'Win-Win' strategy of development[19] on the part of entire human race[20] should be entangled with the games people play in different types of transaction for the purpose of social development through organizational dynamicity of work behaviour, in attaining the goal of human dignity with the objective functions of the entire planning process for matching resources in regard to human up-gradation. As and when, human resource development policy (HRDP) would be suggested in terms of popularizing the method of excellence building for confining organizational activities to achieve the goal of optimum human development, in realistic measure of delivering goods and services towards the advancement of people to the crest of realizing life in free environment of living potentials, then only all types of administrative behaviour would lead to the goal of human salvation of life in the midst of holistic nature of societal emancipation of all backward population around this world of misery as well as dismaying environment.

From the above point of view, it is quite important to remember that human up-gradation principle has to be implemented with the philosophy of truth behind the theory of work, which is propagated in the Vedic sermons in scientific temper. This is the fundamental basis of development, and due to lack of such notion in modern governance policy of organizational activities, the good governance values and ideals is lost; because of lack of adequate knowledge on the art of work in organizational functions entertained for the purpose of developmental objectives[21]. The techniques of management standing on the art of human behaviour could be implemented only when we regard our life as the part of the whole functions of the natural beauty, which is ingrained to the inherent concept of blooming like flower by means of objectifying our goal of leading in a manner of disinterestedness while working for the organizational dynamicity. It will provide holistic development of people by supplying all the necessities of life bringing in coherence as well as harmonious manner, in all types of social developmental activities. The reason behind this is the transactional analysis that would supplement things in balanced manner with all the games people play in organizational nature of leading for performing in optimizing resources. So, the Vedanta version of managing our activities has to be adopted, mainly from the guidelines of Swami Vivekananda regarding human development ideology, and among others, the Complete Works of Swami Vivekananda are treasure of knowledge could be implemented in practice for unifying the goal of modern managing functions, with the concept of human excellence building norms required for optimum development in realization of life process. It is, in my opinion, the concept of beauty for upgrading people by way of reconciling development and emancipation in parallel way to objectify our life in the midst of diversities, and thus human beings will be provided with free environment of existential potentiality in enormous possibilities of the spurt of human personality development from all areas to bloom life in realizing managing values, thoughts and perspectives; in creating and recreating to the nature of emancipating life related problems, to harmonize growing functions in dynamic thought of organizational changing capabilities for human up-gradation, for reducing social disparities[22] in terms of appropriate delivery system.

In interpreting ideas of human development, we have observed that there is the necessity of human cooperation needed in all spheres of organizational managing system, where tasks are performed for the purpose of delivery of goods and services to the maximum number of people for their peaceful and comfortable living requirements, so as to attain the goal of human up-gradation from the pathetic miserable condition to a living environment of harmonious interrelationships between human beings. It is thus very much necessary that human competencies have to be enhanced in organizational activities by way of adjusting with the skill building techniques[23], for which, there should be perfect measure to be framed in the planning process of organizations by taking appropriate measures through right kind of political will, which administers the governing agenda of leading those social institutions that are to be guided in spontaneity of solving social problems of human beings, with the application of varied nature of social developmental schemes as well as implementation of policy resolutions for human up-gradation in judicious, competent and sustainable manner. Consequently, human empowerment consisting of protective nature of growth in realities of living in nurturing organizational cooperative work culture should be infused in mind of the people, so that organizational activities are performed towards bringing people to realize in actualizing the self with the concept of value initiating, concerning growth potential elements of social rejuvenation, in rolling entire wheel of the world order of human living; in a conducive, peaceful and harmonious interrelationships between people. In this way, management would be subject to discrimination between the factors of up-gradation principles in equanimity thought, to reach at the goal of world level upliftment of all humankind who is lagging behind all those scope and opportunities needed for civic living tendencies, in societal order of assimilating for purposive nature of human emancipation. When tasks are performed on the visionary ideals of the perspective areas of urgency in developmental transformation, organizational pulzation in betting the specific areas of human dignity of living in social environment would relate things in objective attainment of the goal of human journey for perfection conditionality, where people will find ample scope of advancement in the way of reaching at the goal of optimum realization regarding meaning of life. This requires again, sacrificial policy in working with the diversified nature of job, because sacrifice would lead to the goal of increasing human potential behaviour in the midst of challenge of change. Hence, the aspects of change[24] management concerned with the dynamicity of organizational journey in the discerning of availability of resources towards the path of optimum development of deprived people, could be conjoined with behavioural proactive situation for the purposive nature of rational growth in all areas of human upliftment, from the basic living needs to the concept of actualizing the self, in order of reaping at the existential freedom of life. So, organizational communication process has to be strengthened by means of looking about the philosophy of human upliftment consideration in terms of providing optimum freedom in the working environment, which is possible to be aided through managerial system of empowering people for excelling more and more in sustainable concept of living, to balance the imbalanced areas by means of organizational transformational ideologies to uproot societal value system in areas of growth, development and spontaneity of organizational dynamicity. Thus, the discriminative functions of management would supplement quality nature of services with the provisions of optimum development potentials, necessitated for human up-gradation, social dimension of coping with change[23] situations, governance philosophy of adjusting resources with the areas of deficient performing situations, reducing human imbalances in social orientation towards the path of global level integrity as well as human dignity in realization of the goal of human emancipation.

Dedicating all actions related to human up-gradation should require an approach of all-round measures like – creation of the facilities for nurturing interpersonal relationships to emulate people from the nature of bondage of work, because human beings are yet to realize that the same work which is the cause of bondage can be a rational counterpart to enlighten people in leading life towards salvation. Here is the importance of the Vedanta version of management thought, once applied in the field of organizational policy through strategic analysis of human causes for deprivation, and solution to this vicious problem in remedial measure of implementing organizational planned activities, with the goals and objectives of making people to have an equal journey to the path of self-realization; there would come rationality in human behavioural prudence to optimize resources for well-being of the mass people, who are still observed living in pathetic conditions, due to lack of basic and other necessities of life. Human beings are surviving in bondage due to the fact that they are deprived off from basic needs of living like – food, clothing, shelter, educational and recreation facilities, among others; which to the extent of pursuing goal of dignity of life are to be supplied by organizational good governance philosophy of work behaviour[26] in communicating things in place of needs in time. The time-space continuum in regard to the conceivability of things would narrate to the solution of the problems in right approach, about the strategy of upliftment principles congruent with the philosophy of beneficial nature of up-gradation, which has to be supplemented in transforming social order where every citizen would feel in mind a nurturing ideology. This is the integral approach of behavioural prudence confining tasks and activities to the specific path of human deprivation, misery and backwardness. Thus, organizational plan has to be made people oriented concept of optimum creativity to bring in social change, the guidelines under such type of social orientation should be framed in the productive ideologies[27] of supplying all the necessities by means of managerial governing agenda, to which the entity of politics should be merged for bringing specific nature of development-related potentiality, ignoring all types of corruptive behaviour on the part of organizational transformational leadership goal. Thus, the discriminative process to verify goals and objectives in supplying maximum to people for their upliftment would require social mobility[28], organizational sustainability, human consistency in work behaviour and worldwide integrity; to correlate issues of development and social advancement of the entire deprived human race. It will bring in common belief in mind of people regarding value of work, the judgment of which should be provided with the correct mechanism of organizational delivery system that would be balanced with the empowerment concept of people, for their self will as well as self zeal for optimizing organizational resources for the highest benefit of universal welfare. In this pattern of management human beings are to be guided for optimum level of understanding, with a fellow-feeling nature of doing tasks for integrating the matching concept of organizational resources to the sustainable impact on reducing social imbalances by means of enhancing human competencies, so as to balance the forward and backward regions in the world environment, to attain the goal of real human up-gradation.

In this way of thinking, our societal environment will be shaped in realities of managing things for providing people better educational facilities in scientific temper of thought, creating more and more employment opportunities for solving social backwardness in artistic manner of doing things for delivery of goods and services to the areas of human needs and besides, managing organizational activities by means of good governance philosophy to administer human upliftment process through different need-based schemes, such as – provisions for electricity and water supply facilities for the needy people who are living in depressed conditions in societal environment of living, due to lack of such amenities of life and also, framing and implementation of organizational policies regarding conducive transportation system to reduce regional imbalances[29] between the backward and forward zones, to restore well-balance in the overall socio-economic environment to deliver to the fullest level possible for the advancement of all population, and to enhance social stability, for increasing goodwill among the people to live in peaceful environment. However, the Vedic norms of equanimity thought is a must for such pattern of competent management under the guideline of spontaneous human skill building capabilities, narrated in aforesaid ideologies of human up-gradation principles, and contained in philosophic nature of value-based managerial approach to emulate things for the overall creativity in bringing human sensitivity with particular type of skill required for doing all these things, in terms of truth, beauty and goodness as the approach of developmental strategy. Human up-gradation, if continued in this way of resolving organizational dynamicity would supplement social mobility to the path of self-realization, on the part of each individual which could be actual existential freedom in matters of providing a system of harmonious human interrelationships among the people, for the purpose of adequate upliftment through managerial challenge in changing social environment where personality development among the masses will spurt like natural growth of the plants. Thus, nurturing harmonious industrial relationships would be made possible by encouraging people towards bringing entrepreneurial abilities in all-round spheres of social upheavals, to which organizational consistency in dealing with different groups would relate to actualize issues of human emancipation from the pathetic nature of living in distressed situations. Because, the Vedic thought in bringing human capabilities will come to open avenues for mutual collaboration between people, strengthen philosophy to change societal system in proactive manner to match resources for transformational dynamicity with all perfections at the work environment, entrepreneurial professionalism regarding democratic reinforcement to the control mechanism system of underlying goals and objectives to get proper feed-back[30] on the scope of development means, natural nurturing of the people in industrial set-up for guiding towards transcendental approach of assimilating ideologies of living as well as value-based concept of managing for human perfectionism, towards the propagation of optimum love for human dignity of living in civic stage by implementing schemes for the orientation of social rejuvenation purposes. All these are expected to be dealt in celebrated as well as sparkling manner in different analysis to be done on scientific revolution of the entire social wheel, where technological achievements of modern age would be tagged with doing business and human services for the ultimate and alternative objective for changing managerial values and ideals, on the notion of organizational behavioural prudence in thinking by means of acting for solving human frustration with the correct mission of human emancipation, for the purpose of upgrading people from the system of slavery to the civilities of their existential dynamicity, for encountering with all possibilities of leading human life in the supreme freedom of eradicating ills and lapses behind all types of sufferings, in reorientation of social pillars to the crest of development potentialities from strategic technological standpoint of application in the field of trade, industry and commerce[31].

Confidence Building Measures

Human beings have infinite potentialities dormant inside inner-mind, which can be activated through proper psychological skills in working out the inner potentiality, for which again, organizational interpersonal relationships are required to be developed in terms of 'transactional analysis'; so that dynamics of behavioural conceptualities could be related to various productive functions of organizations. Looking from this angle, confidence if properly allowed to grow in mind of people at the work environment by mutual as well as collaborative harmonious work relationships, cooperation and mutual trust among the people would be stimulated for motivating groups in producing towards the goal of human development potentiality; and thus, there would come healthy relationships in all spheres of managing things for the enrichment of the goal of organization in regard to embrace people to the realities of life problems[32]. Considering such objectivity, at present political coalition agenda has been going on to different countries at the crises situations for managing sovereign states, to govern people for their utmost developmental needs, to which Indian democratic set-up is one such glaring example, by study and observation of which we can come to a decision that confidence in Indian environment has not been always properly build-up through coalition politics; and due to lack of which adequate development of people has not been achieved for long from all areas of human civic living requirements, conditioned with personal agenda of all the political parties to their respective gains in the name of people's upliftment. Again, another area of confidence like resolving disputes between two countries can be built-up for healthy as well as mutually cooperative relationship in the countries, which go to enrich the pillars of regional disputes between nations of the world, and thus international trade can be strengthened through active participation among the people of different nations in various relationships, like – industrial and commercial activities, games and sports, diplomatic relationships for increasing trusteeship principle in military organizations to combat against anti-social activities and its various elements compounding with the causes of social restlessness situations, and besides various issues pertaining to strengthening the base of human rights activities. From all these, it is clear that appropriate measures on building up confidence through various agencies and organizations of governance would result in increasing active cooperation between people living in different territories of the world[33]. Thus, modern organizations are required to adopt policies on building confidence among the governing entities for the sake of mutual benefits of all the countries, and also matching resources in efficient manner for strengthening the base of organizational effectiveness, in attaining the goal of human development in terms of 'Win-Win' strategy by way of inter-group working relationship. So, the measures of confidence as and when formulated and implemented in right direction can help to cope up with the problems of national integrity, international understanding and universal brotherhood policies to the elimination of human deprivation of all sorts in the ground realities of living in peaceful, harmonious and cooperative environment in the world society. Besides, economic development of people living in different parts of the world would be enhanced through appropriate confidence building measures from organizational entities, to rejuvenate the process of global dynamicity among the masses of the world. World class citizenship would be made through developing the fundamental areas of the social structure in terms of adequate policy, in strengthening confidence to organizational transformational leadership goal of working with the philosophy of human up-gradation, social restructuring and world level proactive change to embrace the goal of human emancipation from backward situations; otherwise, the sufferings of the masses would not be eliminated to rectify social imbalance in right direction.

From the above facts, we must note that confidence has to be built-up on issues of guiding people for inter-activeness in relation to organizational missionary journey of dealing with human upliftment from severe stage of social deprivation, to the directive functions of visionary adjustment with varying tendencies of working situations in different types of organizations, where political will and people's development agenda could be interrelated for healthy human intercourse in social set-up[34]. In this context, it is worthwhile to note that adequate policy on the convergence of confidentiality in areas of bilateral trade would stimulate business related activities for strengthening the base of economic growth in between the nation-states, which is resultantly helpful for interconnecting the cooperative atmosphere to emulate the regional disparities by means of people's development in terms of industrial as well as entrepreneurship activities. Over and above, measures relating to human development potentials like – games and sports, amusements and recreational activities, military arrangements for cooperative environment in reaching at hospitability criterion in enthusing people to augment for mutual collaboration in the field of inter-state human relationship, warfare related activities to reduce hatred between people of the different states, establishment of educational and cultural activities, and also various types of training programmes in different socio-economic areas of bilateral issues pertaining to mutual advancement of world population, health services activities connected to collaborative research programmes, scientific dissemination of technology related programmes in areas of space research related activities, weather forecasting and global environmental issues creating social dynamic movements for worldwide regeneration of human understanding, and international cooperation in the field of communication activities to strengthen organizational consistency in healthy development in all areas of socio-economic upliftment programmes, to pave the way for innovative creativity in sensitizing people to convergence of organizational dynamicity and streamlining human capital formation towards the social undertaking[35], could initiate the growth of the states in the world by means of policy initiation for the purpose of effective man-power development. However, the implementation norms of competencies regarding human cooperation towards the aspects of social rejuvenation process[36] would have to be made effective in increasing social sustainability in terms of global level human cooperation, by means of mutual understanding between governmental agencies, non-governmental organizations (NGOs), international institutions concerning human growth, social mobility in proactive manner and organizational congruency in dealing with the things and activities related to human upliftment programmes and researches towards learning culture, are all necessary areas where confidence once enthused in people by means of effective management would lead to the goal of worldwide peace and social development in connecting people through different ideologies of transformational leadership traits as well as human cooperation. On the other hand, organizational structure would be made more and more flexible to systematize things in realities of management. It is therefore needed measures like international understanding between people, government and various organizational entities so as to attain the goal of integral humanity concept. To this area again, Vedic ideology and value system would be harmonious to actualize things by means of correct notions for implementing confidence building measures – various measures like love and affection between people, self-actualization by realization of empowerment concept for dynamicity of human growth, sustainability for social mobility in initiated path of human integration, organizational acquisition of things for delivery of goods and services requirement to eliminate social poverty and backwardness[37] in terms of human indignity and confluence of thought regarding universal integrity as well as peaceful social environment; among others, are a few of those Vedanta perspective regarding global human rights in matters relating to realization of the concept of social changing instrument of human growth, and global level economic cooperation and human up-gradation towards the path of making organizational journey for social advancement.

The terrible confusion in human mind is that people are different in nature like caste, creed, colour, race, sex, etc. But the modern age scientific investigations regarding human poverty and living stage calls for breaking the slumber of vicious chain in such misconception of living, for which different types of social unrest have been encompassing negative pattern of social growth in between people that has been further, entrusted people to arrive at many types of conflicting elements which are burden for correct implementation of governmental policies in areas of human needs. Hence, inappropriate measures are proceeded for, in the name of development package for emancipation of social poverty. But, the schemes as are undertaken for bringing social change in people create to further social backwardness due to barriers in areas of religious discrimination, caste policies, racial differentiation, gender issues, etc. which relate to organizational interest of divergences regarding goal concept displacement as well as human backwardness. To eliminate all these impact and incidences on development related considerations, measures like democratic participation[38] in activities and involvement of people in decision-making areas of upliftment are much needed in initiating the process of universal human brotherhood philosophy, where scientific investigations are to be implemented to solve grass-root problems of human sufferings, irrespective of any dogmatic ideology in humankind; but rather technological implements are to be used for social dynamic growth bringing abrupt changes in areas of supply-chain management, towards fulfilling social gaps in upgrading people to the valuable path of civic living with all kinds of necessities considered for human propagation of increasing knowledge, and enhancing for motivated learning capacities towards the concept of common welfare of the humanity. This type of organizational policy would result in free-flow of an environment, by which hatred between people will be eliminated automatically in empowerment element of work initiation towards optimum development in equanimity thought, for enlightening leadership goal and organizational stability to cope up with the problematic areas of human backwardness. Thus, confidence in mind of people would be uprooted to feel for working zeal in doing all the services for the attainment of group goal, organizational consistency for matching resources in matchless way, governmental guidance to the enrichment of good governance philosophy for human upliftment, and besides, international agencies would be balanced to encompass global environmental contingencies to systematize things and activities with the norms of human integrity, legal justification and religious proactive thinking towards keeping people in the field of realization for welfare norms of universal harmony as well as human freedom of living, in existential subsistence with the element of initiating self-motivation[39].

All types of confusion of people living in chaotic social environment in this world will go away forever, as and when there would be full empowerment feeling in mind of deprived population of the world. It will then, also solve the problems of terrorism, which are due to frustration of the deprived masses, and where some kind of anti-social elements play their dominant role world-over, taking initiatives in making people to motivate for separatism tendencies in different ways in the name of people's sufferings as well as religious dogmatism – this is the area of deficiency and backwardness of people, which the terrorist counterparts are measuring about the prone areas of governmental weaknesses throughout the world; and which has been followed by anti-social as well as anti-national activities, to which political plate-form has yet to be strengthened by taking corrective measures and also implementing those with active cooperation of people as well as political will force in people's agenda for development of backward masses, to uproot their motivational zeal from inner mind for encouraging them to relate their personal activities for the highest good of the global society. In this way, measures for optimum creativity of people would be supplemented to stimulate adequate responding nature of social dynamicity, world peace and harmony, to tranquil global environment of living with all dignities of life for civil existence; where managerial paradigm shift would be nurtured towards human equanimity of thought for encouraging people in supplementing leadership traits for the sake of integral humanity. Hence, the entire functions of organizational management and governmental governance philosophy[40] in building up cooperation between people would accumulate social resources to channelize in the areas of human problems of civic living, by supplying adequate services to provide themselves in enriching the pillars of harmonious living; so as to accommodate the enormous growth rate in the global nature of organizing people to the embracing of the goal of equipoise entrepreneurship abilities, for enhancing optimum nature of capabilities by means of scientific creativity as well as philosophic idea of sensitivity for universal cooperation. Coming across to such an idea, it is to be noted that measures in areas of – permanent settlement of people for fuller realization of life like, disinterested nature of human performance for the greater humanity, administrative zeal for confining good governance practices for eliminating social distress of human sufferings from all kinds of ills of living, injustices, corruptive behaviour, etc. are required to be remedied through devolution of power and authority with means of decentralizing organizational functional relationship to the pious needs of human beings; so that modern days technological inventive system of management would enlarge the policies of human rights related issues of development, to the path of realistic empowerment concept in compounding a learning atmosphere, to attain the goal of submissiveness in recapitulating human potential growth to assist for dynamic social movement.

Accordingly, confidence[41] must be created in mind of people to nurture ideologies of integral functional relationship between social transformation and people's development to correlate things and activities, in cooperative endeavour of people to confine goal of leadership with the perspective value analysis as well as value judgment, in recreating organizational structure for the procreation of natural journey of human beings encompassing all types of moral building boost-up, to rejuvenate pillars of growth in concrete ideas of value-based management principles. It is highly motivating people, while schooling of the system is entertained in a manner where all types of humankind would be assessed with the philosophy of transformational goal of life. Thus, organizational leadership policy would be strengthened in creative thought of operating all functions of the emancipation base, to which team-building approach should be enthused in mind of people as to their responding nature of working behaviour to abide by the principles of adequate delivery system. It is the good governance practice requires synthesizing about the reformations in the areas of law and order situations, for justified nature of dealing with the concept of human backwardness to advance people in reinventing pattern of social change, with measures of behavioural prudence to cope up with the needs of challenge of change. Consequently, all disputed areas are to be redrafted in policy resolution of political will, to verify the conflicting zones with the reformulation of people's development agenda; which would be consistent to spontaneous growth for empowering people to build-up capacities with measures of social dynamicity. However, this type of confidence building norms should relate to goals of social integrity in structural adjustment of the situations of change[42], for which people's participation should further be made through aided system of organizational managerial leadership goal of each undertaking, to accumulate the resources for development functional relativity with optimistic transparency of bringing abrupt change to uplift the social veil. As per scientific envisagement on the notion of working capabilities of people, organizations are to be treated as social changing element of agency, where measures like – quality leadership principles with all traits of personality development criterion are narrated to the aspects of human growth, social directive mobility, entrepreneurship skill building acumen in working out things for delivering productivity, technological consistency in communicating the role of people's empowerment in advancing social integrity with policy resolving profiles in organizational undertaking, to encompass growth related as well as fundamental development based ideologies to reorient social structure in relation to human upliftment, international understanding in terms of inter-state good cooperative relationship in areas of human rights up-gradation, educational reformation, international trade, industry and business related issues, etc.; among others, could bring in conformity in quantitative delivery between organizational services and people's motivational incentives, to provide for environmental balance between human integrity and worldwide civic mobility among all the people in each and every step of encouraging people, to serve with responding nature of organizational responsibility of giving services for optimum human development process. In this way, confidence building would be molded to encounter for structural reinvention of things in creative performance of organizational leadership goal[43] towards social transformation, with a view to emancipate human beings from all their malnourished conditions, ill-fed qualities, uneducated spectrum of social immobility, inhuman nature of living due to distressed condition of infrastructural means as well as sufferings from health care necessities of leading civic life. So, corruptive system has to be remedied through dynamic behavioural congruency in mitigating needs of human beings, which would relate to motivational training, packages, schemes, etc., to move the society in sustainable direction. Thus, confidence will grow up in between people to systematize things and activities under the guidance of entrepreneurship leadership goal, as sought for human emancipation from severe stage of life bringing survival in backward conditions. As a whole, organizational system adjusting with the kind of goal consistency would thus harmonize human inner mind zeal to serve the society for forecasting everything towards the path providing essentiality for peaceful living norms, leaving all sorts of anti-social thinking and therefore, it is justified to note that human emancipation would result in social reorientation[44] for effectiveness in relating system with human excellence.

Path-Goal Adjustment for Human Living Practices

Human life is not bed-of-roses. It is because of the reason that people have not understood the real objective of life, for which it seems for certain class of human beings in society that concentration of wealth in few hands would satisfy the needs of living in peaceful way. But, the reality of surviving and leading our life bringing process is guiding towards the objective of fulfilling certain other things than we are actually doing in terms of managing our activities in day-to-day to the holistic idea of peaceful living concepts. Here comes the importance of analyzing our goals and objectives, which should be related to the different paths that we follow in course of doing things for getting things done through and with others in systematic order. This order being sequence of parameters in actualizing our self towards the environmental situations, making life process situational to that of attaining maximum happiness for the peaceful attainment of the ultimate objective of life, there is requirement of natural balance in between classes of people who are backward in many conditions of living as compared to forward population. However, social imbalances can be rectified as and when a proper balance between poor and rich classification is remedied in reconciliation[45] to the objectives of human life bringing process through 'goal-path' relational approach from the holistic concept of managerial effectiveness in dealing with the organizational power and authority regarding delivery of the necessities of civic[46] living in all segments of the world population. Today, there is concentration of wealth in a few hands in societal structure, which creates an artificial imbalance among the people and for which, various type of social discrimination have been found in managing for the realities of living in objective attainment of tasks and activities. It has deprived people by organizational system in changing social pattern of conformity in regard to haves and have-nots categorical reduction by adequate 'supply-chain' management potential, to eliminate various dimension of human crises; as it were, to rejuvenate social picture in establishing human goal towards the endeavour of doing all types of socio-economic activities for the common benefit of mass people, and for maximum welfare of the whole society to be found on the crest of human upheavals in realizing life for the supreme existential freedom. Probably, this is the reason for which the Vedanta utters: "Vasudhaiva Kutumbakam" as the philosophy of human living sermon. This is the managerial guidance mantra would supplement proper social balance in order of doing things for common welfare of humankind, and also environmental balance between animal as well as plant kingdom, for the purpose of natural equilibrium which is now, a question-mark for the safety and security of our present generation in this world of living by managing our organizational deeds in terms of contingency, to arrive at a system that could guide the entire humanity to the path of attaining our goal of living.

It is observed that multi-dimensional nature of waves in the great sea and ocean have not now been playing to its course in real sequence for having right type of tides in sea, because of different types of collusion being played through the free intercourse of the naturalistic tendencies to evolve world order in balanced phase of doing the environmental activities[47]. The fundamental aspects of this type of imbalanced situations are caused due to unsystematic management of our industrial and commercial activities in this world, by means of authoritative functions of multi-nationalistic character of organizations; where power and authority has been created in such way in organizational structure that administration of things become quite inter-dependent to environmental relocation of issues pertaining to situational adjustment between 'path-goal' practice, for which mismanagement of resources have been compounded with the natural-environmental dichotomy in prevalence to such circumstances. It is therefore essential that concentration of power for performing industrial activities should be delegated to relegate the affairs on prudence of human behavioural adjustment, instead of concentration of wealth creation for benefits of certain group of people. Modern civilization has to be seen from dynamics concept of social mobility, on which stands human security of living; and hence, organizational activities are to correlate things between economic equilibrium of 'means-ends' relationship, to establish proper or right match between resources convertibility and environmental balancing sustainability to all types of organized human living practices, for eradicating lopsided development in bringing human living order to the path of global existence, in correlating issues of mismanagement through good governance philosophy of guiding organizations, to bring forth abrupt social change in proactive manner in attaining the goal of universal dynamism, in the midst of human diversities of living[48]. Propagating of this theory is possible by means of managerial excellence in providing atmosphere within internal environment of organizational activities, where everything has to be correlated to the issues of performing through embracing the goal of external environmental balance. Accordingly, the principle of doing things must be adjusted to conformity of human living practices for attaining peaceful environment for realization of the absolute bliss in nature, to communicate things in cooperative manner rather than the present pattern of international competition. Because, when there would be common understanding between people of different nations, managerial mutualism will be reflected to the ground realities of multi-nationalistic entities towards the aspect of regarding management for administering to establish unification goal of human integrity, in the working philosophy of peaceful needs to make organizational activities operational for maximum delivery with minimum input costs. Thus, cost-output ratio will relate to the maximization principle of organizational survival concept, to fullest realization of human objectives for attaining perfection in dealing resources to the sustainability of things. In this way, it can further be said that human life in this world order is nothing but conjoining of the principle of spirit to the elements of matter. The matter-spirit dynamic principle is entrusted with the organism character of the entity of beings, which is also found in organizational character to the entity concept of dealing with the performances for path-goal adjustment towards attaining integrity. Thus, the strategy of the co-association principle combining organizations together must be viewed from entity concept, where things are practiced for underlying the principle of the greater natural order[49]. Because, the entity of beings that is the part of the great natural system has its own pulzation with the big system of the Prakriti. Therefore, it is true that all types of organizational entity are concerned with the system of universal process, by which human civilization has been revolving towards the process of evolution of things for attaining higher and higher perfectionism, in rolling towards the end of identities to the greatest aspect of the integrative base of organizational movement, confined with the task of actualizing human all types of endeavour in reaching to the crest of the development pyramid.

From this, it is now worthwhile to note that the strategic idea of human growth is contained in the integrative aspect of organizational 'input-output' relationship, in correlating 'means-ends' opportunities for bringing human life comfortable to the process of dynamic movement by justifying the delivery system through supply-chain management network, in inculcating equilibrium for the sake of organizational changing behaviour to bring in human diversities with the integrative concept of dealing with the norms of human common rolling to the process of universal dynamism, in acting-interacting way of co-associating natural phenomenal episode to the aspects of proactive social change. Hence, organizations as the core of social changing[50] instrument would relate their performance to that of human living practices, which could have certain type of conformity to the consistency of human behavioural prudence. Nevertheless, this has yet to be established in society for the sake of greater unity in human living practices; which must follow the principles of conservatism in evolutionary way of dealing with the techniques of productivity. It is therefore true to say that matching of resources for maximizing productivity with the minimization of cost requires at level of managerial functioning, justify the concept of right leadership practices throughout organizational journey of life. Now-a-days, rampant corruption in actualizing things have created social imbalance due to red-tapes, nepotism; which further results in social disparity as well as separatism in human living norms. Accordingly, betterment of people has not been done in proper way to eliminate social poverty. As a whole, various type of conflicts are aroused in organizational delivery system to make the process of integration more and more consistent towards finding the goal of human competencies, skilful way of dealing with organizational system of effective communication base for enhancing excellence in between groups. This has further ruined the system of human justice[51], which has to be administered by way of judicial reformatory practices in dealing with the policy of universal order of balancing between human development and social proactive change, in each and every fundamental aspect of organizational dynamicity, to produce things for common welfare of the world population. Thus, the strategic idea on common rolling of the world order is consistently maintained through organizational effective behaviour in terms of leadership transformation, to uproot social value to the specific goal of guiding human organizations for the existential freedom and integrative dealing of human beings in means-ends relativity. To bring in optimum development of human beings by way of dealing with the justifiable system of adequate delivery mechanism requires conformity of human empowerment; so that human living practices are balanced in co-association of getting things and attaining goal for the separate identity of beings in organizational entity concept, which should be related to the greater aspect of cosmological beauty in the midst of organizational diversities in dealing with people. Hence, this principle gives an idea that individual goals are to be made in organizations in well-balancing practice of attaining organizational goal-via-group goals, to entertain overall system in creative endeavour of human beings in terms of correct entrepreneurship activities, with the normative aspects of human development for unifying managerial communication system to the organizational structural adjustment between correlation of human growth and development, and also environmental sustainability to optimize resources for universal welfare of human race in the world to the integrative path of dynamic social movement.

For doing with the dynamic nature of changing the societal pyramid[52], organizational planning should have the framework of a road-map which gives people opportunity of utilizing the self-resource in innovative nature of dealing with the tasks, as per goal directed objectives of the organization for deciding about the technological part of human excellence building capabilities; and thus, scientific investigations are required to be made for effective interpersonal relationship in regard to embrace the goal of maximum development of the oppressed people, who are still today, in this age of technological communication could not come-out successfully for the advancement in realities from all sorts of human sufferings. It is therefore leadership perspective should be entrusted with the norms of human equanimity thought of strategic social advancement, with respect to organizational control mechanism to the dynamic behavioural prudence of group cohesiveness, for bringing transformation consistent with the philosophy of nation-states interactive cooperation in dealing with the justice for connoting the principles of human up-gradation, resultant to the fundamental aspects of leadership participation towards social changing in correct way of dealing with the emergent issues of developmental needs of the masses; so that world level model to the level-playing role of decision variables for balancing resources to the cause of bringing social change would be brought forth with the existential mechanism, which is congruent to the principles of international human cooperation and understanding regarding welfare-related projects, to the aspects of human indiscriminative policies encountering human up-gradation and worldwide emancipation from severe nature of sufferings[53] of the mankind. Organizational policies are therefore required to adopt the strategies like: (i) integral humanity commensurate with the principle of optimum development of deprived people; (ii) informal communication strengthening the base of group identity for human cooperation towards matching resources in inventive creativity to supply the needs of the malnourished people; (iii) leadership transformation requiring organizational dynamicity in applying the principles of people's empowerment through 'path-goal' relativity in changing societal environment; (iv) universal rolling of all mankind in diversified way of dealing with organizational resources match, for optimizing 'input-output' convertibility in delivering goods to the areas of human sufferings; (v) international understanding regarding human justice for living in peaceful environment by organizational control mechanism of administered policy, for integrating structure of the society in stratified manner for the sake of advancing people in realization of enormous potentiality, through technological innovative treatment for undertaking resolution on human rights related issues of cooperative living in peaceful environment; (vi) mutual collaborative relationship by means of business combinations, political autonomy, decentralization of power to the needy people for their emancipation, etc.; among others, are a few important guidelines to adopt with the changing potentials of the twenty-first century periods, for attaining integral humanity through nurturing the elements of universal human dignity[54] as well as empowerment approach in realistic scientific envisagement of thought process, requiring human excellence conditioned with universal welfare, environmental sustainability and world class citizenship of the oppressed, depressed and suppressed population living from all corners of civic living necessities. Management decisions are therefore very important in forecasting affairs by means of adequate dissemination of data analysis, for scientific model formulation, statistical simulation of things and activities, and physical relationship in delivery mechanism to attain the task of human psychological treatment regarding motivational objectives towards existential freedom of living with international peace, harmony, cooperation and fellow-feeling nature of dealing with organizational system, to upgrade people in a situation where all the mankind would optimize their self for managerial actualizing to the end of nurturing human dignity, organizational integrity and above all, universal brotherhood philosophy of reaching at the goal of salvation, in terms of synthesizing organizational effective coordination functions, to match resources for common welfare of people. Thus, there would come relevancy in reality towards bringing a healthy balance between reducing human sufferings by way of adequate up-gradation in fields like – educational facilities, healthy living facilities, recreational and other human motivational facilities; besides being supplying of the basic amenities with the provisions of civic living from organizational active counterparts, interactive leadership ideals[55], benevolence of group cohesiveness for attaining human cooperation in path-goal adjustments of human justified living through organizational dynamicity, environmental integrity and worldwide harmony to rejuvenate the process of holistic change.

In concluding about the principle of human entity of living, it is truly required that social dynamicity should be observed while managing things for organizational consistency in dealing different types of resources. For increasing creativity, scientific investigations regarding human backwardness is very much essential, so as to attain conformity of living goals and objectives by means of organizational structural adjustment for bringing adequate level of social change, in synthesizing governance as well as administrative areas, which go to balance a mechanism coherence with the philosophy of international integrity, human dignity, organizational sustainability in confining tasks towards environmental subsistence in conservation, preservation and optimization of the objectives of human living parameters. Hence, synthesizing of the organizational resources in correct way of dealing with the techniques of production, and delivery of the productive goods to the areas of human needs in right way would streamline investment potentials in channelizing manner; so that deprived as well as backward people could be given opportunities for fuller personality development. It is therefore needed that the working schemes and projects are to be framework of human upliftment, on which organizational management will stand to administer things for human emancipation ideologies, with justifiable norms of bringing a balance between haves and have-nots class of human beings. As a matter of fact, organizational management process has to deal with the technological counterparts for supplying towards optimum order to fulfill human needs in scientific adjustment between goals of living and organization as an instrument of social change for environmental balance, human excellence, and organizational structural conformity in dealing with the scarce resources of the world. So, the principles of human dignity, social dynamicity and worldwide peace are all required to be fulfilled in the planned idea of management decision variables, to reduce human conflicting nature of living, and to increase human welfare by justifiable[56] matching of the social resources for both haves and have-nots category of human beings. What is more essential is that the Vedic order of thinking in strategic performances like the principles of equanimity, equipoise nature of dealing, transformational leadership for attaining human transcendental order, etc. are all poignantly requiring for embracing the goal of integral humanity with the philosophical perspective of business relationship with social movement of people, for making journey towards realizing survival necessity with personifying the paths of optimum social mobility for increasing human cooperation, international understanding in existential supremacy by means of organizational deliverance in attaining human emancipation from the grass-root level of sufferings, and all types of ills in living with a pathetic inhuman condition[57]. Thus, the nature of human management compounding the path of up-gradation requires a good synthesis among the permeable parameters of sufferings, which go to say that the technological achievements of the twenty-first century are to relate things of organizational human enterprising autonomy towards the aspects of integrated journey of human beings, by way of matching resources for optimum development of the suffered classes of humankind for their living freedom to illuminate the picture of the society, for attaining world peace through management.

In a nutshell, corroborating the features of human integrity in organizational sustainability of dealing with the resources to the optimality of human welfare calls for 'path-goal' relational adjustment, for which corruptive leadership ideals are to be converted into scientific envisagement of things towards the conformity of dealing with all such resources for universal integrity in organizational activities, international understanding for human cooperation and motivation for delivery as well as excellence building in purposive way of finding out the meaning of human living with the dignity of work, and skill building capabilities for optimizing productivity to deliver in society to the need-based areas for reducing human poverty as well as sufferings; considering innovative leadership goal for attaining human integrity in group cohesiveness to the functional areas of organizations, for propagating the theory of integral humanity with justice of civil living in terms of supply-chain managerial effectiveness, to upgrade people and to reduce social imbalances, which will ultimately go to reduce human social conflicts, eradicate separatism tendencies, and solve the problems of regional imbalances. For all these reasons, at the beginning the sermon of the Vedanta philosophy – 'Vasudhaiva Kutumbakam' has been advocated, with a view to understand precisely managerial functional relativity with the concept of 'path-goal' relational approach in human living tendencies, to the synthesizing probabilities of universal integrity[58], organizational conformity for human living necessities in peaceful as well as harmonious manner.

Twenty-First Centuries – Human Excellence Millennium

The development of human beings in this era of technological up-gradation requires indiscriminating part to be played by modern organizations in the work-related behaviour of organizational importance towards keeping pace with the thought of human sufferings, from all counts of human living parameters, so as to attain human excellence in all-round spheres of societal consistency in regard to human peace from all sources of socio-economic activities, partaking human advancement for the supremacy of liberal practices, in terms of organizational abilities, managerial guidance and good governance conceptualities. It is therefore, human quality at the work place requires commendable transparency to the process of attaining holistic goal of the organizations, which should be backed by technological subsistence, scientific investigations on planning things which are of primarily necessitated by human empowerment considerations, for undertaking organizational responsibility in discharging services by means of productive diversities, in operating technological acumen to people oriented tasks and objective functions; concerning human growth-related potentials to the up-gradation of deprived masses in advancing the civil society to the path of human destiny of life, in encircling towards the peripheral boundary of organizational controlling measures in coordinating the follow-up actions – this is the modern existential challenge requiring human indignity in expounding the realities to the matching principles of managerial effectiveness in organizational consistency, guided by the philosophy of human empowerment in technological renovation of things for observation of organizational delivery system, where leadership norms are required democratic belief[59] in advancing people to the inclination of upward journey in life related prospective goals. This principle is believed to be guiding the path of human liberation, in doing with the techniques of the present day realities, irrespective of any kind of discrimination in human beings; but only one kind of ideology concentrating human up-gradation, social mobility and worldwide dynamic growth of global level organizations, are all required the latest technological adjustments with the corporate policy making resolutions, in revamping organizations towards the path of human work culture in coagulating developmental circumstances to satisfy dire necessities of those people, who are still today remaining in backward situations. Hence, human skill building situations are to be more systematized in the present day multinational corporate entities; so that corporate culture of work becomes instrument of bringing social change in strategic performance of tasks, for the sake of objective analysis on the organizational mission oriented concept of human emancipation role, nurtured for undertaking the urgent social responsibility by means of good governance philosophy of human empowerment conditionality, leadership vision of corporate delivery towards the needy segment of the societal pyramid, democratic consistency of balance in regard to income, employment, savings and investment outlets, technological envisagement towards underlying the importance of sustainable of growth in terms of input-output relationship, and besides, there is the need of global level human advancement in terms of regional distribution function of the resources match, parity of goal concept for adequate advancement of deprived masses to the path of social stratification, human existential challenge of living in civic liberties and worldwide transformational idea regarding leadership objective on delivery system[60], synthesizing all the parameters of growth-related issues for human excellence purpose.

Coming over to such a situation, it is observed that the technological Ombudsman has to be created in industrial houses for excellence building considerations, in propagating ideologies of 'all-in-one' philosophy – embracing the concept of the Vedanta, where every citizen in this world of living would be taken as the resource connect with technological discoveries and inventions, in each part of problems which would supplement global cooperation in human beings that organizational management requires in leading people to the path of human liberation, in living ideologies of emancipation through work culture, excellence building process to the work-out human dormant potentialities[61], and to balance in sustaining growth of the society in correct adjustment of resources for creative development of the backward people. Thus, modern days hurdles of population increase should commensurate with the sustainability of resource innovation, product modification and market segmentation strategies. In all these areas, technology has to be reformulated for organizational diversity, human advancement and global level transformation by means of empowering people at the work place, so as to attain the goal of world peace and human liberation in living with the dignity of work, survival policy with cooperation, unity in diversifying organizational activities in all areas of development-related projects, through managerial effectiveness as well as corporate culture of human nurturing ideologies.

Thinking from such type of managing concept for upgrading human life[62] bringing perspective idea, it can be asserted that modern technological upheavals could be supplemented to utilize in human civilization in the twenty-first century in different areas of social development of the world class beings, like – games and sports, cinematography, museum, antiquarian activities, activities related to transport and communication services, rail-road connectivity, construction activities pertaining to heavy construction of projects like, canals, dams, etc., irrigational activities, say, water connectivity to agricultural fields and others, entire range of human agricultural activities, floricultural and also sericulture activities, weaving activities[63], activities of trade, industry and field of commerce, some other activities like – weather forecasting, space research programmes, dance, drama, gymnasium, music and recreational activities, and besides, many other fields which go to constitute the whole spectrum of human civilization in new dimensional way to the foundation of human cause of development like – elimination of poverty[64], reduction of social imbalances of all types in the nature of misery, distress and sufferings of human beings; irrespective of any caste, creed, colour, sex and racialism[65]. However, it is true that human empowerment through scientific envisagement of social problems can be sorted out by means of technological solution of those problems, so as to ascertain gaps in societal reformation in managing things, for which again, the concept of purity, sovereignty and liberal thought should be exposed[66] in encompassing social elimination of human distress. It is therefore, scientific temper requiring in the framework of organizational policy implications, where man-power related issues like – human fellow-feeling nature of organizational growing dynamicity, technology based training facilities, educational institutionalization of technological version of new thought for human development paradigm, etc. are all required to be assimilated in functional relationship of the entrepreneurial goal of firms and companies; by which every citizen of modern states would be enlightened with the concept of credibility, competency, consistency to open up the door of mental faculty in comprehensive way to understand the need for having human resource development potential[67] in corporate work accountability. To balance all imbalances, to match many types of lapses therefore, technology would find-out means and ways for solving problems of human starvation, malnourishment and all types of mismanagement creating distressful situation in mind of organizational people. Thus, technological achievements should require to be implemented in good governance practice of market-related issues, human psychological background to clean-up internal as well as external environmental situations, to rectify maladies of managerial conflicting situations arising due to problems like – automation and monotony, work behaviour related to de-motivation in industrial environment in areas like production and manufacturing, cost and income disequilibrium, administrative gaps and lapses like legal framework of judgment-related problems and so on.

Another way of interpreting the technological strategy for human development purpose[68] is the foundation of educational background in respect of enhancing quality in man-power resource potential, which constitute the segment of socio-economic parameters to the cause of ameliorating poverty driven aspects of societal existence of people, in terms of quality empowerment zeal for more and more creativity in all types of human organized nature of jobs as well as industrial activities, pertaining to social upliftment of people with certain kind of value orientation. To it again, the Vedanta approach of equanimity thought requires technological assimilation with the transformational type of education needed for adequate research for developmental activities, to percolate all areas of the grass-root people who are till date lying in deprived situations. Hence, government level policy implications with vibrant type of technocrat educational strategic goal for empowering poor people in areas of research related activities find special attention; so that organizational mission for human capability increase would orient towards advancing people with the norms of societal upliftment, where international cooperation and understanding in this respect could have ample scope and opportunities for people to – (i) assess their utmost zeal of performance for quality assurance practice of creative managerial guidance[69]; (ii) enlighten every citizen with the latest technological findings for further research as to how, activities of human civilization could be measured for coming generations of people, along with living in standardization to the present context of the social backwardness; (iii) advance measures and techniques of productive goal as a mechanism of leadership transformation for organizational cohesive nature of dynamicity in areas of social growth, resource sustainability and worldwide transparency in inculcating work culture; (iv) embrace with the environmental paradigm shift in nature of work motivation of people, to entertain every specific area of learning that is concerned with human nurturing for value oriented aspects of overall growth potentials. It thus goes to say that educational strategy must encompass areas of mass communication, which should be proactive towards information sharing in organizational set-up of creative leadership approach to uproot social value in positivistic nature of dealing with human problems of living in social backward conditions. The strategy which is required to be framed in the plan of action of corporate mission statement needs adequate accountability concept with respect to balance sheet analysis of fund issues, where appropriate provisions are to be made for allocation of funds meant reserved for human development through technological research in production function as well as cost benefit-related activities of the corporate structure. The very important notable feature of information sharing strategy in mass media related parameters of study is the scientific investigations regarding fund management diversity, with particular type of project concerning human emancipation through empowerment of technological issues sensitizing at each level of organizational activity, for the specific kind of urgent development necessities backed by people oriented concept of solving social problems[70], with the cost-output measures pertaining to human growth encompassed with variety of developmental needs required for civil living goal, with certain kind of transparency, dynamics in human behaviour and organizational value orientation for increasing people's trust in terms of delivery system. All these are to be propagated with the theories of equipoise nature of disinterestedness in areas of corporate targets, proactive towards reengineering budget outlets for the purpose of upliftment of the distressed people.

In the twenty-first century, it has become essential on the part of developed, underdeveloped and developing countries to upgrade knowledge base of human resources for increasing the quality of industrial productivity, health-care activities, communication services, agricultural activities, banking services, transportation activities, educational learning and research activities, by means of international collaboration, cross-cultural exchange programmes between the countries, government level seminars, conferences, teaching-learning methodological discussions through technical know-how in schools, colleges, and universities in imparting value-based nature of human skill related functional relationships, etc. All these are required a consortium for fund management, on the part of the mutual collaborative affairs amongst the multinational corporations, government agencies, international as well as national agencies, like – NGOs, NPOs and other counterparts; where all should have qualitative norms of social developmental nature of exchanging views and ideas, by management of technical resources for attaining the goal of social dynamics behaviour from all counts of social accountability, governmental responsibility and organizational sustainability for core areas of human understanding towards increasing global cooperation more and more.

This type of understanding would supplement human efficiency regarding production and distribution functions, eliminating social diseases, regional disparities[71], global level cooperation, human motivation and many other issues concerning the synthesizing of the aspects of human development necessities. It is therefore, evident from the foregoing discussions that technological mutuality in areas of human social services call for an urgent decision-making on the part of political administration and corporate social responsibility accounting towards bringing a balance between forward zones and backward zones of the world societies. Again, effective management of man-power resources in business and society for adequate level of socio-economic development has to be corroborated with the organizational functional responsibility to build-up human cooperation in international level; so that cach dose of technological invention could be activated for actualization of organizational activities to the up-gradation of backward people, which can go a long way to reduce social conflicts between man and man. Here, it goes to say undoubtedly that modern technology based on scientific investigations has a tremendous role to play for the scientific development of the distressed people, by giving themselves changes of technological dimensions with the better avenues and scope for increasing democratic participation among the people, who are otherwise, living in behind all types of social backwardness due to lack of proper opportunities. Measures[72] should therefore be adopted in the planning document for the implementation of new types of technology related know-how, with the learning atmosphere in organizational environment in nurturing work culture, with a fellow-feeling nature of human cooperation and managing things for social advancement as well as people's development. This would reduce regional disparities between human beings, and who would participate to work-out in future for more value orientation, by means of acquiring skill and enhancing acumen in different areas of societal foundation. So, coordinating system of organizational guidance should be made more transparent in favouring participative level of managerial guidance through counselling, training, motivating people, exchange and transforming views from one generation to another generation. It would lead to social transformational change in positivistic manner, so as to attain global peace, human cooperation and broadening of understanding in international collaborative atmosphere to reduce human conflicts, and thereby terrorism from the world environment of people's peaceful living in tranquil social order[73].

We have so far assessed on technological backgrounds of human development spectrum in terms of its broader scope, ample opportunities and strengthening the core base of cooperation and understanding. It is also important to remember that technology while applied in proper way with adequate creativity, there would be global level dynamics in social movement in making right journey by managing things and resources for reducing poverty at a speedy rate. We therefore, would like to utter the case of nano technology, robotic technology, which are of immensely helpful for modernization of human economic activities, increasing industrial productivity, learning more for human healthcare-related parameters, reengineering the core areas of construction, architectural functions, musical games for business roles the people play at the work place by means of interpersonal relationship, intrapersonal as well as human cross-cultural fields of industry, trade and commerce, among others. Even in oceanographic study, these are very important technological knowledge can be adjusted through research programmes of universities and colleges, industrial liaison with the technical institutions like – IITs, ITIs, and other management-related institutions. All should have visionary aspect of organizational notion for increasing learning in between people, for the purpose of empowering human beings for variety of skill development activities. To uproot technological development in social orientation process thus, there should be an approach of human interface with the accumulation of knowledge base in industrial programmes, and their research activities[74] – this is the real type of empowerment to be enhanced through government policy resolution for upgrading and advancing technological know-how, for the advancement of backward people living in backward zones of the world environment. Again, there should be surveillance related programmes; especially, for military organizations that go to furnish well-developed system management in the warfare related disciplined activities. The role of NASA in connection with modern technological society would not be exaggerated, because this primer institution, only the best to the organizational level of research programmes with the variety of schemes, could further be synthesized for increase and enhancement of human skills in different dimensions, for ameliorating various types of human social problems and justifying the real cause of human development, in matters relating to advancement of the global society, up-gradation of cross-cultural people in the world, environment scanning for monitoring issues of social backwardness of human population, systematize things in society with adequate feedback approach in consultation with the world governments, along with the UNO. All these are to be attributed in causing human empowerment at the grass-root level programmes to be chalked out from time to time, by means of creating more sensitization among the people through learning by training culture[75], to utmost development of the masses who are primarily, distressed and dislocated from the modern functions of technological benefit.

In a nutshell, human excellence could be developed in many dimensions for empowering people to come-across, in the midst of organizational transformation, governmental transparency and corporate accountability; where modern technological research findings could be activated for increasing global level cooperation for the sake of international understanding and human peace, in correlating issues of global development, human upliftment and worldwide resource sustainability. Again, the role of technology is more strategic towards functionalizing the areas of global warning situations, where human beings could be made more accustomed through propagation of the latest scientific knowledge for enhancing human consciousness, in sensitizing the core issues of peaceful living in tranquil social atmosphere. Thus, organizational capability should enrich people by different means and ways for increasing more and more participation, with a view to manage things in democratic nature for justifiable level of equitable human development, with the freedom of living existentialism through mutually collaborative atmosphere by means of an approach of human integration in overall social environment. So, technology once implemented in proper way and judicious manner could push up[76] the world environment for human skill building, and advancing the social people for betterment of life in all-round areas of human living practices. It is therefore, human skill building requires adequate guidance and counselling services by means of organizational transparent managerial role model practice as well as leadership goal of social change, with the adjustment of proactive challenges for increasing human understanding and international cooperation, with means of coordinating the organizational system of work behaviour. In this way of thinking, human excellence can be brought forth for development purposes in the twenty-first centuries behind the areas of road-traffic management potentiality, animation projects and art related activities for human skills enrichment, hospitability activities development programme implementation, Para-normal as well as para-psychological issues concerning human motivational and clinical survey, highway projects initiative schemes through logistic implications and envisagement of transport route concepts systematization, animal husbandry schemes and related ancillary micro level activities standardization, supply-chain management effectiveness, forestry development programmes, cultivation initiative practices strengthening, flood, famine and earthquake management through effective technology up-gradation and human skill building enhancement, and many more areas of the activities of present human civilization; among others, as already explained in beginning of this topic – are all the necessary attributable factors of human excellence parameters of social development paradigm shift requiring special attention, in inculcating human existential freedom with the nature of living in equanimity approach; wherein mankind would follow the path of civil living in the midst of diversified functional relationships to attain the goal of organizational dynamicity, cultural optimality to flourish for integral humanism worldwide, and at last, pondering hopes and aspirations of growth of human beings with dynamic development transcendentalism[77] in time and space. Thus, technology would be helping to mould human character in scientific temper of managerial thought for enhancement of human excellence at the work place, with value-based effective change of the societal foundation to this century goal; as it were, in the process of making life of mankind easy for survival with all sorts of peaceful mechanism and real justice. As and when, technology would streamline in the field of legal and executive activities for increasing the productive goal of the service distribution functions, by commensuration of the policy of human advancement through participative nature of management, there would come global dynamicity in organizational consistency of making human beings empowered by doing things, in terms of adequate technology-based sustainability for learning situations of social change, human up-gradation and worldwide evolution for incorporating human moral building with a view to salvation of life.

Environmental Sustainability

Environment is the important part in the peaceful survival of human life. It is truly said that development of human life goes in parallel way, along with the sustainable concept of environmental management. Without having a dynamic balance on environmental sustainability, it would have been difficult to think about human development in creative manner. So, environmental technology has to be applied in the way of nurturing the various aspects of human living parameters. In modern times, enormous growth rate of human population over the world at large has caused for environmental degradation, due to uneven exploitation of resources for industrial and business activities. It has thus resulted to a threat to the environment, which is the dependable kind of human living instrument – it is such an instrument, the application of which once made in correct way can help to modify human life for optimum development, taking into consideration all sorts of living necessities, advancing possibilities and survival credibility in sustainable manner. From this judicious ground point, environment can be seen as the good weather friend of all types of human beings, irrespective of any discrimination in mankind due to differences of nationalism, regionalism, racialism, castes, religions and so on. It is worthwhile to remember that environmental balance is a must for matching resources potentiality as usability; because every dose of particular kind of environmental resource required for human industrial activities can help to produce goods in effective manner, with a view to nurture human civilization in uninterrupted way. Knowing thus the concept of environmental importance in human existential balancing[78] framework, it becomes essential on the part of each national government to adopt certain specific policies that would lead to the goal of environmental protection, in the arena of judicial management of the encountering view for exploitative part of sustainability of the resources concerned with environmental dynamic preservation, cohesive conservation and informative interplay of things and activities, from the sides of political administration and executive functional relationships, legal system formulation as well as its implementation in right place to a right manner, economic productivity as well as supply-chain management network in terms of input-output relationship, social responsibility building norms of responding nature of organizational machineries for the sake of effective nurturing optimality, and besides many other issues pertaining to the cause of human upliftment in efficient skill building norms for entrepreneurial possible development; which go to make functioning of environmental technology for organizational effectiveness and national growth in potential manner. Taking into account all these factors inherent in organizational management system for empowering people to serve with efficient environmental consciousness[79] as well as societal value orientation, for management of entire resources of the environment in exploiting raw-materials in profitable, judicious and optimal opportunities of nurturing and sustainable concept of human growth and social dynamicity, it is imperative that adequate mechanism on organizational control behaviour has to be framed for rejuvenating a structural relationship on the aspects of organization-environment interface, to correlate issues of human industrial advancement, productive goal and social development in times of growing population over the world at large.

It is therefore essential that environmental sustainability could be made more purposive oriented towards the effective cause of social building nature of organizational management, in terms of human involvement for forestation activities against the present tendencies of worldwide deforestation; so that efficient management of environmental resources could go in a long way to solve problems of environmental barriers to the path of industrialization, animal protection and weather transformation towards gaining importance of human survival in peace and harmonious manner. Thus, there is the current requirement of having also international thinking on the part of the world governmental agencies, to preserve, conserve and sustain environmental pyramid in balancing phase towards biodiversity, by means of creating nodal agency as instrumental mechanism for the purpose of effective management of environmental resources, good practice of governance qualities regarding judicious exploitation of resources for industrial productivity, natural balance restoration for the sake of harmonious as well as tranquil human relationship of living with the great nature. Another way of looking towards environmental protection is the value orientation as well as value addition on each and every socio-economic function of the organizational agencies, which go to produce and distribute goods for human beings in marketing their products. In this area, there should be adequate mechanism[80] to be framed in organizational policies for controlling environmental resources in coordinating activities of organizations, with a view to emulate a functional relationship[81] between human advancement and environment protective goal; where all types of species in the part of zoological kingdom of life and also, plant protection could be meted out throughout the world, for human competencies in production function activities, organizational credibility in value addition to social building vision, besides being holistic development of mankind in coherence interrelationships among man, animal and plant life. Considering all these areas of social framework of efficient management system, there should be an understanding on the concept of ecological balance that go to build up the biodiversity aspects of human living with dynamic social movement[82], for which again, there is the need of organizational policy implications regarding pollution control mechanism, which causes land pollution, water pollution, air pollution and also noise pollution due to immeasurable practices or uneven causes of productivity or manufacturing related social hazards – this is observed to be underlying detrimental effect on land, air and water, besides being hindering to the aspects of natural ecological balance; which should be curbed by means of environmental technology as well as agencies or organizations that are responsible for maintaining balanced situation on overall socio-economic parameters of environment related activities[83]. Thus, it is quite necessary that organizational control mechanism while implemented in practice could help in healthy way towards bringing harmonious balance to the natural habitation of human beings, along with animal and other species.

Effective measures on environment through deplorable means of technological up-gradation, environmental study on scientific manner by means of proper investigations on the overall aspects of pollution, warm and earthquake related matters concerning peaceful living of human beings and preservation of animals and species by way of protective measures like – natural garden conservation, botanical garden nurture and subsistence through efficient management, sanctuary related projects sustainability, preservation of barren land, forest land and cattle feeding land, etc. are needlessly a matching concept of bringing environmental harmonious situations, to the growth of natural resources for optimal managerial competencies, organizational dynamicity and worldwide interrelationships between living goal and advancement of global society, for embracing the coping nature of environment in fruitful, efficient and sustainable manner[84]. It would lead to call for an urgent solution of the problems of social hazards and destructive impacts on our environment by means of reducing floods and famine, earthquake and tsunami, natural calamities and many other disturbing elements over land, water and air. Another way of adjustment in human behavioural prudence through organizational activities can be framed in policy implications of socio-economic activities of human beings, like waste management and recycle of productivity from the by-products and waste resources, banning of plastic related products and their use in holistic manner, management of industrial pollutants which go to poison water, air and land, and is also affecting human as well as animal life by way of environment degradation, banning of use of pesticide harmful for both species and human beings, and instead implementing environment friendly manures for agricultural productivity, increase of forest areas by means of forestation programmes and new schemes operation for natural balance restoration, etc. are enormous potential element of environment risk management and human capacity building on the areas of sustainability, dynamicity and consistency in environment related hazards and its protective measures to match adequate environmental balances[85] from time to time, in efficient, judicious and profitable manner.

From the above points of view, it becomes clear that environmental sustainability is the overall concept of environment management related to effective production, distribution and exchange of natural resources for the purpose of industrialization and agricultural activities, socio-economic parameters of human organizational service conditionality, legal framework of implementation of government policy resolutions for cooperative atmosphere with a view to coordinating the issues of living situations in peaceful as well as harmonious manner[86], in the growing population tendencies observed throughout the world; which have been seen as the threat on our living goal, along with dynamic movement of the global society in creating things, preserving pious environment and nurturing protective ideas of animal rearing and movement, besides the nature of causing the entire environment for species conservation, human and animal protection, plant life adequate cultivation and forest resource sustainability, natural resource endowment and balanced interface between trade, industry and commerce. However, it is to be noted that an important area of animal life preservation is the project tiger scheme which should be taken into account in environmental planning objective, along with other rare species protection–this is the urgent call of the need of the twenty-first century scientific movement for social reformation, in areas of generating our living goal without animosity and creating further problems that causes for detrimental effect to overall environmental balance. International legal system should further be implemented for controlling mechanism on pollution related emission conditions; so that efficient management of atmospheric movement with balanced thought of living for all could go a long way in rebuilding pollution free society throughout the global environment of human living conditionality, social reformations and environmental renovation to cause for peaceful and harmonious intercourse between industrial activities as well as socio-economic progress of all human beings in this world[87]. We must also be remembered that oceanographic study through information technology, and its connectivity with the environment technology compounding scientific research and investigations pertaining to safeguard of rare species, living in deep-sea area correlate issues of environmental management programmes and protection of the life to maintain human ecological pyramid that needs sustenance to curb against all types of environmental degradation, and human penetrating type of living conditionality in exploitative nature of judicious development of social structure[88] could solve many of the societal problems of peaceful human living condition, towards the aspect of growing necessities of dynamic and dependable factors of human up-gradation as well as nurturing with eco-system; where social stratification becomes quite optimal towards bringing sustainable as well as profitable exploitation of the environmental resources, to attain the goal of cohesive organizational movement in inculcating environment freely atmosphere in the life of civic citizens, to rejuvenate environment-related functions in multi-diversified paths. It is, therefore occupying formidable area of understanding not only in scientific parlance; but there should also be educational and academic pursuits for learning all these impediments of growth related statistics, and by means of such type of learning in institutionalizing the concept of ecological system for managing existential process of human socialization needs could help in harmonizing healthy way towards the specific path of human survival with dignity[89]. The employable opportunities are also there when such issues are planned and implemented properly by means of national policies of the state governments, international programmes on the part of the world body of different agencies, and global technological framework of a consortium regarding advancement of the society in creative, sensitive and sustainable manner. It is, therefore essential to come up with stringent policy measures which go to solve problems of environment study in areas of watershed management programmes, channelization of rivers for adequate agricultural development, construction of small dams after proper study of ecological balance situations; instead of big river dams which are highly affective for human and animal life, matchup schemes through river-sea projects for efficient inculcation of harmonious interplay of species in combination with severity study on natural habitation, and exploiting the forest products for which forest related study centre in national and international level, etc. could strengthen academic movement in the way of learning atmosphere; so that human life becomes more manageable towards specific area of human resource development process[90].

The overall discourses justifying the sustainable concept of environmental issues pertaining to human living in peaceful atmosphere, requires management strategies and organizational approaches for increasing human consciousness with a view to encouraging healthy capacity building towards social orientation process, and value addition to human industrial productivity-related considerations, and also existential peaceful norms of human survival with adequate level of growth–all these parameters are to be made creative, balancing and sustainable by means of efficient environment management technological development, human learning with innovation, organizational guidance and managerial counselling, governmental legislative modifications, executive level good governance policy resolutions, and judicial equanimity towards social orientation[91] process could enlarge dynamic social movement by means of institutionalizing the system of environmental study with scientific temper of thought. It will thus, advance social learning cooperative atmosphere in national as well as international level to propagate the goal of harmonious societal nurturing culture, making thereby the concept of environmental sustainability a boon to eradicate problems of human sufferings, species rearing, plant life nurturing; so that adequate management policy of both national and international agencies streamline the issues of social growth, human living and environmental consciousness in advancing human present generation towards realization of overall survival goal in a manner as narrated in the Vedic scriptures and religious philosophy of the ancient Hindus. We therefore, would like to mention here that 'Vasudhaiva Kutumbakam' is nothing but the inner most idea of coherence of interrelationships between living beings and their environment. To which goal this environment of ours is created is to see carefully that we take utmost attention for its judicious management for causing adequate level of sustainability, as and when exploiting environmental resources for industrial and business activities. So, equanimity of thought in areas of environmental growth for human development purpose is the Vedanta version of Kutumbakam ideology[92]–matching and managing of which, life on this Earth could be made more sustainable towards embracing goal of social movement in dynamic nature. Hence, all types of environmental technology should be developed for exploiting our natural environment in free atmosphere of human living tendencies, with all manageable situations of nurturing existential freedom of human beings on the part of organizational changing concept of social development issues as well as human growth perspective ideas.

In brief, environmental management with the effective strategy of human development and societal rebuilding necessitated the cause of environmental overall reengineering on issues of sustainability, to renovate the superstructure of human goal of peaceful living in tranquil social atmosphere, which the Vedic nature of environmental thought had envisaged long back in human history, by means of sermons of the Vedic Rishis, Sages and Seers in their Kutumbakam ideology merged in environmental thought. This kind of manageable idea would be propagated in the present system of social crises[93], where all living beings would further be benefitted to uproot social value system in terms of preservation policy, conservation theory and sustainable concept of equipoise nature of human development in social existence. What is more necessary is the free atmosphere, which is observed to be a threat in the present day need of growing population in the world. So, good environmental governance philosophy guided by adequate policy implementations in time and space, would be healthy practice in balancing human civilization; where only the alternative idea of the Vedanta could be optimally utilized for effective environmental sustainability, along with efficient human nurturing in environment freely atmosphere of living goal. When the equanimity approach in managing and matching resources would be sensitized and evolved in preserving nature of industrial activities, and conserving idea of supplying eco-friendly productivity, there would come actualization of self-subsistence and thus, the holistic idea of sustainable concept[94] on environment would supplement to the goal of human existential freedom of life, in equipoise strategic nature of global integrity.

Global Human Balance

The development of human beings over the world at large in balanced manner would be the strategy of international agencies, along with national boundaries by the sovereign governments in underdeveloped, developing and developed nations. This is now very important because, the world development reports on human beings, as against the growth rate statistics as submitted by experts in various countries reflect on the gloomy picture of human development parameters. From the reports at different intervals, we get an idea that human beings suffering a lot from many areas of their socio-economic life, which confront themselves for augmentation of regionalism as well as separatism tendencies; as for example, the case of South-East Asian countries is the glaring point of enormous situations of such tendencies prevailing in these countries, and causing thereby restlessness throughout this zone of the world. Again, the case of African countries has been showing pathetic picture on human starvation death and malnourishment situations[95]. All these are attributed to the cause of arms race, terrorism and the real story of sea route disturbance, etc. However, the resultant idea of mismanagement of human beings by the authoritarian governments in respective countries, in terms of development issues have gone for irrelevant social practices and causing thereby social discrimination in many ways, like – caste, creed, colour, race, religion and cultural differences; besides many other factors of global importance of human imbalances narrating to the aspects of chauvinistic tendencies between people of the world[96]. Thus, global human balance in living parameters and competent development structure could go a long way to eliminate human distressed situations, not only on socio-economic scenarios; but also various other social disturbances would be minimized by means of proper planning by the respective state governments, and their timely implementation towards the realization of the goal of human upliftment programmes. As we know that human development has no colour, so also; in question of development strategy application of science and technology has to be made more and more broader to the aspect of social rejuvenation process of the entire humankind living in this world in a pathetic malnourished as well as downtrodden situation, in terms of food, clothing, shelter, medical and educational facilities; which we have already mentioned in the foregoing analysis of this Chapter.

From the above discussions, it cannot be ignored by anyone else that when we say about human development, it means bringing a balance in all human beings with respect to living facilities and social infrastructure development throughout the world environment; where there will be international brotherhood between people in the world, instead of international chaos as well as warfare activities prevailing now-a-days, which has been observed in this age of technological reformation and global mass-media development activities. As a matter of fact, it could be mentioned without any doubt in mind that mismanagement of national wealth and imbalanced distribution of natural resources for some private individual gains, there has been discrimination in human development process, which have caused for the failure of national plans of various democratic governments from time to time in continuous manner. Accordingly, human imbalances[97] in respect of living civic life, and leading towards the path of dehumanization process to the entire societal structure have cropped up with many of the problems, for which governmental machineries are busy with maintaining warfare activities to that of the dissatisfied population; who are living below standard of humanitarian conditions of surviving civic life, or in poverty which is shame to the present age of scientific development society – called global society based on information technology, and a cybernetic age of human civilization. The bitter experience of poor people from the side of governmental machincrics and agencies in long periods to the human history has paved the way for social separatism tendencies, human restlessness due to terrorism, regionalism, communalism, racialism, religion and like other tendencies; which have caused people for their derailment from the mainstream of the society. Not only it is enough, but there are also international conflicts between people of the world due to their distressed situations, being caused by inadequate application of government/public funds for gaining benefits with personal interests by the bureaucrats, civil servants and corporate houses. In this way, elimination of poverty from the modern societies has not been made possible, because of unsystematic type of management which goes against ethical code of conduct in managing business as well as other socio-economic activities[98], meant for people's development with the public scarce resources. Thus, scientific temper of human development perspective has been ruined due to corruptive system of the society and looting of public resources by a group of dishonest people, who run the wheel of the society in terms of the present system of bureaucratic model of management. To restore global balance in human beings with the parity of living goals and ideals, it is necessary that the latches and lapses are to be eradicated from the organizational system of management; and to the contrary, there should be moral guidance of people through national as well as international oriented concept of leadership strategies for increasing human competencies, strengthening credibility and optimizing managerial communication system towards the highest level of human emancipation, by means of proper implementation of private and public schemes and activities. In this way, human development should be correlated to the process of social development by means of upliftment of people from the grass-root level of social backwardness. Then, and then only, global human balance in terms of living parameters could be restored for the purpose of bringing world peace, and thus; human fellow-feeling nature of organizational work culture would be strengthened by motivating themselves to produce for maximum welfare of mass people, connoting thereby the concept of integral humanity in the process of living dignity, managing optimality and guiding society towards the theory of maximum social advantage[99].

As regards strategy on human development issues, there is confusion in mind of people whether it is possible to restore a harmonious social balance in human beings, by managing things with the vested interest of politicizing development related agenda for the gain of certain classes of people and political parties; which have been observed from the present tendencies of governing the administrative machineries from the side of corrupt political groups. In this context, it has become essential that people should be developed, and only development related performance criteria should go to make a framework of political administrative policies of different interest groups; otherwise, human emancipation from all types of social ills and maladies for which people are suffering severely would not be possible to rectify mismanagement in the administrative system. Thus, the slogan of social engineering could be the best measure for human equanimity of thought regarding perspective development, as and when this is being permeably looked at, by the expert of economics as well as social scientists who go to decide about the fate of distressed human beings. It is regardless to mention here, that good governance imperatives of human strategic guidance throughout[100], for the sake of moral boost-up and social journey in dynamic way, would relate to the issues of human sufferings caused due to maladjustment and uneven distribution policies in the nature of reaching out of the government schemes, for which these are actually meant to develop backward human beings; as it were, for there is no justification of human development and social balance without organizational guiding competencies, in throwing light on such conditionality of downtrodden people. Because, imbalance in the nature of human nurturing philosophy through development strategy could be rectified by all means and ways that are to be dedicated towards human up-gradation, in terms of supplying basic necessities for surviving civic life, where there is always mismanagement being observed, from the side of administrative agencies and organizational changing instrument of social existential foundation. So, legal machineries are also to be involved for managing things in effective manner, for the safeguard of people's interest in areas of social infrastructure building emergent necessities, along with managing for good governance conditionality[101] which go to decide about human civic living situational system. Again, the aspects of development as we know, is concerned with agricultural activities along with industrialization, which would be helpful for social change in proactive manner – these are to be continued by operation of service giving principles in the areas of irrigation, cultivation, construction of dams, cannels, road construction, railway services network management, etc. for causing human beings to move forward for their development opportunities; which are of immensely needful areas of eradicating regional imbalances over the world at large. Hence, service code of conduct in organizational system of management could be made more socially oriented[102], by means of application of technology in irrigational fields, and employing 'research and development' (R&D) related programmes to the path of industrialization, which go to solve many of the problems of human sufferings and backwardness. Service to man, service to God should therefore be the agenda for development, with a view to understand human equity concept of living goal, and realization of the principles of the 'maximum social advantage' ideologies, propagated in the theory of economics and social change mechanism for the restoration of human balanced development process and existential freedom of management thought.

The challenging ideal of human emancipation goal could be meted out in terms of redesigning social structure, from the view point of Indian Vedanta concept of management, where it is given that humanity should be cared, motivated and nurtured from the background of development issues. In this way of thinking, management of organizational activities should be related to social development meant for the elimination of poverty from the grass-root level, where the agenda of such development must be adopted for inclusive growth of all segments and kind of social people; irrespective of any type of discrimination in castes, creed, colour, sex, religions, culture and regional thinking. But rather, there should be a framework of policy decision regarding integral human upliftment programme, in terms of up-gradation of people by giving themselves all opportunities for leading justified civic life, in the organizational guiding system of development strategy and social changing mechanism[103]. In this area of thought, religious issues are to be based on human moral building and counseling regarding managing things, only for the betterment of all classes of social people and pursuing thereby organizational reengineering of social renovation with respect to human emancipation, and social radical changing philosophy by way of correlating issues of human development in transparent, sustainable and dynamic manner. Thus, the problems of human hatred in connection with social discrimination could be eradicated through organizational motivated leadership goal, which go to build-up the societal pyramid from the areas of human common understanding for optimum development of mass people, that has been observed to be redundant in the present system of human existential superiority from the side of corrupt administrative machineries and inadequate legal system, incapable of doing things for the effective implementation of goals for human upliftment programmes in different measures and schemes. It is, therefore, an understanding should be made innovative for increasing human efficiency with the help of training man-power resources, with a view to regenerating human skills by different types of employment opportunities, to be created in organizational journey of human life in terms of transformational leadership and decision-making towards augmenting social reformation in human beings, to motivate people to serve for the optimum development of the backward people who are living in distressed as well as pathetic inhuman situations[104], in advancing towards dynamic progress in life from vitiated cycle of socialization, in correcting life process with harmoniousness for accommodating tendencies to be stationed in betterment with the fulfillment of civic living necessities[105]. Thus, the goal of corporate policy should be to include people who are lagging behind opportunities for development, and the strategy for management of regional imbalances, along with reducing human sufferings and hatred from the society should be incorporated to corporate social responsibility in responding towards effective development of people, by means of proper implementation of organizational objectives for the realization of the goal of human salvation as well as efficient emancipation from all types of social crisis.

The above idea can be dealt in reformative manner, as and when national policy for human development and international planning to reduce human discrimination with respect to living ideologies are sorted out to excel things in proper delivery system, managed by means of real democratic movement for people's development and to curb anti-national as well as international warfare tendencies of human activities, acting and interacting for the display of artificial role model seeking the cause of human development and restoration of social balance, in the name of administrative guidance by the elected governments in different parts of the world, terrorist activities playing dominant role and bargaining with the sovereign elected government agencies for the mischief cause of humanity and social orientation, regional politics with partisan base as well as divisive role being played in the name of development of certain classes of human beings, etc. In this way of thinking, integral concept of human upward journey of life with harmonious nature of living in civilities[106] should be redrafted in organizational guiding framework, and governmental planning strategy to develop human beings in equitable nature of forward growing tendencies, creating thereby managing zeal for excellent service orientation philosophy of human life. So, the present legal system has to be reformulated caring about human sufferings from basic needs required for civil living goal in societal orientation process, making people to feel that optimum development of downtrodden human beings[107] are necessary condition of social rejuvenating towards the realization of human soul, national goal and international dynamicity of growth as well as social radical changes, proactive leadership ideas and also transformation in organizational integrated system of making a common understanding regarding human efficiency building, skill development and social balance restoration, in perfecting things for universal emancipation of human beings conditioned by social responsibility accounting and moral code of conduct to manage human business, and other activities for the adequate implementation of organizational resources, government funds and international legal system.

The above facts and figures regarding global balance restoration in case of human development perspective are quite relevant, in analyzing the reasons of human backwardness as well as underdevelopment over the world at large, in this age of technological development and scientific research activities, to which we would like to note that– (i) human development should be made by organizational activities of public and private sectors in holistic manner, to universalize the concept of human emancipation from the living stage of slavery, due to administrative mismanagement and corruptive work culture pertaining to common understanding regarding universalization of all the basic needs for the upliftment of people from misery to happiness in living atmosphere; (ii) securitization of human life by rule of law as well as code of conduct regarding supply-chain management system, to fulfill agricultural development, industrial advancement, interface between agriculture-industry by means of application of modern technology and research for human improving development indices; (iii) to develop the tools and techniques of modern educational activities to bring in quality in human life for capacity building by means of creating new employment opportunities, entrepreneurship development programmes, government guidance and counselling for human creativity[108] and sensitivity development, so that backward and forward regions are made at a pace of balanced nature of undertaking for increasing social cooperation, eliminating human starvation death and ills of various sufferings; (iv) eliminating international competition in productivity approach to international confidence building by way of human cooperation and public-private interface towards developing needy areas; and thus, 'action louder than speech' should be the framework of the philosophy of human development in realization of the goal of integral humanity; (v) social infrastructure building in backward zones of the nations, so as to increase international understanding and bond between man and man to eliminate social conflicts, restore human cooperation, and bring in administrative quality in working life; (vi) information technology and mass-media should be applied in holistic concept of human development programmes and to streamline social equity between people, with respect to socialization of corporate activities[109], democratization of government fund management system; and besides, there should be transparency regarding good governance in administrative activities, to eliminate all types of unjust behaviour which go to create barriers in the path of development parameters[110]; (vii) philosophizing development as the mantra of human emancipation and salvation of life, and thus; quality of work life (QWL) should be made an important model for social development, to reduce regional disparities[111] and increase human efficiency so as to empower people in understanding value of life; (viii) to curb anti-social activities by effectuating legal instrument of social change, and government machineries would thus be made more responsibility oriented to perform tasks speedily at a judicious manner, with the responding nature of job in fulfillment of the policy of human up-gradation, social rejuvenation and worldwide transformation. However, there are many other strategies could be adopted for increasing human competencies, organizational credibility and social rationality, to pave the way for global balance restoration in connection with human development paradigms shift in nature; so that everything becomes manageable in society not at the cost of humanity, but at the dynamicity of social movement in making balanced development of all human beings, for the purpose of attaining global leadership that would increase human excellence in different sectors of the socio-economic activities. Thus, balanced development philosophy as and when propagated at micro as well as macro level study on parameters of growth needed for increasing societal peace and harmony, in terms of universalizing of the concept of maximum social advantage; it would lead to the path of existential freedom and salvation of life, in perpetuating people to understand social equilibrium policy of the present market-oriented economy. In a nutshell, international understanding between countries of the world should be strengthened by eradicating human misfortunes through organized pattern of management in societal value orientation process, for which separatism tendencies prevailing worldwide would be reduced automatically at the lowest level, and global warfare activities would also be eliminated in naturalistic way, to safeguard human civilization from the optimum possibilities of catastrophic destruction[112], and to restore a natural balance in human living tendencies in creating universal brotherhood to realise the concept of integral humanity.

Scientific Temper in Development Strategy Formulation

Development of human beings in the world is dependent on the formulation of governments planning and proper strategy regarding creation of opportunities for employment in different segments of human living parameters. So, empowerment process in managing human resources for the sake of human potential analysis through skill building system of organizational activities, supplement for the competencies as well as sensitizing people to the norms of human credibility in involving with the various nature of job, pertaining to employability goal for living standard in a way would be the social strategy for their development in coherent, dynamic and continuity manner[113]. In this respect, it is worthwhile to note that human resource management with sustainable nature of surviving potentiality is the basic background of human development concept, considering which all planning activities are to be performed in modern organizations and corporate houses. With a view to initiate this goal in a sovereign country, every government should be responsible to frame its policies considering the urgent necessities of human development perspective; so that unemployment problems created due to lack of adequate strategy towards developing people from the side of democratic system of management would relate to the goal of human advancement, in terms of increasing standard of living, taking into consideration all severe stages of human sufferings in their day-to-day life. Thus, scientific temper of thinking regarding human resource potential building could go a long way to solve many of the problems of sufferings in human life related conditions[114]. Here, comes the importance of thinking on the aspects of human creativity the result of which, while strengthened in potential manner would help to nurture human beings in right perspective, with strategic ideology and in dimensional manner of social emancipation of the world people. This is the emergent issue, concerning which all types of social disturbances are created in the overall societal environment as well as organizational effective work culture. Once work culture is strengthened for social transformation, there would be enlightenment throughout the social structure, which would also enlarge people to think for human cooperation building enterprise inculcated for strengthening the base of social pyramid, by means of managerial reorientation of things for development goals, organizational guidance for social advancement perspectives and leadership issues of innovating social activities for the purpose of development dynamicity, changing strategy and coping behaviour in human upliftment programmes. In the formation of development strategy[115] thus, there should be scientific temper in framing government policies, organizational objectives of management which should consider the case of humanity and human dignity of living in people like human beings, who are the supreme important factor constituting the structure of the social reformation movement in causing relevant social change, to bring in human competencies building for the purposive idea of social rejuvenation, human salvation of life and governmental guidance as well as organizational counselling system by means of leadership transformation, legal justice for human equity, integral concept of human fraternity and fellow-feeling nature of coherent interpersonal, intergroup and intersociety relationships.

It is fact that scientific investigations regarding investment potentials while done in managing funds for organizational effectiveness, quality level of man-power development perspectives has to be enhanced with caring about human backwardness, social stagnant situations and worldwide human restlessness due to severe crisis in the field of living with civilities, surviving with dignities and leading life with enormous opportunities[116], to excel for human perfectionism, social dynamism and organizational existentialism. So, effectuating human cause through organizational strategy formation for build-up of integrated way of human personality development, human resource potentiality enhancement and human empowering for survival as well as consistency of growing necessities are concomitant to the scientific aspects of development strategy, in formulating the social foundation with the spirit of 'espirit de corps' principle, where cross-cultural people from different segments of societies would run to hold positions for understanding view points of universal integrity and societal harmonious relationships. Thus, framing of the organizational policies in considering development issues require adequate formulation of strategy regarding unified nature of social growth, by means of equal level human participation in development related activities of social advancement of mass people. Initiating thus, the technological counterparts to the path of development strategies correlating human up-gradation principles to confine things into changing paradigms would result in scientific envisagement of human empowerment related policies, employment related practices and holistic growth of modern organizations; which go to safeguard manpower resources from decaying nature of ruin, draining mode of human quality swing and perverting ideology of mankind. For these reasons, it has become now quite important that scientific development of people for nurturing coherent base of human excellence building process through adequate guiding initiatives is the cornerstone of organizational policy formulation towards framing strategies from all sides[117], which will be supplemental to the process of social balance restoration in harmonious work culture as well as human developmental core idea of strengthening the nature of perfect growth, liberal management of resources and justified practice of bringing human equity of thought for living goal, to assess human competencies, creditability and existentialities in realistic management attitude. Accordingly, scientific notions are to be build-up to strategic areas of confining things for human uproot of social value with productive goal, which should be related to organizational framework of policies for the formulation of social transformation with the means and sources of resources match in potential manner, to add human social value in initiating each task for advancing social dynamic nature of growth with all the correlatives of living foundation in peaceful, harmonious and sustainable manner to manage things and activities of modern organizations for human perfection.

At present, it is observed that some political and social organizations in many countries of the world, in the name of public services are creating trouble to run smoothly the public administrative system, either through their political, or social activities which are going against the moral ethics of humanity and polluting social environment, for which general people who had been suffering normally from the long past, have now, further been disturbed in their process of development. Consequently, the elected governments are made incapable in managing things, because they could not decide going against such will of the social interest groups; who are actually voicing for people's interest with some vested interest of a few class of people or groups, and trying to take advantage of the situation of the social backwardness. Again, it is further observed that a few political parties running the sovereign administration of the governments in many parts of the world have no realistic will or agenda to change[118] the lot of their representatives or citizens, who are suffering severely day-after-day. To the contrary, they run the system by managing things in corruptive way to ruin the countries and loot public fund from government exchequers in their personal gain. So, for all these reasons we have found that social restlessness as well as conflicting situations has always been prevailing throughout the environment of the society[119]. The repercussions of these have been played with dominant role in replacing either governments in power frequently, or creating a panic situation on the advantage of taking mileage by the vested interest groups, going against the sovereign entity of the countries. Under all these circumstances, control mechanism of the system of public administration has been going out of the hands of the elected governments, and poverty of population has also been increasing with the no work culture or slow going stage of socio-economic situations. Thus, there has also been strikes, lock-outs, etc., which have disturbed for industrial productivity and business activities. In this way, unscientific system of managing things for people's development has cropped up problems further more to deteriorate social sufferings of mass people or general people, who are already in distressed situations. In this area of public oppression, suppression and repression from the side of elected governments, or even from groups of people who are raising voice for development with mischievous spirit and personal interest of taking advantage in mind for their self propagation of disowning something, or remaining abstained from power politics have resulted to social anarchism; which should be remedied by means of scientific system of management and administering public activities for the adequate and timely development[120], to elevate social poverty and to restore a balance between haves and have-nots, by locating problems and solving those by creating opportunities for the suffered population. As and when, social infrastructural projects, like – road and railway transportation system, water supply facilities, industrial and agricultural activities for public services, public management system by adequate deployment of public funds and resources, housing and sanitation facilities are created and given to poor people, health-care activities are provided by means of medical services and opening new health units in needy areas, and besides those which are necessary for civic living in society, then only these are essentially becoming part of development; which go to eliminate sufferings of people. Consequently, development policies of the governments are required to be resolved[121] with the framework of judicious cementing of public relationships, by undertaking social responsibility shouldering accountability in scientific envisagement of issues concerning backwardness of people, due to pathetic sufferings and living in an environment of societal impoverish nature of human growth elements. All these are attributed to the urgent necessity of the recall to the principles of good governance goal of public administration as well as private management system, so that development of common people becomes the slogan of the present era in restructure of the social system in new dimensional way, where every man should get all opportunities of civic living; irrespective of any type of social discrimination or personal interest, or even vested political interest of a few class.

In this way, scientific system of development would build-up social structure to make people free from the clutches of the corruptive tendencies, and in the long-run there would be healthy social atmosphere to motivate people to produce things which will be for the safeguard of the country[122]. It is therefore, required leadership principles and practices based on trusteeship norms of administration, creating things to eliminate social distressed conditions of mass people who are malnourished due to non-availability of their basic and other needs in surviving human life legitimately. Another way of looking about the scientific process of social development is the eradication of concentration of power in few hands; along with empowering backward people by involving themselves in the decision-making process of human development considerations. Democratic system of management by participatory level of framing strategy to formulate things in the policy resolution in deciding for the lot of the suffered classes in society, would result in radical as well as proactive social change to commensurate ideas of social upliftment of deprived people, in terms of carrying organizational activities for the safeguard of the interest of poor human beings who have been suffering from many kinds of ills and diseases, as are observed to be prevailing in the present society due to inefficient as well as unscientific system, and lack of proper administrative guidance and organizational management – this is the most important and common phenomena of social backwardness of people, requiring still now, scientific nature of prolonged strategic idea of human well-treatment from all sides of living perspectives, for encouraging people to perform things willingly from their mind and thus, synthesizing for the formulation of human growth perspectives in organizational missionary way of leading with the things[123], concerning human strategic development for social forward looking tendencies, in this age of technological upheavals as well as scientific research in the field of socio-economic parameters of development consideration. In the field of agricultural system of management, it is essential that development policies are also to be considered for watershed management, construction of irrigational projects, dams, canals, etc., supply of good seeds, manures and agricultural implements to the poor village agriculturists, their credit finance to harvest by means of adequate banking facilities and creating provisions for institutional fund management system to increase agricultural productivity, in elevating poverty from the society, and besides; some other important amenities, like – marketing facilities, stock of agricultural produce by means of creating provisions for state level as well as public-private system of managed warehouses, centres of distribution, marketing networks for productivity, etc[124]. Again, agricultural universities and institutions are to be opened up widely to the areas of need and they are further to be developed for people, in training manpower efficiency to produce things in effective solution of the problems of human hunger and starvation. Also, mining activities are to be balanced with adequate legal system for harmonious industrial development and upliftment of people who are remaining in backwardness, environmental activities are to be cared for nurturing atmosphere as well as safeguarding animals and species, rare plants, medicinal plants and plants in general for forestation purposes, in maintaining floods, famine, earthquake, tsunami, etc. In this way, all the important social infrastructures necessary for human development are required to be managed with scientific planning in new and modern technological means. There should be 'river-sea' good network formulation policy on development related yardstick of performance management appraisal, constituent with the nature of social rebuilding concept of growth parameters, judging efficient system of good governance policy implications regarding development of the social structure[125].

From the above discussions, it is clear that things are to be taken strategically on humanitarian considerations for social development purposes, to curb all types of social ills for which people have been suffering in continuity for long. Hence, scientific vision on management ideologies for human development in proactive approaches and leadership goals with the practice of things, to keep pace with people's agenda in the policy formulation concept of human growth initiative perspectives, would streamline organizational efficiency for channelizing resources in social orientation process, to enlighten the goal of human advancement and reengineering human civilization in new dimensional way, to recapitulate the social structure based on human existentialism, world dynamism and international understanding on the philosophy of social building approach for human survival, organizational nurturing and global integrity. These are required to be expounded to match philosophy of human equanimity of thought regarding management effectiveness, entrepreneurship transformational ideas towards bringing radical social change and organizational initiative for human integrity with the dignified thought of living ideologies, surviving principles and growing issues of human upliftment programmes. So, while formulating strategy by the governments, there should be keen interest in favor of human development[126]; especially development of the needy people in terms of providing organizational services and techniques of equipoise nature of human rolling towards some kind of perfection, in the midst of managing diversities, leading optimality and producing things for up-gradation of common people; to a stage of societal upbringing throughout the all-round process of development effectiveness, meant for the attainment of the goal of unified social journey of all people in effectuating for the commanding height of human perfectionism[127].

In recapitulating the process of human development with the social services, we would like to note that there is the extreme necessity of framing policies by the democratic government for creating provisions in social building activities like supply of electricity facilities for poor people and, for agricultural and industrial activities in increasing productivity, for generation of power in regard to agricultural fields, educational institutions, hospitals and to many other socially oriented projects; so that speedy development of the foundation of society has been made possible to alleviate poverty from the society, and also to solve many of the problems of human life that people are suffering for long in different underdeveloped and developing countries of the world. As for example, the case of India, Pakistan, Bangladesh, etc. can be taken into consideration with the severity of their problems within enormous growth rate of increasing population year-after-year, causing people of these countries to suffer more and more without having such facilities. It is therefore permeably said that adequate power generation, among others; could be a great instrumental picture of social reformative movement, in the midst of various human crises. In a nutshell, policy of development should be strategized with the scientific temper of management philosophy of doing human activities by the Vedic value-based principles of social value orientation process, from all-round spheres of human advancement of all classes of people living in this world, for which the slogan: "One in all and all in One" should be adopted as the approach of organizational system of management as to the mantra of universal human development ideologies. Hence, the justification of human living with fraternity could be assimilated to the core idea of human coherence interrelationships in managing things and activities, by means of modern corporate world which are, for all these reasons, to be reformulated in new dimensional order to change the societal orientation in congruent manner, to the thought of integrated system of living through spurt of human personality development as well as social diversification process of employing all resources to the needs of time and space[128]. This is the real nature of scientific temper of development thought should be envisaged in good governance philosophy of organizational management as well as administrative system, required to be compounded to grow people with living freedom and coordinating social activities for realistic team building approach, in connecting everything with the formulation of strategic policies to augment social orientation in terms of human up-gradation and worldwide development.

Sanatana Practices for Technological Development

Technology is the modern day's vehicle carrying people to the path of development. It is thus apparent to say that the seed of human civilization is being propounded by technological part of development, concerned with the notion of human upliftment from the severe causes of social sufferings to a stage of enlightenment for realization of the life problems, in terms of integrated performance in confining all things and activities to ameliorating social backwardness, in shaping technology as the instrument of social changing machinery to cope up with the challenge of time. It is, therefore, human civilization could go for forward looking tendencies in advancing people to all kinds of facilities of healthy living practices, by means of adequate pace with technological up-gradation and the implementation of organizational policies for integrated human development, in course of managing human socio-economic activities by modern developed technological means and services. Thus, an important concept of balanced development is encompassing with the issues of social reengineering[129], where technology as the guide of modern civilization would stimulate people to manage things effectively for the well-being of common people who are, still today; in this age of technological development living in different types of crisis situations which has no other alternatives, but to modify things for social order of movement in leading people to their path of optimum development. In this way, management of social resources could be balanced for effective as well as harmonious human development in pursuit of social progress, as and when technological counterpart is looked at for global emancipation of human population. This idea is already reflected in previous discussions under the concept of human excellence theory in this Chapter, to which we have to note that technology and human progress go in parallel line with the thought of human development perspective. Because of thinking thus, our idea on technology is conceptualized herein with the development paradigm, for initiating appropriate strategy towards managing organizational activities by all means of technological profound concept of modern world; so that real developmental issues would be addressed for social reformation to meet-out problems of human opportunities of development and scope of the study on social renovation of things, for the sake of bringing managerial integrity in the system of organizational work culture. When this is studied with empirical research findings, it becomes highly relevant to say that ancient Vedic sermon: "Vasudhaiva Kutumbakam" is the only idea of technological integrity for scientific development of the world population, who are spiritually united in one common bond of human relationship called as the 'integral humanity'[130]. For this purpose probably, there were ethical practices in Vedic periods in realizing the core concept of human beings, which is ingrained in human soul that is universal in nature. For the understanding of such realization in goal of human practices for judicious performance, there is the necessity of revealing the fact that technology has its own strategy for development, besides modern warfare activities–it is meant that human peaceful living should be the endeavour on the pursuit of technological development, for which there is every possibility of increasing human empowerment with the existential freedom of doing things for advancement of the goal of human civilization to the salvation of life, in an approach of cementing ideas of social unification, worldwide dynamism and organizational transcendentalism; as it were, in the 'Sanatana' practices, and is being followed for more and more progress of the societal pyramid.

Considering thus[131], all the essential elements of human civilization in propagating things for encouraging people to perform organizational activities in achieving goal of universal development, the strategic view on technology for industrial productivity as well as social services and communication activities has to be confined towards human motivation and morale building aspects of social foundation, where governance criterion should be emphasized for optimum development of people living in grass-root level, and thus; all the activities of modern organizations are required to be based on technological 'Ombudsman', which is the real agency to audit for the actual level of technological development and human up-gradation policy to commensurate the goal of maximum social advantage, in principles of democratic management system. So, it is apparent to believe that leadership goal of organizational guidance requiring innovation in doing tasks by means of human skill building operations and training necessities, has to have convergence philosophy on the policy implications of human competencies, organizational credibility and social dynamicity in relating technological researches for industrial activities and social services, to encounter a balancing nature of match between haves and have-nots class of human beings[132]; otherwise, social transformation needed to an approach of human upliftment from the social backwardness of people would not come to realize the goal of global human equity in living potential, in ascertaining things and activities for the purpose of human integrity through technological diversification and channelization of social resources to the path of social rolling in reformative way. In this context, the Vedanta ideology of 'truth, beauty and goodness' should be followed in management practices of technological shape towards confining things for social building activities, the destined role of technology development programmed will then, carry all people in journey towards social ramification for undertaking a shouldering responsibility to initiate the goal of human advancement, by way of occupying an important place in civilization forward looking tendencies for human capacity building as well as empowerment quality to the cause of enhancing acumen, which should rebuild the concept of technological development thought in new dimensional order. Thus, the reasons inherent with the theory of absolute poverty mentioned in economics study with certain parameters, drawing a 'silver-line' in the historiography of thought provoking ideology in human civilization for long, would be strengthened in terms of real technological findings to the effective means of guiding human society in visionary way. Accordingly, it is to be noted with great care that technology should not play dominant role in course of carrying out only warfare activities, but rather there should also be refinement of the idea of world dynamicity in inculcating human existentialism with the freedom of peaceful living[133] – this is possible, only when there is worldwide managerial consensus regarding consciousness for human unanimity in the spheres of common development, and so technology and human development peripheral stages are to be balanced in equilibrium to reach at a situational condition, in which organizational management resources are controlled for mass productivities and human activities for the purpose of eradicating social misfortunes of suffered people. Thinking thus, the Vedanta philosophy of human core of living for universal integrity with the developed structure of technological civil social foundation should be taken, in an approach of strategic social movement for unifying people to choose the path of integral humanity[134] with the seed of spiritual management system, in scientific envisagement of technological productivity for industrialization goal as well as socialization of human services motive. The structural adjustment in reformation of social dynamics will, therefore, be reinforced with the feedback of technology based managing concept of social rejuvenation process, to monitor control mechanism for achievement of the goal of human sufferings, due to lack of the fundamental necessities required for living in civic manner. In this way of guiding organizational activities in terms of technology related programmes, human excellence in skill building enrichment idea would be narrated to different planning of organizations, meant for human optimum development in the action-oriented principles of management leadership as well as administrative dynamicity in modern days world of corporate social responsibility, to accommodate things and activities in innovative technological research; so as to bring in social transformation, human advancement for realization of life and global dynamism in civic foundation of the world society.

The above discourses on the path of technological development for human belief towards the possibility of reaching at the goal of organizational integration process, in terms of Sanatana practices requiring social reformation through human understanding for optimum development from the present stage of slavery in condition of living situations, as observed to be the social course in this age of scientific discoveries and inventions, on new paths against social sufferings of mass people have to deal with the system of electoral reforms in every country of the world. Thus, there is the urgent recall on the part of mass communication discipline to uproot social values for increasing human capacity building initiatives[135] in nature of participative system of management, by voicing the role of human empowerment areas in considering the democratic plans for the devolution of power, to transfer all means of social development schemes and human advancement opportunities in decision-making process of governmental administrative agencies, which go to select/elect their people to implement organizational policy implications. Hence, the system of adult franchise process in augmentation of social good should be reflected by the electronic and print media, so that social diseases of human sufferings and backwardness could be addressed in time and space. In incorporating such values in corporate social responsibility accounting system to impose technological development for common good of all people, there should be electronic movement on the part of mass communication system in managing things for the betterment of people in universal nature. However, the present system of corruptive management followed by organizational entities as well as government bodies, are all required to be reframed on technology – because, it is only means of human development seed in the hands of modern corporations and government authorities. Thus, power and autonomy should be mutually collaborated for social reformation activities, in confining things for the ameliorating of poverty from the modern scientific world; so that human civilization has been rolling towards the path discovering all kinds of proactive approaches in managing resources for social transformation, connoting the all-powerful elements of spirituality inherent in all human beings, without having any religious dogmatism in question of developing people for realization of the value of life. It is, therefore, technology modification programme to which, in doing activities for increasing industrial productivity for optimum development of society, distressed population will be helpful for opening the door of human freedom of living in all kinds of environmental barriers by segregating the principles of work in equanimity thought[136], in which modern civilization in making real journey to the path of human emancipation would be nurtured in the process of democratic planning for electorate justice, corroborating the principles of industrial democracy and human advancement in parallel way. Considering all these aspects of balanced development philosophy in the plan of action of corporate strategies, in confining things for technological development in new dimensional way, there is the urgent necessity of restoring a system of faithful management in organizational guiding motives, which would result in social transformation to flourish for the spurt of human excellence qualities in the areas of interpersonal relationships, and thus, the points noted below are verily necessary to be taken into account for initiating real social growth as well as rolling of mankind for free existentialism: (i) human participation in innovating ideas for industrial research by means of technology development programmes and organizational policy formulations for greater social responsibility of doing things to the cause of human sufferings, social importance of growth in rectifying conditions of human imbalances in living situations, worldwide integrity[137] in managing social resources for advancing people with creativity and sensitivity development process; (ii) technological 'Ombudsman' in international sphere as the vigilance for making democratic system of management more socially oriented towards well-being of mass population; (iii) considering technology related programmes for both animate and inanimate causes, as propounded in the Sanatana principles for the purpose of global balance restoration and human peace in living ideologies; (iv) nurturing environmental sustainability by means of organizational creativity and human upliftment programmes, confining people to serve in brotherhood practices in increasing social good for 'all in one' concept of human integrated development; (v) fixing corporate responsibilities in course of dealing with technology related human development programmes by means of providing adequate training facilities, for creating opportunities in every field of social activities; so that

modern civilization is taken as the core of human relationship for increasing
social cooperation, human dignity of living and universal understanding for
welfare of human race in holistic manner; (vi) equilibrium in principles of
economic growth for balanced regional development throughout the world as
the mission of corporate social responsibility, in responding towards common
good of backward people; (vii) policy initiatives for encouraging people to
participate in motivating personality, in guiding organizational system of social
change and therefore, technology-related development paradigms have to
be created for establishment of productive foundation of the social base;
(viii) universalizing of the system of social reformation movement for
increasing human cooperation to the commanding height of civilization
pyramid, in terms of technology based developmental goals in propagating
human original spirit of realization[138] for the 'self' in work-related atmosphere,
conducive towards dynamic social orientation process in managing global
resources for innovative and judicious practices.

In brief, all permutations and combinations in macro as well as micro
level study regarding management of modern organizational activities through
developed means of technological findings, should spell out the real picture
of social sufferings of backward people in considering the reasons of human
marginalized stage in society, and therefore, it is expected that rejuvenation
of social structure is possible with the help of information based administrative
mechanism pertaining to human efficiency building and, carrying thereby to
reorient social foundation to the path of human dignity of living necessity
with peaceful means of running organizational activities, in procreating
goodwill in terms of nation building objectives. Following these guidelines,
technology related programmes are to be implemented in organizational policy
resolutions, for which people's upliftment agenda should be placed in priority
to seek for channelization of resources and funds in balanced development
process, in the leadership approach of modern corporate objectives; where
system of management mingling towards connoting the principles of the
Sanatana practices[139] of business, trade, industry and whole range of commercial
activities will be embraced for analyzing reasons for human backwardness –
this will give solutions for encountering the problems of human sufferings,
indignity of living due to malnourished conditions, impoverish situations, etc.
in resulting balanced level of social growth in diversification of funds to right
channel[140]. Thus, the role of management in social transformation will be made
more transparent by means of modern developed technological ideas, where
competencies of human beings in their work relationship at organizational
atmosphere of dynamic performance will commensurate innovative results
for the purpose of attainment of human welfare objectives, and to treat
organizational policies as the instrument of radical social change for human
free interaction as well as work relationships. Group dynamics behaviour would
thus be supplemented to technology knowledge transfer from generation to

generation, and one society to another society, with a view to understand human spirit of work culture in cooperative organizational leadership approach. It is therefore judicious to decide about dynamics of innovative leadership goal, in which technological know-how should be merged in relation to imbibe the Sanatana practices of universal human excellence quality improvement, in regard to achieve the objectives of common human welfare, in the midst of managerial challenges[141]. However, it is further to be remembered that technology should be considered as the bridge in eradication of social gaps between haves and have-nots, by which regional imbalances would be eliminated to the lowest possible level. So, organizational mission, work vision and leadership goal are all to be assimilated in strategic approach of Vedic management perspective for integral humanity as well as global dynamicity, in incorporating ideals of the Sanatana practices in doing all business and socio-economic activities of modern organizations, for bringing global peace, human existentialism and transcendental order of transformation of human civilization, in connoting ideas of harmony in living perspective with respect to balancing resources through organizational technocrat system of management. Thus, the evils of modern society and nepotism in administrative structure should be modified[142] in terms of technological balance in systematizing human developmental goal, to rectify social ills and lapses by means of the Vedic values and code of human conduct.

Global Empowerment of People

Global development is possible by means of creating conditions which go to empower human beings worldwide, and therefore, we have assessed on the strategies for human development in terms of scientific management thought; conjoining with it various notions of technology related aspects of human activities, pertaining to the cause of human upliftment programmes in organizational pattern of dealing with the types of human behavioural postulates of development thought. It is now, expected to conclude this idea with the effulgent of light on the screen of social structure, where things of realizing on parameters of human excellence building goal concerning such pious knowledge would reflect to expose ideas of human growth-related paradigms shift in nature, as inherent and concealed in ethereal environment of dealing with the conditions of human competencies, organizational credibility and social transformation – this is the strategic idea of scientific temper of thought on managing resources for human up-gradation, creating thereby all conditions for social dynamicity, in context of human realization regarding the integral concept of management. Thus, exhorting the causes of technological development has already been analyzed for encompassing dynamic social reformative movement in terms of social activities and governmental guidelines, for emanating the roots of universal rolling of mankind should be entitled with the norms of social building atmosphere in shaping environmental issues, to cope up problems of regional disparities, social imbalances and human sufferings[143]. Coming over to such incidences of the conditions of human living barriers, it is noteworthy to mention here that devolution of power by means of appropriate decentralization process in decision-making affairs of organizational system of good governance criterion should be addressed to human sufferings; and so, there is the urgent need of having approach of equanimity concept of human growth perspectives in social living structure, which should further be restructured through employability aspects as well as delivery system of organizational effective management base. Creating all these essential possibilities of social reorientation could well be approached in relation to human work atmosphere and interpersonal relationships, confining thereby organizational tasks for universal human development process in scientific investigations where; there are problems of mismanagement due to lack of adequate opportunities being not yet possible to be created by the present system of organizational consistency in dealing with the things, for eradication of poverty from the world society which is believed to be a great curse on the part of scientific civilization and democratic movement for social development. So, coordinated work culture should be prevailing in organizational strategy of deciding about the factors responsible for the causes of balanced growth of the world society. Reasonably, global empowerment with creative means of opportunities by democratic movement of socialization process concerning human dignity of living, along with existential freedom of participation in organizational activities have permeably shown importance in these days of technological reformation; for which the present scientific researches, and discoveries and inventions in the field of efficient management of resources could go a long way to eradicate social misfortunes[144], in deluding the concept of human pathetic stage of survival in social atmosphere. Thus, global empowerment of humankind irrespective of any type of social discrimination should be made possible in reality, to manage things with the help of lifting the corporate veil as well as deciding about the corporate social responsibility part, for social orientation process in innovative nature of human growth. In this pattern of management, there should be legal framework of establishing judicious policy for encouraging social growth by means of human advancement, in an approach of equipoise nature of dealing with organizational tasks, and functional responsibilities of respective government agencies in different countries of the world.

The scope of management in objective fulfillment of social diversification of resources through project proposals and their implementation at the grass-root levels, for social reorientation purposes has been well warranted from the viewpoint of ameliorating poverty from social set-up, and therefore, it is expected that people's involvement in supplying necessities for fundamental change in the lot of suffered population would stimulate productive goal of human upliftment, in terms of carrying out programmes of social welfare activities[145], like – (i) education for illiterate people by means of institutionalization schemes at a rapid rate in backward regions of the world society; particularly, in case of underdeveloped and developing countries; (ii) healthcare activities for treatment of diseases to poor people who cannot afford to resort in this area, due to lack of scarce resources and low rate of income; (iii) housing facilities to those who live below the sky in shelterless condition; (iv) sanitation and clean drinking water facilities in remote villages to the starving population; (v) facilities of food, clothing, etc. with the availability in small means for surviving life with comfort ability; and besides, there are many opportunities like road transport and communication means, rail connectivity, infrastructural facilities for agricultural as well as speedy industrial development in backward zones, electricity facility, etc. – these are all socially oriented projects can be started for fast growing of the society in the twenty-first century periods, taking important attention towards environmental sustainability in connecting people to remove all the difficulties of human sufferings, as observed to be faced by different countries of the world. Hence, the systematic development of the social structure by democratic means of participative level of management can be helpful to strengthen the base of social foundation. So, it is very much urgent need now that opportunities of living in the above areas are to be covered by government policy formulation and its timely implementation at the grass-root level, with the value of judgment for social change in proactive manner[146]. It will thus help in solving problems of social restlessness situations and derailment of human beings from the mainstream of societal foundation. Another efficient thought provoking ideal in regard to people's involvement can be seen from organizational transcendental order of modifying things, narrating therein the principles of the maximum social advantage philosophy in scientific temper of managing resources for the distressed population, in creating more and more employment opportunities for eradication of the severe nature of poverty from the backward regions of the world society. Thus, schemes of social upliftment are to be advanced for unprivileged as well as underprivileged marginalized categories of human beings, who will go to restore a balance in society in terms of reducing gaps between haves and have-nots population. Again, these activities would lead to increase income of low paid or underpaid people who resort to many means of unsocial as well as anti-social activities, due to lack of tremendous sufferings and living priorities. It is thus, the responsibility of the elected government in every country of the world to open up doors of involving capacity for their deprived citizens; so that efficient management of social scarce resources and diversification of funds becomes a balanced match for empowering people to enhance civility in their survival conditions in society. From this standpoint, it is invariably to be noted that the spirit of managing social activities by modern multinational corporate houses are to unify goal of human cultural transformational change, in redefining the concept of development strategy with the notion of creativity and sensitivity analysis for encompassing social diversification of resources net-work system of effectiveness, in relating issues of empowerment so as to attain the objective function of social development for the sake of human integrity, to cope up challenges of change in environmental threats against the checks and balances narrating the different aspects of human de-motivation in groups dynamics concept of organizational consistency, to deal with the problems of human sufferings, social mobility and economic growth at macro as well as micro levels[147].

From the analysis as depicted in the above factors considering the causes of human empowerment conditionality, it is well known fact that cooperation in international level from the side of international agencies, and also from respective world governments side there should be enough confidence building measures by means of bilateral or other kinds of trade agreements; so that integrated system of management becomes the slogan of the present century[148], where humanism should be placed in the focal point at the prism of developmental mechanism – this would happen in practice, as and when humankind should be treated with the idea of nurturing concept, ignoring the concept of religious, castes, linguistic, racial, etc. differences in question of empowerment possibility; but only integral being of humanity in motivating people to reconstruct human civilization with the thought of universal dignity in mankind will be preserved in corporate work culture ethics, in guiding themselves with the motive of scientific method of involvement in the participatory role of organization. Thus, it is essential that corporate policies are to modify things on the basis of international understanding[149] for enlarging goal of human fraternity and brotherhood concept of dealing everything, with the objective of fulfillment of social transformation by way of radical change in cooperative manner. If things are delivered on the basis of such missionary objective for human development purposes, there will be arising universal diversification in maintaining consistency towards resources match, for enlarging people to the path of free existentialism with the coordinated system of leadership goal confining towards bringing social equality in between people. Good governance atmosphere will prevail due to all such understanding in empowering people to rebuild social structure in new dimensional way, where there will be peace and tranquility in entire society. Interpersonal relationships will also be enriched in this sort of management ideology, to occupy a position in the world system of cultural free flow of human participative nature of management goal, in creating things for the innovative redesigning of the social gamut, in accounting for human resource potential excellence to inculcate norms of democratic values, and living justice for the efficient cause of bringing human equity in social set-up. In this way, global development through organizational adjustment will be propounded to exemplify the idea of integral humanity, in an approach of social transformation, leadership role playing model for optimum human development process and causing empowerment an important instrument of social changing mechanism.

When there is adequate organizational convergence in mitigating such issues in practice of human involvement policies for increasing social welfare, the root of managing with all social values and human dignity will prevail in work atmosphere of organizational challenges for radical social change, and this would be supplemented to provide for efficiency in the delivery system to the needy areas of the social backwardness[150]. Everything should be built-up automatically in connecting people to realize for human integrity in living diversities, to propagate universal upliftment by reducing social wastes and eradicating corruptive practices of management system. Governmental agencies would be more responsible towards confining things in judicious manner for increasing human cooperation, and guiding people to think for universal development. By way of participating all people in areas of social reconstruction process[151], there would come optimum social diversification in channelizing government funds and thus; portfolio management for social infrastructure building will go to commensurate people's welfare by means of shouldering initiatives through leadership programmes, and people will further be motivated to produce more and more in team building approach of management objectivity, in question of social transformational as well as universal upliftment ideology[152]. Challenges of change would be made a proactive concept of human development conditionality, in strategizing organization as the plateform of human cooperation building enterprise for increasing social good of all people. This is the real picture of human emancipation policy should be practiced in organizational work culture, to attain the goal of global development with a view to supplement effective managerial guidance in regard to enhance human participation level to industrial rationality, social dynamicity and governmental optimality in utilizing all types of social resources for common welfare of human race. It will thus dignify the concept of democratic notion of human participation in correcting social imbalances[153], to curb ills of mismanagement and to restore well balance in matching scarce resources of the environment. Economic crisis from the society will be reduced by such means of democratic process of organizational system of efficient management, in order of increasing human excellence towards social building conditions in positive attitude. It will thus, lead to the goal of human empowerment process for global balance with the fabricated means of organizational work ethics as well as human scope of exhibiting things for producing outputs, to the fullest level possible development of needy people, in sensitizing themselves to understand broadly about the group dynamics behavioural postulates of human capacity building, organizational credibility to deliver goods in solving social problems[154], and in the long-run; the entire civilization of mankind would be strengthened to realize for universal brotherhood principles of social existence, in coherence as well as harmonious manner to excel human qualities for embracing with the ideologies of integrated opportunities for dynamic social development.

From the above discourses, it becomes important to remember that organizational policy of involving people with the democratic ideas of participating nature of work responsibility will be instrumental towards sustainable social development, in so far as the goal of management is concerned with rectifying social imbalances for eradicating human sufferings, balancing resources match to produce goods needed for backward regions, and redesigning the concept of human upliftment programmes in terms of various schemes operated for the sake of eradicating poverty from the global society. Scientific techniques are to be applied for investigating social problems, automation process in industrial productivity will have to be enriched to attain the goal of human empowerment through employment opportunities; being created by organizational system of management for the deprived population of the world[155], and besides; there should also be innovative practice for utilizing technological background in realizing things for optimal order of social transformation, by way of bringing universal level playing role in human development model, to encompass with the scope and opportunities of management reengineering in the establishment of scientific social movement, to enhance the goal of integral humanity with all the means and ways of dealing with organizational resources. In this pattern of leading modern organizations, there will be coming human quality which will enrich interpersonal relationships at work culture, and thus, people will feel themselves more motivated to participate with will-force in work related matters, so as to produce effectively. Management of love as the practice of universal empowerment process should emanate from the top level in organizational structure, so that human accountability is strengthened to stabilize organizational performances in challenging manner, to overcome problems of human backwardness in society[156]. Under all these circumstances, managing with the ecstasy of divine love for humanity should be entrusted with the work culture and organizational leadership dynamics, in complementing towards mutual participation with a view to augment human fellow-feeling nature of team building approach in organizational structure. In this way of understanding responsibility, global human existentialism will prevail in practice by means of scientific resource development programmes, and technological strategic policies of human capacity building through organizational credibility, to realize the ultimate goal[157] of social development in holistic manner.

Notes and References

1. In India, organizations, from the apex level of the Indian Parliament down to village panchayats, from society to family to the individual, from universities down to the schools, all make a vivid display of how much we have distanced ourselves from the true spirit of organization as enunciated by Swamiji ... ... Rights, rights and rights, and fights, fights and fights – that is the grammar of organizations in India". – Shuddhidananda, Swami (Ed.): "Vivekananda as the Turning Point – The Rise of a New Spiritual Wave", Advaita Ashrama, Publication

Department, Kolkata, 2013, p. 206. In an understanding on human activities, it is immensely required unity, integrity and to see the questions therefore, to investigate well – where is the mind, where go the common goals and objectives? The key to the solution would lie in the dictum of "service of God in man". – *Ibid.*, p. 207.

2. This salvation of human life process is like – "In the moral world, unselfishness is the basis of all morality. We give up the individual, the little circle of diluted selves, and march toward the universal". – Chaudhuri, Asim: "Swami Vivekananda in Chicago – New Findings", Advaita Ashrama, Publication Department, Kolkata, 2012, p. 161. Again, the path of salvation in life has to influence on our profound knowledge about the science of spirituality, which would open up new horizons before all of us, for enlarging and unifying all of our ideas and ideals of modernity as well as development potentiality ingrained in the core of pious living goal, for highest level of perfectionism and antiquity of eternal solitude for advancing in blissful progress of the entire human civilization.

3. The world order can be balanced through self-sustaining process of development. According to W. W. Rostow, it is the order that economic and social development should reach a stage when the economy and society propel themselves to further progress. Policy makers should make an attempt to boost up economic progress by way of export promotional measures and import substitution provisions to adjust with market competition in between countries of the world. Further, it is essential to increase foreign direct investment for the purpose of efficient production and distribution system, and for rendering services such as banking in which large chunk of profits can be made quickly. Infrastructure investment such as construction of high-speed four or six line express ways, high-speed railway connectivity, by means of operating bullet trains and high-speed trains services, and improvement or reconstruction of ports, etc. are all required for appreciation in exchange rate of the rupee value. Besides, employment generation programme should concern major policies to balance social progress, in terms of human capacity building and social development in speedy manner. In context of upliftment of people, the message that Swamiji wanted to give through his observation was loud and clear. Because, Swamiji ceaselessly inspired and exhorted Indians to arise, awake and struggle on till they achieve their self-mastery as individuals and as a nation. – Shuddhidananda, Swami (Ed.): "Vivekananda as the Turning Point – The Rise of a New Spiritual Wave", Advaita Ashrama, Kolkata, 2013, p. 217. It is therefore obvious that human work behaviour has to be made development oriented, instead of petty quarrelling over trivial questions of caste, creed, race, colour, sects and faiths; but to stay united and strong and reach their desired goal thereby, for which Swamiji voiced again and again, in roaring like lion throughout the world. This way, decaying nature of social progress can be rectified.

4. In discourses on human development strategy, we would like to analyze – how economic geographers have often discussed the relative importance of different factors – an early start, proximity to raw materials, access to a disciplined or skilled labour force, capital, entrepreneurs with vision and ability to take risks, professionals with innovative skills and proximity to large markets in explaining

location of industries. Industries processing raw materials – steel, heavy machinery, cement, paper, sugar, jute, wheat and oil mills, and petroleum refineries, factories producing chemical fertilizers and other petrochemicals, are important part of social transition, requiring special attention to science and technological development, for which; our analysis on various strategies will illuminate the picture of modern management thought. Hence, a comprehensive approach is essential, taking full account of the concrete historical conditions of development of particular countries and regions, and the basic economic and political goals pursued by the countries concerned in creating the integration groups. – Maximova, M.: "Economic Aspects of Capitalist Integration", Progress Publishers, Moscow, 1973, p. 143. Thus, the strategy for development requires a further stepping up of joint efforts by the socialist countries in the external economic sphere, heightening of the struggle of the developing countries for economic self-reliance, a tightening of the links between them, including those in the form of regional economic associations of an anti-imperialist character, and growing economic cooperation between the socialist countries and the developing countries. These are all reflected in different Chapters, as and when discourses are made to understand the idea of human development policies.

5. A major problem in planning for every large country is that of development of its different regions. It raises questions of regional allocation of resources, location of major projects, and rates of growth of production, income and employment in different regions, and allied questions of inter-regional movements of goods and people. Planners in every country are concerned with these questions. Plans must contain clearly articulated policies in respect of them and appropriate programmes to implement the policies. In case of large countries, such as India, the national plan must be accompanied by regional plans for States and smaller areas. – Nath, V.: "Economic Development and Planning in India", Concept Publishing Company Pvt. Ltd., New Delhi, 2010, p. 51. To conserve and protect national economies, it is undoubtedly to be mentioned here that the formation of an integration mechanism, like the establishment of concrete forms of economic integration, is not an arbitrary process. – Maximova, M.: "Economic Aspects of Capitalist Integration", Progress Publishers, Moscow, 1973. This is the work translated from the Russian by Bryan Beam into English and is first printed in 1973. However, we suggest here that a common technological production chain to boot, a system of international cartel agreements on various forms of cooperation, international production cooperation for creating permanent technological ties by a system of long-term agreements, long-term programme for production development and corresponding plans for organization and management structure, industrial cooperation, creation of multinational horizontal and vertical industrial complexes in different countries, with a similar or complementary technological structure of production, etc. could be important part of economic sustainable means of human development process. Hence, global sustainability should be made through economic integration, which is regarded primarily as process of human development paradigm. Also see, for further study – Kamecki, Z.: "Pojecie i typy integracji gospodarczej", Ekonomista, No. 1, 1967, pp. 93-94.

6. Our model for optimum development could be adopted from the visualization of Swamiji's thought regarding the motherland. He uttered: "Do not be dragged

away out of this Indian life; do not for a moment think that it would be better for India if all the Indians dressed, ate and behaved like another race … … The lord knows how many thousands of years are in your blood. Therefore, make way for the life-current of the nation. Take away the blocks that bar the way to the progress of this mighty river … … and out, it will rush by its own natural impulse, and the nation will go on careering and progressing". – Singh, Vidyotma: "Swami Vivekananda: Pioneer in Social Revolution", Vista International Publishing House, Delhi, 2008, pp. 210-211.

7. It should also be said that scientific parlance in work relationship has its spectacular successes in the context of modern technological society and its competence to eradicate poverty and human misery, a value-system permanently dedicated to the rational spirit of enquiry. Again, defending both religion and science, Needham was nevertheless painfully aware of their deficiencies. So, he was much concerned with the "religious opium", which is depicted in explanation in Chapter 3 of this volume. In relevance to human strategy – science, religion and politics can be assessed, according to Vedanta, which enumerates the whole idea thus: "Ignorance of the Reality breeds desire, and desires propel one into action, and this chain of ignorance, desires, and action is the cause of human misery. – See foot note by Swami Shuddhidananda in edited works of "Vivekananda as the Turning Point – The Rise of a New Spiritual Wave", Advaita Ashrama, Kolkata, 2013, p. 273. So, the betterment scheme of population should confine worldwide view like given by Swami Vivekananda. Swamiji speaks about ignorance, inequality and human desire, but predicts that in this, inequality is the natural corollary of ignorance … …-*Ibid.,* p. 273. Again, another way of looking about ignorance in political functioning of the State can be said by example that political influence and threats of unpleasant references in Parliament tend to dissuade bright men to join top positions. – Ramaswamy, T.: "Public Enterprises in India – Objectives & Performance", Meenakshi Prakashan, Delhi, 1972, p. 108. So, it is correct to say that goal of human development could not be achieved for real poverty eradication and reducing misery from the country.

8. About right conduct and the way of our value judgment, it is treated to be progress in morality, which is dependent on the progress of knowledge, among men … … and the basis of right conduct. – Laurie, Simon S.: "The Philosophy of Ethics – An Analytical Essay", Cosmo Publications, New Delhi, 2008, p. 104. However, it is said that the higher quality determines the right act; but where the antagonism arises among sentiments, desires, or felicities of the same general quality, though of varying intensities, the element of quantity can alone determine the right act. – *Op. cit.,* p. 106. Moreover, Swami Vivekananda says, "one must first know how to work without attachment, then one will not be a fanatic. When we know that this world is like a dog's curly tail and will never get straightened, we shall not become fanatics". – Bodhasarananda, Swami: "The Complete Works of Swami Vivekananda", Mayavati Memorial Edition, Vol. I, Advaita Ashrama, Kolkata, 1986, p. 79. Thus, a good practice in human life is said to be "sacrifice", has been propounded by the Upanishadic Order in the Hindu religion, - called the Sanatana practice of life; and so, economic value should be given the highest priority for human development, in bringing freedom toward realization of beings existence in social system.

9. The way of looking about the strategy for upliftment of human beings in the present stage of sufferings can be set to the objective idea of Sociology. It is because, Indian Sociology or Sociology in India, today, is a very large discipline and one of the largest in the world. It is reasonably said that the concern for quality of social science is vitally linked to the development of what may be called the development of scientific culture or ethos as distinguished from the development of scientific skills, even though the two are not unrelated. – Bhai, L. Thara (Ed.): "Studies in Indian Sociology", Sage Publications India Pvt. Ltd., New Delhi, 2012. Refer to the Series of this work – "Indian Sociology: Issues and Challenges", Vol. 1, p. xxxii. It is fact that scientific culture includes the cultivation of values, attitudes, norms and methods appropriate to the growth of social science. Accordingly, it is evident for the fulfillment of its humanistic objectives, as one can distinguish between sociological problems from social problems and sociological issues from political problems. While human development perspective is taken into consideration, there is no need to shun Western models, but we should selectively use relevant ones for understanding the society under investigation. Thus, social wheel can be scientifically in movement by way of assimilation, and destruction.

10. In this context, we have observed that personal and political changes are highly important factors of bringing global development process. Accordingly, Veerabhadrappa's views on this matter can be reflected for the purpose of broad understanding. As he says: "Personal and political changes are very much interrelated and both will be the product of learning process". – Veerabhadrappa, R. P.: "Teaching of Peace and Conflict Resolution", Lotus Press, New Delhi, 2007, p. 74. Religious sermons are also having positive impact on social changing goal. It is for this reason, that peace studies central to the task, not only of paradigm change; but also in the achievement of structural and systems change in the global order. Hence, 'teaching-learning' process can bring forth abrupt changes in society, by means of leadership training and patriotism. It can strengthen human mind in excelling best to the need of changing society in time.

11. In human civilization, it is observed that creators are generally average people with a given talent which they discover only through great effort and tremendous patience with themselves. In regard to the techniques on human invention of things, satellites are one of the more recent gadgets which scientists have invented to improve man's ability to sense things. It is true that nature provided many hints for early man's ideas. Weaving was probably suggested by a bird making a nest or a spider building a web. It was probably women hunting for roots and berries who discovered that seeds grow. And women may also have invented tilling the soil – perhaps even the early plow. Again, man must have observed the bee storing its honey or the woodpecker or squirrel hiding its food, and gotten the idea of storing food to withstand a severe winter. Weapons may have been suggested by the tribes of apes who flung sticks and throw stones. In this way, some accidents like the liberation of fire surely gave rise to many other inventions. – See also, Mueller, Robert E.: "Inventive Man", Lancer Books, New York, 1963, for understanding – how order of human development in global civilization can be made possible through inventing things, by means of human creativity as well as sensitivity analysis.

12. About upliftment and human advancement through sacrificial nature of doing things, it is worth-noting to reflect the ideas of Swami Vivekananda, which goes like: "Give and take is the law; and if India wants to raise herself once more, it is absolutely necessary that she brings out her treasures and throws them broadcast among the nations of the earth, and in return be ready to receive what others have to give her. Expansion is life, contraction is death. Love is life and hatred is death. We commenced to die the day we began to hate other races, and nothing can prevent our death unless we come back to expansion, which is life". – Editors: "India's Contribution to World Thought and Culture", Vivekananda Rock Memorial Committee 12, Pillaiyar Koil Street, Triplicane, Madras, 1970, p. 650. Again, Samar Deb opines: "The management by love has therefore, benefits in group dynamics because by this method the management creates a confidence, oneness, and sense of belonging in the minds of its people through its attitudes, approaches and policies". – Deb, Samar: "Contemporary Issues on Management", Atlantic Publishers and Distributors, New Delhi, 2001, p. 136. Thus, a sense of commitment should be commanded by virtue of management's policy of love, i.e., love should start at top and flow to the bottom. The term group dynamics has been adopted here from the definition of Keith Davis, who has rightly remarked the concept as: "The social process by which people interact face to face in small group". – Davis, Keith: "Human Behavior at Work", McGraw Publishing Company, New Delhi, 1975, p. 439.

13. In this matter, along with scientific temper of thought, religion has its own contribution for enhancing the core idea of equality. And again, in practical life, the Swami, as we know by this term to famous Vivekananda, advocated the encompassing ideas of social equality of Islam, for human development purposes. This idea is like: "... ... Advaitism is the last word of religion and thought ... ... we believe it is the religion of the future enlightened humanity ... ... yet practical Advaitism, which looks upon and behaves to all mankind as one's own soul, is yet to be developed among the Hindus universally. On the other hand, our experience is that if ever the followers of any religion approached to this equality in an appreciable degree in the plane of practical work-a-day life ... ... it is those of Islam and Islam alone. Therefore, we are firmly persuaded that without the help of practical Islam, theories of Vedantism, however fine and wonderful they may be, are entirely valueless to the vast mass of mankind ... ... For our own Motherland a junction of the two great systems, Hindusim and Islam,- Vedantic brain and Islamic body – is the only hope. I see in my mind's eye the future perfect India rising out of this chaos and strife, glorious and invincible, with Vedantic brain and Islamic body". – Sharma, Suresh K. (Ed.): "Swami Vivekananda the Patriot-Saint of Modern India", Vol. 2, Vista International Publishing House, Delhi, 2008, pp. 68-69. Thus, religious unity can bring in human integrity for enlarging ideas of social equality and solving many critical problems of human life in this world of peaceful living.

14. In going through liberal practices for enhancing socio-economic progress, the case of India can be well set to predict that "India is beset by an extraordinary diversity of economic, regional, communal, and caste interests". – Joshi, Vijay and Little, I. M. D.: "India's Economic Reforms 1991 – 2001", Oxford University Press, New Delhi, 1998, p. 264.

15. With a view to understanding about the picture of human development, it is clear that in earlier phase of economic planning the main objective of the plans was a modest rate of growth and it was hoped that with its realization the country would automatically solve the unemployment and poverty problems. In Indian scenario, when such a thing did not happen the planners started listing some other objectives also along with economic growth, and ignoring the incompatibility between the objectives expected that success might be achieved in all the directions within India's mixed economy framework, the objectives of rapid economic growth and alleviation of poverty are not always in harmony. It was thus felt in case of India, that along with the world economy, there were three main aspects of the strategy of development plans during the post-Independence periods and thereafter, except in some years, like: (1) building up of a sound base for future economic growth; (2) a high priority to industrialization when actual development started; (3) emphasis on the development of capital goods industries. – Misra, S. K. and Puri, V. K.: "Development and Planning (Theory and Practice)", Himalaya Publishing House, Delhi, 3rd. Edn., 1988, pp. 718-19.

16. Underlining this fact, Dandekar and Rath wrote: "A plan of development, which accepts a national minimum and aims at assuring the same to all within the shortest possible time, cannot depend entirely on a high rate of economic growth. Without a deliberate policy to ensure an equitable distribution of the gains of development, the processes of development benefit the upper middle and richer sections of the population much more than they do the lower middle and the poorer sections. As a result, even a high rate of growth, probably beyond the range of feasibility, cannot lift the bottom of the society to the desirable minimum within the foreseeable future. This is not a plea for a lower rate of growth but a warning that a high rate of growth is not a substitute for deliberate policies to ensure equitable distribution of the gains of development". – Dandekar, V. M. and Rath, Nilakantha: "Poverty in India", Economic and Political Weekly, Bombay, 1971, p. 51.

17. A good picture of social structure can be attributed to Indian system of agricultural societies. According to Charles Bettelheim, "Cooperative farming societies in India are essentially capitalist agricultural societies. The only advantage of forming such societies is that they can be of use in disseminating more advanced cultivation techniques". – Bettelheim, C.: "India Independent", Khosla & Co., Delhi, 1977, p. 195. As a result of such things, public distribution system has been ruined, which could not be made efficient to enhance social equality, so as to strengthen human foundation by means of real poverty alleviation programmes from time to time, among others. This can be readjusted through agricultural reformations, in line with social subsistence and transformational guidelines.

18. In modern organizations, participative techniques in changing need of time are highly suggestive. Because, modern participative techniques like – empowerment of employees at lower levels, enabling them to take decisions. Another way of looking is the modern self-managed teams. These teams will help in enhancing employee satisfaction and commitment towards organization goals. – Bhatia, S. K.: "Managing Organizational Behaviour", Deep & Deep Publications Pvt. Ltd., New Delhi, 2008, p. 339. Hence, to uproot social value system, it is essential to

implement organizational policies, keeping regard to the quality circle (QC) to provide in carrying out in-depth study about identification of causes to problem. It will offer for alternative solutions of the practical problems. Samar Deb, again, suggests: "It enriches the organization in the spheres of results in operational areas, along with other objective basis of the organization, being the subject-matter of the concept is all-comprehensive as it results to an expected way of development of the organization and its members for the greater creativity, less hostility toward others, and greater sensitivity to social psychological influences on work behaviour, etc. It thus, inculcates a wide range of behavioural goal towards the success of the organization for bringing a balance between group members, by coordinating different aspects of development in harmonious manner in universally accepted principles ... ..." – Deb, Samar: "Unified Thought on Management", Kalpaz Publications, Delhi, 2004, p. 81. In a nutshell, Japanese techniques of QC concepts can be enthusiastically applied in Indian industries for increasing participative values, so as to enhance adequate nature of human development in holistic manner.

19. This 'Win-Win' strategy by reinforcing the Vedic worldview can help to develop ideas of transformational leadership by developing sttva and reducing tamas. – See, Robbins, Stephen P., Judge, Timothy A. and Sanghi, Seema: "Organizational Behavior", Prentice Hall, Delhi, 2008, p. 457. So, the study has important implications for organizational behaviour in getting proper worldview to optimize organizational functional role of social development dimensions. – See also, Kejriwal, A. and Krishnan, V. R.: "Impact of Vedic Worldview and Gunas on Transformational Leadership", Vikalpa 29, no. 1, January-March 2004, pp. 29-40.

20. As to the subject of "race", it has long been a topic of concern for those interested in the dynamics of human societies. Indeed, since the very beginning of recorded history philosophers and physicians, sages and scientists, politicians and pundits and pamphleteers have written on the nature of "racial" and "national" differences and offered explanations for the bases of intergroup conflicts. – Rose, Peter I.: "The Subject is Race. Traditional Ideologies and the Teaching of Race Relations", Oxford University Press, New York, 1968, p. 1. The best way to the critical, systematic and objective assessment is, at bottom, to approach this subject of race and race relations for the purpose of social development.

21. In this context, the Administrative Reform Commission, Study team on Economic Administration Report (1969) in India had observed thus: "Industrialization is necessary for reconstruction and development of agriculture. Besides, lightening the burden of agriculture, the industrialization will provide the means for supplying agriculture with more power, better transport facilities, marketing and similar services, and by increasing the number of income earners and hence the demand for foods, it would stimulate agriculture and more specifically mixed farming. Expanding industrial system absorbs a part of the rural labour force". For further study of the Report see, The Economic Administration Report, 1969, The Administrative Reform Commission, Government of India. Thus, it is required a structural transformation in the overall economy for the positive social change, along with the change of population in the country in time and space.

22. Social disparities can be reduced by massive industrialization programmes. It is imperative as a growth propelling force, has been generally acknowledged in

the developing nations. One common feature as noticed in all such developmental endeavours has, however, been the special treatment accorded on the development of small scale industries as an important part of the industrialization programme. – Mishra, P. C. and Achrya, G. C.: "Working of the State Financial Corporations", Indian Publishers Distributors, Delhi, 1995, p. 3.

23. In this field, post-reform India has emerged as a growing power of soft skills mainly in the service sector. – Deb, Bimal J., Sengupta, Keya and Ray, B. Datta (Eds.): "Globalization and North East India", Concept Publishing Company, New Delhi, 2008, p. 344. On the other hand, China's hard skill in manufacturing provides preliminary advantage to China. Thus, it is suggested, in ASEAN nations our organizational activities could be performed in such way which will help in gaining the status of a dependable partner in steady manner. So, skill building techniques are to be redrafted with the models of incorporating soft infrastructure like regulatory frameworks, financial markets and recognized and transparent property right. About considering perfection in our measures, global electrification can be said to hold a key trend over the next few decades, and it will be the shift in technology dominance from supply side to demand side, as the electricity delivery system becomes integrated with communications to form a new mega-infrastructure with new functions. New skills therefore, are helpful for adopting as well as adapting with government policies from time-to-time. It requires leading will to have faith in the capacity of the masses to struggle. – Chandra, Bipan: "Indian National Movement. The Long-Term Dynamics", Har-Anand Publications Pvt. Ltd., New Delhi, 2008, p. 77. Hence, the leadership strategy in confining all these factors requires – basic goals, objectives and values,... ... demands and aspirations, to create people who would struggle together, to evolve correct strategy and tactics which correspond to the specific historical situation. – *Op. cit.,* p. 78. To enhance human competencies, we are to go back to the ancient Indian history, wherefrom, the extraordinary nature of such history may be perceived, which Ganguly mentions, there is little room for doubt that these characteristics of history ... ... evaluating the authenticity of the Vedic tradition. – Ganguly, D. K.: "History and Historials in Ancient India", Abhinav Publications, New Delhi, 1984, p. 30. Again, the implementation of the measures is to correct things in organizational order of performances alike to that of the characteristics of history, which R. G. Collingwood writes: (a) that it is scientific or begins by asking questions; (b) that it is humanistic, or asks questions about things done by men at determinate times in the past; (c) that it is rational, or bases the answers it gives on appeal to evidence; and (d) that it is self-revelatory, or exists in order. – The Idea of History (London, 1970), p. 18. In upgrading people from social sufferings, we should adopt appropriate teachings in bringing human skills; so that a planned approach is followed for administering all types of governing agenda, to lead social institutions to the path of human efficiency as well as organizational effectiveness. Because, Majumdar writes: "The nature of these corporations is now a matter of general knowledge and there are reasons to believe that things have not changed much, except in the lax observation of rules in recent days". – Majumdar, Ramesh Chandra: "Corporate Life in Ancient India", Cosmo Publications, New Delhi, 1994, p. 171.

24. The reasons behind this can be attributed to the contingency of a nation which could be well admitted, if we consider Rabindranath, for instance, who

categorically stated about poetic practice thus: "... ... it was the width of leisure which was the location of poetic practice, thus wishing such practice away from the everyday and the ordinary time of life and labour". – The Philosophy of Leisure, VQ, 7 (1929-30), p. 8. For change, therefore, we are to be practical, because imagination signified a future beyond the familiar, beyond what one was equipped by knowledge to anticipate. – Mayaram, Shail, Pandian, M. S. S. and Skaria, Ajay (Eds.): "Muslim, Dalits, and the Fabrications of History", Parmanent Black, Delhi, 2007, p. 320. Thus, change aspects of management should be free from imagination, but rather it will take into consideration the practical expositions of human life as well as national policy-making issues, to overcome problems of environmental issues. Further, every change in society should care for sub-cultural diversity. Weisgran therefore, remarks rightly this view: "Yet, one of the unintended consequences of this institution building has been affirmation of dominant values and erosion of sub-cultural diversity". – *Op. cit.,* pp. 206-208. We are to make our journey in doing business and social activities in dynamic order; so that change elements are well-warranted to open avenues for all people for the fuller personality development. In this way, change can be said to have the religious spirit of human beings. Henderson suggests: "It is firmly rooted in everyday life, and it ranges across a huge variety of belief systems". – Henderson, Carol E.: "Culture and Customs of India", Greenwood Press, London, 2004, p. 28. For bringing change in society, Jawaharlal Nehru also advocated for helping both the sectors of our economy. He remarks thus: "In present circumstances, the public sector itself will fail to function adequately if it is not helped by private enterprise in many ways in the consumption and the products of heavy, medium and light industries. We shall require a net-work of well-spread out industries of all levels and types". – Nehru, Jawaharlal: "India's Independence and Social Revolution", Vikas Publishing House Pvt. Ltd., New Delhi, 1984, p. 153. So, change is ubiquitous. It is universal for human development in rationalistic order, as we have observed that the most important aspects of change are coming from people, technology, information processing and communication, competition and social trends – it is essential on the part of the management to handle these forces quite consciously, ... for all types of changing forces acting on the enterprise and their employees. – Deb, Samar: "Contemporary Issues on Management", Atlantic Publishers and Distributors, New Delhi, 2001, p. 95.

25. Jagannath Mishra, in terms of social dimension asserts: "What is amazing is the fact that side by side, in all modern countries, the people are experiencing a process of change affecting everything but controlled by no one. It is in a sense spontaneous. Men are being transformed. – Mishra, Jagannath (Ed.): "India's Economic Development", Vikas Publishing House Pvt. Ltd., New Delhi, 1984, p. 133. Positive change will bring in societal value system, and so, a value system has no doubt a relevance to a period of time on the basis of the needs and expectations of people as well as on their own faith in such a value system. Social dimension of change has its relevancy with that of bringing qualities in human beings, for which, from early times, it had always been the concern of great thinkers, philosophers and saints to put emphasis on certain qualities in every human being.

26. This type of philosophy of good governance for our work behaviour has been cited by Dr V. K. R. V. Rao thus: we want to combine the best in our national past with the best in the global present so that our future will be based, to use Acharya Vinoba Bhave's language, on science and spirituality. The work behaviour should be guided by Indian values and ethics. In this context, work of Dr S. K. Chakravarty of Indian Institute of Management at Calcutta is quite illuminating, who has brought out ten ingredients of Indian values which have direct relevance for Indian management. It is suggested because, Dr Chakravarty is the pioneer in exploring this area, and his thoughts are in the process of going through searching enquires for recreating values in managerial profession. – *Ibid.,* p. 143.

27. However, on going through such ideologies, Keynes in his "Essays in Persuasion" has given long-term prescription thus: "The pace at which we can reach our destination of economic bliss will be governed by four things – our power to control population, our determination to avoid wars and civil dissensions, our willingness to entrust to science the direction of those matters which are properly the concern of science, and the rate of accumulation as fixed by the margin between our production and consumption" (p. 373). Hence, the perspective of productive ideology for supplying necessities could get useful attention when we consider Minhas and Srinivasan. – For details, refer to Minhas, B. S. and Srinivasan, T. N.: "New Agricultural Production Strategy: Some Policy Issues", Readings in Indian Agricultural Development, Pramit Chaudhury (Ed.), p. 132. Thus, agricultural strategy in increasing production through extensive cultivation, and a correct diagnosis of the problem of raising agricultural production, namely, the insufficiency of modern inputs has to be made socially-oriented in nature for governing things with the effectiveness of its value judgment for people's development. Productive ideologies should also be made through land reform measures, which is essentially to be completed very quickly. Again, small farmers should be given adequate credit facilities to buy necessary inputs like seeds, fertilizers, etc. and there should be adequate arrangements for the supply of farm-machines on hire, to be provided by the government. Among others, farmers should be encouraged to join cooperatives for cultivation. – Agrawal, A. N.: "Indian Economy. Problems of Development and Planning", Vikas Publishing House Pvt. Ltd., New Delhi, Eleventh Rev. Edn., 1985, p. 319. Thus, the framework of productive ideologies should be made a holistic concept of development, by means of managerial delivery system in organizational pattern of controlling things and activities for citizen's welfare.

28. An example can be cited in this regard by saying that implementation of plans and programmes for agricultural development are seen as a difficult task in Indian environment. – Phukan, Umananda: "Agricultural Development in Assam (1950-1985), Mittal Publications, New Delhi, 1990, pp. 101-102. In bringing scientific mobility in this field, particularly, human factor played a vital role in the process of implementation. However, it is suggested that extension agency should be made responsible in giving to our agriculturists' research support, to improve efficiency in agricultural productivity. – See also, IADP – Second Report (1960-65) of the Expert Committee on Assessment and Evaluation, Government of India, p. 401. We should be further careful for supplying maximum to people for improved agricultural technology that were offered so far, has not been found

adequately location specific. It is observed altogether that Research and Extension activities had no proper link in previous years. – For clearing doubts, readers are also suggested to go through – Borah, D.: "Role of Contact Farmers on Transfer of Technology to Follower Farmers under T and V System: AERC for N. E. India", Assam Agricultural University, Jorhat, 1983. For verifying our goals and objectives in discriminating order, keeping men at the center-stage, we should also take advice from the West, like Rousseau proposed long back: "An ideal which, though constantly exceeding our limited grasp, is capable of inspiring humanity toward a brighter future. – Havens, George R.: "The Age of Ideas", The Free Press, New York, 1955, p. 277.

29. For doing this, we are to increase in society the number of suitably technically qualified people, because the inadequacy of technically qualified people has been one of the most important factors for the backwardness of the north eastern region. – Ahluwalia, Shashi (Ed.): "Social and Economic Development in North-East India", Gian Publishing House, Delhi, 1986, p. 40. In reducing regional imbalances, evidently the correspondence is likely to become closer the greater the progress towards equality of opportunity. – Robertson, D. H.: "Lectures on Economic Principles", Vol. II, Staples Press, London, 1959, p. 142. Thus, for serving depressed people we are to dedicate for supply themselves with all necessaries requiring for civic living, and this way the regional imbalances will be reduced with the sacrificial nature of our services performed for have-nots class of the society.

30. The European Economic Community (EEC) must have to be reformulated for getting feed-back in an approach of international mechanism, along with other economic forums and agencies of the world. Thus, the EEC tariffs, quotas and other trade barriers are to be adjusted with that of Asian countries like – India, China, Japan, Malaysia, Singapore, Pakistan, Bangladesh and many other countries. Besides, SAARC countries will require some anticipated models for disposing things in regard to their national development. In understanding development thus, for economic advancement might be expedited by import restrictions, development efforts also require assistance from the Development Fund of the Community, which has to be enhanced by financing with the contributions from member countries, and therefore, the introduction of an agricultural programme should be acceptable to all members, which has proved to be one of the more difficult problems encountered. – Wasserman, Max J. and Hultman, Charles W.: "Modern International Economics: A Balance of Payments Approach", Eurasia Publishing House (Pvt.) Ltd., New Delhi, 1970, pp. 449-50. Coming over to the Indian concept of development, it is predicted that our underlying goals and objectives must have the scheme of life as chalked out by the seers of the Vedas had "spiritual liberation of the individual" as its supreme goal. – Shuddhidananda, Swami (Ed.): "Vivekananda as the Turning Point. The Rise of New Spiritual Wave", Advaita Ashrama, Kolkata, 2013, p. 167. Probably, this is the reason for which Vivekananda shared his unshakable love for humankind and the bodhisattva ideal with this promise to all: "And may I born again and again, and suffer thousands of miseries so that I may worship the only God that exists, the only God I believe in, the sum total of all souls – and above all, my God the wicked, my God the miserable, my God the poor of all races, of all species, is the special object of my worship". – *Ibid.*, p. 440. Thus, the feed-

back approach of nurturing people has to be assimilated with that of the Indian Vedanta philosophy, which believes the divinity in men.

31. In consonance with the World Trade Organization (WTO), it is said that technical cooperation is an area of WTO work that is devoted almost entirely to helping developing countries ... ... The subjects covered deal both with trade policies and with effective negotiation. – Jain, N. K.: "WTO Concept, Challenges and Global Development", Regal Publications, New Delhi, 2008, p. 201. Technically strategies are to be framed for global level cooperation so as to ensure that the multilateral trading system results in mutual benefits for all countries. – Op. cit., p. 221. Development strategies also require that less developed countries are to be provided with special attention by making provisions in most favourable treatment for this group in terms of rights as well as own level of obligations. In looking towards technical standpoint, we are to note that the Asian region has the possibilities of exploring trade, for which every state should have the intervening to give a strategic edge to its domestic firms by way of favourable exchange rate. – Thakur, Devendra (Ed.): "International Business for Third World Countries", Deep & Deep Publications, New Delhi, 1997, p. 121. For holistic development process, our idea of technological cooperation should be merged with supreme peace. In this regard, Kuppuswami comments: "Knowledge is superior to making the mind steady and steadfast and meditation is greater than knowledge. But the abandoning of the fruits of karma (action) is far superior to meditation ever. Deliverance or supreme peace is easy to be attained by abandoning the fruits of action. – Kuppuswamy, A.: "Bhagavat Gîtâ", Chaukhambha Orientalia, Varanasi, 1983, p. 350. The philosophy of such remark can be attributed to realize our life in the supreme freedom of doing things, for eradicating human ills and sufferings, by means of sacrificial nature of job while performing in organizational status with the nature of disinterestedness, so as to raise people to the higher ladders of life in terms of trade, industry and commerce.

32. Under such circumstances, it will be useful to refer Gaurinath, who observes in the context of human life: "Surrender is thus the point of convergence of all the efforts displayed by the human disciple and the powerful current of love flowing from the divine source. It is the goal towards which the Triune Path leads the seeker. Absolute surrender perpetuates the union between the knowledge of Truth and the love for the Supreme". – Gaurinath: "The Triune Path", Sampurnananda Sanskrit Vishvavidyalaya, Varanasi, 1982, p. 79. As a solution of life problems, it is to be suggested that we are to develop the state of harmony and peace, in the midst of doing our activities for human beings, and thus created, is the ideal coalescence of the divine and the human. Because, it is the Vedic wisdom had never sustained a divorce between scriptural and empirical life.

33. Thus, it is observed that in social experiments initiated by the U. S. Department of Housing and Urban Development (HUD) in the early 1970s to test the use of direct-cash housing allowance payments to assist low-income families improve the quality of their housing through the open market (Trend 1978 a). Again, the U. S. Agency for International Development (AID) to train community health workers, observed that the health problems of people living in Colombia, plus Ecuador and Indonesia were mainly related to the conditions of poor nutritional status and bad economic conditions, which could be revived through – (1) vaccination; (2) sanitation; (3) nutritional level to child; (4) level of health care

and nutrition to mothers; (5) providing to families health education concerning prevention and treatment of disease; and (6) improvement of knowledge and access to effective family planning practices. – Tyagi, Darshna (Ed.): "Applied Anthropology", Anmol Publications Pvt. Ltd., New Delhi, 2006, pp. 219-22. About appropriating our measures for human development, the techniques of music have a great resemblance. We may quote here the works of William Pole, as he remarks: "It is a rule existing in many other cases that the sequence of ideas must be connected and logical ... ... and in the ordinary course of things, prefers that in harmonic, like other progressions, some definite and logical relations should be preserved". – Pole, William: "Introduction to Philosophy", Cosmo Publications, New Delhi, 2008, p. 264. Thus, we require active cooperation for governance in progressing through inquiry into the facts, that there are grounds or justifications in implementing things with natural and philosophical principles, for adequate confidence building measures in developing social structure.

34. We are to believe in power of truth – where human healthy relationships are to be based. About the belief of Rabindranath Tagore, it is also uttered like: "On the basis of these ideas Truth was considered in ancient India to have its cosmic power". – See also, "A Centenary Volume of Rabindranath Tagore 1861-1961", Published by the Sahitya Akademi, New Delhi, Fourth Printing 1992, p. 377. Our development agenda should be framed, keeping in mind the policies for socio-economic activities in different ecosystems, which will also be helpful for sustainable tourism development. In this context, Sandeep Kumar remarks: "It is imperative to provide incentives for the wide range application of environmental management systems". – Kumar, Sandeep: "Biodiversity Environment and Suatainable Management", A. K. Publications, Delhi, 2009, p. 102. Therefore, human healthy intercourse has to be built on the pillars of strengthening integrated management policies in consistent manner; in which the strategy, integrated management of biodiversity resources and sustainable tourism, with ample participation of civil society and in coordination with the government, are all considered as the top priority for national development.

35. We are to streamline measures through a comprehensive risk management framework in banking system, as it is the parameter of human growth and social stability. Hence, capital formation with human face of organizational undertaking requires: (1) credit risk policies and procedures; (2) organizational structure for effective credit administration and risk management functions; and (3) credit risk rating framework. For innovative creativity in sensitizing people for dynamic growth potentials, we may suggest for risk scoring and rating models of two Indian banks, as furnished by the work of M. Y. Khan in this regard. – Khan, M. Y.: "Indian Financial System", Tata McGraw Hill Education Private Limited, New Delhi, Sixth Edn., 2009, pp. 13.11-13.29. Besides, the socio-economic upliftment programmes have to be guided with the provisions of "Avoidance of Double Taxation Agreement", in case of global convergence, national transformation and human indignation purposes. – *Op. cit.,* p. 18.36-18.42. Thus, for international cooperation and human development, the technology of thinking should be like, as Gide and Rist remark: "But every connection with practical politics had to be removed and a new body of closely knit doctrines had to be created before social thinkers could have this new point of view from which to

cooperate". – Gide, Charles and Rist, Charles: "A History of Economic Doctrines. From the Time of the Physiocrats to the Present Day", Authorized Translation by R. Richards, Second English Edition, Oxford University Press, Delhi, 1983 (Third Impression), p. 382.

36. It requires adequate industrial and economic policy, the lack of which as S. C. Raychoudhury has opined: "Impoverished the village community more than the urban economy ... ..." – Raychoudhury, S. C.: "Social, Cultural and Economic History of India", Surjeet Publications, Delhi, 1987, p. 113. Industrial labour requires not only training and working in an industrial unit, but also commitment to an industrial way of life. – See Mayers, *Op. cit.,* p. 36. The severe problem of India's rural population is that there is still impoverished land, aptly observed by Shiva Rao, "is incapable of supporting socially and economically they represent the most backward sections of the population". – Rao, Shiva: "Labour in India", The Annals of the American Academy of Political and Social Science, 1944, p. 128. For social rejuvenation, we are to adopt ideas of the Vedic age, because Khurana remarks that: "The morals of the people (Vedic) were very high ... ..." – Khurana, K. L.: "Ancient India", Lakshmi Narain Agarwal, Agra, 2013, p. 40.

37. For establishment of peace, we are required that prosperity shall return to the entire human race, and therefore, Singh remarks: "Science, technology and development, gradually leading people to higher standards of life". – Singh, Brig. Jagdev: "Growth of Hindu Religion and Culture", Gyan Publishing House, New Delhi, 2006, p. 319. Thus, for delivery of goods and services, India has to work to take their industrial revolution to fruition, in order to bring prosperity to the people. – *Op. cit.,* p. 320. Dhar observes, economic difficulties disrupted the planning process in India in the mid-1960s. ... ... Major shortcomings include insufficient improvement in income distribution and alleviation of poverty, delayed completions and cost overruns on many public-sector projects, and far too small a return on many public-sector investments. – Dhar, R. N.: "History of India: Social and Economic", Cyber Tech Publications, New Delhi, 2010, pp. 165-69. All these consequences prove that we are to enhance our services by expanding employment opportunities and building the rural infrastructure as a means of encouraging rapid economic growth.

38. The feeling of such democratic thinking requires the mind-set for bringing international cooperation. In this line of thinking, we may predict that Rashbehari Bose (1880-1945) had a dominating personality, and was a nationalist, who believed in international cooperation. – Raman, V. V.: "100 Great Names from India's Past", Bombay, 1989. Again, Sarat Chandra Bose (1889-1950) always thought of India as one, resisting regionalism and communalism ... ... he was an ardent liberal in social matters in thought and conduct. He spared no efforts to warn his countrymen against the evils of caste and untouchability. – Majumder, R. C.: "History of the Freedom Movement in India", Vol. III. In this way, we can observe from the Gita, that our democratic participatory norms should be guided by the philosophy of sacrifice for doing well to others. Thus, another Indian personality, named Satyendra Nath Bose (1894-1974), can be considered a man of genius, a scholar in the best meaning of the word, a lover of music and of literature, a creator in science, an ardent teacher, simple in outlook, indifferent to name and fame, had professed himself for whatever is best in the Indian love

of learning. – Aiyar, R.: "Biographical Vistas", Bombay, 1966. To pave the way for people's development, his mind had been interacting with the notions of the past of India, and the consequent of such thinking had resulted in his holistic approach for such intellectual acumen and growth to the cause of humanity. In this way, it may be predicted that involvement of people for deciding to their upliftment requires much needed philosophy of the democratization with radical principles of integral humanity concept, as found also in Subhash Chandra Bose (1897-). It is evidently, said that: "The Indian people, hungry for freedom, participated in their thousands in the struggle launched throughout the country by the Forward Bloc on April 6. – Singh, Nagendra Kr. (Ed.): "Encyclopaedia of the Indian Biography", A. P. H. Publishing Corporation, New Delhi, 2000. All these explanations are commendable to predict for the real theme of democratic nature of human participation for values, ideals and social emancipation. For developing societies, political leaders must have the will force to involve people to prepare themselves for the heroic adventure, as remarked by Lt. Col. Philip N. Pierce and Karl Schuon, in case of providing America's technical, man-into-orbit skill. – Pierce, Lt. Col. Philip, USMC and Schuon, Karl: "John H. Glenn Astronaut", Ballantine Books, New York, 1962, pp. 69-81.

39. For self-motivation in our existential freedom in realizing all norms of legal justification for the religious proactive things, we may refer to Nanac, the founder of this faith, was born 1469, at Talwandi, a village on the river Beas. It is asserted in a Gazetteer thus: "Being of a contemplative disposition, and it is said devout and benevolent, he became an ascetic, remarkable for his austerities, ever among the Hindoos". – ESQ., Edward Thornton: "A Gazetteer of the Territories under the Government of the East India Company, and of the Nation States on the Continent of India", Low Price Publications, Delhi, 1993, p. 911. So, the motivational path should be followed for preaching the unity and omnipresence of God, the necessity of good works, of pure and of good-will towards men. – *Ibid.,* p. 911. For bringing inner zeal in motivating people we are to take things enthusiastically for learning new trades, without fighting and winning. – Also refer to "A Tour of Soviet Uzbekistan", Foreign Languages Publishing House, Moscow, 1954. It is a translated work from the Russian. Further, it is noted in this work that we are to follow our decisions widely, simply and with inspiration. – *Op. cit.,* p. 243. In a nutshell, it is worthwhile to note the lines for our existential freedom, which would be motivating people much: "Seek not that the things which happen should happen as you wish; but wish the things which happen to be as they are, and you will have a tranquil flow of life". – Beatty, John Louis and Johnson, Oliver A. (Eds.): "Heritage of Western Civilization", Prentice-Hall, Inc., Englewood Cliffs, N. J., 1964, p. 146. Remember that in life you ought to behave as at a banquet. So, live like: as the captain calls you, you run to the ship. This is called sincerity and discipline, should be propagated for holistic development.

40. This philosophy of governance should be free from concentration of power in a few hands, and therefore, it must be observed that finance capital and its foreign policy, which is the struggle of the great powers for the economic and political division of the world, give rise to a number of transitional forms of state dependence … … but also the diverse forms of dependent countries which,

politically, are formally independent, but in fact, are enmeshed in the net of financial and diplomatic dependence, typical for this epoch. – See "V. I. Lenin Selected Works", Vol. I, Progress Publishers, Moscow, 1977, p. 697. In this context, we are to remember that our leadership traits are to be developed for bringing human integrity to social reconstruction means, in attaining objectives of devolution of power for the sake of suffered human beings, to enlarge the vista of political activities on the superstructure of socio-economic equalities. Coming over to financial governance, it is worthwhile to note that the Indian financial system till the early 1990s was a closed, restricted, highly regulated, and segmented system. – Pathak, Bharati V.: "The Indian Financial System. Markets, Institutions and Services", Second Edn., Dorling Kindersley (India) Pvt. Ltd., Delhi, 2009, p. 37. In the 1990s, there was a paradigm shift in development from a state-dominated to a market-determined strategy. This shift was a result of the government's failure in achieving a higher growth rate. Hence, the deregulation of industry, liberalization of foreign exchange markets and convertibility of currency require an efficient financial system. Globally, book building is a recognized mechanism for capital raising process. Here, it is truly said that it was book building which built the US market almost entirely in the 1940s and 1950s. In connection with governance philosophy, we may thus quote: "The unity of government which constitutes you one people is also now dear to you". – Blum, John M., Catton, Bruce, Morgan, Edmund S., Schlesinger, Jr. Arthur M., Stampp, Kenneth M., Woodward, C. Vann: "The National Experience", Harcourt, Brace and World, Inc., New York, 1963, p. 149. Therefore, our organizational management functions should justify for its own pillars in the edifice of real independence in terms of work principles, liberty through people's empowerment, and a spirit of innovational techniques upon the principles of the conviction of the truth. All these will support for our tranquility at home, and peace abroad. Thus, traits of integral humanity will be strengthened, as and when development philosophy is guided by such governmental policies for social building notion.

41. Confidence will come from such circumstances, when there is the possibility of rebuilding economy for common people of a nation-state, who are assured of a means of livelihood. In this regard, inaugural address of Chiang Kai-shek is quite relevant, which goes like: "Within the limits set by the Allied Powers, Japan should be allowed to rebuild its economy so its common people may be assured of a means of livelihood". – Yanaga, Chitoshi: "Japan since Perry", McGraw-Hill Book Company, Inc., New York, 1949, p. 645. Thus, mutual relationship has the dominant role to play for peaceful industrial progress, agricultural development and social reformations to open new avenues for every citizen in respective nation-states. Evidentially, Japan has now been considered successful not only for bare necessities of the Japanese people, but also to expand the output of her industries, and to grow in all fields of business. Today, in Asia, Japan has charted a course for peace and international cooperation, intent on regaining her position and prestige in the family nations.

42. For doing this, we must expand the field on our diplomatic relationships in positive direction. Internally, government agencies are to be rectified through restructuring bureaucratic system for increasing people's welfare through efficient delivery mechanism. With the situational change of time and population increase

in every country, there should be efficient productivity in all fields of national economy; so that the entire nation comes up as: when tiger-forces together going for pray. Our challenging notion to fulfill hopes and aspirations of people will bind them in changing social structure to the path of salvation. Thus, Samar Deb opines: "The social structure is required to be considered for the ultimate development of the social wheel to the pious journey of human life, to a stage of global civilizing norms; in concentrating the idea of universal upliftment of human beings in a unified nature of living". – Deb, Samar: "Global Principles on Management", Dominant Publishers & Distributors Pvt. Ltd., New Delhi, 2014, p. 309.

43. For this, we must have to review our policy for joint and continuous efforts from time-to-time. Thus, organizational leadership should have the mind-set to rectify things in bringing strength of their people. As an example, the "reversion" campaign in Japan can again, be cited about the "Treaty of Mutual Security and Cooperation" which was as due in 1970. However, this had in consequence, that the United States promised "joint and continuous review" of Okinawa's status, and as a manifest of ultimate intentions, the Johnson Administration permitted the reversion to Japan of the Ogasawara (Bonin) Islands in June, 1968. – Clyde, Paul H. and Beers, Burton F.: "The Far East. A History of the Western Impact and the Eastern Response (1830-1970)", Prentice-Hall India Private Limited, New Delhi, 1974, pp. 469-70. So, the goals and objectives are to be redefined in new dimensional order for eradicating problems of the socio-economic scenario, so as to strengthen international cooperation, financial support, technical aid policies, and enlarge ideas of international responsibilities.

44. Social orientation process in German is quite elucidative in this context, because it is observed that they (German people) can have weight in international law. The reason behind this is that ever since the twelfth century the eastern provinces have been cultivated and almost exclusively settled by Germans and by them brought to economy prosperity and cultural efflorescence. ... ... And that all alterations of such frontiers can be established only through a free-negotiated peace settlement. – Arntz, Helmut: "Germany in a Nutshell", Public Document Published by the Press and Information Office of the Federal Government of Germany, 1960, pp. 20-21. In this document, it is laudable to suggest that: "The educative aim of all schools is to inculcate independent thought and responsible action, to develop an independent personality and the idea of public responsibility, respect for the convictions of others, love of one's country and its people, to advance devotion to peace and to stress cooperation between peoples". – *Op. cit.,* p. 99. Thus, the system of schooling should be made an instrument of holistic social change by means of harmonizing a learning culture, as observed in case of Germany.

45. In reconciling our objectives for poverty alleviation, we should use latest development of scientific inventions. Poverty alleviation can be made through renaissance in technological reformations, which could be applied in all fields of human living parameters. Thus, the discovery of America and the exploration of Asia, the demands of industry and the extension of commerce, turned up knowledge. – Durant, Will: "The Reformation", Vol. 6, Will Durant Foundation, USA, 2002, p. 849. But that, we should not ignore traditional beliefs and encourage people through fresh thoughts, which helps in social building process

by all means of scientific investigative mind of human beings. By means of scientific investigations and technological renovation of things, social reconciliation should be strengthened to communicate things for human upliftment, progress and social moving in right directions. Again, Gandhi held the view on such reconciliation thus: "My conviction is that as long as we do not enter into political field with 'Dharmic' aims, so long we will be unable to succeed in the pure and true amelioration of India". – Quoted by Chakravarthy, Gargi: "Gandhi and Communal Problem in Twenties", Mainstream, September 29, 1973, p. 35. Probably, this is the reason for which he (Gandhi) talked of Indian independence as Ram Raj, the rule of the Hindu God, Rama; the struggle for it was to him Dharma Yudha which to anyone would mean Hindu religious war". – Hansan, K. Sarwar: "Gandhi and the Congress: A Muslim View", in Lews, M. D. (Ed.), "Gandhi Maker of Modern India", p. 44. All these utterances were made by Gandhi, because he was inspired by the religious faith of the Gita, a holy scripture which can solve problems of human life; if perfectly followed for social emancipation of human beings, in making journey towards the path of liberation.

46. Regarding delivery mechanism, we must care for scientific and technological development. – Datt, S. C., Pandey, T., Joshi, K. V. and Srivastava, S. B. (Eds.): "Sources of India's Strength", Vani Educational Books, New Delhi, 1984, p. 154. For civic living pursuits, we are to narrow down the disparities in the distribution of income and wealth. Thus, V. K. R. V. Rao has stressed the need for framing programmes according to the needs of different states. – *Op. cit.,* p. 342. P. R. Brahmananda, a noted economist, further giving a serious warning for halting our population. He said that unrestrained leap in our population will result in poverty, hunger, unemployment and social tensions. Hence, it can be safely predicted that necessities of civic living will be provided easily, when we go to curb population increase. Again, serving all segments of the population requires cooperative federalism; because, it emphasizes the inter-dependence and cooperation between the various levels of government. – Maheshwari, S. R.: "Comparative Government and Politics", Lakshmi Narain Agarwal, Agra, 1985, p. 106. It will strengthen organizational entities for bringing effectiveness in civic living parameters and is suggested for the reason that development is a total concept. It thus, makes for the deeper economic pressures, which go to follow that political development emerges as a dependent variable in the social system. Thus, Binder, referred to political development as: "Changes in the type and style of politics". – Binder, Leonard: "Crises and Sequences in Political Development", Princeton University Press, Princeton, 1971, p. 66.

47. For doing this, the case of the Janata Party Government can be referred here, because after assuming office, this government under the leadership of Prime Minister Morarji Desai traditionally maintained friendly relations with the Soviet Union. – Khanna, V. N.: "Foreign Policy", Vikas Publishing House Pvt. Ltd., New Delhi, 2012 (Reprint), p. 298. For regional economic cooperation, we are to strengthen relationships, particularly, SAARC areas – this could help in brotherhood relations in trade, industry and commerce for mutual benefits of the respective countries and their citizens. Nationalistic tendencies in behavioural prudence should be reviewed. In this regard, it can be said that Vajpayee's visit to Indonesia, the country with largest Muslim population, was highly significant.

– *Op. cit.,* p. 353. This way, we can strengthen our policies for "East-West" cooperation in building all nations through mutual environmental relational approach as well as socio-economic activities.

48. Thus, we may use the concept of Giuseppe Mazzini (1805-72), a nationalist theorist, who inspired nationalist liberation or unification movements (e.g. Young Italy, Young Poland) in various parts of nineteenth-century Europe. It is because, his vision of the coming age of international harmony was ecstatic. His remarks in this context are like: "... ... As children of the same mother, as brethren gathered together, the peoples shall assemble around those altars, and make sacrifice in peace and love". – Cited in Hayes, P.: "Industry and Ideology", Cambridge University Press, Cambridge, 1987. It is the recall for human diversities in living pursuits in unity and integrity. Again, green economics, organized now-a-days has been considered to the alternatives to the traditional economics of growth. Because, it necessarily introduces a new dimension into economic decision-making: the needs of future generations. – Eatwell, Roger and Wright, Anthony (Eds.): "Contemporary Political Ideologies", Rawat Publications, New Delhi, 2003, p. 240. Thus, it seems that living diversities are to be made universal in terms of thinking for the future generations.

49. In this connection, we may quote Kirkpatrick, an American Bio-regionalist: "Nature works with more flexibility and fluidity. But the general contours of the regions themselves are not hard to identify, and indeed will probably be felt, understood or sensed, in some way known to many of the inhabitants ... ... or those still in touch with a culture that for centuries knew the earth as sacred and its well-being as imperative". – Sale, Kirkpatrick: "Mother of All", in Satish Kumar (Ed.), "The Schumacher Lectures", Vol. 2, Abacus, London, 1974, pp. 226-7. For a useful discussion of the relationship between ecologies and liberal principles, see Mark Sagoff, "The Economy of the Earth", Cambridge University Press, Cambridge, 1988. Our goal is to attain integrity by all kinds of developmental strategies adopted for human emancipation.

50. For making positive change, it is enclosed in nothing but an empirical framework, predicts thus Rathore. – Rathore, L. S.: "Relevance of Political Theory", Rawat Publications, New Delhi, 2010, p. 50. So, human living practices are to be guided by the philosophy of co-association principles, which give birth to human cooperative endeavours in attaining goals. In the absence of a philosophic framework in life, theory is 'bound to be without direction and barren of meaning', further comments Rathore. – *Ibid.,* p. 50. The scale of change in technological field can be felt from the Japanese organizational positions and social environment. – Deb, Samar: "Contemporary Issues on Management", Atlantic Publishers and Distributors, New Delhi, 2001, p. 96. It is therefore, communication and information processing requires effective implementation by modern organizations to make human life orientation, as it is the biggest force of organizational change. – *Op. cit.,* p. 97.

51. In restoring human justice, we are to reduce regional imbalances by all means of technological set-up. It requires separate economic policies for vulnerable states, like the North-Eastern region of India, in order to create avenues of employment for the unemployed youths. – See also, Baruah, Apurba and Dev, Rajesh (Eds.): "Ethnic Identities and Democracy", Regency Publications, New Delhi, 2006,

p. 35. Further, there should be administrative and judicial reforms to look after interests of ethnic groups living in these remote areas of the country. It is helpful for reducing armed violence within the states of the N. E. Region. So, tribal groups are to be protected well in time, so as to democratize socio-economic activities for their upliftment, along with all other people living in this backward zone of the country. Altogether, human justice should prevail for holistic development.

52. The dynamic path which is showing illuminated picture for social changing phenomenon requires assessment of the contributions of Sufis. In this regard, works of Aquil has predicted that we shall also see the Sufis' valuable contribution to what is traditionally referred to as syncretism and synthesis in the field of religion and culture. – Aquil, Raziuddin: "Sufism, Culture, and Politics", Oxford University Press, New Delhi, 2007, p. 205. Thus, there should be a good planning for social reconstruction, taking all in the ship of development, which would supplement human growth potentials for social rejuvenation purposes. Nevertheless, the economic compulsions must equally govern foreign policy. In the context of Indian scenario, V. P. Dutt predicts that it would be India's economic health, the well-being of the people and social and political cohesion that would determine India's place and role in the world. – Dutt, V. P.: "India's Foreign Policy in Changing World", Vikas Publishing House Pvt. Ltd., New Delhi, 2010, p. 19. Every country, in this age of technological development has two types of responsibility – (i) Firstly, it has to strengthen its internal policies; and (ii) Secondly, there should be international cooperation in dynamics behavioural relationships. In this way, we are to plan for harmonizing our relationships with the larger interests of the people of the world, and must have a close interaction with the global communities. This is the challenge of change ahead for collective development, which we are to utilize with energetic as well as passionate courage for developing nations with the road-map of only one mantra – "development mantra".

53. It cannot be denied that the vast increase in the population of most of the countries has immensely complicated the problem of providing food, shelter and other necessities of life to their citizens. – Basu, Rumki: "Public Administration – Concepts and Theories", Sterling Publishers Private Limited, New Delhi, 2012, p. 84. Our reasons behind adopting indiscriminative policies are guided to the facts that inequalities, among men and nations have been one of the most critical social, economic and political characteristics of our time. For worldwide emancipation of human beings, it is very much necessary that the world communities should go for reconciliation policies, which will be fruitful for making a definite step in the way of the decolonization process adopted under the auspices of the 'League of Nations'. It could thus satisfy all parties to some extent. – Haas, E. B.: "The Reconciliation of Conflicting Colonial Policy Aims: Acceptance of the League of Nations Mandate System" in International Organization, Vol. VI, 1952, pp. 521-36. So, while encountering with the policies of organizational system of human up-gradation, developed nations should recognize in the most solemn manner that the helpless and underdeveloped people and nations are carefully taken into consideration, for overcoming their problems of poverty, increasing social stability and transforming the technological base in reformative paths, to create socially viable environment of peaceful living in

this world. Hence, the principles of international human cooperation are to uphold views regarding holistic welfare – it is welfare in the sense of solution of human problems of life, culmination of equal rights and powers, nationalism practices through universal quest for living together in between nation-states, tolerance in terms of equal rights in doing trade and business activities, mutual collaboration for technological up-gradation and utilization of knowledge-base in all areas of social rejuvenation process, and among others; instrumental policy for international brotherhood philosophizing aspects of human potential growth as well as all-round development. For eradicating thus, sufferings of people the world policy of President Roosevelt addressed on 4 March, 1933 could be much useful, which goes like: "I would dedicate this Nation to the policy of the Good Neighbour – the neighbour who resolutely respects himself and, because he does so, respects the rights of others. – Johari, J. C.: "International Relations and Politics", Sterling Publishers Private Limited, New Delhi, 1985, p. 290. It is therefore, permeably said that economic reconstruction contributes to national and international well-being, as well as to peace among nations.

54. The pillars of human dignifying principles are to be based on human empowerment in scientific temper of thought. In this context, it is notably said that peaceful collaboration between representatives of various States and the development of intellectual interchange among their peoples is conducive to an understanding by each of the problems of the other as well as of problems common to all, and makes more readily possible the peaceful adjustment of international controversies.

55. These ideals are reflected thus: "Countries without great economic power but with a great cultural wealth should regard the projection of their culture as a political operation of the first order and should entrust it to high-powered and competent persons". – Hayter, Sir William: "The Diplomacy of the Great Powers", Hamish Hamilton, London, 1960, p. 40. As such it needs to draw on all its resources of skill and on the great riches of its national heritage. – *Ibid.*, p. 41. Thus, it is worthwhile to note that the French diplomacy in areas of leadership skill, that is only the diplomacy of country, and has made it a "Great Power" illuminate commendable example of the task for initiating our inter-activeness, in the group leadership cohesiveness for civic living goals and objectives, to bind people with such kind of benevolence thoughts.

56. In justifying so, it can be said that there should be "a spirit of enquiry and search for truth which are the guiding principles in judicial approach characterize judges' pronouncements on social, educational, and cultural matters". – Gajendragadkar, P. B.: "Law, Liberty and Social Justice", Asia Publishing House, New York, 1965, p. 14. It seems thus, in matching resources we must put attention towards reducing problems of human beings, particularly, which are of immensely requirement for civic living, like – education, health and cultural dimensions. Hence, equanimity as well as equipoise nature of doing things can be real judgment in scientific parlance of serving the society.

57. All such things are attributable to unscientific thoughts for our religious philosophy. Actual idea of religion is consistent with the norms of social-building. In modern society, according to Stephen Fuchs: "Religion rouses and gives expression to the consciousness of the community in its members; and by so

doing it stimulates and strengthens the intention to maintain the common life". – Fuchs, Stephen: "The Origin of Man and His Culture", Munshiram Manoharlal Publishers Pvt. Ltd., New Delhi, 1983, p. 211. Thus, this would eventually indicate the unexplored chapter which is the base line for implementing future program. – Vidyarthi, L. P. and Upadhyay, V. S. (Eds.): "Development of Researches in Anthropology in India", Concept Publishing Company, New Delhi, 1981, p. 114. From a comprehensive picture of the genetic composition of the groups concerned in societies, it can be predicted that pathetic ills are created by multiple forces of fission and fusion, which are operating in this particular field. It is thus evident, that there should be a unique base to study some of the processes of human evolution. Again, Harris suggested that the task of discovering human laws could be done by studying the material constraints to which human existence is subjected. Such material constraints rose from the need to produce food, shelter, tools, machines, and to reproduce human populations within limit set by biology and the environment. – Sharma, A. N.: "Anthropology in Human Welfare", Sarup & Sons, New Delhi, 2007, p. 107.

58. Universal integrity in raising the living standard between the tribal and non-tribal requires an aim to bridge the gap by improving conditions – socially, economically and educationally to minimize their social differentiation. – *Ibid.,* p. 156. In this way, transformation caused by the impact of modernization could change economic pattern of living in beings, which will result in good interaction and cultural contact with different groups. This is the peaceful as well as harmonious way of leading with the things. For integrative thought, our idea of performing duty can reach at the goal of organizational objectivity. Thus, Kant assumes the duty and self-interest are the only two motives of actions. – Paton, The Moral Law, pp. 14-15. Rationalization also emphasizes the notion of duty or moral obligation. – Sinha, Jadunath: "A Manual of Ethics", New Central Book Agency (P) Ltd., Calcutta, 1998, p. 148. Hence, human living necessities are to be guided by the principles of the highest good, for which our conscience has to be identified well. Perfectionists also stressed on this point of identifying our conscience, like – J. M. Murihead has said that we are to identify conscience with the whole self legislating for its parts or aspects. He asserts therefore that conscience is original, intuitive and universal; it is the whole self apprehending the highest good. – *Op. cit.,* p. 78.

59. While Ayer avoids the crude view that all ethical judgments are really commands, he agrees with Carnap that whereas all judgments proper have two characteristics – that of expressing a state of mind and that of asserting something, ethical judgments assert nothing, and mere expressions of a state of mind in which we are liking certain kinds of conduct and wishing others to behave accordingly. – *Op. cit.,* pp. 254-55; Ross, Foundations of Ethics, 1939, p. 34. Again, Russel regards value-judgments as expressions of our emotions, and he predicted that conscientious feelings are explained by the operation of the unconscious wishes. – Russel, Bertrand: "Religion and Science", 1935, p. 227. But, H. A. Prichard recognizes the uniqueness of the concept of good; whereas the Deontologists deny that an action, to be right, ought to make the greatest total contribution of goodness to the world. Finally, C. D. Board does not regard good as pleasantness or any other non-ethical characteristic, but considers it to be unique. – Board, C. D.: "Five Types of Ethical Theory", pp. 164-65. All these are the backgrounds

of our belief on which we are to stand erect for the inclination of making a right journey in our. In a nutshell, it is required full freedom in the choice of making our life realizable through work perfections as well as uniqueness in empowering people for their correct vision on democratic methods of work. At the present time, opinion plays a dominant role in the selection of a criterion of leadership. – Zelst, R. H. Van: "Empathy Test Scores and Union Leaders", Jour. Appl. Psychol., 1952, 36, 293-295. For further understanding on such issues, readers are suggested to go through Meyer, H. H.: "Factors Related to Success in the Human Relations Aspect of Work-Group Leadership", Psychol. Mono., 1951, 65, 1-29.

60. By recognizing the value that already exists, it is possible to establish methods of remuneration which increase production by encouraging the expression of individual differences, and which, at the same time, do not conflict with the needs for social development and progress. – Maier, Norman R. F.: "Psychology in Industry", Houghton Mifflin Company, Boston, 1955, p. 398. Hence, objectives of leadership should be guided by the philosophy of classifying jobs, comparisons, technical knowledge, and a typical approach to solve problems of human life in transforming societal foundation. Also, Lincoln, J. F.: "Incentive Management: A New Approach to Human Relationships in Industry and Business"; Spriegel, W. R.: "Personnel Management" (5th Ed.); Viteles, M. S., *Op. cit.;* Whyte, W. F.: "Economic Incentives and Human Relations", Harvard Bus. Rev., 1952, 30, 73-80 is all important guidelines for assessing the factors of social stratification in coming to human existential norms of living.

61. To work-out dormant potentialities 'Role-Playing' is an important area which could be useful for knowing that people grow with the trust and responsibility with proper kind of consideration for care with the characteristic nature of human beings. Hence, workers in industry should be treated like, the child and the employer, are human beings. These are all having reflective feelings in mind of people, which could be reflected through association of people by means of 'give-and-take' relationship. In this way, counselling can help in working out skills of individuals with the free learning environment, which favors both – the employers and employees.

62. Up-gradation of human life means knowing the bliss of Brahman, he does not fear anything. – Taittirîya Up. ii. 8. In this context, the Rig Veda gives: "May I reach the light on reaching which one attains freedom from fear". –Rig Veda, ii. 27. Thus, Radhakrishnan while explaining the Hindu view has remarked: "When one is in contact with the universal source of life, one is filled with vitality and freedom from fear. – Radhakrishnan, S.: "Eastern Religions and Western Thought", Oxford University Press, Delhi, 1989, p. 45. Commenting on the Chapters of the Gita, Kuppuswami explains: "The blissful grace of Brahman is experienced by those ascetics (sannyâsins) who have freed themselves from attachment (kâma) and anger, who have control over their minds and who have understood âtman (self) being experienced both in the life here (while living in this human body) and in the life hereafter (and after the death of this body). – Kuppuswami, A.: "Bhagavad Gîtâ", Chaukhambha Orientalia, Delhi, 2005, p. 169. Thus, managing our activities for human up-gradation requires knowledge of Indian scriptural order.

63. North-East India has a special identification in the areas of spinning and weaving and handicraft. The people here produce cloth for themselves, and in addition they, very efficiently weave furnishing cloth, carpets and shawls. These help them in improving their financial condition. – Bhushan, Chandra: "Terrorism and Separatism in North-East India", Kalpaz Publications, Delhi, 2007, p. 57. But in the North-East India, terrorism has played a dominant role for which people of this area have been suffering a lot. Consequently, it has regionalism due to backwardness and undue advantage being taken on those.

64. Poverty alleviation, first of all requires elimination of corruption, castes, religious dogmatism, etc. For developing people, an agricultural country like India should produce enough so as to spare for exports. – Nanda, J. N.: "Conflicts and Co-existence India", Concept Publishing Company, New Delhi, 1991, p. 53. Political parties are now, to put their attention for social-building and nation-building activities. Again, the entire technical manpower could be relatively easily harnessed to education, sanitation and recycling of materials. It is the excess of agricultural production which eventually will finance all industrial and service projects. Government should look into matters like – anti-poverty, environmental issues and conservation programmes, including monitoring of the great programmes. Thus, we require harnessing poverty by means of mutual co-existence for peaceful living in society as well as reducing social imbalances.

65. These are all coming under cultural identities, which Malinowski's view reflect that it (cultural identity) could not be defined by its form alone. – Sarana, Gopâla: "Sociology and Anthropology and Other Essays", Institute of Social Research and Applied Anthropology, Calcutta, 1983, p. 61. Thus, there is a process of refinement in life of a nation to fulfill the growing aspirations of her citizens as well as to play a constructive political role at the global level. – Jha, Makhan: "An Introduction to Social Anthropology", Vikas Publishing House Pvt. Ltd., New Delhi, 1994, pp. 123-24. Modern nation-building activities are to be implemented through a particular ideology for the welfare of the citizens of the world.

66. All these require value-based education and spiritual wisdom of human beings. It is because, today various reports indicate that there is a sharp decline in morality in not of India but all the societies of the world. – Mazumder, Arundhati, Datta, Devasree, and Biswas, Sarbani (Eds.): "Human Development: Perspectives and Dimensions", Research and Publication Cell, Wemen's College, Silchar, 2013, p. 73.

67. It can be asserted that the International Biological Programme provides a great opportunity to take stock of human adaptability as it is manifested at the present time in a wide variety of terrains, climates and social gaps, to deepen our knowledge of its biological and to apply this knowledge to problems of health and welfare. – Malhotra, R.: "Bio Anthropology of High Altitude People", Mittal Publications, New Delhi, 1989, p. 15. Thus, for human development potentials we are to do all this satisfactorily, for communities ranging from the very simple to the highly industrialized, requires an integrated approach and an application of methods drawn from many fields, particularly those of human environmental physiology, population genetics and developmental biology aided by auxiliary disciplines, for example in medicine, anthropology, ecology and demography.

68. To make the technology of human development successful, Malinowski's version of thought is illuminating, when he comments: "This somewhat pedantic discussion of the scientific quota in social studies needs no apology. There is no doubt that in the present crisis of our civilization we have risen to vertiginous heights in the mechanical and chemical sciences, pure and applied, and in materialistic theory and mechanical engineering". – Malinowski, Bronislaw: "A Scientific Theory of Culture and Other Essays", Oxford University Press, London, 1944, p. 13. But, it is sure that we have neither faith in all, nor respect for the conclusions of humanistic arguments, nor yet in the validity of social theories. So, our behaviour should correspond closely to our concept of institution and its component parts. We should be also instrumental in performance in terms of objectivity, techniques, cooperation, transmission, as well as orientation; in so far as science and technology relates to human development perspective.

69. As to this fact, management personnel in different organizations have expressed that they consider it possible to evolve a national wage policy for industrial workmen in India. – Mathur, A. N.: "Dynamics of Wages", Popular Prakashan, Bombay, 1986, p. 136. Again, government officials and employers' representatives have also indicated that they consider national wage policy feasible. But, in regard to all such assumptions, disagreement is expressed more clearly by internal trade union leaders who consider their role being reduced in the wake of emergence of national policy framework. Thus, creative managerial guidance could not arrive at a qualitative pattern of human performance. Accordingly, quality assurance practice requires two methods, particularly, in areas of revenue earning and government expenditure, by which inflation and rising prices can be countered. These are: (a) to bring the government expenditure below its revenue, and (b) to raise the government revenue above the expenditure. – Agarwala, R. K.: "American Economic Development. History and Analysis", Kitab Mahal Private Ltd., Allahabad, 1965, p. 42. Hence, there should be scientific idea behind the social security program, for which initiative and cooperation should be from the state governments, if at all, quality has to be enhanced in public organizations; besides administering and exercise central control mechanism. On the other hand, basic policy in China is determined by the Communist Party, on the principle that the Party provides leadership for the state (the administrative organs of government), and the state manages the economy. Thus, Morris Bornstein remarks: "China's economic management system is by international standards, extraordinarily centralized and characterized by strict vertical control, with relatively few horizontal linkages". – Bornstein, Morris: "Comparative Economic Systems. Models and Cases", Surjeet Publications, Delhi, 1987, p. 244. So, the response of units at the bottom to changes of policy at the top is remarkably quick and uniform. In this way, managerial guidance has its relevance to achieve quality in modern organizations, and to assess the zeal for utmost performance, it is regardless to be said that: "Money has a social existence. It does not exist in a Crusoe economy". – Chand, Mahesh and Lohkar, R. N.: "Aspects of Economic Theory, Liquidity, Growth and Policy in India", Chugh Publications, Allahabad, 1973, p. 97. To restore quality thus, we are to be careful in handling money which makes hoarding and black marketing, and even smuggling convenient. Our quality assurance should therefore be attempted through discharging social responsibilities for general

welfare of people, with the honesty, integrity and dignity of work culture, propounded by the concept of technological reformations and the practice of its uses which leads to scientific pricing of factors of production, goods and services in terms of money. – *Op. cit.,* p. 97.

70. Otherwise, the free play of the market forces, as Myrdal expresses as a result of circular and cumulative cauzation normally tends to increase rather than decrease inequality between regions, and the 'spread effects' of the growth of the advanced regions will be too weak to flow to the backward regions which will remain steeped in poverty unless State intervenes with an effective redistributive policy. – Myrdal, G., *Op. cit.,* p. 31. It is no wonder, that intrastate disparities are as glaring as the inter-state disparities. – Mahajan, O. P.: "Economic Planning and Regional Development in India", Ess Ess Publications, New Delhi, 1982. If, however, increase in the prices of the products of the backward regions does not bring about increase in their production, and low elasticity of supply in the backward regions themselves to act as drag on the advance of the growing areas through adverse terms of trade, they may begin to develop their primary resources or shift to imports, and thus the spread effects may not trickle down to the backward areas which would be further left behind. Such conditions had existed in the backward regions like Brazil's Nordeste, Colombia's Oriente and Italy's Mezzogiorno. – Hirschman, A. O., *Op. cit.,* p. 189. As a matter of fact, the problem of regional imbalance is mostly the problem of a few developed, urbanized, metropolitan regions in a few states – less developed as well as more developed – surrounded, beyond the immediate periphery, by backwardness. So, it is suggested that in modern technological upheavals, we are needed urgent attention towards solving human social problems, for which people-oriented tasks are to be assessed as the measure of human development strategy.

71. Castes and sub-castes were seen essentially as a system of a restructured hierarchy in case of India. – Chakraborty, Rabindra Nath: "National Integration in Historical Perspective", Mittal Publications, Delhi, 1985, p. 113. Thus, regional disparities in India have increased day-by-day and years-after-years, which must be curbed through "methodology" which involves the interpretation or "rationalization" of the procedures used by individuals in their investigations. – Tarascio, Vincent J.: "Pareto's Methodological Approach to Economics", The University of North Carolina Press, Chapel Hill, 1968, p. 85. Again, we observe that Comte attempted to "generalize" science. He aimed at creating a "philosophy of the sciences". – Lewes, G. H.: "Comte's Philosophy of the Sciences", George Bell & Sons, London, 1904, pp. 8-9. We therefore, require methodologies of the physical and social sciences to arrive at a valid source of scientific knowledge, which will go to reduce social disparities in time and space, reduce human diseases, increase human cooperative endeavors toward reaching at social as well as regional balance, in terms of human up-gradation through all the tools and techniques of modern age.

72. Modern science has adopted so many techniques of human development process, of which, according to the Vedanta thinkers, it is the human psyche, the mind that is chiefly instrumental for man's all bondages and salvations. – Barche, G. D.: "Shakespeare's Select Tragedies: A Post-Colonial Study in Patanjali's Psychology", Yking Books, Jaipur, 2010, p. 45. So, the vision of the path leads to the better and higher life. For this, human beings are needed the right knowledge

which is utmost significance, as it alone helps one reach the Kaivalya, i.e., a liberated state. – *Ibid.,* p. 144. It is therefore truly suggested that our measures for technological innovative practices should be guided by the philosophy of the eternal truth of life regarding the operations of the human mind. – *Op. cit.,* p. 137. Because, man's bondage is caused by the mind, and liberation too is caused by the mind alone.

73. About this, we discover that Rousseau has proposed an ideal which, though constantly exceeding our limited grasp is capable of inspiring humanity toward a brighter future. – Havens, George R.: "The Age of Ideas", The Free Press, New York, 1965, p. 277. In regard to understanding on the concept of tranquil social order, Rousseau's book on the 'Social Contract' has its illuminative discourses, in which the basic relationship between people and ruler has been reflected quite in a lucid manner. It is evident from the picture that Rousseau cries: "Man is born free and everywhere he is enslaved". Again, in a speech on May 10th, 1793, Robespierre, obviously imitating Jean-Jacques Rousseau, exclaimed: "Man is born for happiness and freedom, yet everywhere he is unhappy and enslaved". – Thompson, J. M.: "Robespierre", Oxford University Press, London, Vol. II, p. 47. Thus, by means of understanding human freedom and reducing corruptive behaviour, we can think of attaining a tranquil social order; instead of various modes of social conflicts which have been prevailing in world environment of living.

74. My research findings (1993, 19-41), comments thus Makarand, regarding the folkloric intertextuality support Hindoo's views. – Paranjape, Makarand (Ed.): "Nativism Essays in Criticism", Sahitya Akademi, New Delhi, 1997, p. 181. Thus, to acquire these values by living them is usually to make a permanent addition to one's mental make-up. – *Op. cit.,* p. 37. Because, we have observed that Adam Smith's 'Wealth of Nations', J. S. Mill's 'Political Economy' and 'Application of Science to the Economic History of England' have all represented and supported modern bourgeois economic thoughts and views born in the modern economic world. – *Ibid.,* p. 38. So, our research activities are to be based on the concept of the Vedanta, as enumerated elsewhere in this Chapter, to try to work-out the best out of the serious Indian thinkers – to understand the capitalist economic system. About the use of knowledge of classical Economics made by the nationalist leaders, Professor Bipan Chandra writes: "Though India was changing, the transition, the intellectuals came to hold, was from traditional, pre-colonial or feudal pattern of backwardness to colonial backwardness where limited modern development, especially in the fields of trade and transport occurs, transforming the country into a new material producing and processing as well as capital absorbing country, leading to backward agriculture, repressed industry, and foreign domination of economic life". – Chandra, Bipan (Ed.): "Ranade's Economic Writings", Gian Publishing House, New Delhi, 1990, Introduction, pp. IX-XI. Thus, knowledge base programme should be undertaken for making research activities effective towards the path of holistic human development process in modern times.

75. Today's English literature is full of exposures which are made to contribute mainly for explaining cruelty, unscrupulous intelligence, conventional and traditional methods of discussions connoting ideas of wholly unmoral grounds.

To the contrary, to overcome romanticism of life, we are to add values in society through our creative writing system and training skills, like: "A special, express, and unique communication from God to lead mankind to truth and virtue". – Diaches, David: "A Critical History of English Literature", Vol. IV, Allied Publishers Limited, New Delhi, 1994 (Reprint), p. 261. The techniques of learning by training can in this way be viewed in reality, for renunciation and self-discipline in human life. Further, our creative thoughts in writing should be reflected for sensitizing people to the path of liberation, humanism, historical and psychological interpretation of religion, culture to set the values and ideals which could strengthen social pillars, primarily for developing all kinds of human beings through the latest modern technological communication system. Robert M. Gagne and Edwin A. Fleishman comments on culture thus: "Each culture has a distinctive pattern of its own which is reflected in the behaviour of all its members. This fact is especially important because it makes possible certain predictions about human behaviour. Knowing the culture of which the person is a part helps us predict certain aspects of his behaviour, just as knowing about his abilities and skills help us to predict other aspects". – Gagne, Robert M. and Fleishman, Edwin A.: "Psychology and Human Performance", Holt, Rinehart and Winston, New York, 1959, p. 294. Linton has said that in case of learning, our cultural background has tremendous role playing impact on personality development. So, when he considers culture, it is defined as the "sum total of behaviour patterns, attitudes and values, shared and transmitted by members of a given society". – Linton, R.: "The Cultural Background of Personality", Appleton-Century, New York, 1945. To develop masses there should be effective supervision, and for doing this, Hemphill had recorded long back ten categories which seemed to cover the range of supervising activities. Initiation, representation, fraternization, organization, domination, recognition, production emphasis, integration, communication down and communication up – these are classified as the sorted points included into his categories. – Hemphill, J. K.: "Leader Behavior Description", Personnel Research Board, Ohio State University, Ohio, Columbus, 1950. Hence, it is reasonably to be noted that our programmes for human development requires planning scientifically for increasing training skills and learning qualities, which will accommodate free cultural assimilation; along with environmental conditions to sensitize people in understanding social values with creative thought.

76. In this regard, you have got to treat with disrespect whatever does not fit into the physical world, remarks thus Bertrand Russell. He further explains: "But that is really very unfair to the things that do not fit in. They are just as much there as the things that do. The physical world is a sort of governing aristocracy, which has somehow managed to cause everything else to be treated with disrespect. That sort of attitude is unworthy of a philosopher. We should treat with exactly equal respect the things that do not fit in with the physical world, and images are among them". – Russell, Bertrand: "The Philosophy of Logical Atomism", The Bertrand Russell Peace Foundation Ltd., New York, 2010, p. 96. In that way you can have established continuity. You have not in fact done so. It seems therefore that in implementing technological ideas, we must have holistic views. Because, Sri Jibendra comments: "Now with all this data of creation given, of involution and evolution of the divine consciousness, it will not be difficult to

follow the evolutionary process which is the sole theme of the Divine life". – Jibendra, Sri: "Sri Aurobindo's Philosophy and Yoga. Some Aspects", Sahityasree, Calcutta, 1983, pp. 60-61. In pushing through human skill building ideas, we should consider all these at the summits of human mental intelligence have still to work under the shadow of the ignorance cast on them when the Divine created them and gave them freedom to separate their consciousness from the supreme divine consciousness, that is, these intelligent human beings are still subject to the original in-conscience illumined to some extent by progressive growth of knowledge and consciousness culminating in the attainment of the supreme divine consciousness through various turns and vicissitudes of ignorance in several lives of continuous self-progression towards the supreme self-knowledge. – *Ibid.*, p. 61.

77. For this, we are to remember that which is painful leads to aversion. – *Ibid.*, p. 149. In transcendentalism, the main motives for action — pleasure and pain has to be taken carefully. Because, Sinha summarizes: Visvanatha analyses a positive volition (pravritti) to realize a good into the following elements: (a) a desire to act (chikirsha) or perform a voluntary action; (b) the cognition that it can be done by one's volition (kritisadhyatajnana); (c) cognition that it is means to one's good (ishthasadhanata jnanam); (d) the absence of the cognition that it is productive of a stronger evil (balavadanishth-anaubandhitva jnanabhana); and (e) the perception of the materials of action (upadana pratyaksha). – Sinha, J.: "Indian Psychology – Emotion and Will", Vol. II, Sinha Publishing House, Calcutta, 1961, p. 505. In the Gita, it is shown that theory of motivation assumes that action based on mere desires and hatreds, likes and dislikes, belong to the lower level of personality and that principles should govern actions". – Kuppuswamy, B.: "Elements of Ancient Indian Psychology", Vikas Publishing House Pvt. Ltd., New Delhi, 1985, p. 164. So, dynamic development through transcendentalism will be made possible, when attention is also drawn to the concept of 'lokasangraha', that human action should be conducive to the well-being of society.

78. Here, Sri Aurobindo's teachings are interesting, indeed unique for a major Indian philosopher, in that he presents a very theosophical-anthroposophical cosmology, involving specific planes of existence, subtle psychic faculties, spiritual entities, and long processes of evolution. – Verma, Rajeev: "Faith & Philosophy of Hinduism", Indian Religions series: 1, Kalpaz Publications, Delhi, 2009, p. 185. About the spheres of such balancing phenomenon, again, Tillich notes that the symbols of creation and salvation are reflections of something real in the nature of the divine. – ST, III, p. 283. Thus, the existential balance is opined by Masih in this way: "It should be conceded that and belief and practices which aim at evoking-invoking an all-pervasive attitude, leading to a culture of the soul should also be regarded as religious". – Masih, Y.: "Introduction to Religious Philosophy", Motilal Banarsidass Publishers Private Limited, Delhi, 2012 (Reprint), p. 7. Our policies are therefore required the transcendental idea of a necessary and all-sufficient being, which is so overwhelmingly great, so high above everything empirical, the latter being always conditioned, that it leaves us at a loss, partly because we can never find in experience material to satisfy such a concept, and partly because it is always in the sphere of the conditioned that we carry out our search, seeking there ever vainly for the unconditioned –

no law of any empirical synthesis giving us an example of any such unconditioned or providing the least guidance in its pursuit. – *Ibid.,* p. 206. So, each national government should adopt such policies, by which human existential core of living with technological investigations and applications are confined toward the path of salvation in life, along with satisfying the goal of environmental protective measures.

79. It is experiencing nature as a work of art has been problematized in the twentieth century and yielded a form of aesthetics which can be broadly called "environmental aesthetics". – For a detailed discussion of the various perspectives in environmental aesthetics, see Carlson, Allen: "Aesthetics and the Environment: the Appreciation of Nature, Art and Architecture", Routledge and Kegan Paul, London, 2000. In recent times, different theories of aesthetics of nature have emerged in the West. It also encompasses other dimensions of art (and tradition) such as music, spirituality and the very conceptualization of time through nature. – For interrelationship, and its detailed discussion, between music, painting, aesthetic emotions and experience, see Kaufmann, Walter: "Rasa, Râga-Mâlâ and Performance Times in North Indian Râgas", Ethnomusicology, Vol. 9, No. 3, Sep., 1965, pp. 272-291. Internalizing nature in art would therefore involve using popular markers of time. Hence, nature can be evoked through markers (say, trees, flowers, clouds) which also express nature at a specific time. Again, time in Indian music (not musical time of rhythms and beats) is often experienced through seasons. – See also, Prajnanananda, Swami: "A History of Indian Music", Ramakrishna Vedanta Matha, Kolkata, 1963. Thus, aesthetic experience distinctively involves sensitivity to the subtle nuances of nature and its deep appreciation is achieved here through a process of internalization of certain cultural codes, which where correctly evoked bring about not only an aesthetic experience, but almost bring back nature to be experienced in all its immediacy. – Sivaramakrishnan, Murali and Jana, Ujjwal: "Ecological Criticism for Our Times. Literature, Nature and Critical Inquiry", Authors Press, New Delhi, 2011, p. 144. Thus, environmental consciousness has its relevance to a wider spectrum of human living phenomenon, which requires scientific inquiry into its reach in terms of continuity and interdependence. In comparison with the rapidly changing fields of the hard sciences, it has tremendous role playing value in the humanities as a whole. The modern management in resourceful creativity should therefore, attempt to exploit our environmental resources for the wider benefit of humankind, so as to find-out 'path-goal' relationship toward the utility concept for human development strategies.

80. The ever-renewing organization (or society) is not one which is convinced that it enjoys eternal youth. It knows that it is forever growing old and must do something about it. It knows that it is always producing deadwood and must, for that reason, attend to its seedbeds. The seedlings are new ideas, new ways of doing things, new approaches. – Gardner, John W.: "The Individual and Today's World", Macfadden-Bartell Corporation, New York, 1966, p. 65. Thus, in an organization the mechanism we are concerned here requires, many points of initiative and decision, and also an innovation which stands to better chance of survival. Again, Surti comments on such mechanism which is based on human wisdom, like: "Let us not hold the hand of evil in our hand. Something that is not worth talking about is like a tree which is barren of fruit and devoid of

fragrance. ... ... Instead of uttering evil words, it is better not to do anything. When words are matched with wisdom, they are pleasant to hear". – Surti, Bahman Sohrab: "Shah Namah of Firdaosi", Vol. IV, Dr Bahman S. Surti, Andhra Pradesh, 1988, p. 799. Hence, adequate mechanism on organizational activities requires policies based on human wisdom in coordinating with environmental issues, for societal peace and healthy living practices.

81. As a functional relationship, it can be well asserted that the acquisition of knowledge has therefore been the thrust area throughout the world. Thus, knowledge has always been the prime mover of prosperity and power. Again, during the last century the world has changed from being an agricultural society, in which manual labour was the critical factor, to an industrial society where the management of technology, capital and provide the competitive advantages. – Kalam, Abdul A. P. J.: "Ignited Minds. Unleashing the Power within India", Penguin Books, New Delhi, 2002, pp. 121-122. Thus, our functional relationships need special attention toward the aspects of utilizing efficiently the existing knowledge base for innovative creation as wealth production, in the form of health, education and other indicators of progress. A. P. J. Abdul Kalam therefore writes: "The ability to create and maintain the knowledge infrastructure, to enhance skills and increase productivity through the exploitation of advances in various fields will be the key factors in deciding the prosperity of this society". – *Ibid.,* p. 122. Hence, functional relationships in organizational perspective should be found through societal foundation and transformational processes, leading to develop the core areas like – education, healthcare, agriculture and governance; and all these will ultimately, lead to the process of employment creation and generation, increasing productivity and, at the same time, rural prosperity in parallel way.

82. As a pollution control mechanism for building notions toward the concept of biodiversity, there is a great challenge today of treating sewage which is more than installing a technology that will do the job. – Rana, S. V. S.: "Environmental Biotechnology", Rastogi Publications, Meerut, 2010, p. 164. Dynamic social movement requires that the solid waste, often called the third pollution after air and water pollution, and those materials which arises from various human activities should be controlled through effective management of human activities. We should not therefore, normally discard these materials as useless or unwanted. In an age of information technology, our endeavor should be devoted to reduce solid waste, like – domestic, commercial, industrial and agricultural activities, by means of adequate management system and value-based techniques of production, and also creating human consciousness about this fact.

83. To suggest measures on this standpoint, it can be said: "By further judicious control and selection of the herbivores on which humans could come to depend as intermediaries in energy flow, there is a potential for increased efficiency and production at that level". – Kormondy, Edward J.: "Concepts of Ecology", PHI Learning Private Limited, New Delhi, 2012, p. 416. The Earth is ultimately finite in its resources; they are ultimately of limited quality. Demand must come into balance with supply and that portion of the supply that can be recycled must be recycled if human are to survive as a species; and along with the explosive growth rate of population, this is an important point, for meeting the world's

food needs not only a quantitative but also a qualitative matter, with protein needs being the most difficult to meet. – *Op. cit.,* p. 417. So, development must be environmentally sound and sustainable without any constraints to quality of life. – Sharma, P. D.: "Ecology and Environment", Rastogi Publications, Meerut, 2009, p. 353. As the intensive agriculture led to problems of land degradation, water depletion, salinity, mineral deficiency, pest infestations and loss of genetic diversity of crops, so there is the urgent need of initiating programmes to protect, reclaim and manage the land, water and the biological resources which support agriculture and animal husbandry. Thus, a balanced situation should be created through ecology which plays an important role in human welfare, as it influences the areas of agriculture, range management, forestry, fisheries, animal husbandry, wild life management, national park and wilderness preservation, pollution control, oceanography, terrestrial ecosystem, etc. – Verma, S. R., Sharma, R. S. and Shukla, Gopi Rani: "Ecology and Animal Behaviour", Jai Prakash Nath & Co., Meerut, 1995 (Third Edn.), p. 370. Hence, it is essential for human beings to protect its natural environment, as it implies for natural checks and balances through ecological study which involves the role playing model as the control mechanism between the animal and plant populations, and maintains equilibrium between populations.

84. For doing this, we must follow the 'principle of equivalence'. This equivalence is needed to be established through the earth, sun and other bodies of the universe (stars). Bishwanath Chakraborty remarks: "All types of gravitational fields are of the same nature and follow the same fundamental physical laws of nature". – Chakraborty, Bishwanath: "Principles of Electrodynamics", Books and Allied (P) Ltd., Kolkata, 2010 (Reprint), p. 455. This way the principle of equivalence means that the gravitational fields of the earth, sun and other nearby masses cannot be made to disappear by any choice of the reference systems. – *Op. cit.,* p. 456. So, we are to following natural balance in terms of soil, because people's activities are a major influence on the quality and amount of soil references. – Hudson, Travis: "Living with Earth. An Introduction to Environmental Geology", PHI Learning Private Limited, New Delhi, 2011, pp. 327-28. Our policy of protecting soil should be framed in curbing its erosion, by which soil is degraded or lost all around the world. It is very important part of human development, because – soil is a mix of interacting Earth systems. – *Ibid.,* p. 328. Again, it is carefully observed that several diseases, pests and weeds have found their ways from one country to another along with introduced plant materials and have caused tremendous damage and other problems in India. – Shukla, R. S. and Chandel, P. S.: "Cytogenetics, Evolution, Biostatistics and Plant Breeding", S. Chand & Company Ltd., New Delhi, 2009, p. 511. For maintaining organizational dynamicity in work behaviour, to benefit the world society, agricultural resources, climate condition maintenance, weather friendly environment and industrial projects – all require a scientific system for good governance practices, where technology should be connected to illuminate picture of quality human life, in overcoming problems of social hazards.

85. In recourse to such fact, 'Biosphere Reserve' network programme was launched by the UNESCO in 1971. The objectives of such programmes are to – (i) conserve representative samples of ecosystems; (ii) provide long-term in situ conservation of genetic diversity; (iii) promote and facilitate basic and applied research and

monitoring; (iv) provide opportunities for education and training; (v) promote appropriate sustainable managements of the living resource; (vi) disseminate the experience so as to promote sustainable development elsewhere; (vii) promote international cooperation, among others. Hence, in order to evolve a sound strategy for management of endangered species, especially medicinal plants, programmes on seed biology and tissue culture should be initiated effectively, to conserve in situ and mass multiplication of species. To have a sustainable impact, such progress should include identification and enumeration of endangered species on regional basis, systematic studies on reproductive biology, gene pool conservation, artificial propagation in natural habitats, and development of tissue culture techniques for mass multiplication, domestication and of selected threatened species. – Sharma, P. D.: "Environmental Biology", Rastogi Publications, Meerut, 1997, pp. 257-58. These are good suggestions for environmental balance with protective measures, required to be implemented with efficient, judicious and profitable manner for scientific nature of human development process.

86. In this context, A. P. J. Abdul Kalam remarks: "The unification of science and spirituality will be essential to take the benefit of science and technology to mankind". – Kalam, A. P. J. Abdul: "Ignited Minds. Unleashing the Power within India", Penguin Books India Pvt. Ltd., New Delhi, 2002, p. 92. So, it requires equanimity regardless of circumstances in our living situations, by which human beings will be able to transcend the limitation of the physical world and realize the higher self. For this purpose, we have already cited examples of the Vedic thoughts and the Gita's teachings elsewhere in preceding discussions.

87. Thus, Man and Biosphere Program (M&BP) which is in fact, the outcome of the experience of those involved in the International Biological Program (IBP) and has its relevance to environmental problems and its real solution, where interdisciplinary approach is felt by means of emphasis and collective efforts by natural and social scientists. The M&BP therefore, helps bringing together the planners, policy makers, managers and scientists for arriving at a rational decision on the issues of resource management. – Sharma, P. D.: "Ecology and Environment", Rastogi Publications, Meerut, 2009, p. 527.

88. Social structure of the Ao Nagas tribe in the north-eastern part of India is still very much vivid, because the whole territory in which they live consists of one mass of hills, and there are no level stretches, but hill after hill and ridge after ridge with deep valleys between. The hills rise gradually from the low ranges skirting the Brahmaputra valley until in the inner ranges, where there are some peaks above 5000 feet in height. However, in the smaller streams they bridge with bamboo or a single tree trunk, and the bare-footed natives carry their heavy loads, glide over these paths; and though the climate where they live is generally cool, hills are clothed with evergreen forest. The jhum system is the process of their cultivation. – Smith, W. C.: "The Ao Naga Tribe of Assam", Mittal Publications, New Delhi, 2009, pp. 1-3. Thus, it furnishes the view that this tribe has not yet been developed in adequate manner, since independence of India. The Ramos of Arunachal Pradesh who lives in also generally cold climate area has their communications with the bridle paths, and their area is severe to travel in rainy season. Because, during the rainy season the foot track they use becomes muddy and the log bridges used in different places get slippery. –

Dhasmanna, M. M.: "The Ramos of Arunachal", Concept Publishing Company, New Delhi, 1979, pp. 1-33. They live in poverty and malnourished condition. Khasi hills people in the north-eastern part of India are also undeveloped from all counts of modern day's developmental activities. – See for further study, Raft, Mrs.: "Khasi Folk Tales", Spectrum Publications, Guwahati, 1985 (Reprint). Thus, to reconstruct the social structure of the tribes who live in the north-eastern province of India, the Ministry of Tribal Affairs, Government of India; along with the agencies in the North-East region provincial states should take adequate steps immediately, to develop all these tribes in holistic manner. It is voiced because; we have observed that the conditions of the tribes living in and around forests and particularly, in forest villages are far more precarious and vulnerable. – Aggarwal, P. K.: "Tribal Development Planning in India", Mahaveer & Sons (Publishers and Distributors), New Delhi, 2007, p. 16. The social structure requires the middle path and the right path. In this context, Nanda remarks: "The middle path and the right path as preached by the Jains, the Buddha and the Vedantists become the universal common thread in all Indian religions". – Nanda, J. N.: "Conflicts and Co-existence India", Concept Publishing House, New Delhi, 1991, p. 95. The Gita summarized the approach by declaring that all religions lead to the same God, or same bliss. We therefore require equanimity system of thought in restructuring the entire society. In restructuring modern social structure, peace should be placed as the highest priority of development of mankind, because peace also spreads from one region to another as we have observed that an international conflict spreads and engulfs one country after another. So, we should voice for peace and against conflicts regarding co-existence. Hence, it is suggested that security in freedom is necessary for each nation to develop according to its genius. – Nanda, J. N.: "Conflicts and Co-existence India", Concept Publishing Company, New Delhi, 1991, pp. 56-60. There should be models of more work opportunities, so that skilled and trained manpower can be increased in society for eradicating human backwardness, and also the availability of infrastructure should be made through scientific problem scanning with objectivity. For this, at least some channel of trustworthy communication is required to be kept open. – *Ibid.,* p. 145. In the present circumstances, we are required for holistic development technology and the capital as well as management skill, to overcome problems of regionalism. Thus, judicious thinking could ameliorate human problems, uplift people through holistic nature of social development and reduce conflicts by means of sustaining environmental balance with the perspective of peaceful living atmosphere.

89. In regard to dignity of human living potential Erasmus predicts: "In a showcase scheme to improve water supplies, a social scientist, a geologist, a public health expert, an engineer, and an anthropologist may be required". – Erasmus, C. J.: "Man Takes Control", Minneapolis, 1961, p. 179. Again, corruption is main disease in modern times, which should be totally eradicated for improving human conditions; otherwise, mere application of science in work place will not be helpful for national development, because, corruption acts as the psychological obstacle to growth. Corruption free society will bring in a stimulating influence to bear in many directions for achieving the ultimate goal of human development. David Cushman Coyle remarks: "In response to such appeals the government is likely to speed up various kinds of public works, such as roads, power plants,

seaports, even public schools, if the money can be found, at home or abroad. This speeding is normal and desirable. It all helps the big push". – Coyle, David Cushman: "National Development and How It Works", The New American Library, Inc., New York, 1963, p. 53.

90. For this purpose, community development is a must. It should be thought of as an abnormal and unusual form of development ... ... It is necessary to concentrate on ideas of self-help by utilization of existing resources. Glynn predicts thus: "If strategy in community development becomes traditional, again it would yield a genuine form of development, because it would make clear the distinction between imposition from without and evolvement from within the community". – Cochrane, Glynn: "Development Anthropology", Oxford University Press, New York, 1971, p. 54. Again, Foster has said: "In my experience the biggest blind spot of administrators is inability to understand the principle of scientific capital, the accumulation of theory and fact, general and specific that has been built up painstakingly over a period of many years". – Foster, G. M.: "Traditional Cultures and the Impact of Technological Change", New York, p. 248. Thus, scientific investigations are to be carried for developing specific areas for utilizing potential in mankind. There should be human interface of technological findings to accommodate people in realizing values of life through development parameters of living ideals.

91. Social orientation has its own secret name, and therefore, Aggarwal remarks: "Its secret name is the Truth of truth". – Aggarwal, D. D.: "Upanishads. The Real Truth", Kalpaz Publications, Delhi, 2003, p. 114. Since this secret name always has a transcendental import, it is difficult to understand. Thus, peace, progress – material and spiritual progress; as well as universal peace, economic prosperity, and spiritual progress are assumed in the Vedic mantras (Atharva Veda). – Rao, T. N. Achyuta (Ed.): "Vedanta. The Knowledge Supreme", Kalpaz Publications, Delhi, 2004, p. 54. Hence, there should be equanimity to realize soul, which requires the 'art of karma (work)' and governance philosophy for bringing society a holistic path of human development in leading holy life. So, institutionalizing the Vedic values, environmental scientific management will be made possible in reorienting modern societies to the noble path.

92. It is the power of history that guides the destinies of man. On the seashore of eternity, it plays the eternal game of making and breaking, of building and rebuilding. – Chaudhuri, Haridas: "Modern Man's Religion", South Asian Publishers Pvt. Ltd., New Delhi, 1966, p. 47. Thus, the 'Kutumbakam' ideology helps whenever there is a crisis in history. It is an eclipse of higher values; an upsurge of the forces of ignorance and evil, the evolutionary world-spirit is manifested in finite form for the good of humanity. In order to subdue the forces of darkness and discord and to ensure the reign of love, truth and righteousness – Kutumbakam idea is the only alternative to the world for human scientific development.

93. We should therefore, perform our activities in selfless way. Selfless service actually means doing service without selfish considerations. – Bhajanananda, Swami: "The Light of the Modern World: The Universal Significance of Sri Ramakrishna's Avatarahood and Message", Advaita Ashrama, Kolkata, 2012, p. 65. The Bhagavad Gita propounded the discipline of selfless work, and

consequently, depicts various guidelines for doing selfless work, which we have also suggested in the foregoing analysis.

94. About this concept, it is better to remember that when used effectively, it has tremendous strategic potential for governing employee behaviour and, in turn, organizational direction through its dynamic links to selection systems, training and development (T&D), career-planning systems, and reward structures. Aligned with corporate strategy, it can be used to reinforce the path towards the attainment of the organizational mission. – Mukherjee, Jayant: "Designing Human Resource Management Systems: A Leader's Guide", Sage Response, New Delhi, 2012, p. 130. Thus, the implementation of things through this concept requires human and cultural aspects rather than being technical. Hence, organizations are required to meet the needs of time to balance the measurement culture with the performance culture. Morris Bornstein remarks thus: "Such a calculation could be made only in money. We could not do it by comparing various classes of expenditure and savings in kind. If it is out of the question to reduce to a common unit the quantities of various kinds of skilled and unskilled labour, iron, coal, building materials of different kinds, machinery, then it is impossible to make them the subject of economic calculation. We can make systematic economic plans only when all the commodities which we have to take into account can be assimilated to money. True, money calculations are incomplete ... ... If we abandon them, economic calculation becomes absolutely impossible". – Bornstein, Morris: "Comparative Economic Systems. Models and Cases", Surjeet Publications, Delhi, 1987, p. 113. Thus, it is clear that in today's world, a stationary economic system can never exist. We should therefore think about sustainability in terms of rational economic system, which would be able to operate the wheels of the entire economy in moving towards self-sufficiency with the changing conditions; along with the collective expression of the will and distributional attitudes of the working community. In this context, it requires participative model, because the participatory firm will be more likely to support education, training and retraining of its members, when a strict profit motive might not suffice to do so. It is observed that in poorer countries, the community of the labor-managed firm may be the only group powerful enough, financially and organizationally, to initiate and carry out projects for collective consumption, such as housing projects, recreation facilities, and even school facilities.

95. Whereas, the American people have the advantage of extensive education facilities; they enjoy a very favorable health status; social security and public welfare measures have made available several forms of assistance to the needy, the old, the disabled and the dependent orphans. – Agarwala, R. K.: "American Economic Development", Kitab Mahal [W. D.] Private Limited, Allahabad, 1965, p. 21. Thus, it is observed that in American region, the gross average weekly earnings in manufacturing industries went up and the average weekly hours of work are reduced since the World War II. In this way, in America, higher income and more leisure make possible better health and greater happiness. In short, the saga of American economic development is as thrilling as it is stimulating. But, in African countries, we have observed that there is lack of consensus amongst management personnel, workmen, trade union leaders and government officials on rational and acceptable earnings criteria with the exception of overwhelming acceptance of the cost of living factor. – Mathur, A. N.: "Dynamics of Wages",

Popular Prakashan, Bombay, 1986, p. 145. However, all such pathetic conditions of living can be balanced through scientific models of determining the wage level, so as to reduce poverty from the society. With the increasing emphasis on skill and technology, along with zero level tolerance for corruption can build up social structure to maintain increasing level of earnings in many backward countries of the world. For doing these activities, legal system should be reformed with strict measures for delivering needs required for civic living of human beings. The advantage of mathematics lies chiefly in this, that it permits us to treat problems far more complicated than those generally solved by ordinary logic. – Tarascio, Vincent J.: "Pareto's Methodological Approach to Economics. A Study in the History of Some Scientific Aspects of Economic Thought", The University of North Carolina Press, Chapel Hill, 1966, p. 107. Thus, human starvation and malnourishment is the necessary part of positive science, should require full realization of the methodological judgment; where it is required that it is precisely here that the significance of their contribution to the issue of ethical neutrality is to be found for adequate development of human beings. Again, Leo Strauss remarks: "This fact is not understood even today". – Strauss, Leo: "Natural Right and History", University of Chicago Press, Chicago, 1953, pp. 35-80. His contention is that Weber was referring and argued for completely value-free social science. Hence, we conclude that it is time to integrate economies of the world, by which terrorism will also be reduced, if the activities of governments in different countries of the world are run by means of social transformation. So, transformation will come only when: "Corruption in the public life of the landed aristocrats, oppression of the feudal lords and their armed retainers over the agriculturists and the failure of the government to protect individual life, liberty and public peace in the countryside". – Chakravorty, R. N.: "National Integration in Historical Perspective", Mittal Publications, Delhi, 1985, pp. 178-79, is handled with strict principles of the rule of law. Again, Swami Vivekananda asserts that the task of organization is to proceed equally taking all, and therefore, the world order can be made a free living system, when we will try to remove all types of discrimination between man and man and provide food, shelter, and other amenities of life to all human beings.

96. In this regard, Dean Cotel once said: "All the corruption, all the decay of the church, all the offences in the world come of the covetousness of the priests". – Das, P. G.: "History of Political Thought", New Central Book Agency (P) Ltd., Delhi, 2013 (4th Edn.), p. 149. So, we require now abrupt social change very urgently, to change positively the onslaught of the population of the world, for which reformation along with renaissance is the only mantra for social development, to be carried in terms of human development strategies with scientific temper of thought. Thus, chauvinism can be overthrown from this world for ever.

97. Capitalism is the cause of all types of social imbalances in this world of living. Marx has said: "Communist society, not as it has developed on its own foundations, but on the contrary; just as it emerges from capitalist society, which is thus in every respect, economically, morally and intellectually, still stamped with the birthmarks of the old society from whose womb it emerges". – *Op. cit.,* p. 654. For eradicating human living imbalances and bringing social peace, we require to securing economic welfare of people. – Gauba, O. P.: "Western Political

Thought", Macmillan Publishers India Ltd., Delhi, 2011, p. 305. Human emancipation is possible through large scale practices of the subtle methods having scientific enquiry into subjects like – economic, sociological, political, cultural and psychological levels, where principles of justice have to be understood and determined by 'rational way of doing things'; because inquiry into the principles of justice is a complex issue. – *Ibid.*, p. 162. There should be rational choice in adopting these principles. Again, the World Bank's fifteenth annual World Development Report (1992) emphasized for the first time the link between unchecked population growth and environmental degradation, slow economic growth, declining health care, and declining living standards. – McWilliams, Wayne C. and Piotrowski, Harry: "The World since 1945: A History of International Relations", Viva Books Private Limited, New Delhi, 2006, p. 255. Toward the end of the twentieth century, industrialized nations became concerned with the issue of climate change caused by global warming. – *Op. cit.,* p. 453. Thus, various imbalances in production, distribution and other modes of human living – have caused for breaking mutual trust between people in different countries of the world, due to increasing level of human sufferings and dehumanization processes.

98. It is worthwhile to mention that Tagore asserted that the people in the villages could achieve real swaraj if, like the villagers of ancient India, they themselves managed most of their affairs. – Tagore, Rabindranath: "Samuha", Calcutta, 1335 B.S., pp. 64-69 and 97-98. M. N. Roy believed in humanistic ethics, and therefore said that Gandhi was the champion of national capitalism, as Jawaharlal Nehru was the apologist of National Socialism, and they complemented each other. – Ghose, Sankar: "Modern Indian Political Thought", Allied Publishers Private Limited, New Delhi, 1984, p. 416. Further, he (Roy) claimed that the social basis of Gandhism was: "Cultural backwardness; its intellectual mainstay, superstition ... ... The Gandhian Utopia is a static society – a state of absolute social stagnation". – *Op. cit.,* p. 417. Code of conduct in doing all kinds of social and business activities should be backed by national interest, by which people must be developed to realize the infinite power of the soul. Dealing with "national interest as an end", J. Bandopadhyaya refers to realism and idealism and concludes that, "on the whole it would be correct to say that there is strong accent on realism in the modern Indian thinking on international relations ... ... than in any other country in the world". – Khanna, V. N.: "Foreign Policy of India", Vikas Publishing House Pvt. Ltd., New Delhi, 2012, (Reprint), p. 15. Also see, Rajan, M. S.: "Studies in India's Foreign Policy", New Delhi, p. 286. It is suggested because; idealists hold national interest with universal moral aspirations like eternal peace and human brotherhood. Again, Sardar Vallabhbhai Patel is often regarded as a Realist par excellence. – Misra, K. P.: "The Conceptual Profile of Non-Alignment", in Misra and Narayanan (Ed.): "Non-Alignment in Contemporary International Relations", p. 197. Thus, human activities require holistic mind-set for development perspective, so as to eradicate human ills and social sufferings.

99. Accordingly, the most important key to successful economic development without loss of independence is the development of a workable governmental system that can show the mass of the people a reasonable hope for a better future. – Coyle, David Cushman: "National Development and How It Works", The

American Library of World Literature, Inc., New York, 1963, p. 15. In this regard, it is observed that the search for foreign technological improvements still goes on, and much of it is now a part of the government's technical cooperation program. It is suggested therefore, that the U. N. technical agencies would require doing more in managing for the exchange of experts and technology among member nations that rank as "underdeveloped". Social security as well as benefit should be provided to each country on the basis of customs and traditions that have deep emotional roots. – *Op. cit.,* pp. 17-18. Again, it should be our primary aim to provide an adequate amount of carbohydrates to those who are not getting enough carbohydrates. – Agrawal, N. C.: "The Food Problem of India", Vora & Co. Publishers Private Ltd., Bombay, 1961, p. 89. In a nutshell, besides the provision of an optimum amount of calories in our diet, all the essential constituents of a diet must be provided in proper proportion. Whether measured by economic and material loss or by human suffering and wasted skills, the cost of unemployment is high. Unused natural resources remain to be used in the future. But work, the creative activity of man, once wasted can never be recovered; what might have been produced is lost. The damage to individuals and to society from unemployment often cannot be repaired. – Okwn, Arthur M. (Ed.): "The Battle against Unemployment", W. W. Norton & Company, Inc., New York, 1965, p. 7. The social efforts of unemployment vary considerably according to the age, length of unemployment, the economic level of the unemployed and other factors, but there is a common pattern of unfortunate consequences. Housing demand also responds, to some extent, to changes in disposable income. Thus, tax reduction will have some direct effect on residential construction. – Op. cit., p. 94. Fiscal and monetary policies can ameliorate, moderate, and perhaps even compensate fully for such tendencies toward sluggish investment opportunities. Just as people decide their day-to-day decisions about consuming and non-consuming in the marketplace for goods, for bonds and saving accounts and for equities, so they may voluntarily come together at the political polls and vote for an additional rate of capital formation to be brought about through government action. – See also, Friedman, Milton and Meiselman, David: "The Relative Stability of Monetary Velocity and the Investment Multiplier in the United States, 1897-1958", in the Commission on Money and Credit Stabilization Policies (Prentice-Hall, 1963); Smith, Warren L.: "Debt Management in the United States", Paper No. 19, U. S. Congress, Joint Economic Committee (January 1960) and White, William H.: "The Flexibility of Anti Cyclical Monetary Policy", Review of Economic and Statistics, Vol. 43 (May 1961). Further, the rural sector of the Indian economy has a low degree of monetization. This may be brought out by analyzing the proportion of cash and non-cash components in consumption, production, investment and income in the rural households. – Sinha, M. R. (Ed.): "Modernising Indian Economy", Asian Studies Press, Bombay, 1965. Readers are further suggested to consult various series of 'The National Sample Survey', Government of India, New Delhi, along with 'The National Sample Survey', No. 2, Second Round, April-June 1951, Government of India, New Delhi, and December 1953. The above analysis depicts the picture of governance ideology on which stands human development structure.

100. In this context, it is asserted that a policy step adopted with a view to correcting this state of affairs will bring in a very crucial welfare decision as to the priority

to be accorded to the satisfaction of particular types of consumer demand. – Datta, Bhabatosh, Chakravarti, Santikumar, Bhattacharya, Manoranjan and Ghosh, Gouri: "Economic Development and Exports", The World Press Private Ltd., Calcutta, 1962, p. 203. Again, when there is scope for external borrowing or getting donations, results can be achieved in a much shorter time than would be required for securing export-expansion with a comparable quantitative impact on the balance of payments. Empirical research findings give the idea that the long period problem of the economy is basically one of productive capacity, costs and domestic prices. However, in the present situation, what is important – the extent to which technical economies can be undertaken in the existing export industries. So, wages and raw-material prices really hindering in the export-efforts have to be curbed through scientific planning as well as administrative system; so as to stabilize export oriented measures through domestic control mechanism which are affecting in production, costs and domestic prices. The strategic guidance should be viewed like: "If just a few firms invest, this would be taken up by the multiplier and we will have the beginning of a cumulative upward movement". – Sachdeva, M. B.: "Welfare Economics", Sublime Publications, Jaipur, 2010, p. 115. We might liken economists' success in forecasting the economic future with that of meteorologists forecasting tomorrow's weather; they are usually accurate but can often be wrong, sometimes spectacularly so. It is because, the chapter of the 'Economics' is subject to fluctuations in activity, are therefore, scientific measures are to be judged from psychological as well as political aspects of governing things and activities. Thus, it requires a vast range of policy issues. Among others, we may quote Peu Ghosh as: "They include global environment concerns, the epidemiology of AIDS, legal and illegal migration, including refugee movements, human rights, reform of the U. N. and its agencies, extension of international law, and the prosecution of crimes against humanity, whether involving terrorism, religious fundamentalism or international organized crime activities that range from drug production and trafficking to money laundering, smuggling goods of all kinds including weapons, diamonds, endangered species and people and 'new wars' arising from 'identity politics' linked with religious, ethnic or cultural factors". – Ghosh, Peu: "International Relations", PHI Learning Private Limited, New Delhi, 2012, p. 16. It is therefore, that the 'throughout' concept in strategic guidance should be scientifically adopted in making policies for global business, and to the framing of human development agenda.

101. Of the different conditions of good governance, one important aspect is the quality of leadership which should be concerned towards the poverty as well as to eradicate such poverty, for the good of poor people. Thus, Lal Bahadur Shastri, the then Prime Minister of India, who belonged from a very poor family living in a village near Banaras, denied the basic luxuries of life. He had a distinct "feel" of the pangs of poverty (so natural to the majority of Indian) and turned out to be a humble, down-to-the-earth person. – Pal, R. N.: "The Office of the Prime Minister in India", Ghanshyam Publishers & Distributors, New Delhi, 1983, p. 42. Besides, truthfulness is another important image can deliver for the people. In this area, the quality of Atal Behari Vajpayee, the then Prime Minister of India is quite laudable. We are now required, at the present system a vibrating leader having qualities of lion, which Swami Vivekananda advocated for the

roaring speeches with the honesty of interest and dedication for the services of the poor people. Thus, the philosophy of good governance policy requires that things we want to perform should be deeply connected to people, which would be helping in the process of human liberation through civic living possibilities. Good governance, from international perspective requires resolution of boundary disputes between countries, for which every country will get benefit from their mutual as well as judicious negotiations, for withdrawing from border disputes. Here, it is remarkable to note that: "Pakistan was told by all major powers to restore the sanctity of the Line of Control. Pakistan kept on harping on the occupation by the freedom fighters till the United States said categorically to Pakistani leadership to withdraw its regulars and other intruders". – Khanna, V. N.: "Foreign Policy of India", Vikas Publishing House Pvt. Ltd., New Delhi, 2012, p. 103. Thus, there should be friendly relationship and hopeful environment in between countries for increasing trading and commercial activities, industrial progress and other kinds of social development norms, to get mutual benefits for their citizens living in respective countries throughout the world. Bilateral relationship should therefore be strengthened by popular talks and discussions on the part of governance authorities. For good governance practice we must follow the principles of social orientation, which Parkinson predicts that: "Although they are necessary to establish true general principles ... ... which contain not only the act or the fulfillment of possibility, but also an original activity". – Parkinson, G. H. R. (Ed.): "Leibniz Philosophical Writings", Everyman's Library, London, Reprinted 1983, p. 117. So, it is worthwhile to note, this is why God governs minds as a prince governs his subjects, or as a father cares for his children; whereas he disposes of other substances as an engineer handles his machines. – *Ibid.,* p. 117. Thus, no hypocrisy should prevail for good governance philosophy to be implemented in practice. It all requires the Vedanta philosophy of sacrifice for the highest good of human beings, cited elsewhere in foregoing discussions.

102. It will perhaps be said that one must be equal to the other; but as matter has more perfection than empty space, reason demands that a geometrical proportion be observed, and that there should be more plenum in proportion as it is worthy of preference. For what is necessary is so by its essence, because the opposite implies a contradiction; but the contingent which exists owes its existence to the principle of what is best, the sufficient reason for things. – *Op. cit.,* p. 221-22. We shall, again, find that everywhere and in every effective performance the individual can satisfy his interests or needs one carry out any and every effective action only within organized groups and through the organization of activities. – Malinowski, Bronislaw: "A Scientific Theory of Culture and Other Essays", Oxford University Press, New York, 1944, p. 46. Thus, in the study of the environmental setting with the specific objects which belong there, the buildings, the equipment, and the capital sunk into an institution. In our socially oriented path, we would also find that to understand an athletic club or a scientific laboratory, a church or a museum, we would have to become acquainted with the rules, legal, technical and administrative, that coordinate the activities of the members. – *Op. cit.,* pp. 47-48. So, the relation between belief and the organization of human institutions is one of those which play a great role in modern times for holistic human development system. As a whole, there should

be pragmatic approach in the significant policy and forms of development strategies to management of things, which are naturally fertile in implementing our technological issues.

103. Whereas economists, following the long tradition beginning with Adam Smith, believe that it is very important and very good, to have a wide ranging division of labor. – Liebenstein, H.: "Economic Theory and Original Analysis", New York, 1960. However, we are concerned with the implication for management, the free flow of information, ideas, technology, and the maximum of individual talent. Again, Carter, Herz and Ranney in their joint work have remarked on such mechanism thus: "But even though many controls, such as food rationing, for example, have been relaxed, the government must keep a continual supervision over the workings of the whole economy if it is to support not only extensive social services but also wide external responsibilities". – Carter, Gwendolen M., Herz, John H. and Ranney, John C.: "The Government of Great Britain", The World Press Private Limited, Calcutta, 1958, p. 17. Today, in the changing world scenarios, the demand for social welfare, the need for defense, and the struggle to increase the export surplus require inevitably the massive expansion of governmental activities. Hence, local government is important not only for all these reasonable grounds, but also because it enables the people of local communities to take an active share in managing their own affairs. Further, to establish policy of justified civic living system, the civil servants should have a commitment to Constitution … … Democracy makes administration a politically committed function". – Bhattacharjya, A.: "Recruitment Rules and Civil Services", Prachi Prakashan, New Delhi, 1984, pp. 121-22. The civil servants should be dedicated towards transforming the society with their administrative zeal for functioning in eradicating all problems, for which civic citizens have been suffering for long. Their services are to be provided to all means of down-to-the-earth in alleviation of social poverty as well as amelioration of people's sufferings.

104. Thus, much have to done for a rapid sketch of Rousseau's political system, of which the historical importance is that it is in great measure answerable for the 'Declaration of the Rights of Man'. – Pollock, Frederick: "History of the Science of Politics", Akashdeep Publishing House, Delhi, 1990, p. 83. As the birth of all men free and with equal rights, the collective sovereignty of a nation depends on rectifying conditions of people who have been living in distress. In many countries of the world today, communal riots have become common, instead of people's development. So, it is remarked by Baruah: "Almost all communal riots are urban, and many begin and are sustained in areas where a large Muslim population is living among Hindus. Riots often take place in the old parts of cities, where roads and lanes are narrow and crowded. Over the past 50 years, the government has developed a routine for controlling riots and dealing with the problems of post-riot administration". – Baruah, Sanjib (Ed.): "Ethnonationalism in India. A Reader", Oxford University Press, New Delhi, 2012, p. 35. To make human emancipation for better living conditions, our political establishment must be now, busy with doing social activities most emergently, and the administrative functions are to be run for not controlling riots and violence, but to serve people with the disinterested way of working as depicted in the Hindu religious scriptures; which are backed by scientific

philosophical concept of social reconstruction measures and norms of human sacrifices. Rousseau's view on democracy predicts: "It is unimaginable that the people should remain continually assembled to devote their time to public affairs". – Das, P. G.: "History of Political Thought", New Central Book Agency (P) Ltd., Delhi, 2013, p. 300. In this manner, it is said that people's development should be the mantra of modern age, for which entire instrument of science and technological inventions should be divested in making the world societies for world class citizenship. Friedrich lists all these objectives as: (i) Protection of individual in the sphere of genuine autonomy; (ii) Right or freedom of religion and other rights; (iii) Maintaining rule of law on the basis of constitutionalism; (iv) Division of political power both functionally and spatially, among others. – Friedrich, Carl J.: "Constitutions and Constitutionalism", International Encyclopedia of the Social Sciences, Vol. 3, p. 319. It is worth noting fact that his constitutionalism is both the practice of politics according to 'rules of the game'. – Maheshwari, S. R.: "Comparative Government and Politics", Jainsons Printers, Agra, 1985, p. 64. In the West Asia, there are now pathetic situations and therefore, we must be careful to measure up to internal and external challenges and by the ascendancy of conservative regimes hostile to rational and humanistic concerns. – Agwani, M. S.: "Religion and Politics in West Asia", Vikas Publishing House Pvt. Ltd., New Delhi, 1992, p. 19.

105. We are enriched when we acknowledge the excellences of others, may they be physical, intellectual, moral or spiritual. When Wordsworth danced with joy on seeing the daffodils or when Shelly sang, inspired at the experience of the west wind, or when Keats raised to our view the beauty of the autumn season, they enriched their minds and the minds of mankind. – Kanal, Satyavan P.: "To Be Good", Dev Samaj Publications, Delhi, 1989, p. 121. Thus, our life process will be revitalized when we will try to appreciate the good points in another. In this way, we would be able to bring in truth into the world, as a poet brings goodness and truth into the world when he sings about the beauty of a flower, of a heroic action, or of a great life. The science behind human development is based on appreciation for the experience of truth, and not by making conflicts on our ideological differences. It thus, adds to the total value of the world order. Hence, we must be able to learn with the clearest proof, by which we would be also able to overcome problems of our lack of appreciation of the excellences of others. So, Kanal remarks: "Our self-love in the form of vanity covers with fungus the excellences of others". – *Op. cit.,* p. 120. It is right, too, that the great poets, the ideal interpreters of life, should be dearer to us than those who stop short with mere deciphering of what is real and actual. But it is no less true that the enduring weight of historian, moralist, political orator, or preacher, depends on the amount of the wisdom of life that is hived in his pages. – Morley, John: "Aphorisms", Macmillan and Co., London, 1887, p. 14. Thus, the fulfillment of the betterment condition, from time to time, has been observed to be concerned with such activities where the ego gives up its connection with the external world and withdraws into the state of sleep, in which its organization undergoes far-reaching changes. – Freud, Sigmund: "An Outline of Psycho-Analysis", The Hogarth Press, London, 1955, p. 3. It is interesting to note in this connection that the Buddhist view on this point, as explained by Dharmottara, came nearer the Jain view by identifying pramāṇa and pramāṇa-phala in jñâna ("knowledge"). –

Dasgupta, Surendranath: "A History of Indian Philosophy", Vol. IV, Motilal Banarsidass, Delhi, 1975, p. 167. In reality, we have observed that it is not possible to speak of any difference or distinction between God and His qualities, and therefore, it is expected that quality work should lead to the goal of attaining to the God-head, once everything we intend to do is done in pure sacrificial nature for the greater interest of mankind. Thus, we may refer to Swami Vivekananda for correcting our life process like: "This universe is helpful to every being and every being is also helping this universe, for they are born part and parcel of each other, the development of the one helps the development of the other; but to the Atman, the self-effulgent one, nothing can be helpful because it is perfect and infinite". – Vivekananda, Swami: "Science and Philosophy of Religion", Udbodhan Office, Calcutta, 1931, pp. 104-105. The above explanations give the idea that development is a holistic concept and it requires human face for realizing life order in living through civilized pattern to the tendencies of attaining human liberation.

106. While it is true ... ..., it is theoretically conceivable that there should be ethical theory that concerns scientifically and objectively with the casual conditions and the concrete consequences of this and that desire. The practical difficulties in the way are immense. Only a slight beginning has been made. – Dewey, John: "Problems of Men", Philosophical Library, New York, 1946, pp. 178-79. The attack upon science is now an attack upon the attitude, the standpoint, the methods, which are science, with especial reference to their bearing upon human institutional problems, focussing on the supreme issue of who and what shall have authority to influence and to give direction to life. – *Op. cit.,* p. 162. However, it means something quite different from what it means to the inventor who is engaged in translating mathematical-physical formulae into machines and other power devices. For it does not mean to him technology in the abstract; it means technology as it operates under existing political-economic-cultural conditions. Thus, John Dewey predicts: "Here and not in science, whether pure or abstract, is where materialism as the enemy of the humane is found; and here, not elsewhere, is where attacks should be directed". – *Ibid.,* p. 163. In redrafting therefore, our organizational guiding framework it is notable: "But were the enterprise pursued, it would develop, as it matures, techniques for dealing with human nature as we now have them for physical nature". – *Op. cit.,* p. 179. Hence, integration, to bring our knowledge of the relation of means and consequences with respect to human desires and purposes, requires that social knowledge and actions to anything approaching should be alike what already exists in physical knowledge and power; so that harmonious journey of life is being made possible through living in civilities.

107. The development of agriculture is important, because the whole progress of our modern technological civilization depends even more nowadays on this surplus of production from the land. – Calder, Ritchie: "Science in Our Lives", The New American Library, Inc., New York, 1962, pp. 113-14. In India, agricultural production remains at a relatively inefficient level, because of the vicious circle in which the cultivator is entailed. He is poor; therefore he cannot buy efficient implements or fertilizers; he plants his seeds laboriously by hand on land which he has scratched with his ox plough. He himself, his family and his animals are under-nourished, lacking energy for hard work ... ... Because he has no surplus,

he remains poor, and his poverty is increased by his usual indebtedness to the money-lender and by the incidence of such heavy expenses as providing marriage dowries for his daughters. – *Op. cit.,* pp. 114-15. Again, the source of materials are abundant in regions which are themselves underdeveloped industrially – the Congo, South Africa, northern Canada, Australia, and (for thorium) India and Brazil – and which are not prepared to remain only the miners of atomic ores. These areas need energy for new industries; they need a short cut to industrial development. – *Ibid.,* p. 184. In such ways, traditional ingenuity and twenty-first century science can combine to quiet the restless ghost of Malthus and answer those who would renounce humanity and deny the benefits of modern medical science to those who, "breeding like rabbits, should die like rabbits". – *Op. cit.,* p. 188. If people are condemned to live like animals, they will breed like animals. And while, obviously, the population increase should be restricted, there should not be the threat "Unless". So, we must believe now that modern science belongs to the humanities.

108. Recent research has demonstrated that the standardized tests of intelligence are not effective in identifying creative individuals. Similarly, creativity requires mastery of the medium in which the work is to be done, but is something more than sheer mastery. The great artist, writer, scientist or architect has first of all mastered his craft – mastered it to the point where one might almost say that he can forget it. But all masters of a craft are not creative. The average scientist, author, artist or musician may be a solid craftsman, admirable in many ways, but not necessarily gifted with originality. Gardner therefore makes a comment: "In science one finds a relatively thin line of innovative individuals working at the frontier of discovery, and behind them a vast army of competent people doing routine work". – Gardner, John W.: "The Individual and Today's World", Macfadden-Bartell Corporation, New York, 1966, p. 39. Thus, human creativity is possible in most forms of human activity. It is unpredictable, digressive, and capricious. As one scientist put it, "I can schedule my lab hours, but I can't schedule my best ideas". – *Ibid.,* p. 39.

109. The remarkable range of such professional and technical services that are available, forces the flexibility of the contractual relationship, gives the modern organization a wide range of choice in shaping its own future. – Gardner, John W.: "The Individual and Today's World", Macfadden-Bartell Corporation, New York, 1966, p. 79.

110. In this context, it is observed that the exploiters have used Islam as a cloak for their nefarious designs to go on looting the people. We have to fight this cynical exploitation of Islam. – Bhutto, Benazir: "Pakistan the Gathering Storm", Vikas Publishing House Pvt. Ltd., New Delhi, 1983, p. 26. The real way of resolving the issue is to interpose a truly popular programme to end all exploitation. Thus, a mixed economy, informed with an egalitarian spirit, is the inevitable need. That is all. We are to follow the principles of the ancient Indian Sanskrit Kâvya Literature, where it is preserved that ancient India was rich in craftsmanship. It portrays before us the picture of a guild of silk-weavers, proud of their own profession, and true of their own organization, but displaying within these limits an activity and keenness for all-round progress that is really surprising. – Majumdar, Ramesh Chandra: "Corporate Life in Ancient India", Cosmo

Publications, New Delhi, 1994, p. 27. Hence, problems of social development should be eradicated in terms of scientific utilization of our old valuable as well as resourceful things as depicted in scriptural order of ancient Indian people, where the science of astrology was cultivated by them while the finer arts like poetry were not neglected, as is abundantly evidenced by the brilliant resources of poem before us. – *Ibid.,* p. 27. The guild in ancient India was thus not merely the means for the development of arts and crafts, but through the autonomy and freedom accorded to it by the law of land, it became a centre of strength, and an abode of liberal culture and progress, which truly made it a power and ornament of the society. – *Op. cit.,* p. 28.

111. The extreme backwardness of the productive forces prompted by insufficiency of cultivation imposed collective labour on the people making impossible the existence of private ownership over means of production and land. – Dange, S. A.: "India from Primitive Communism to Slavery", Bombay, 1949, p. 40. In short, there was no provision to integrate the economy of the communes in any way with that of nation. – Peterson, Joseph: "The Great Leap – China", B. I. Publications, Delhi, 1966, p. 254. So, regional disparities were created by such means, among others, which require effective agricultural planning, industrial modernization and social sector reforms for people's development purposes. North Korea has long had her own emulation movement, the Flying Horse movement, to stimulate popular effort in industry. – *Op. cit.,* p. 353.

112. The social insecurity, crisis in the agrarian economy, complexities in the urbanized money market degraded the status of the women folk where women's sexual role towards male sexual hunger became a commodity for sale and purchase. The tragedy in the life cycle of the womenfolk, sufferings in their family life mirrored the overall degeneration in the productive system brought about by the societal change with a lust of affluent urban life consequent to the Muslim conquest and superimposition of an alien community over the decaying feudal Hindu social structure. – Chakraborty, Rabindra Nath: "National Integration in Historical Perspective", Mittal Publications, Delhi, 1985, p. 142. So, it requires scientific understanding of the problems of reality by which modern societies are to be rejuvenated for transformation in areas of human developmental needs in holistic perspective. International understanding should be made more harmonious for the safeguard of human civilization from all types of warfare and human sufferings.

113. On this premise there is ground for supposing that, in spite of differences, trusted leaders may be able to exploit a common tradition to the degree of achieving political unity in action at least when the cry is liberation from a foreign yoke. – Caroe, Olaf: "Soviet Empire: The Turks of Central Asia and Stalinism", Macmillan, London, 1967, p. 255. A nation has its own idealism – its own romance. Life moves forward and nothing can prevent a nation from developing. – *Op. cit.,* p. 268.

114. In Indian situation, our problems arrived before independence. And when Tilak held up Swaraj as the Indian's birth-right, he meant that Indians claimed complete political independence and were free to go outside the Empire. – Guha, A. C. (Ed.): "The Story of Indian Revolution", Allied Publishers Private Limited, New Delhi, 1972, p. 63. So, amelioration of human conditions requires the way only

of a fully awakened nation. All these premises made Aurobindo Ghosh, also conclude that the sloth and slumber of the people must be brought to an end layer after layer. – *Ibid.*, p. 63. Problems of human sufferings will be meted out through good educational policy, along social reformative activities. It is because, Hamilton who was too willing to "encourage" Besant's scheme of education saw in the Western education a real danger to the British rule in India, though he miscalculated the time. – See also, Hamilton to Curzon, 20 September 1899. Hamilton Papers, Reel No. 1. It is remarkable to note that Annie Besant's Hindu College at Benares proposed to impart now "by undertaking the task of giving religious and moral education on Hindu lines to its youths". – Besant to Curzon, 17 January 1899, Letter No. 18, Curzon Papers, Reel No. 7. All these references are quite evident to say that human resource potential could be developed through the Hindu lines, which are highly scientific for solving problems of human distressful conditions of living, even in today's technological world of social reformative means. It is the Vedanta speaks about human infinite possibilities of development for going to the path of liberation.

115. In India especially, banks are required to modify their performance in profit-making if that clashes with their obligations in such areas as social welfare, social justice and promotion of regional balance in development. In any case, compared to other business concerns, banks in general have to pay much more attention to balancing profitability with liquidity. It is true that all business concerns face liquidity constraint in various areas of their decision-making and, therefore, they have to devote considerable attention to liquidity management. But with banks, the need for maintenance of liquidity is much greater because of the nature of their liabilities. – Bhole, L. M.: "Financial Institutions and Markets – Structure, Growth and Innovations", Tata McGraw-Hill Publishing Company Limited, New Delhi, 2004, p. 129. Thus, social reformation movement also requires formation of strategies in regard to financial services, and so, government policies are to be guided by principles of financial liquidity, profit-making decisions; along with optimum level of public services. In this way, relevant issues of human development are to be addressed for making positive social change in bringing people towards the purposive idea of social rejuvenation.

116. Depending upon the commitment of the various governments to eradication of poverty among the rural poor – landless agricultural labourers belonging to the scheduled castes, in villages in the plains; members of the scheduled tribes in the hilly, tribal areas of peninsular India; both farmers and landless labourers in the western and eastern Himalayan regions where the fields are small and there is heavy soil erosion during the summer seasons, the fate of human population can be changed enormously. It is observed that the summer monsoons create problems in these areas, as many fields get washed away; the semi-desert and desert areas of western Rajasthan also face such problems. – Nath, V.: "Economic Development and Planning in India", Concept Publishing Company Pvt. Ltd., New Delhi, 2010, p. 98. So, opportunities of swing can be created by – (i) building up or repairing of roads; (ii) construction or repair of drinking water sources; (iii) construction and repair of irrigation sources; (iv) conservation of soil-cum-irrigation works. It is therefore suggested that construction and repair of roads, cheek dams and drinking water sources will constitute for the most widespread work to be undertaken by the elected governments in all such regions, where

people have been suffering a lot for long time. In areas of socio-economy, it is further observed that there is clear cross-country evidence that high rates of inflation are associated with the low rates of sustained growth. The negative link is not due to costs of inflation per se. Rather, "The inflation rate serves as an indicator of the overall ability of the government to manage the economy. Since there are no good arguments for very high rates of inflation, a government that is producing high inflation is a government that has lost control". – Fischer, Stanley: "Macroeconomic Factors in Growth", Journal of Monetary Economics, December 1993. See also, V. V. Chari, Larry E. Jones, and Rodolfo E. Manuelli, "Inflation, Growth, and Financial Intermediation", Michael, Bruno and William Easterly, "Inflation and Growth: In Search of a Stable Relationship", and Robert J. Barro, "Inflation and Growth", all in Federal Reserve Bank of St. Louis Review, May-June 1996, and M. Bruno, "Does Inflation Really Lower Growth", Finance and Development, September 1995. Hence, we should find out means and ways to curb inflation in providing people dignities of living norms through government packages and their right implementation in the field in time. Again, Nelson and Plosser showed that the method used to model the trend plays a critical role in identifying shocks. – Dornbusch, Rudiger, Fischer, Stanley and Startz, Richard: "Macroeconomics", The McGraw-Hill Companies, Inc., Boston, 1998, p. 174. We should excel perfectionism in socio-economy through potentials of production function which provides a quantitative link between inputs and outputs, and also policies of the government are to be redrafted for human capability building notions so as to assure people for their legitimate rights of civil living pursuits.

117. Here, it is also important to mention that the mode of reproduction in crop plants may be broadly taken into consideration for human advancement, for which organizational policy regarding breeding system in crops is immensely helpful, as it facilitates in the overall genetic system which is a must, in today's world of population increase for supplying with the growing demands of people. – See also, Kar, Dipak Kr. and Halder, Soma: "Plant Breeding Biometry Biotechnology", New Central Book Agency (P) Ltd., Delhi, 2008. Again, nation building process also requires scientific training in the architectural archaeology in these days of earth quake prone proximities over the world at large, and things of such subjective issues are narrating rightly to apply these principles [Altchin, F. R. and Chakrabarty, Dilip K. (Eds.): "A Source Book of Indian Archaeology", Vol. I, Munshiram Manoharlal Publishers Pvt. Ltd., New Delhi, 1978, p. 33], so as to find-out solution of the problems of human settlement in different parts. Further, we have observed that dams are constructed on rivers so that they form reservoirs which improved water that is later used for irrigation, water supply and industrial purposes, power generation, recreational purposes and flood control. – Garde, R. J.: "River Morphology", New Age International Publishers, New Delhi, 2011, p. 301. Hence, framing of strategies for reservoir sedimentation could be useful for implementation of various socially-oriented projects which will illuminate the picture of human civilization in going through right path.

118. We are to overcome therefore, problems of shortage by means of creating mobility of resources; the agenda which is highly important to change social structure. Thus, W. Arthur Lewis comments: "The shortage disappears when all that is wanted can be purchased freely at a reasonable price, and a reasonable price is that which corresponds to the normal average cost of production. Shortages are

therefore the result of the immobility of our resources, and so also is such need as there is to use planning by direction. If we could greatly increase mobility we could eliminate all shortages, and could rely exclusively on planning by inducement". – Lewis, W. Arthur: "The Principles of Economic Planning", Dennis Dobson Ltd-George Allen & Unwin Ltd., London, 1954, p. 75. Sovereign governments should therefore try to the quickest way to get rid of shortages and of licences by concentrating on immobility. By means of scientific investment and public expenditure, governments in different countries would be able to set a balance in both public and private sectors, to harmonize resources balancing use, and therefore to be fitted into the budgets for the whole economy. Consumption pattern will also be maintained steadily and consequently, employment opportunities will be created for setting in motion the forces of inflation As a whole, such policies will commensurate a balance to the producing disequilibrium in the foreign balance. Hence, our agenda to change should be made holistic process of human development to reduce sufferings of people, and to eradicate unnecessary pressures of the various interest groups, as observed worldwide.

119. To reduce conflicting tendencies of human beings, government policy should be reformed through moderate wage rates enhancement for the workers working in industries. Again, trade union policies require that there should be healthy relationship between employers and employees for congenial industrial productivity and good coordination between union leaders, employers and the government authorities. As we have observed that the Wagner Act of 1935 had given opportunities to wage earners through the 'New Deal' policy in providing many social security measures to strengthen labour (Chakrabarti, Sudhindra Chandra, Kundu, Kuja Bihari and Patra, Madan Mohan: "Economic Development of America", Nababharat Publishers, Calcutta, 1962, p. 139), so it is suggested that reforms are needed to rationalize industries in modern line in recapitulating government's efforts and programmes to the establishment of export guilds in promoting cooperation among less affluent exporters for the development of foreign markets. – Shaikh, A. J. and Mannur, H. G.: "A Short Economic History", S. Chand & Co., Delhi, 1971, p. 230. So, skilled and unskilled labourers in industrial undertaking have to be well-trained for the purpose of collective responsibility, cherished with the goal of social emancipation of human beings. In this way, social environment will be reformulated for conflict less work culture and brotherhood industrial relationship, and the democratic performance will be maintained in guiding people towards the existentialism as well as civic living objectives.

120. It is assured that the study of different economic system prevailing in different countries definitely would make us less dogmatic in our attitude towards our own economic system and more tolerant of other people with their different economic systems. The study will thus broaden our view point and approach which will serve as basis of better relations among different countries of the world. – Desai, S. S. M.: "Economic Systems", Himalaya Publishing House, Bombay, 1982, p. 24. Thus, it will help to mould our issues for developing the economy in speedy manner, so as to find-out means and ways for effective public administrative system, in encouraging people to shoulder responsibility, and transformative norms of managerial values and beliefs in considering

development as the pillar of social reconstruction, with strategic foundation of human work related opportunities. Remedial measures are to be adopted by means of appropriate reporting system, to reduce human anarchism. Thus, it is argued that large organizations have so important an impact upon a country's economy that everybody in the country has a right to know what such organizations are doing, and that the information necessary to explain activities fully should be provided in annual reports. – Guter, A. and Guter, M.: "Financial Accounting", Teacher Yourself Books, Holder and Stoughton, 1981, p. 301.

121. While resolving policies, a sense of commitment should be commanded by virtue of management's policy of love, i. e., love start at top and flow to the bottom. – Deb, Samar: "Contemporary Issues on Management", Atlantic Publishers and Distributors, New Delhi, 2001, p. 136. At the organizational levels, it is the 'management by love' which can be experimented as a methodical way of solving various problems and bringing an atmosphere for the overall development of organization; which is ultimately helpful for group dynamics. It is group dynamics that considers things in social intercourse and therefore, Keith Davis has said rightly: "It is the social process by which people interact face to face in small group". – Davis, Keith: "Human Behavior at Work", McGraw-Hill Publishing Co., New Delhi, 1975, p. 439. By this method, organizational management creates a confidence, oneness, and sense of belonging in the minds of its people through its attitude, approaches and policies. It is fact that love is never glad about injustice, but rejoices whenever truth wins out. It is loyal, no matter what the cost, and it also believes and expects the best while contributing the best. Hence, people's sufferings will be eliminated, as and when social building activities are to be performed in terms of selfless services by modern governments; because, love is never selfish at the cost of others. – Michael, V. P.: "Management by Love", reproduced from the Seminar Paper presented at the Indian Institute of Management, February 1988. Considering scientific aspects of human development parameters, it can be asserted that Buddha gave the highest priority to the principles of fraternity as the only real safeguard against the denial of liberty or equality. Hence, it is true that the science behind human development is the brotherhood concept which can protect freedom and equality in beings. So, organizational policies and government decisions are to be guided by the philosophy of the entire fabric of the vitality of life in commonness of thinking, and therefore, diversifying the goal of life in an unending journey. – Deb, Samar: "Unified Thought on Management", Kalpaz Publications, Delhi, 2004, p. 97. The civic living essentialities are required that to get the ultimate perfection by human organization, it is needed to guide people through numerous social activities. – *Op. cit.,* p. 98. The productive functions are to be carried out by modern organizations in a goal oriented manner, so that organizational balance is maintained in converting the social, financial, natural, and other material resources into effective productive resource that go to increase human welfare in terms of solving most of the burning issues and problems of the society, and managing thus, all types of human social crises will be supplemented in efficient manner, which is the challenging need in the present system of the growing world order. – Deb, Samar: "Global Principles on Management", Dominant Publishers & Distributors Pvt. Ltd., New Delhi, 2014, p. 277. Behind development therefore requires that less developed countries are to be given due

importance in the share of the world trade. Thus, in the context of a society we should feel that a man must not be a burden on the society; but rather, everyone should be promoted to the highest ladder of life in terms of generation of employment opportunities through creation of different infrastructural projects and social amenities, which will only bring in social peace and harmony. – *Ibid.*, p. 229.

122. In producing things for safeguarding our country, the role of nonprofit service organizations has been observed to be commendable because these organizations work voluntarily with dedication and zeal – both for nation-making and man-making. Many of them are inspired by religious idealism, some by social and national idealism. The primary aim of most of these organizations is socio-economic growth, leading to cultural, moral and ethical elevation of life. The government proposes plans and nonprofit organizations deliver the goods, sometimes with government assistance, sometimes without – just by collecting funds from the public. They are a vital factor in the rise of India today. Swami Jitatmananda remarks: "The activities of voluntary organizations are vast and varied, and stretch from tribal development to education and medical service activities. The missionaries among nonprofit organizations have been running outstanding institutions of education since the last 100 years, producing academic giants having high moral standards, with their roots in India's cultural heritage. They organize camps for blindness prevention, polio vaccination, general health, eye operations, hygiene, and so on. They nurse the sick in cities, in villages, on war-fronts. They work towards elevating the status of slums. They fight for women's justice. They enrich the rural population not only through the Green Revolution but also through the 'evergreen revolution', as M. S. Swaminathan calls it, with developed agro-based technology". – Jitatmananda, Swami: "The Role of Nonprofit Organizations in Tomorrow's India", in Prabuddha Bharata or Awakened India, Advaita Ashrama, Calcutta, Vol. 104, November 1999, p. 863. Thus, today many nonprofit institutions have drawn world attention and have earned international fame. It is therefore scientific in systematizing development oriented tasks which could be useful for reforming India's socio-economic pattern of human upliftment programmes, along with government's plans and policies for eradicating social sufferings of downtrodden human beings.

123. It requires, three things are necessary for great achievements, according to Swami Vivekananda. Firstly, feel from the heart – the heart brings human inspiration. Love opens the most impossible gates; love is the gate to all secrets of the universe. Secondly, think for way out, any practical solution, some help instead of condemnation, some sweet word to soothe miseries of human beings, to bring them out of this living death. Lastly, have your will force to surmount mountain-high obstructions. Dare to do what you think is right. – Vivekananda, Swami: "To the Youth of India", Advaita Ashrama, Kolkata, 2002, pp. 72-73. Hence, our prolonged strategic idea of human well treatment requiring scientific envisagement in encouraging people to serve for miseries of human beings in disinterested way, by forgetting all about our name, fame and own bodies. This is the urgent requirement because, at this time, the whole world has been waiting for such notion of scientific path of services in overcoming problems of social sufferings of deprived human beings, in working like miracles. Vivekananda rightly asserts: "If there are holes in this national ship, this society of ours, we

are its children. Let us go and stop the holes. Let us gladly do it with our hearts' blood, and if we cannot, then let us die". – *Op. cit.,* p. 74. Thus, our mission, vision and strategies for development should be guided by the philosophy of human upliftment and social forward moving tendencies, in this age of technological upheavals as well as scientific research in all fields of human progressive foundation. It is therefore truly mentioned that policymakers ought to take heed of uncertainty about the best target for the economy. Dornbusch, Fischer and Startz have rightly noted: "Once a target is chosen, policymakers need to remember that we are unsure of the exact magnitude and timing of the effects of policy actions". – Dornbusch, Rudiger, Fischer, Stanley and Startz, Richard: "Macroeconomics", Tata McGraw-Hill Publishing Company Limited, New Delhi, 2004, p. 181. Hence, policymakers must account for the effects that policies have on the public's expectations of the future.

124. It has been observed by Sharma (Sharma, S. K.: 1981) that development of agriculture is an essential though by no means a sufficient condition for rural development in the developing countries. Although agriculture may not initiate industrial development process, its progress will strengthen the rate of industrial development, by increasing food production capacity, capital formation, in providing market for industrial output of consumer's goods and lastly, by utilizing agricultural inputs originated in industrial sector (Schultz, T. W.: 1968, pp. 3 and 6). With the interpretation of the concept of development, as the improvement of social welfare; the agricultural development has also become a wider concept incorporating considerations of social justice and ecological conditions, along with the performance in terms of economic gains in fields (Kishan, 1979). We must therefore keep in mind that agricultural development planning should not divorce all these objectives, because the package programme of agricultural development benefits not only a certain section of the cultivators, but also certain regions as well. – Bhargava, Archana: "Resources and Planning for Economic Development: A Case Study of Sagar Division, M. P.", Northern Book Centre, New Delhi, 1991, p. 79. Again, Lipton puts it that breeding for nutrient response has done little for regions suffering both from poor soils and from lack of water (Lipton, 1978). Agricultural development envisaged through improved seeds thus remained a localized phenomenon, concentrated in favorable regions. Culturally and politically conscious regions have managed to adopt new yield raising technology, but regions of poor, small and marginal farmers are lagging far behind. This situation also necessitates the examination of the conditions of agriculture and its relation with the geography of the region. Thus, scientific examination will give result for systematizing agricultural activities by way of making networks as well as public distribution measures, along with productivity enhancement plans and programmes from time to time; particularly, in the very needy areas where people have been suffering a lot for long. The problems of marketing of handloom products, as for example, in the north-eastern region is evident from the observation made in the report of the Planning Commission which notes "marketing activity is not well-organized and is limited to the establishment of Emporia in Delhi and State Headquarters where fabrics purchased sporadically are sold at fairly high prices. There is no direct link with the weaving community ... ... they have in turn to depend on a disorganized supply system". – Report on the Development of North Eastern Region – Some

Aspects, Government of India, Planning Commission, 1977, p. 114. The weavers have not been able to dispose of their products in the absence of good designs and assured marketing facilities. – Weaving Industries in Assam, Government of Assam, May, 1976, p. 44.

125. In pursuit of this objective, the interface between national regulatory structures and international regulatory norms is bound to be critical. And this interface is likely to be not only important but also complex in the sphere of capital controls. In contemplating this task, there is a fundamental distinction that should be drawn between countries where capital controls exist and countries where such controls do not exist. – Nayyar, Deepak: "Trade and Globalization", Oxford University Press, New Delhi, 2012, p. 274. It is therefore essential that good governance policy implications are to be modified for regulating such type of social structure where man, animal and the earth have been managed with performance efficiencies for building social infiastructures which are immensely helpful for human development, and also internationally conducive towards all types of changes that are being abruptly faced by nation-states against social peace and tranquility. Lack of good governance has now been observed as the outcome of patterns of development where economic growth is uneven between regions and the distribution of its benefits is unequal between people, so that there is growing affluence for some, combined with persistent poverty for many. – <i>Op. cit.,</i> p. 345. This may be the consequence of strategies of development, as a similar economic performance in the aggregate could lead to egalitarian development in one situation, and growth which by passes the majority of people in the another situation. Hence, human development has to be made through good network of policy formulation for correcting regional imbalances and solving problems of human hunger as well as civic living needs in this age of technological revolution, so as to safeguard human civilization from catastrophic destruction. Ludwig has considered his view in an understanding thus: "If we do not begin to try to improve the life of our people, we are undermining the basis of technical progress. Then we shall leave the circle of civilized nations. We can only participate in a further happy and healthy development if we have the courage to consume". – Erhard, Ludwig: "Prosperity through Competition", Asia Publishing House, New Delhi, 1959, p. 56. If we lack the courage to fight social resentment, if we cannot bear it that without being especially deserving some become consumers of the new product before others, then we shall have to continue living in an artificially preserved poverty. <i>Ibid.,</i> p. 56. We must do everything to solve this serious social problem. We must not give up the idea of modernizing of the economy for the greater interest of human upliftment from social sufferings.

126. From the measuring incidence of direct and indirect taxation, which is often regressive in developing countries, it becomes clear that the educational system is not a vehicle for promoting equality. It often works in the opposite direction to reinforce and/or widen inequality. – Todaro, Michael P.: "Economic Development in the Third World", Orient Longman Limited, Hyderabad, 1993, p. 349. So, human integrity should be placed at the highest level for rejuvenating educational activities in bringing social equality, by which social and economic activities should be reformed for human dignified living oriented thought. It is true that equality of educational opportunity can have little meaning if financial

assets and income-earning opportunities are very unequally distributed. Besides, strategy for human growing issues are required to be guided by 'stabilization' policies, which are often viewed as measures primarily designed to maintain the poverty and dependency of Third World nations while preserving the global market structure for the industrialized nations. – *Op. cit.,* p. 421. However, management effectiveness is the criterion for organizational transformation towards bringing abrupt social change. In this context, Bhatia asserts: "Transformational leadership leads to superior performance in organizations facing demands for renewal and change". – Bhatia, S. K.: "Managing Organizational Behaviour", Deep & Deep Publications Pvt. Ltd., New Delhi, 2008, p. 261. Transformational leaders are more democratic, because they are visionaries, and their characteristic features are like – courageous, believe in people, value driven, lifelong learners, ability to deal with complexity, ambiguity and uncertainty. Thus, dignity of living can be found through transformational leading goal, where tasks are performed for holistic nature of human development with the integrated concept of organizational guiding philosophy.

127. It is because of the fact that the present century is considered to be 'Human Relation Era'. The workers are to be treated not as 'cogs in the machine', but rather they should be treated like partners in the industry where they are working. So, the commanding height of human perfectionism requires that participation of labour in any commercial enterprise should envisage the principles of – 'equity, equality and voluntarism; and also there should be concept of involvement of workers in the decision making process of organizations. This kind of attitude invigorates a sense of belonging and love towards the establishment. In this context, remarks of S. N. Singh and others are: "You can buy a man's time, you can buy a man's physical presence at a given place, you can even buy a measured number of skilled muscular motion per hour in a day, but you cannot buy enthusiasm, you cannot buy initiative, you cannot buy loyalty, you cannot buy devotion of heart, mind and soul. You have to earn these and they are the things that go to make a happy and prosperous enterprise". – Singh, S. N., Narain, (Kr.) Amarendra and Kumar, Purnendu: "Socio-Economic and Political Problems of Tea Garden Workers", Mittal Publications, New Delhi, 2006, p. 204, cited in Patel, S. K., Tatai, R. C. in article: "Workers' Participation in Management", Quarterly Journal of Workers' Education, Nagpur, March 1994. In other words, all-round social development needs that the organization of society should run on a competitive basis and the nationalization of railways, telephones, tramways, etc. does not itself accomplish the transition from individualism to socialism......
This is the truth which many Fabians have been compelled sadly to acknowledge. – Vide Pease, History of Fabianism, pp. 242-3. With the conclusion of the Peace of Versailles in 1919, the movement for the establishment of universal standards in industry entered on an entirely new and most hopeful phase. The signatories to the peace treaty stated in the preamble that universal peace 'can be established only if it is based upon social justice', and they proceed to enunciate a number of principles of which the declaration that labor is not to be regarded 'merely as a commodity or article of commerce' may be taken as typical. – Birnie, Arthur: "An Economic History of Europe 1760-1939", Methuen & Co. Ltd., London, Reprinted 1964, p. 198. Thus, the attainment of the goal of unified social journey requirement constituent is concerned with global economic and social

development on a sustainable basis, which requires further: "Solid rates of economic expansion". – Jain, N. K.: "WTO Concept, Challenges and Global Development", Regal Publications, New Delhi, 2008, p. 243. A new global enabling environment can only be built on the foundation of an open and integrated global economy. Also, in some instances, the exports of developing should benefit from a better treatment with respect to measures taken by other WTO Members. To reach at the commanding height, technical assistance should also be provided to developing countries to assist them in assuming their obligations and more effectively realizing the benefits of the multilateral trading system. In this way, unified social rolling in bringing human perfectionism could be reached at a high where the world order will be moved for universal peace and social tranquility.

128 Coherence interrelationships, in today's world of commercial complexity require that bank industry should be reformed in new dimensional order. Mehta depicts: "The success of the banking industry is based on, among other things, your successful role performances". – Mehta, R. R. S.: "A Story of Cheques", Himalaya Publishing House, Bombay, 1985, p. 1. Changing phase of social orientation process needs that the collecting bank has to prove that it has acted in good faith and without negligence. Social diversification further needs realization of the fact that even though agricultural exports contributed a lion's share in the total exports of our country, there is a large scope to improve the situation by streamlining and revamping the export policy in general and marketing of agricultural commodities in particular. – Prasad, A. Sivarama: "Agricultural Marketing in India", Mittal Publications, Delhi, 1985, p. 419. Under these circumstances therefore, there is every need for creating a situation where the cultivator will have greater confidence in being able to sell his produce in the market without being exploited. – *Op. cit.,* p. 422. This is a good example for bringing interrelationships to reformulate the path of social orientation. There is the permanent-income theory of consumption, which is propounded by Milton Friedman, and it considers the steady rate of consumption a person could maintain for the rest of his or her life, given the present level of wealth and the income earned now and in the future. – Dornbusche, Rudiger, Fischer, Stanley and Startz, Richard: "Macroeconomics", Irwin/McGraw-Hill, New York, 1998, p. 304. In this context, it is worthwhile to note that income policies are to be coined in a manner which can shape the fate of deprived masses to change their life-styles in realizing the scientific norms of social building process. Our integrated system in reforming human personality should be made free from bondage of action. According to our Indian system, there are two existences: nature on the one side and the self, the Atman, on the other. So, human personality should also be confining to the fact that the reality in nature is spirit. Swami Vivekananda therefore rightly asserts: "Reality itself – the light of the spirit – moves and speaks and does everything [through our bodies, minds, etc.] It is the energy and soul and life of the spirit that is being worked upon in different ways by matter......The spirit is the cause of all our thoughts and body-action and everything, but it is untouched by good or evil, pleasure or pain, heat or cold, and all the dualism of nature, although it lends its light to everything". – Vivekananda, Swami: "Thoughts on the Gita", Advaita Ashrama, Calcutta, 2000, pp. 61-63. In this way scientific temper of doing things will enlighten the picture

of real development, when we will try to assess Indian concept of the Vedanta, in time and space.

129. The social reengineering thought as mentioned in Ramakrishna's principle of inherent divinity and his teaching about serving God in the human being should be given the highest priority to solve human life problems, and integrated human performance in this line of thinking for confining our tasks must be taken into consideration in reshaping our technological foundation for coping with the changing nature of social building notions; so as to manage human socio-economic activities to guide the world order to the path of salvation in life. Thus, teachings of Ramakrishna have the uniqueness which lies in the fact that he put everything to test, found them true, and then told the world about them. – See also, the article: "Genetics and Sri Ramakrishna", published in the Monthly Journal of the Ramakrishna Order, Prabuddha Bharata, Advaita Ashrama, Calcutta, November 1999, pp. 844-45. Balanced development will come in society when we will try to perform our activities in serving human beings, which is the only road to God-realization, and is the only goal of life.

130. This integral humanity, according to Sri Ramakrishna's opinion is concerned with the Divine Mother. So, he gave the idea to all that lust was the enemy of human beings. We must therefore consider rightly the idea of sex and the idea of money, for doing things, as he (Ramakrishna) thought, that these prevented him from seeing the Mother. Accordingly, he comments about integral humanity concept, which is ingrained with the whole universe – the manifestation of the Mother and She lives, as per his estimation, in every woman's body. – Vivekananda, Swami: "My Master", Advaita Ashrama, Calcutta, 1990, p. 33. This is the idea of common spiritual unity in beings should be preserved for social reformations, if we want to change this world order in positive direction through development policies and activities implemented for the purpose of upliftment of masses from severe sufferings to a stage of civilities.

131. Of great interest are the first communications on the subject. Indian scientists D. Lal and N. Bhandari, after subjecting rock samples returned from the Moon to special treatment, have discovered unusually long tracks of some particles in the crystals of lunar matter. – Komarov, V. N.: "Science for Everyone", Mir Publishers, Moscow, 1989, pp. 94-96. Similarly, we are to judge things with the scientific temper of mind to work-out the reasons behind the development. It is said so, because Caird thinks: "A partial knowledge may be conveyed to us of things that are in themselves within the compass of human thought". – Caird, John: "An Introduction to the Philosophy of Religion", Surjeet Publications, Delhi, 1997, p. 69. Thus, ideas which we are as yet incapable of grasping in their highest form may reach our minds in a form which, though less adequate, is still essentially true. But any such combination of knowledge and ignorance, if we examine what we mean, will be seen to be contradictory and impossible. – *Ibid.,* p. 69. Hence, in terms of the real story of development, it is asserted like these words: The revelation of a mystery, if by that we do not mean merely the revelation of the fact that there is much in the universe which we do not know, must be the revelation of something which can be construed by the mind, which is conveyed to it in terms of human thought, which can be expressed in coherent propositions.

132. It requires to bring to the notice of organization's activities through the mission statement which sets out the organization's ground rules to its approach in doing business, and good statements usually address: (i) The shared beliefs and values; (ii) A definition of the business which covers the needs being satisfied, the chosen markets, how those markets will be reached, what technologies will be used in delivering the products/services; (iii) It may also include the legitimate claims of relevant stakeholders (e. g. employees, shareholders, customers, society, the City); (iv) Attitudes to growth and financing, decentralization, innovation, etc. – Bowman, Cliff: "The Essence of Strategic Management", Prentice-Hall of India Private Limited, New Delhi, 1990, p. 6. Till today, all the desires of even a single person have not been satisfied nor can be satiated. If a desire is born but it is not satisfied, it causes much pain. Therefore, if a person wants to escape pain, the remedy is the renunciation of desire. Here a doubt may arise why we should perform an action, when we have no desire. The clarification is that an action is performed in order to reap its fruit and also to renounce the desire for its fruit. – Ramsukhdas, Swami: "For Salvation of Mankind", Gita Press, Gorakhpur, 2003, p. 125. This is the real truth should be discovered for spiritual discipline in making all our technological researches for balancing our works which will immensely be helpful for reducing social gaps, with correct nature of human competencies as well as abilities, and through organizational credibility in initiating dynamic nature of social change.

133. Peaceful human existential condition rests on divine prayer with the surrendering attitude like: "He whose brilliance vies with the brilliance of innumerable suns, whose coolness is equal to that the countless moons, who possesses the luster of crores of Fire-gods, and the prowess of numberless wind-gods, whose affluence is equal to that or countless Indras, who possesses the beauty of crores of Cupids, whose forbearance is equal to that of innumerable Earths, whose gravity is equal to that of countless oceans, whom none can explain by any simile, whose real nature has only been assumed even by the Vedas and scriptures, and could not be fathomed by anyone, to that matchless Úrî Hari I offer obeisances, again and again". – Goyandka, Jayadayal: "Gems of Truth", Gita Press, Gorakhpur, 1994, p. 47. This is the meditative nature of work should be performed with surrendering attitude for bringing world peace with the freedom of living necessities. It rather, according to Samar Deb has been playing a dominant role to interplay between technology and human real development with the kind of 'SWOT' analysis. Thus, Deb opines that the world dynamicity can be reinforced through SWOT – which is the catchword and means for our strengths, weaknesses, opportunities and threats. – Deb, Samar: "Unified Thought on Management", Kalpaz Publications, Delhi, 2004, p. 222. The prestigious joint venture of IBM of the US and the Tatas – Tata Information Systems Ltd. (TISL) which was started formally in January, 1992 had also undertaken its SWOT analysis. In this way visionary guidance to human society can be brought forth in reconciling the process of inculcated existentialism for the greater interest of mankind; otherwise, all types of human vanity will be failure process in trying to solve human distress and miseries. Again, the Vedanta's ideology of 'truth, beauty and goodness' in managing activities through technological shape should be propounded in terms of 'Being and Becoming'. In this matter, D. N. Banerjee writes: "Being and Becoming are different aspects of the same reality and are only relative to our

intelligence. Man has the promise and potentiality of divine realization, of spiritual perfection and therefore is God in the making, for even his humanity is intelligible only if regarded as an individualized self-expression of God". – Sharma, Suresh K. (Ed.): "Swami Vivekananda the Patriot-Saint of Modern India", Vol. 1, Vista International Publishing House, Delhi, 2008, p. 103. In this way, the world dynamicity in inculcating human existentialism should be propounded through the claim of Hinduism which is to be the universal religion, in the sense that it preaches principles of human development, but does not demand any loyalty to persons in return of doing good to others.

134. Human core of living is ingrained with the universal integrity from the view point of civic living process required in social foundation, in which integral concept of humanity is better to be understood for human equality and performing things on the basis of equanimity principles, as depicted earlier in the previous Chapter. However, in this regard, we may also adopt sayings of the Bhagavad Gîtâ which goes like: "Knowledge is superior to making the mind steady and steadfast and meditation is greater than knowledge. But the abandoning of the fruits of karma (action) is far superior to meditation even. Deliverance or supreme peace is easy to be attained by abandoning the fruits of action". — Kuppuswami, A.: "Bhagavad Gîtâ", Chaukhambha Orientalia, Varanasi, 1983, p. 350. In going through adopting strategy towards managing human activities in terms of spiritual system requires such kind of notion; so that people would realize scientific temper of delivery system in changing societal veil through all kinds of services, be it industrialization or reformation by means of social services. It shines out clearly, therefore, that the subject-matter of all kinds of development should dwell in some form or other on the contact of the individual self with the Lord or the Supreme Principle. Gaurinath rightly remarks: "It shines like a priceless diamond set in the velvety words of the Divine Song which gives it a shelter and a luster of its own. It sends out its fiery rays from the many-folded facets which had been cut into it by the inquisitive mind of the spiritual seeker". – Gaurinath: "The Triune Path", Sampurnananda Sanskrit University, Varanasi, 1982, p. 26. Integral humanity should therefore be followed by the way of overcoming our duality – good and evil, and correct understanding of this concept in reality needs the resting of our idea eternally in Consciousness and Truth. The approach of such strategic idea should be made common to all, as for the one who is endowed with the inner vision; the discrimination between an ordinary rock and a precious gem is spontaneous and immediate. – *Op. cit.,* p. 27.

135. This kind of initiative requires also vision for the feminine power, along with all classes of human beings. Here, remarks of Vivekananda are worth nothing: "Without Shakti [feminine power] there is no regeneration for the world". – Complete Works, Vol. 7, p. 484. The magic wand that could bring about this regeneration was, according to him, education. So, he further comments: "Only let woman and people achieve education! All further questions of their fate, they would themselves be competent to settle". – Nivedita, Sister: "Woman in Modern India", Prabuddha Bharata, March 1928, p. 238. The modern women, as Vivekananda believes, have their intellect stuffed with information, but for him, this mattered very little. It is because; he always placed purity and chastity above mere intellectual attainments. – Shuddhidananda, Swami (Ed.): "Vivekananda as the Turning Point. The Rise of a New Spiritual Wave", Advaita Ashrama,

Kolkata, 2013, pp. 173-74. In his view, the future women would be the fusion of the soft heart of a mother and a hero's will. Thus, we require first, to uproot social value system for increasing human capacity building in reorienting society to give birth to spiritual giants for the sake of innovating the world order, by all means of developmental activities through human empowerment system as well as redrafting our democratic plans for the devolution of power in terms of real and scientific educational schemes in a decisive understanding.

136. Principles of work to be performed in equanimity thought are also prophesied in the Holy Bible. It is therefore noted in the Bible: "A good tree cannot bear bad fruit, nor can a bad tree bear good". – The Holy Bible, The Gideons International, Andhra Pradesh, 2008, p. 937. The balanced development philosophy is therefore actual equanimity thought which must have the ideal of the Bible comments: "Every tree that does not bear good fruit is cut down and thrown into the fire". – *Ibid.,* p. 937. But, the Gita goes above all these ideas, while saying that we should perform for human beings with the notion of sacrifice, as we offer to God. Hence, the Hindu philosophy of work dignifies the concept of equanimity to the disinterested notion for serving and doing well to others. Modern corporate strategies are required to be adopted all such balanced thoughts for eliminating social distress of suffered and downtrodden human beings. It will lead to the path of salvation to all, and in the long-run, universal peace will also be restored for coherence human interrelationships to the envisagement of industrial democratic path in parallel way.

137. To cite an example, there was once, the method of clearly stratified sequence of three cultures – (1) The Brahmagiri Stone Axe Culture, (2) The Megalithic Culture, and (3) The ndhra or Sâtavâhana Culture as observed by the 'Archaeological Mission' which is the shining reflection of Indian antiquity to the destiny of the world-wide integrity, prevailing thereby an aspect of human craftsmanship and scientific parlance of living foundation. In other words, the three cultures represent a continuous occupation of the site through three successive phases and can therefore be interrelated chronologically. – Wheeler, Mortimer: "My Archaeological Mission to India and Pakistan", Thames and Hudson, London, 1976, pp. 63-64. It is therefore submissively said that technological considerations are to be meant for nurturing human environmental sustainability with the creative path of human brotherhood feeling, so as to solve problems of misery, hunger and distressful social living situations in coordinating corporate responsibility accounting tasks, in initiating social balance through scientific human development process; which demands for efficient utilization of social resources in rectifying conditions of human imbalances in living parameters.

138. In pursuant with the spirit of realization, it can be noted in the language of Frank Davy who states in the Preface to 'From There to Here': "When the very diversity and looseness of contemporary structures invite commitment and participation, the values of detachment and impersonality fade. The classical artistic concept of the totally integrated whole has no incarnation in a sensory reality that is everywhere fragmented, discontinuous, post-logical (Davy, 1974: 20). To quote Kroetsch, "The spirit of high modernism was to assert the validity of a single cosmology and, with it, closure. Modernists wanted things to be all of piece again. And a lot of the things that were happening then – physics, comparative

religion, anthropological studies were undermining notions of a single cosmology" (Kroetsch, 1982: 28). We thus have a falling out of cosmologies and a falling into language. But to the conducive view on dynamic social orientation process, it needs to mention that we should move forward with original creative movement and invention, in returning to our judicial practices for human emancipation from sufferings with great inspiration, in invigorating, analyzing and theorizing power of utilizing resources for the purposive management, which goes to attain the goal culturally, in initiative and thoughts of making strategies for human real development. New relational conceptualization of identity politics should be confined the visionary hope for postmodernism's future rather than as one of its achievements, as Jardine argued for the French project of uniting feminism and modernity. – Kudchedkar, Shirin (Ed.): "Postmodernism and Feminism: Canadian Contexts", Pencraft International, Delhi, 2005, p. 90. Hence, the spirit of realization must not be in conflicting situation for any divergences, but rather there should be assimilating tendencies which will depict technological innovations for human effective system of communication. In this way, we can develop our activities in all means of modern organizational communication system, with the coordinated path of social upliftment of marginalized sections that have been looking to intellectuals, leaders and strategists for their advancement in modern day's technological society.

139. The Sanatana practices bring in people joy and happiness for doing works and services with the selfless sacrifice or motive. It is permeably said that this principle follows for the good of others in performing with energy and in time. There is the concept of unconditional deed under this philosophy and the science behind acting is concerned with the notion of salvation initiatives, for which requires communication skill profound with spiritual knowledge, and the means of personality development which are guided by the scientific envisagement 'man-making services and leadership qualities', have been conceptualized in organizational pattern of managing human activities, for the great cause of humanity. Our activities pertaining to trade, industry and commerce should be performed in making society dynamic towards confining people to the path of existentialism in positivistic assumptions of the meaning of life, which connote to the principles of humanism, universality and eternal practices of life bringing possibilities; directed towards attaining the goal of universal brotherhood in terms of cooperative international understanding as well as eternal peace in making social foundation based on the pillars of tranquility. All these are accentuated through the principles of – "Vasudhaiva Kutumbakam" ideology exemplified in foregoing analysis.

140. Channelization of funds in right path must have the scope for making use of household financial savings through capital market. But in facing the challenges of the 21st century, serious and immediate attention must be given to the persisting problems of interfacing between the primary and secondary markets and the prevalence of rampant speculation. However, Sengupta remarks: "It (capital market) must start functioning effectively as an effective watch dog policing against the on-going reckless speculative and attendant evils like insider trading, gambling on the kerbs, manipulations with the unofficial premia". – Sengupta, N. K.: "Government and Business", Vikas Publishing House Pvt. Ltd., New Delhi, 2001, p. 185. These tasks must be given utmost priority if the Indian

stock market is to continue to be a barometer of economic progress. For social growth, we must have a vision to the diversification of funds, and which is further concerned with the speculation process; and to turn to Keynes again, we may say that speculations may do no harm as bubbles on a steady stream of enterprise. But the position is serious when enterprise becomes the bubble on a whirlpool of speculation. In terms of efficiency it can be said: "Under conditions of perfect or near-perfect competition a more general tax, whether direct or indirect, is better than a less general tax". – Ganguly, S.: "Public Finance A Normative Approach", The World Press Private Ltd., Calcutta, 1992, p. 78. In this way, correct speculative measures should be adopted in restructuring overall economy for setting an order through equilibrium; so that tax reform may actually increase economic welfare by effectuating a better allocation of economic resources.

141. Managerial challenges are now also constituent with the moderate and effective pricing strategies, as Dwivedi comments. "The pricing strategy varies from stage to stage over the life-cycle of product, depending on the market conditions". – Dwivedi, D. N.: "Managerial Economics", Vikas Publishing House Pvt. Ltd., New Delhi, 2008, p. 393. In pursuant with business cycles, managerial challenges could be predicted by quoting Burns: "… … men who wish to serve democracy faithfully must recognize that the roots of business cycles go deep in the economic organization, that the ability of government to control depressions adequately is not yet assured, that our power of forecasting is limited and true foresight requires policies for coping with numerous contingencies". – Quoted from Gordon, R. A.: "Business Fluctuations", Harper and Brothers, Publishers, N. Y., 1952, p. 4. Again, managerial challenges can confront with the influence of the character, quality, and content of their educational systems by manipulating important economic and non-economic factors. Excellent surveys on economic issues relating to education to development can be found in Simmons, John: "Education for Development Reconsidered", World Development 7 (1979): 1005-1016. Blaug, M.: "An Introduction to the Economics of Education", Penguin, England, 1970. So, challenging phase in managing resources is concerned with the objectivity which should commensurate with the goal of human excellence quality improvement considerations.

142. The modification is also necessary from the viewpoint of the interdependence of tasks which has to accompany interdependent social relationships at work. – Bhatia, S. K.: "Managing Organizational Behaviour", Deep & Deep Publications Pvt. Ltd., New Delhi, 2008, p. 213. If the two are not in harmony, the people concerned with the task will not perform the job as though it was interrelated. To overcome problems of nepotism, we may choose to prefer few hierarchical positions in organizations, because it becomes less bureaucratic and flexible in approach. In this way, we may be able to rectify social ills and lapses for maximum amount of delivery with the minimum governance in administering our tasks in structural adjustments, to simplify values and identify aspects of working models. In terms of balancing with technological innovation, human civilization's positive works are possible to be transformed into social goal of human development, if it is done only after mastering language that a deaf-blind person becomes capable of comparing his own actions against the cultural standards evolved by mankind in relation to all spheres of life. Similarly, it goes without saying that, once language has become established, it exerts an extremely powerful influence on a

child's established patterns of behaviour and on his mind, enabling the latter to advance to the higher level of development, one that would have been attainable without language. – See also, Judelson, Katherine: "Awakening to Life", Translated from the Russian, Progress Publishers, Moscow, 1974, pp. 291-308. Transformation of human beings takes place through initiation, and so, the realization of this potential which is called forth by social factors has to be given special attention. It is the special form of learning can help in the process of development and to the manifestation of increasing scientific skills in capacity building in a holistic approach of teaching as well as teaching with reinforcement.

143. The roots of universal rolling in regard to integral concept of management should confine all activities of human organizational pursuits, now here referred to as "rights-based" theories and principles. In this context, readers are advised to consult Wong, David B.: "Moral Relativity", University of California Press, Berkeley, 1984. To be sure, some contemporary western moral philosophers are questioning the "rights-based" concept cluster of modern morals, turning away from highly abstract rules, logical principles, and calculations, turning instead to qualities of personal character, in many ways attempting to reinvigorate the concept cluster surrounding the Aristotelian virtues. The significance of this shift notwithstanding, it is almost certainly the case that non-western ethical systems will not better described by an updated Aristotelian terminology than by the terminology of "rights-based" moral theories; more will be needed. For the trend away from the latter in contemporary philosophical work, see Foot, Philippa: "Virtues and Vices", University of California Press, Berkeley, 1978; Wallace, James D.: "Virtues and Vices", Cornell University Press, Ithaca, N. Y., 1978; Williams: "Ethics and the Limits"; Sommers, Christina H. (Ed.): "Vice and Virtue in Every Life", Harcourt Brace Jovanovich, Orlando, Fla., 1985. In this way, ethical rules are standardized for social building norms of human environmental issues, connoting principles of social imbalances, regional disparities and human sufferings. Science behind dealing with all these conditions should perpetuate human knowledge regarding strength and courage producing the elements of a higher culture as well as improving all these through mental activity. Halbfass mentions therefore that the human spirit may only be enticed and able to grasp its own nature in thought where it is conscious of its own specific dignity. – Halbfass, Wilhelm: "India and Europe. An Essay in Philosophical Understanding", Motilal Banarsidass Publishers Pvt. Ltd., Delhi, 1990, p. 152. In coping with the problems of social disparities thus, philosophy, as a science would be able to demonstrate practical situations wherefrom people should be streamlined for harmonious and resourceful unity to their mental power in assorting things to the reformative movement with the conduct of organizational activities to nurture people, who have been deprived by the present system for long.

144. If one looks to the vertical context, it is evident that the pursuit of the contemplative path to a "higher" kind of consciousness is crucial. – Larson, Gerald James and Deutsch, Eliot (Eds.): "Interpreting Across Boundaries. New Essays in Comparative Philosophy", Motilal Banarsidass Publishers Pvt. Ltd., Delhi, 1989, p. 181. The efficient match of resources requires scientific backgrounds of the Upanishads to overcome problems of extravagant absurdities. Thus, Indian scientists of ritual and grammar as Bandhāyana, Pāṇini, Āpastamba,

Kātyāyana, or Pata jali have contributed great insights which could be useful in applying to the principles of social reconstruction for eliminating human misfortunes. It is therefore, in modern sense of social orientation process, can also be suggested that the works of Marx, Freud, Darwin, Einstein or Chomsky should be found from the scientific researches' angle, so that modern civilization can find-out all the principles of existential freedom of living. Social misfortunes have to be eradicated through oneness principle. Because, it is the essence and so, oneness is essential in God also, which will help people in illuminating idea of the absolute unity; and in the case of all other beings, it is relative and dependent on God. Hence, the theory of unity is ingrained in human development with the multiplying principles of the synthetic notion of social unity. All our discoveries and inventions are therefore required such efficient concept of management.

145. In doing social welfare, Vallabbhbhai Patel was therefore the man who was best able to reconcile the impracticalities of Gandhian philosophy with the realities of peasant politics. – Hardiman, David: "Peasant Nationalists of Gujarat Khedia District 1917-1934", Oxford University Press, Delhi, 1981, p. 128. This leads us to suggest that the chief initiative in the peasant movements of the 1917 to 1934 period came not from the elites, not from the petty bourgeoisie, and not from the middle peasants, but from the more substantial peasant communities. – *Op. cit.,* p. 255. The past experience thus reflects when in 1931, after the Gandhi-Irwin Pact, the Congress leaders tried to call of the movement, the poorer peasants refused to comply ... ... there were clashes with the police. – See also, Sanyal, H.: "Gandhian Political Movement in Southwest Bengal 1921-1947", pp. 6-12. All these past references are still today, relevant in ameliorating our present poverty, which require radical social reformations with the kind of land reformative initiatives in which people will be empowered for utilizing their potential resources in confining social assets to the path of human welfare activities, along with government initiatives which are primarily lagging behind all such amenities required for people's development. Hence, it is expected that land reformation will change the modern society in positive direction to bring in human welfare through different programmes of the governments. It is therefore the absolute need of the time in the changing pattern of socio-economic process of human development initiatives as well as government's action plan in the scheme of eradicating poverty from Indian economy, along with advancing the country to be able to a good world community in reshaping societal standard of living parameters.

146. As behaviour, models, and standards for knowledge evolve, so can goals ... ... As thought and mental models guide action and further thought, we adopt clear thinking and accurate models as goals in themselves. – Heller, Knut H., Mehmud, C. H. and Tumbult, W. H.: "The University Textbook of Nanotechnology", Dominant Publishers and Distributors, New Delhi, 2008, p. 231. The evolution of goals thus brings forth both science and ethics. Organizational innovation in analyzing the wealth of nations is important part of human development. History shows how crucial organizations are for the achievement of human goals; as the sad story of centrally planned economies so clearly shows, without the organizational genius of the modern private-enterprise firm, all the land, labour, and capital would work for naught. – Samuelson, Paul A., Nordhans, William D.: "Economics", McGraw-Hill, Inc., New York, 1995, p. 103. The value

judgment for social change requires that the project which are nearing completion need to be funded adequately so that they can be completed within their schedule time and no cost and time overruns are created. – Kapur, P. K. & Sehgal, V. K. (Eds.): "Operations Research Theory and Practice", Spaniel Publishers, New Delhi, 1995, p. 271. Thus, proactive nature of work reflects that we should realize the goals of the organization in terms of its functioning, for which we need to ensure timely completion of socially oriented projects in successful manner. This helps in consumption along with saving. Lipsey and Steiner remarkably said: "If we know the dependence of consumption on disposable income, we will also know the dependence of saving on disposable income. – Lipsey, Richard G. and Steiner, Peter O.: "Economics", Harper & Row, Publishers, Inc., New York, 1981, p. 511. Our policy decisions are therefore important for implementing government schemes of work in changing the societal foundation, which can utilize resources for timely implementation at the grass-root level.

147. All these are required creativity and innovative entrepreneurship development programmes to start new ventures through environmental factors and events encompassing background, education, careers, family, etc. Finally, there should be a sense of purpose. So, we need to create in a business ideology to serve customers, not to exploit them. New laws, economic influences, social changes and new technologies should not be viewed as threat, but to industrial stability providing for the ample opportunities to entrepreneurs. – Holt, David H.: "Entrepreneurship New Venture Creation", Prentice-Hall of India Private Limited, New Delhi, 2004, pp. 23-57. Again, a comprehensive study of environmental issues would be necessarily done with the aspects of human motivating factors – they must take into consideration cultural, legal, political and economic characteristics that exist overseas. – *Op. cit.,* p. 333. Hence, growth perspective analysis should also be made for the foreign environment of business, to accommodate a system backed by scientific analysis. The battle between rational, left-brain behaviour, and creative, right-brain behaviour, is a common problem for technological innovation. Because innovation is often explained in technical terms – tangible products or processes that result from technological development – there has been a preoccupation with rational, analytical innovation models. – *Ibid.,* pp. 38-39. So, it is suggested that problems of human sufferings should be solved in terms of supportive strategic decisions that encourage creativity and innovative development. R. R. Paul writes: "Economic progress is a dynamic process and the study of economic progress is a study of economic dynamics". – Paul, R. R.: "History of Economic Thought", Kalyani Publishers, New Delhi, 2013, p. 221. Thus, we have two forces working in the opposite directions: technological improvements promoting growth and the tendency of diminishing returns retarding growth for this reason, macro as well as micro aspects are required to be seen from both quantitative and qualitative framework of decision variables, to uproot social value, enhance productivity and to restore organizational balance in changing social dynamics. In a nutshell, production of material wealth is the basis of human existence and the mode of production of wealth is the determining factor of social development. – *Op. cit.,* p. 289. In bringing social mobility, particularly in underdeveloped and developing countries, governments should monitor the economy through international market

prospective, internal human development deficiencies and technologically guided norms of human up-gradation. Besides, two structures should be changed in such a way which would help in reducing gaps between rich and poor people. It is to be done for overall social efficiency. Overall, any study of market and theory of value must be associated with money, price, trade, industrial fluctuations, etc. – Das, Debendra K. (Ed.): "Economics of Markets Theory and Evidence", Deep & Deep Publishers, New Delhi, 1993, p. 35. Significantly, we must consider the fact that there is also possibility of developing a set of criteria for defence output irrespective of cost and technology. – *Op. cit.,* p. 192. As technology and circumstances are changing rapidly, we need to apply principles of integrity to deal with problems from practical situations and realities of management. Thus, diversification of resources network should be maintained for innovating human skills, to cope up challenges of change in the environment.

148. It is observed that markets will fail to achieve allocation efficiency when there are externalities. So, there should be enough confidence building norms prevalent through bilateral or other kinds of trade agreements. On this line of thinking, the government will have to assume progressively a predominant and direct responsibility for setting up new industrial undertakings and for developing transport facilities. – Lekhi, R. K.: "Public Finance", Kalyani Publishers, New Delhi, 1988, p. 743. A progressive country should therefore adopt right policy in looking through forward tendencies with great hopes for development. To elucidate the idea of integration, corporate tax should require simplification procedure in moving economy towards the advancement, for empowering people to interact with other nations profitably, and to solve problems of development within the country by joining hands with the sovereign governments.

149. Many that have followed Machiavelli's percepts have ended in disaster. – MacIver, R. M.: "The Web of Government", The Free Press, New York, 1965, p. 7. In modern times, intensive growth has turned a large number of country-governments into national governments. So, international understanding has now been placed as the focal point of study for intensifying corporate beliefs and removing bottlenecks of human developmental paradigms. This requirement holds not only for a large range of economic issues but also for numerous arrangements necessitated by technological developments, such as the assignment of radio channels and generally of the facilities of intercommunication, quarantine and other regulations affecting public health, patents, and copyrights, the rights of travelers, migrants, resident aliens and journalists reporting from foreign countries, and so forth. Some of these matters are regulated by the body of customs called international law, others by agreements made at international conventions. – *Op. cit.,* p. 273. From all such, among others, the advantages of international understanding and its impact on human development cannot be exaggerated.

150. In this context, it is worthwhile to note that the contrast in economic and social organization between the advanced exchange economy and the backward indigenous economy is one of the most striking characteristics of a poor country. – Meier, G. M.: "Leading Issues in Economic Development", 1984. The development of human and technology will exert an ever increasing influence on economic development too. Khachaturov remarks that there are reasons to expect the following major achievements in science and technology in the future:

the use of thermo-nuclear power in the power industry and the widespread use of fast reactors; the synthesis of super-hard materials and metals without dislocations in their crystalline lattice; the introduction of lasers in different fields – communications, detection, the processing of materials; micro-miniaturization; fourth- and fifth- generation computers; automatic libraries; whether control; widespread use of the sea-bed for the development of the mining industry; solution of problems in the struggle against malignant tumors; chemical control over the ageing process; regeneration of organs; artificial foods; new types of artificial leather – durable, fine and porous, the production of motor vehicles that do not pollute the atmosphere, and of battery driven vehicles; disposable consumer goods. – Khachaturov, T.: "The Economy of the Soviet Union Today", Progress Publishers, Moscow, 1977, p. 171. So, the targets of increased production, higher labour productivity, lower material requirements per unit of output, and so on must be based on the introduction of new technology, its performance and scale. Data on the performance and the scale of use of new machinery, machine-tools and materials can be taken as the foundation for calculations of future output, increases in labour productivity and cuts in production costs. This requires fundamental improvement in the planning of technological progress, coordination of plans for technological progress and production, and their organic interconnection.

151. Each function involves some process and is discharged for a certain section of people residing in a particular area or region. To quote a few examples, the development of agriculture dealing with agriculture is evidently based on functional principle. Since the department benefits agriculturists it can be categorized as clientele principle department. Likewise Foreign Affairs Department concerning foreign affairs is based on functional principle. Since the department deals with affairs pertaining to foreign countries it is based on area principle. The Department of Defence is not only based on functional principle but also process, as war which is to be conducted by the Defence department is an activity as well. – Bhagwan, Vishnoo and Bhushan, Vidya: "Public Administration", S. Chand & Company Ltd., New Delhi, 2003. We, the citizens of this degenerating world, have responsibility to help in the transition of the existing value system of the international society. – Kumar, Pravin: "Contemporary India", Abhijeet Publishers, Delhi, 2011, p. 254. To quote Vijay Sharma: "Whereas most other regimes would derive their legitimacy from law, as distinct from morality, the environmental regime is distinct. Its legitimacy rests quite substantially on its being perceived as moral in redistributive and equitable frame". – Economic Times, 17 Aug., 1993. This is what the experts and environmentalists would like to encourage, the development and promotion of environmental purity, simultaneously, a concept which may be defined as environmentally sustainable growth and development. Again, the dominant mode of production in the rural areas taking into account the process of interaction and the forms of economic exchanges among different strata of rural population based on caste/status on the one hand, and the size of holding and other economic capabilities on the other. The caste-class framework (Kumar, Dharma, 1965: 48) needs slight modification when applied to tribal sector. The village headman and the village priest normally have more land than other individuals. Such pre-existing inequality is getting exacerbated in the face of new opportunities leading

to some sort of class formation (Pathy et. al., 1976: 399-417: Agro-Economic Research Centre for North-Eastern India, 1969: 221-23). Hence, status-class approach might be useful for such kind of social reconstruction. It is observed that in spite of the poor socio-economic resources with low potentiality for production in the rural sector, people borrow from the 'exploitative' informal sources rather than the 'cooperative' formal sources. – Baboo, Balgovind: "Economic Exchanges in Rural India", Manak Publishers Pvt. Ltd., Delhi, 1992, p. 271.

152. For this, materialism may be an over-simplification of the world – all matter is probably instinct with life, and it is impossible to reduce the unity of consciousness to matter and motion, but matter is a good weapon against the Church and must be used until a better one is found. – Shanta: "Marx and Contemporary Materialism", Printwell Publishers, Jaipur, 1987, pp. 27-28. Thus, the essence of Marx's philosophy is that it is a 'Philosophy of action', 'Philosophy of deed', or 'Philosophy of praxis', that it is such a 'theory' as does not retain just they but also demands the act of changing the world and also at the time participates in this work. – Petrovic, Gayo: "Dialectical Materialism and the Philosophy of Praxis", in Boston: "Studies in Philosophy of Science", Vol. IV, (Ed.) by Cohen and Wartofsky, Holland, 1969, p. 265. Nehru thought that Appleby was right in saying that the Indian administration machinery was slow and was fettered by the old procedure suitable only for the stagnation of the colonial days and totally unsuitable in the days of social change ... ... However, his approach was not free from major shortcomings arising from the underestimation of the class nature of the officialdom. – Martyshin, Orest: "Jawaharlal Nehru and His Political Views", Progress Publishers, Moscow, English translation 1989, pp. 145-46. It is thus, obvious that the problem of governing and of the government machinery was very much on Nehru's mind. Further, the withdrawal of the British was so unexpected that even till the last moment, Gandhi was thinking in terms of resuming another struggle for freedom ... ... after the vital role Netaji Bose played ... ... Control over the decisions of the Congress Working Committee, all the important leaders abandoned him and paid only ritual homage to his leadership. – Lahiry, Ashutosh: "Gandhi in Indian Politics", Firma Klm Private Limited, Calcutta, 1976, pp. 182-85. Under such circumstances, it is clear that social transformation requires a broad view on human emancipation from severe social sufferings, for which the Vedanta version of universal human upliftment ideology is most suited in today's world of discrimination.

153. In rectifying social imbalances, the governments should consider that steps need to be taken to ensure, as enjoined in the Directive Principles of the Constitution referred to, that concentration does not operate to the common detriment. – Srivastava, S. K., Nigam, R. S., Sahai, Bishamber and Banerjee, Mrityunjoy: "Industrial Economics", S. Chand & Co., New Delhi, 1967, p. 506. Again, in line with participation, they remark: "Where an industry is not reserved for the public sector and where the more difficult capital intensive industries are concerned, which call for the acquisition of foreign collaboration facilities, foreign exchange from private or semi-public lending agencies abroad and the provision of experienced managerial talent, naturally, the applications from the larger industrial groups in the country have to be considered, if the Plan targets have to

be expeditiously achieved. Otherwise, the policy is to prefer new entrepreneurs wherever possible". – *Ibid.,* p. 506.

154. Social problems erupting mainly when restrictions of this nature are coupled with local political instability, the threat of war or revolution, communistic leanings, the fear of expropriation or of increasing harassment by the government, the "culture for investment" is obviously unfavourable. – Wasserman, Max J. and Hulfman, Charles W.: "Modern International Economics: A Balance of Payments Approach", S. Chand & Co., New Delhi, 1970, p. 228. Hence, there should be a good investment climate to deliver services with organizational capacity building and competencies, along with all credibility. However, in delivering goods to the crisis areas, as for example, in this time of water energy and environmental purity crisis, the hyacinth can be a very effective tool in water pollution control, water recycling and energy generation. It certainly calls for far greater efforts than are being put currently. – Trivedy, R. K. and Goel, P. K. (Eds.): "Current Pollution Researches in India", Environmental Publications, Karad, 1985, p. 138. Thus, organizational work ethics have great scope for exhibiting things in producing outputs, to the fullest level development of needy people in reducing social problems. Bergson remarks: "Our freedom, in the very movements by which it is affirmed, creates the growing habits that will stifle it to renew itself by a constant effort: it is dogged by automatism". – Bergson, Henri: "Creative Evolution", Macmillan & Co. Ltd., London, 1960, p. 134. Like eddies of dust raised by the wind as it passes, the living turn upon them, borne up by the great blast of life. They are therefore relatively stable and counterfeit immobility so well that we treat each of them as a thing rather than as a progress, forgetting that the very performance of their form is only the outline of a movement. – *Op. cit.,* p. 135. It is true that all orders necessarily appear as contingent. Dialectic is necessary to put intuition to the proof, necessary also in order that intuition should break itself up into concepts and so be propagated to other men; but all it does, often enough, is to develop the result of that intuition which transcends it. About embracing our ideologies, finally it is observed that things, once constituted, show on the surface, by their changes of situation, the profound changes that are being accomplished within the Whole. In trying to excel organizations through productive kind of human social existence, it is high time that taxation policies are to be reformed for civilization's goal of forward moving tendencies. Here, Mongia's view can be quoted: "High taxation often adversely affects private enterprise and initiative, and contributes a decline in the net investment capacity (and thereby, in the employment level too) of the economy. – Mongia, J. N.: "Impact of Deficit Financing on Economic Growth in Underdeveloped Countries", Associated Publishing House, New Delhi, 1971, p. 5. In solving social problems, we are to curb inflation for bringing stability in societal structure, where people have been living in a stage of slavery. Any encroachment on the already low consumption standards of these people is likely to be offset in part through disinvestments, such disinvestments taking many forms, among them failing to maintain worker's houses and other durable personal property, and less investment in the training and education and health of themselves and their children. – *Op. cit.,* p. 17. Integrated opportunities could be viable through dynamic investment climate, and it requires encouraging the flow of investment into the desirable channels. So, international trade policies

are to be redrafted to enhance the outcome through factor prices, not only in promoting employment generation; but also to the protection of the overall economy. – Mankar, V. G., Sadasivan, C. R., Kulkarni, C. Y. and Shah, J. H.: "Public Finance Foreign Trade and Development", Himalaya Publishers, Bombay, 1982. To strengthen harmonious business relationships, it is to be noted the amount of employment, at any moment, depends upon the amount of capital in existence and the techniques of production. – Robinson, Joan: "An Essay on Marxian Economics", Macmillan & Co. Ltd., London, 1960, p. 29. Thus, this ideology of doing business can reduce social equalities by increasing quality of living, if this system is used, which can work as the last link with the theory of value in realizing social dynamicity.

155. Attempts are to be made to promote the development of the backward regions through autonomous public investment. – Mahajan, O. P.: "Economic Planning and Regional Development in India", Ess Ess Publications, New Delhi, 1982, p. 15. Concentration of the limited public investible resources on the growth centres is bound to provoke strong reaction from the less developed areas. So, measures like transfer of funds from the developed to the less developed regions for direct investment and for provision of infrastructural facilities, loans and subsidies, and special tax concessions to induce investors to locate their enterprises in the backward areas, etc. are required to be adopted. This type of management can balance regional disparities to overcome problems of human deprivation. Ludwig Erhard opines: "Convertibility and a liberal trade policy could merely prepare a way to a solution of the difficulties connected with balance of payments ... ... and that an interconnection can be established between markets for other commodities than goods". – Erhard, Ludwig: "Germany's Comeback in the World Market", George Allen & Unwin Ltd., London, 1954, p. 147. In organizational system of management, a proper analysis of the financial affairs of an enterprise can certainly throw up useful signals about overall managerial effectiveness. – Gupta, L. C.: "Financial Ratios for Monitoring Corporate Sickness", Oxford University Press, Delhi, 1983, p. 111. It is here importantly to be suggested that less trade restriction and exchange manipulation, are the right diet for all phases of the trade cycle or the right remedy for all the economic ills of the world. – Robertson, D. H.: "Essays in Monetary Theory", Staples Press Limited, London, 1948, p. 113. To solve problems of human deprivation worldwide, the rapid technological progress that has been observed in the environment could well be channelized to suit conditions for uneven economic development as well as distribution capacities and human skill building operations.

156. If the economies of developing countries have diversified structures, regional economic cooperation or customs union among them would promote trade and lead to an export based growth. For eradicating human backwardness, reduction in or elimination of trade barriers among such countries is a necessary condition for coordinated industrialization. To overcome problems, there should also be coordinated planning and more to a common market as in case of EEC (European Economy Community). To settle disputes of trade, it is suggested that the East African Common Market, Latin American Common Market, Central American Common Market, Andean Common Market, etc., are expected to provide gains of trade creation and economic integration. – Avadhani, V. A.: "International Finance: Theory and Practice", Himalaya Publishing House, Delhi, 1987,

p. 146. So, mutual participation can help countries in international transactions, in rectifying trade barriers on a multilateral basis, and thus, regional economic cooperation is a must for international strength in currency settlement, trade negotiations, international cooperation building atmosphere for reducing regional imbalances. Human conditions can also be remedied through improving system of agricultural productivity. Hence, for scientific utilization of reclaimed wastewaters for crop irrigation, it is necessary that the wastewaters are carefully and completely characterized with reference to various parameters that are known to influence the soil conditions and plant growth. – Trivedy, R. K. and Goel, P. K. (Eds.): "Current Researches in India", Environmental Publications, Karad, 1985, p. 93. Like the magnitude scale that had been developed on the basis of measurement of brightness of stars (Basu, Baidyanath: "An Introduction to Astrophysics", Prentice-Hall of India Private Limited, New Delhi, 2003, p. 52), we require developing human society in such propensity to advance people in realization of their life problems. Backwardness can be dealt in a position; we are able to see the manner in which a refinement of the conception of position has been developed. – Manjunath, P. R. (Ed.): "Gravitation and Relativity", RBSA Publishers, Jaipur, 2007, p. 181. So, we should assume its 'truth' in geometrical propositions.

157. The scientific theme of working attitude should be converted to service, in which everything will be professed, and so, every religion teaches that – see God in everything and everywhere. – Chetanananda, Swami (Ed.): "Vedanta: Voice of Freedom", Advaita Ashrama, Kolkata, 2011, p. 111. In Advaita system, there is wonderful unity can be felt through work and this can be implemented at least, to a few hundred million citizens of India who are observed to be ill-fed, ill-clad, poorly sheltered, ill-treated, despised, exploited and cheated (Aleaz, R. P.: "The Gospel of Indian Culture", Punthi Pustak, Calcutta, 1994, p. 184), to realize the ultimate objective of human civilization. Technological strategic policies are to be adopted for the world development in a set pattern and order. —Nakamura, Hajime: "A History of Early Vedānta Philosophy", Part One, Motilal Banarsidass, Delhi, 1983, p. 497. It is translated into English by Trevor Leggett, Sengakul Mayeda, Taitetz Knno and Others.

Chapter 3

Religious Perspective for Human Development

Confluence of Thought for Human Development – Religiosity for Humanity

There are different strategies adopted in social science studies for human development from different dimensions, of which religious perspective in strengthening the base of human development issues can be analyzed in terms of philosophical understanding regarding various aspects of social upliftment ideas of humankind, that go to shape the present world in scientific temper of thought for binding people, in considering core concept of living elements[1]. As to this objective assessment, it has become imperative to know about various backgrounds of human religious philosophy, with reference to organizational system of management in effective guidance of people, to nurture work ethics in cross-cultural dimensions of multinational corporate objectives to unify goal of human living parameters toward reaching universal humanity, concomitant to radical change element perspectives of the societal background. It is therefore, confluence of human unanimous thought necessary for understanding the ecstasy of religious universal philosophy, ingrained in conceptual foundation of social development pyramid, noting which the present system of corporate activities could be merged in the process of cultural unity regarding the thought of universal fabric of social harmony, in terms of organizational guidance in making human life realizable towards living perfections by way of adequate performance as well as effective delivery, to meet social challenges in time and space. Thus, universality for understanding on the strategy of human development perspective has become a catch-word, in knowing exactly the role of religion in changing the social spectrum from multi-phases of developmental activities that would be measured, in dignified manner to amplify the goal of integral humanity aspects on religious plat-form. Consequently, it is said undoubtedly that no religion in this world guides people to think for selfish motive[2], either for individuals, or for any groups in society; in orienting the societal foundation to the rationalistic attitude of human upliftment programmes. Probably, this is the reason, that which religion is the background of human understanding with a view to realize modern organizational activities based on universal performance criteria, to which everyone should have the right to participate in the process of making socialization an idea of universal subject, for the objective attainment of managing social resources towards all endeavours of human beings; in encountering for optimal order of human development where each human being will find scope of expressing the self for others, in connection with development activities, to aid for advancing the social journey in dynamic rolling of the world order to the fullest level of human personality development. More or less, we have become slave of our limitation of thinking with respect to religious ideology, which has not given scope of expressing people to mould the character of human civilization, for which there is bloodshed in society as observed, in question of religion. The reality of religion[3] stands on the pillars of thinking for humanity regarding condition of human life surrounded in social environment. Everywhere, in society we find, now-a-days, there is unnecessary debates going on in question of religious ideologies; which is termed by a group of people to politicize development of human beings, as the communal or secular agenda, to gain something out of such mischievously created problem. Actual science behind religious thinking is nothing, but humanity should be objectively taken into consideration in the present set-up of backwardness prevailing in society. It is, therefore, confluence of thought should be made from the strategic ground realities on developing social structure, rolling people to move for advancement and considering all socio-economic activities as worship for the welfare of mass people. In this way, nurturing cultural humanism should be accounted for organizational guidance[4] by means of vibrant leadership techniques in dealing with human activities, to consider for social change, in which religion should be entrusted to play role in democratic participative nature of human challenges to radicalize social development to the path of making dynamic growth of the world societies. In short, the entire subject of religion should be made a discipline of human development oriented concept of scientific socialization process, in dealing each and every activity of modern organizational progressive idea of social changing philosophy as well as human existential freedom of life.

The idea of humanity is thus conceived from the religious concept of development-related aspect of truth, bliss and absolute in matters of understanding on human activities, to be performed for integrating the base of the world society on pillars of integrated social development in sustaining, conserving, and preserving will of the universal interrelationships between religious institutions on the one hand, and organizational agencies for social changing mechanism, along with government counterparts on the other hand, so as to complement the process of social upliftment programmes with a view to emulate picture of illuminated social rejuvenation to the path of human dignity, social survival of human beings, and worldwide harmony among religious leaders. It is pity to mention that the scientific enlargement of ideas on the practice of social activities are concerned with religious bigotry, in course of dealing with people's agenda; which has to be balanced in realistic manner for encountering issues on human backward conditions in different parts of the world economy. We should therefore be flexible while a framework of policy resolution will be adopted for universal development of humankind, as this policy will help increasing social good in nurturing concept of integral humanity, by way of following approach of honesty and truth as the leadership criterion to the goal of religious works[5], meant for universal human development activities. Consequently, religious information are to be made more and more socially oriented towards all endeavors of human activities, concerned with carrying out of the objectives of man-power development process, in terms of organizational guidance as well as governmental supervision. Narrating thus the concept of universal human cooperative base in organizational agenda of social changing mechanism, religious perspective should be enlarged in effulgent ideological system of correlating issues of human growth, based on social reformation in dynamic order in rolling the entire humanity towards the idea of finding out optimum level of human emancipation, by maximizing social welfare through common good of deprived masses; irrespective of any kind of religious narrow sectarian viewpoints. Measuring all these aspects of religious supremacy in creating social foundation on structure of strategic movement for unifying the causes of religious truth, which go to advance people in regard to survival as well as existential possibility in highest order of excelling things, will require integrated approach of social rolling on the developed platform; where there is only slogan of human capacity building and universal integrity towards binding the whole human race in one common agenda – universality of human core idea of living as well as realizing human life for optimum order of perfectionism through all positivistic religious ideologies, ingrained in different beliefs of respective religion of individual beings. Further, there should be interrelatedness of religious values[6] which will be sorted out to produce healthy human relationships, instead of managing things in conflicting nature of social environment. Religious ideologies are therefore, cementing grounds on the floor of reconstructed social innovative rebuilding process of making a universal pattern of journey, in the midst of diversified organizational performances, which is highly essential to commemorate world heritage in nature of underlying a process, in systematizing organizational integrity for human challenges of social growth potentials; so that integral humanity finds way to express the democratic participatory role of every groups of religious people[7], to common good in socializing organizational pattern of socio-economic activities, in unifying world set-up towards harmonious human cooperative inter-group relationships.

Equality of status and fraternity in living principles will be embracive ideology on complementing religious values, and propagating human development paths on trusteeship principles of management; which are all, to be narrative ideas of integrated social development in nurturing organizational work-culture towards the attainment of welfare objectives, judging which from such background, humanity should be represented in scientific motivated personality that inculcates human development cohesive forces, in encompassing goal of socialization in stratified manner. It is thus, prerogative for religious belief in underlining social distressed conditions of worldwide human beings, and if, organizational philosophy of work practices are sustained for this nature of reasons to work-out human lapses, and ills of management through universal human cultural system; there should be enrichment of the idea of human core order of living goal to unify the process of organizational accountability as well as social transformation, in advancing people towards the door of harmonious living ideals[8]. Substantiating these views in correlating issues of religious principles for obtaining human behavioural prudence to recapitulate social development ideologies on the path of organizational sustainability, in creating people to innovate practices of living conditions; there is the urgent necessity of understanding about the sectarian views on religious propagation towards fanatic assumptions, which are negative policies going against the philosophy of mankind's welfare in correct dimension – it is therefore needed religious superiority on educational foundations, where humanity should be placed priority, and other conflicting nature in politicizing developmental issues should be accepted in matters relating to human backward conditions. All should find importance, who are still today in scientific development living in distressed inhuman conditions. Thus, it is permeably said that the superstructure of the societal foundation can be made to prescribe for religious democracy, in managing all human activities toward such endeavour. Consequently, there is also urgent necessity of establishing integral social humanity concept on religious background of social architectural inscription; so that moving of humankind in making journey towards the path of perfectionism could be made erect all negative approaches, by means of organizational performance meant for optimum development of backward people[9], without having any discrimination in the administrative pattern of managing the change elements, entitlement process in terms of challenging the ideas which go to safeguard in favour of bringing good to the onslaught of the suppressed population, in matters of living crises. All these are propounded in the Vedic thoughts for encountering with the religious philosophy in human development perspective. We are therefore to remember that universality is the only motto of human religiosity, which helps in social building reformative thought in course of utilizing organizational resources, to strategize human development process in dynamic way. It will pave the goal of integral religious prosperity in unifying the concept of management to the path of global development consistencies, and so; following points are to be noted in the framework of organizational policies adopted for good governance[10] practices:

(i) Making religion an instrumental idea of changing social order in scientific parlance, to uproot human value, strengthen political set-up to administer things only for human development and social sustainability;

(ii) Eradicating irreligious beliefs from human mind, as observed to be practiced over the world, in the name of religiosity. To the contrary, ideas of humanity like honesty, sincerity, and integrity should be followed in correlating issues of development for humankind, which are to be imposed in guiding people to perform in scientific temper of thought for the purpose of global unification, in terms of leadership approach of benevolence thought applicable for human upliftment programmes;

(iii) International understanding[11] has to be strengthened for motivating people to believe that all human beings are same species of the Almighty creator, and they are created for social orientation purposes; and not for conflicting in matters of religious ideologies which go to destruct human civilization but rather, in making welfare a regular practice in leading their way of life;

(iv) Safeguarding religious truths and ideologies implementing for the practice of socialization goal, narrating thereby human integral idea of development base, for making journey in societal order of sustainable movement throughout the process of reorienting organizational transformation, towards the principles of universal human development tools and techniques;

(v) Considering religious institutions as the social changing instruments, and so; religious activities are to be backed by the philosophy of human sufferings, and their adequate solution to eradicate social problems of human backwardness;

(vi) Religious fanaticism as well as politicizing religious beliefs for propagating vote-banking instrumentalism to the paths of communal practices, are all to be curbed and nipped in the bud for undertaking social development[12], by means of entrepreneurship principles, governance justice and liberal business practices; so that world class human citizenship is reconstructed to regenerate forces of free democratic leadership as the vista of human development foundation as well as social architectural norms and ideologies.

In a nutshell, it is worthwhile to note that religious philosophy on human development has to be construed for solving problems of human living parameters, in connection with peaceful survival as well as coexistence of leading happy life, towards binding humankind in work related matters of socio-economic liberation; in practicing all types of organizational values and ethics guided by human conduct of unity, integrity and fraternity, in the nature of social existence by all kinds of religious groups and entities to complement for orienting the foundation of societal pyramid encrypted through the concept of integral humanity. In this way, it is found in the Vedic sermon that 'Vasudhaiva Kutumbakam' has already been mentioned in Chapter 1, have to be interpreted as the all time philosophy on the strategy of human developmental core idea of religiosity, where multiplicity of cultural entity merged with economic sovereignty of the national entity concept should correlate issues of business practices, and managing goal of identifying human potential towards enlarging process of social unification, in terms of human supremacy of living ideals in congruent manner[13]. Where, there is tendency of assimilation, maintaining respect for each type of religious values and social ethics of human performance based upliftment character, from the present condition of slavery in human living situations to a stage of humanity for existential freedom with the fraternity of all religious bodies or groups of people; it will be healthy practice for understanding organized pattern of socialization through various business practices, in connecting people to attain the goal of universal development – this is the real idea of social sustainability in economic sense of the terminology, which requires adequate endeavours on the part of respective religious institutions existing in this world, for encompassing social growth potentialities and dignifying people to live in peaceful manner, by managing various conflicts in society arising out of politicizing religious behavioural prudence; which is never expected in the Vedic theories on realization of human fraternity principles as well as justice in strengthening human cooperative base of interpersonal, or intergroup relationships. As and when, all such innovative things are empirically made emphatic to understand harmonious organizational management practices, to rejuvenate social nurturing of distressed people living in different parts of the world[14], forgetting religious fanaticism; there would come universal peace and social conflicts will be reduced thus, in transforming positively human living situations, to aid for human integrity and dynamic social movement towards creating tranquil as well as celestial world order. Hence, the fundamental principles of all kinds of religious ideas are to be based on the business practices as well as socio-economic activities of truth, beauty and goodness philosophy in bringing thereby universal integrity in humankind; so that all people in this world live in coherence relationships in terms of balancing a civic order to survival conditions. This will help tremendously in supplementing human excellence building ideas and motivate people to nurture innovation creativity for enriching pillars of integral humanity, by eradicating all types of negative thoughts practiced in the name of religions to politicizing human development issues from governing administrative grounds to accumulate healthy understanding between various religious groups for social development purposes. It is therefore, highly essential that compulsory education should be urgently universalized in scientific temper of human development thought, so as to strengthen the process of socialization of human organizational entities in fulfilling to bridge all types of religious beliefs meant for common upliftment of human race, to solve different types of social crises and human problems of living in perfect order[15].

Human Development and Religious Organizational Common Responsibility

Religious organizations are backbone of human development thought and social reconstruction from ancient times, which can be proved from the scientific as well as scholastic studies made on human civilizations, as depicted in religious scriptures, and also in different types of encyclopedias; like the encyclopedia of social sciences, encyclopedia of commerce and business, encyclopedia of Britannica, encyclopedia of Americana and so on. Again, this fact can further be examined from the study of the world history, the European history, and the ancient Vedic literatures, the Christian literatures, and much other resourceful information as available in religious scriptures; which go to reflect about the discourses on human development aspects in civilization's part to various periods of human living conditions. It is therefore true to say that human up-swings are found in treasure-house of knowledge, as prescribed in above sources of materials; among others, where there is mentioning of the fact that irreligious behavioural traits of mankind were the reasoning grounds of pitfall of human beings. Accordingly, civilization's foundation, based on which human race as a whole, in historical perspective was confined to the process of a kind of obligation to manage socio-economic and other activities, depending on respective behavioural prudence to scientific facts of religions related ideologies, concerning social reconstruction with a view to reformative analysis, on humanization situations in societal living style peacefully. Thus, every organization having religious background[16] to their solidarity of existential entity should be involved with the kind of common responsibility, in so far as human development is concerned to their survival goal for social building process, in connoting ideas of human real growth potentialities. This fact cannot be ignored, because management literatures are having full of available information regarding such kind of scientific views on human living parameters in various narratives, giving thereby ample scope of the study with respect to social responsibilities of religious institutions that modern human civilization should follow, for the purpose of artistic play of things in favour of bringing human development to the limelight of the social picturesque – this type of social responsibility as observed to be made in common, also in ancient times, has now been called for once again as the urgent need of the hour in emergent social reformative thoughts, necessitated by human backward conditions of living over the world at large.

The above ideas are required to be innovated for human development in sustainable manner from holistic concept of social rejuvenation process, as there is the unanimity in religious philosophy towards understanding about the ultimate truth[17] of human upliftment considerations, from the view points of human sufferings that has been made as the discourse of the present civilization. Realizing this philosophy of management in utilizing social resources, humankind should follow the path of undertaking religious responsibility in shaping human fates from the institutional segments which represent people's voice for maintaining their religious ideologies from time to time. Hence, social building notion should be taken in celebrated as well as sparkling manner as the common religious responsibility, from the side of religious organizations, or institutions, which have actually existed in the world for this sole aim as the mission, in many kinds of religious activities to be provided for human upliftment programmes, in the nature of performing organizational tasks that human civilization demands now, in the periods of growing population at a galloping rate over the world as well as crying demand of distressed human beings, who have been living for long in a stage of pathetic inhuman conditions to their survival situations. If this has to be managed to solve vicarious problems, to change onslaught of suffered human race in an emergent approach, religious philosophy in guiding the entire social scenario has to be treated as the true instrument in challenging manner; so that management of social resources could be made more effective towards channelizing human growth potentials in positivistic social orientation purposes. Coming over to such an analysis, we must follow the rules of religious scientific practices in innovating human socio-economic activities, directed towards attaining human development goal by all such means and ways, which are required to be planned in the administrative system of modern sovereign governments in each and every country. This is universal responsibility, because when we go to discover ancient civilizations, it is observed from historical perspective that basically, there were two hemispheres in the time of creation of the present world system – (i) eastern hemisphere where people were observed, living in fully developed pattern, due to religion-based[18] ideologies propagated to nurture human beings by those ancient social institutions; and (ii) western hemisphere where people were found to be living in a stage of fully de-humanized condition, due to irreligious practices in maintaining social activities, by means of their institutional informal bodies, and entities. All these, gave birth to an idea of religious responsibility and its belief regarding human developmental notions, so that social reformations would be undertaken for the purpose of human peaceful living conditions. In a nutshell, at later dates in human history, like in periods of Buddhism, Christianism, Islamism, and Sikhism and so on, we follow that there were various types of up-swings in civilization's part, due to lack of adequate respect towards every religious counterparts; and instead of all these, there were human conflicts as well as catastrophic destruction because of human warfare activities prevailed in societies of the world. So, it is clear fact that religious ideologies[19] backed by truths of human development-related activities, can help to rebuild foundation of the world society in connecting people to realize for matching balance, in eradicating human problems of living, and thereby healthy social relationships would be strengthened to encounter positive nature of growth in holistic manner.

From the discussions and analysis made so far, it has clearly depicted us the picture of human development realities, which are fundamentally related to the original ideas of religious organizational common beliefs on the responsibilities of human participative[20] nature of democratic management system; without which, it becomes quite impossible to think about the concept of global unity and sustainability principles of human growth potential incidences. However, to arrive at a decision regarding effectiveness of all the religious institutions in making people oriented to social transformation, it is worthwhile to note that we should follow inter-religious scientific truths regarding management of human cooperative activities, in encompassing social upliftment of backward population throughout the world environment, so as to maintain social peace and tranquility by reducing gaps between haves and have-nots. This will help further in solving human conflicts in between religious entities from organizational perspective, and thus; scientific socialism as the root cause of humanism-via-religiosity should be established in the world order, in bringing whole humankind to the path of global unity, universal integrity in living parameters, and human existential freedom of choice in creating social foundation[21], to illuminate social development picture up to the crest through religious diversity. In this line of thinking religious organizations should be made responsible, to raise curtain up to the level of development oriented doors, where every individual will be allowed to participate in the nature of conducting socio-economic activities, pertaining to human empowerment consistencies in innovating things which go to mould plan of actions of organizational entities, for the cohesive nature of human work behaviour in terms of religious leadership counselling affairs – it should be seen carefully that corporate cultural entity of human pluralism is maintained positively, as and when social welfare terminology is conceived with the growth perspective ideals, combined with the nature of religious activities to that of political administration meant for common benefit of the entire humankind. This is the narrative ideas of the Vedic norms of social building concept, enlarged in religious practices to the long past history of human existential choice, for reaching at global balance restoration in terms of organizational entities; so that human beings are placed in a position to underline silver-mark in correlating issues of development and social unification, through all means of emancipation guidance.

In practice, the nature of responsibility for social development is vested to religious truths[22], because without having the philosophy of common understanding in between different religious groups, no society can be expected to supply human needs in view of covering all types of people to the containment of the process of holistic social growth. It is thus, permeably said that responding nature of positive as well as scientific behaviour in complementing religious ideals to social orientation process, will come to reflect on the responsibility part of management for human development paradigms, in which organizational truth, beauty and goodness philosophy will further accumulate common benefit to all categories of people, in considering themselves for the purpose of making universal journey towards realization of human goal of living dignities. Hence, the kind of responsibility here we are concerned with various religious principles, has to be made more and more strategic in regard to manage things with creativity, along with the sensitivity approach of dealing with the nature of human development-related social orientation objective; otherwise, the narrow concept of religious ideological perspective will be more detrimental towards bringing social restlessness situations, as we have observed so far, in the present context of the world order. Evidentially, it is religious practices which are required to be applied for human emancipation from the stage of slavery; as it were, and is being consistently stressed in Vedic literatures for salvation of human life[23] – this is the scientific envisagement on the manifestation of human pluralism, as expected to be undertaken in organizational system of management, while social resources are utilized for balancing regional imbalances by means of reducing gaps between rich and poor; and is suggested by the ancient Eastern Vedic thought in matchless way. Here, all types of social problems of humanity regarding ifs and buts are recommended to fulfill human satisfaction in considering value of life and meaning of social activities, to solve by religious optimum realization of truths in covering human development potentialities. In this nature of dealing with organizational entities, there would be social reconstruction in terms of providing all the basic and fundamental services, needed for distressed populations who have been suffering a lot for long, from the emergent crises of civic living necessities required for the purpose of survival existentialism in social set-up. As and when such responsibilities are commendably shouldered by religious leaders, they could be able to guide political administrative bodies and social organizational entities for increasing common good of mankind, who are found to be suppressed, oppressed and depressed in various manners to stage of their social living conditions[24]. However, it is immensely important to realize from the above facts that coordination of activities, in between religious institutions and administrative counterparts are increasingly demanded from the view points of managing people for effective nature of social growth. The underlying characteristics of such relevancy arise due to human excellence building process, and social sustainability norms of developing humankind to optimize their maximum participation, in areas of organizational diversity to bring in innovative nature of human social foundation. Thus, the role of religious responsibilities enshrined with the policy of universal development has no other alternative, but to adjust with the situational challenges of time and space, in considering organizational instrument of social change mechanism[25], and is required to be discovered in religious ideological thoughts, in motivating people to produce things for the greater interest of backward classes of human beings; so that the concept of integral humanity is nurtured through optimum utility of social resources, in solving problems of human hungriness, poverty and starvation deaths. Under all these circumstances, it is scientifically observed that relationship between human civility of living and realization of religious absolute principles of truth searching, in the context of development oriented concept of social building perspective idea has the root in finding out the goal of human peaceful living conditions, so as to assure people to unite for universal integrity and organizational dynamicity.

From the above discussions, we may come to note that religious organizations should not follow any kind of hype in making development as the agenda of taking any advantage of political benefit out of its philosophy, contained in their organizational guiding goal; which assesses development policies in terms of communal or secularism perspective. But rather, there should be scientific investigation regarding division of human mind and their separatism tendencies, for which religious leaders should come forward in making people to realize this thing that without development, the core idea of humanity could be ruined by political leaders in taking out challenges to uplift people from sufferings of poverty. Thus, religious truths are to be based on human development issues, while making decisions at organizational level to change the fate of the entire humanity, by means of handling such vibrating issue as the religion (dharma) of mankind. When each individual being is taken care of, in eliminating the doubt for irreligious process of dehumanizing by way of utilizing human beings for creating a line of demarcation in society, in the name of religion; which go to separate people from the mainstream of living environment, there is the probability of increasing social conflicts in leading life peacefully[26]. Hence, institutional obligations are there to emulate things for spreading religious education in society related to developmental issues, and then scientific uplift of all kinds of human beings could take place without any hesitation regarding the concept of religious responsibility for social transformation in transcendental order. Human conscious will be raised for doing activities in participating religious movement, for the purpose of social building process undertaken with a view to solve many of the complex human problems of life, in sustainable manner to occupy a pivotal role in managing things for human democratic nature of living existential freedom. Thus, the real differentiation between religious truths and hype once made for applying religious sermons based on scientific nature of guidance, as an indicator of social changing instrument, it can go long way to build up people for healthy practices of organizational good governance ethics, which is immensely helpful for creating favourable environment of development atmosphere throughout the socio-economic culture – it is highly essential now, in the present set-up of social environment; where we find that in many countries of the world religious practices are undertaken for certain kind of separatism tendencies, and making thereby life of innocent people more risky in turning the entire social picture, in which selfishness tendencies are increasing day-by-day. Consequently, social restlessness have been increasing due to many sufferings, that the innocent or general people are observed to be ruined in making their life happy as well as easy to survive.

For the reasons, as explained above, we therefore suggest here that religious organizational role in making society and life of human beings pious can be remodelled in restructuring social pyramid[27], where there will prevail universal brotherhood philosophy in connecting people for development agenda as the motto of social living mantra, to realize human core ideas of life related issues of understanding for the sake of broad religious ideologies, to assimilate; but not to divide, in the path of making society a celestial heavenly abode of living parameters. Evidentially, it is necessary that social responding behaviour in the process of upliftment of people through organizational responsibility, on the part of religious entities could be harmonized for coherence business practices; so that human development is made in holistic approach by way of playing strategic role model in all areas of administrative activities, to embrace the goal of human development as well as universal social welfare. Thus, the base of integral humanity will be strengthened more and more, to recapitulate development as the main religion[28] (dharma), in which entire mankind would find optimum satisfaction for producing things in rationalistic attitude. Cooperative human relationship will find place in managing organizational resources, to channelize productive output towards the benefit of backward people. In this line of thinking, religion can be made as the fundamental instrument of social change, forgetting any type of political interference on religious organizations. People to people motivation will be enriched by these philosophical assumptions, in making policies at organizational levels, to uproot social value in providing guidance through different types of positive religious leadership ideologies; which will go to reorient things in increasing social development potential. In a nutshell, organizational role of playing social responsibility will be made thus, more effective when people would be made to follow the path of undertaking liberal religious practices[29], in attaining social reconstruction, based on human development goal and universal integrity of all religious ideologies, concerned with the practice of human justice for living in tranquil social order.

Religion for Human Growth

Religion is the key to open the door of human life, because it enlightens people to acquire knowledge – how to attain salvation in life. For this reason, it is truly said probably, by the highest order of the Hindu monk in India, Swami Vivekananda that expansion is the real order of human life, and not contraction; which is equivalent to death. In this context, everything should be managed in our organizational life based on the science of religion, as it were; so that growth in human life comes from the eternal stage of leading everything, depended on the various truths concerning scientific beliefs for religiosity in embracing the goal of humanity, in all sorts of socio-economic activities for the highest order of manifestation in realization of the life process, which the evolutionary scientists as well as social thinkers are dedicating for understanding about the growth perspectives of human life related issues in the real world. Thus, religion and human growth indicators go in a parallel line, to measure up human efficiency for appraisal of various organizational performances, leading towards human upliftment process through strategic development of the entire gamut of social life. It is therefore, assessed in synthetically approach of combining the effectiveness of human organizational activities with that of social building notions[30], when each individual entity in the system of institutional guidelines is observed to be mingling towards the aspects of human perfectionism, for the sake of understanding the entire creativity. This is the real picture emerged in the depth of the ocean of human life, when mankind will be in a position to find out the reasons for social existence, there would come social emancipation of human beings. In this way, religion can be undertaken in handling tasks carefully to illuminate the picture of social survival, confined with the need related aspects of human satisfaction for advancing life process, to attain the goal of integral humanity, in terms of organizational consistency, social diversity and human creativity.

Judging from this angle, we have considered our attention on religious analysis to arrive at a decision – how it can be focused for human growth related issues of organizational performance, where psychological parameters of behavioural truths are observed to be scientifically related to orient the system of strategic goal for social reformation. This is the perplexing notion of dealing with the process of organizational delivery system, confined to human understanding for realization of actually interrelating issues of growth. As and when, this practice will go to reflect human 'life-cycle' originality, and religious supremacy in bringing humankind towards all possibilities of social excellences, the excellence norm of human legacy encompassing growth parameters will also come to give results of organizational performances, where every work of mankind should be treated as the forward looking steps for making journey to the paths of optimum order of realization; by means of organizational involvement in conjugating the holistic system of organizational diversity as well as existence problems, in spiritualizing[31] all human performances to attain the goal of universal development, in terms of organizational planning process and its proper implementation in the real world situations. It is thus obviously, said that religion is not the opium for sleeping in permanent way that has been observed in case of few underdeveloped and developing countries of the world, like India, Pakistan, Bangladesh and others, among which, there is enormous consciousness growing day-by-day; due to fair policy on educational tendencies being increasing these countries than before. But the rate of education in raising people to feel that fanaticism is not the real education, which can be said to enhance people for increasing amount of social growth, by way of creating new paths to open up the door of humanity from the present stage of slavery. When people are observed in both the underdeveloped as well as developing countries suffering due to political restlessness, it is religion and its unscientific base can be made responsible to such incidences. However, religious truths backed by people oriented principles of growth can be scientifically focused for enhancing human integrity, in the multi-polarity tendencies of human understanding; so that intelligent and literate people who are running the political system can be challenged by people of scientifically educated ones, who constitute only a few in the class of social reformation movements. Therefore, humanitarian considerations are to be allowed as the priority in bringing religion to book for human growth, which is otherwise; going against the scientific parlance of religious thoughts – truth, beauty and goodness for whole people, which are the fundamental assumptions of human growth potentials, taking into account all types of religious ideologies in the balance sheet of human progressive development, for social building approach in strategic manner, to arrive at a decision regarding organizational diversity and working order of social transformation. Hence, there is no other alternative, but to resort to abide by the principles of organizational ethics to follow up human actions bound by the concept of human integrity; where religions are not to be looked at, as the barrier in social building process; but rather, all people should be well trained to learn about common religious beliefs[32] that are interpreted to optimize human growth in holistic concept, from different socio-economic paths, in which no politicization should be made to twist in skewed nature to make up religious strategies for social conflicts. On the other hand, in managing organizational activities for effective social growth and human emancipation from the stages of pathetic living conditions, religions are to be made more and more responsible to enlighten people for understanding the real nature of human personality as well as crying need of the hour – to accumulate human happiness by way of matching social resources for increasing an orderly balance between all types of mismatches, so as to unify the process of scientific religious understanding in reducing human conflicts, and increasing growth potentials to illuminate the picture of universal human development.

In this connection, it is worthwhile to note that religions are backbone of human skeleton, where lies the spirit of social movement in right direction for motivating people to understand the celestial beauty of the ecstasy of management thought in vibrant manner. Consequently, it is true to say that universal order of maintaining religious beliefs would help society strengthening the course of human learning habits regarding integrated characters of organizational unification, for encompassing with all threats that can be made to solve challenges in reforming human social orderly arrangement of synchronizing all irrelevant issues, by means of common humanitarian needs of advancing human life for the sake of diversified living order, in the midst of various problems. Here, religion is the only criterion in narrating principles of human growth in challenging nature of managing organizational tasks, where the mantra human development should be assessed as the strategic goal of implementing religious basis, for making fundamental social change; in connecting to realize the real meaning and objectives of religion, coming across in way of human unification for increasing common good of all people, by way of accepting good governance philosophy as the positive guidelines for religiosity as well as human integrity. In this order of thinking on religious beliefs[33], there is the optimum possibility in reducing gaps between rich and poor in society. Ultimately, the foundation of the society will be inscribed for estimating religion, in the measurement of social dynamicity to the congruent nature of human growth; along with mapping for the entire ecological balance, to realize social welfare perspective through religious characteristics, and their ultimate truths implemented for human salvation in life.

It is highly important to note that religion as the instrument of social change can help to strengthen mind of organizational managers, to remold human characters from all types of evils and animosities, to realize the absolute potential of human capacity in balancing radical social transformation; so that optimal order of human growth is initiated in all-round spheres of the social structure, in restructuring social set-up on the foundation of existential perfection, knowing which human beings would be stimulated to reorient social dynamism in proactive manner. From this true assessment, we may be thinking that religion is the mechanism which converts the nature of animosity[34] inherent in men into real humanity, by way of organizational innovative creativity in nurturing people to help in the process of social reformation, with all policies of modern organizations dedicated towards nation building activities and unifying the scientific cause of living peacefully, in societal order of human dignity, universal integrity and worldwide socio-economic positive dynamicity. All these are resurgent resilience in the reconstruction path of human fate in new dimension, where religion is considered to be the primary as well as fundamental instrument of bringing people towards social building in scientific nature of human growth, philosophic order of social development compounding acceleration of human productivity for the sake of rational reformative goal, and artistic play of things in creating humankind free from all types of irreligious thoughts[35], to accumulate social welfare in recapitulating truth-oriented beliefs of religious harmony. In this way, organizational entities are expounded to eliminate social differences between man and man; which is further helpful for reducing regional imbalances in mankind, that we have observed in the present situation of the administrative latches and lapses of the judicious application of organizational policies; in implementing packages which go to restructure society towards balancing growth potentials enormously. It is here pity to mention that the system of public governance is politicized by religious slogans from different angles, where vote-banking pattern, particularly in countries which follow the rules of administrative justice for restoring governance criterion on the principles of humanity, like India; among others, religion should be taken into consideration for bringing positive social change – this type of change is only possible when the Vedanta philosophy of human core idea of 'oneness in all' principle is followed, in maintaining organizational work culture, eradicating all legal problems to rectify irreligious beliefs and tendencies from the social environment by means of transparent management system; so that integral concept of human unification order is balanced for initiating social growth as well as human development paradigms shift in nature, to emulate nurturing potentials in mankind in terms of organizational guidance and administrative counselling. Hence, accommodating religion in the compartment of human growth strategies, to reduce conflicts at the social level could further shape human mind, for increasing higher level of productivity which can be utilized for the purpose of solving human problems of misery, distress and malnourishment. Thus, religiosity in management strategy by way of implementing the highest truths can be adjusted without any doubt in mind, for initiating social change through positive nature of human growth, in redefining the concept of integral humanity[36]. In a nutshell, human growth by means of spiritual order of employing all policies of organizations, and adaptive religious behavioural prudence, can be substantiated to reorient modern societies of the world, in regard to match resources mismatches in the name of people's development, to which level playing of religiously implicated ideas of political administration would be reformed in liberal as well as transcendental order.

From the above discussions, it can be safely remarked that religion (dharma) as the principle of work (karma) can be taken into account to measure up human efficiency at the work place, for which; human attitude towards confining organizational activities in terms of statistical measurement as well as econometric analysis (done in the form of curvilinear studies to ascertain skewed nature of graphic representation for the issues of developmental trends, where mathematical assumptions find place in correlating various parameters of human growth potentials), have to be made more and more strategic in realization of the goal of emancipation in holistic nature, to inculcate human participative nature of employability, so as to eradicate all types of unscientific hate mongering speeches and debates from the social environment – without this kind of principle contained in the work philosophy of organizational guidance towards bringing social balance would be quite impossible. Consequently, if such atmosphere is presumed to be underlying with the principles of management, human growth from different perspectives will be a problem of administrative system of management. Hence, principles of religion should be based on human justice, equality and fraternity thought for enlarging issues of social backwardness, and its solution by means of applying religious philosophy[37] of human advancement process, where – 'truth, beauty and goodness' should find as the priority for organizational transformation of the societal foundation, to guide people in nurturing innovative thoughts for creating things, for the sake of common good of mass people; irrespective of religious differences, but rather considering human beings as the central point of study on all such issues, pertaining to growth related analysis in scientific temper of human development related thoughts. In connoting thus ideas of religion for bringing social diversification in strategic development consideration, dynamics of human behavioural prudence to curb anti-social activities will be made more and more sustainable to preserve humanity, in the midst of organizational diversities and human dignity of living in coordinating work culture with the scientific nature of enriching the goal of religious guidance, to confine things for optimum order of development of all kinds of people; who are otherwise living in a stage of inhuman conditions throughout the social foundation. This is the real balance between religion and human growth oriented concept of social transformation, must have to be undertaken for empowering people in initiating sustainable development with the approach of universalizing of religious beliefs[38], that would supplement in the process of establishing global peace by means of fundamental social change brought forth in kind of innovating human excellence potentials. It would further lead to the areas of interpersonal relations in increasing work qualities, which go to rationalize industrial productivity as well as human living equity. Religion should be judged from this measurement of guiding people, ignoring all other political behaviour that has been found; while empirical studies are providing learning knowledge about human condition of social orientation stage. Managing social resources in methodical channelization towards bringing human upliftment, by means of implementation of various schemes of the sovereign government entities, would be fruitfully healthy for enlarging social diversification goal, to occupy legal justice in the framework of religious foundation[39] which takes into account good governance philosophy as the norms of organizational empowerment conditions, with a view to understanding the broad concept of human core principles of living in peaceful way. Thus, optimization of human participation level regarding delivery system would be innovated in cooperating people to render efficient services, for the sake of social welfare, where the principle of the Vedanta order of socialization process – 'Vasudhaiva Kutumbakam', has already been analyzed in Chapter 1, will be intermingled from religious perspectives to find out the realities of human growth[40] related deficiencies; so that social organizations are viewed as the scientific instrument creating abrupt as well as positivistic nature of social dynamicity, in kind of making social change in all types of communal threats prorogated for, in the nature of artificial voicing on secularism agenda of the different political parties; as it were, in the social level transactions of vested interest groups and people.

We may conclude that religion is the fundamental choice for establishment of the social foundation on the pillars of human salvation of life principles, in which individual entity of each human being should be merged with the whole spectrum of human race, unifying the realities of social living in tranquil order to illuminate the picture of the global society in diversifying socio-economic activities of the world organizations; where all classes of people are to be educated by imparting lessons of universal human dignity, democratic participation in work atmosphere to uproot social value system, in terms of organizational mechanism of finding the original sources of human fraternity of living in unified order, to represent the world societies in the 'Committee of Nations' for enthusing integrated brotherhood principles, in creating healthy human interrelationships to rejuvenate social organizations, in correlating principles of human optimum necessity[41] of finding-out goals and objectives of social existentialism in mankind to holistic approach; where there would be enormous peace that will prevail in social fabricated platform, in synthesizing common backgrounds of human growth related ingredients to the cause of elementary wisdom, for religious guidance and motivated personality building in all-round human development possibilities. Thus, religious beliefs and faiths are to be nurtured and inculcated in organizational setting for the purpose of blooming distressed people in this world, like budding flowers, in the garden of human industrial harmonious entity; wherefrom cool breeze will flow to social atmosphere that should be harmonized for cooperative human living principles, in an understanding of integral humanity. Here, growth perspectives are to be contained in reducing human conflicts in organizational system of management, with a view to increase social good for backward areas, in which people are getting no such opportunities for overall development. It is therefore, essential that religion sermons are to be propagated for unifying people to reconstruct the social foundation on the path of universal upliftment philosophy, to which; further the leaders of various religious organizations have to initiate the process of level playing role model, in framing society towards the achievement of the goal of human justice for living in society, in practicing activities of modern organizations to embrace unitary principles in diversified means and ways; so that the world order in making journey of mankind to the path of perfection becomes heavenly abode of God[42], in realizing living necessities for civilities of life bringing principles with optimum nature of human development, in order to personify each individual's personality towards reaching at the golden door of tranquility. In brief, religion as the breakthrough in management system has its own existence for changing human life, to percolate all types of valuable ideologies in organizational foundation, to the characteristic attributes of unifying goal of human growth initiatives, by means of effective managerial communication base to match social resources in increasing human welfare, and social transformation in reformative approach to strengthen radical nature of social change in time and space.

Religious Policy for Scientific Resource Match Technique

Religion is the backbone of human development process, because irreligious policies can lead to social restlessness, for which; there is the possibility of human conflicting tendencies in societal environment that might create distrust in human mind regarding each performance of social organizations, directed through demoralizing system of leadership guidance. So, religious policy in finding out goal of human development with the scientific temper of social sustainability could help in solving problems of human misery and distress tremendously[43]. In this area of thinking, religion can be focused in relating human backwardness and its various reasons, and also assessing on the aspects of human malnourished conditions in social living situations of all classes of human beings; who are otherwise, guided by the philosophy of unscientific behavioural traits in human interpersonal as well as intergroup relationships, at the organizational constituencies of changing social norms. Thus, management of organization can be made potential in terms of religious truths for enlarging areas of human participative nature of organizational dynamic movement, for creating innovative ideas in leadership challenges to overcome problems of human dissatisfaction towards unifying social building conditions. In this context, it is undoubtedly noted that policies of management in utilizing social resources with the techniques of scientific model formulation are to be redrafted, taking into consideration fundamental truths of universality in applying religious backgrounds to correlate human development, in strategic foundation of innovative leadership to eradicate human demoralizing tendencies which go to strengthen social pyramid[44]. It is therefore universal understanding on the basic policies of religious guidelines in enthusing people to shoulder responsibility, to attain the goal of social diversification, to which organizational planning premises are to be molded in scientific investigations in controlling things that lead people to chalk-out solutions of human peaceful living in social strata. Hence, there are various common policies could be founded on changing onslaught of deprived people, who are not getting any benefits in their stages of life, due to irrelevant issues confined with the religious philosophy in understanding the scientific reasons for balanced human development process. Accordingly, anti-social activities are observed to be done by some vested interest groups, who claim to maintain themselves as religious guides as well as people's responsible representative for sustaining religion, from the dangers of social unrest tendencies[45]. In reality, such kind of unscientific holding on religious issues have ruined the very structure of the democratic social fabric, due to which; further people are directed to revolt against all types of social goods. This is the reason for which religious ideology has been going to be misguided in politicizing development issues, in the name of social welfare. In reality, such an affair on religious strategy to occupy a strong hold in development platform should be interrelated to grass-root problems of human sufferings; so that management of organizational activities are carried on the basis of fruitful analysis of religious truths, and its implementation in practice to motivate people to analyze things on realities of human backward situations.

It is therefore predicted undoubtedly that religious policies are required to be reformulated on the basis of utilizing social scarce resources for increasing human welfare, by means of systematizing organizational guidance; where efficient diversification in fund management[46] could take place for accumulation of organizational profitability, that can be deployed for the purpose of construction of social infrastructural projects necessary for solving problems of regionalism. Consequent on this nature of organizational urgency for eradicating people's sufferings, religious thoughts are required to be made scientific oriented towards attaining resource sustainability. As a result of all these incidences on the screen of societal picture of human deprivation, policies of modern organizations are to be framed on the notion of human resource development potentiality, which further demands for organizational guidelines on the specific ideas of strategic human growth perspectives. Hence, we would like to look into affairs of social reformations through religious policies, which should stimulate organizational productivity in rational norms of utilizing social resources with all the techniques of resource diversification process. As a whole, the following points are suggested for increasing effectiveness of resource match for bringing balanced nature of social development, to eradicate problems of human sufferings, and also for reducing the regional imbalances in living parameters by scientific reasons between haves and have-nots classes of human beings[47]:

(1) Foundation of religious backgrounds for increasing social welfare have to be adjusted with the policies of modern multinational character of social organizations, so as to enhance effectiveness in question of exploiting scarce social resources, and thus; environmental sustainability could further be accomplished with a view to increasing human comfort and happiness, to usher all-round social development

in terms of adopting scientific religious policies in organizational activities, from time to time;

(2) Human integrated undertaking should be infused in religious thoughts, for empowering people to judge organizational activities from the viewpoints of human advancement in social set-up[48]. We are therefore to follow the path of universal nature of human progress through perspective guidance of organizational leadership practices, oriented towards unifying religious policies for utilizing techniques of resource match in effective manner; so that integral concept of human efficiency building rests on the fundamental truths of religious beliefs that, it is possible to encourage people in producing goods for the common betterment of deprived population, who are still observed to be living in inhuman stages in their social order of survival goal;

(3) Religious policies are to be justified from the grounds of human participative nature of industrial democracy, which has its origin to the basic concepts of human personality development and its various issues which motivate people at the work place. Thus, religious policies are to be redrafted for unifying input-output relationship in nature of human socio-economic behavioural prudence, and organizational efficiency in guiding people to reorient social system on the foundation of human consistency for living in healthy practices. Thus, it is essential that all broad frameworks of organizational policy resolutions should cover human dignity of living by solving problems of mistrust in regard to religious understanding[49];

(4) Redefining organizational policies on the practice of human justice for equity in living goal, requires that religious guidance should be inculcated to human perfectionism for attaining the goal of speedy social development, in terms of increasing resource outlets to diversified manner so as to add value to social orientation system in balancing orderly distribution of organizational output, for reducing human crises regarding happiness in life. It is therefore, religious scientific policies could help in initiating organizational innovation towards unifying resource exploitative potentiality, in enlarging human motivation to produce for social welfare for the greater interest of deprived population, who are malnourished due to lack of basic necessities for leading a civic life;

(5) Human creativity should be the foundation of employing religious policies in organizational activities, where people would get a learning culture to excel for optimum nature of human growth, social development, and worldwide transformation in positive

direction; to reduce human conflicts in question of irreligious faiths and beliefs. To the contrary, there should be universal idea in connecting religious philosophy with the welfare concept of human emancipation to the severity of living injustice, guiding inequality, and progressing problems. As a whole, there should be international cooperation in religious philosophy to uproot social value system[50]. In this perspective order of managing religious ethics, organizational policies are to be redrafted to orient human beings in order of necessitating optimum human development through work culture, which should be adopted in organizational planning process;

(6) Religious policies must commensurate the goal of resource match in innovative way to solve problems of climate change, which has been observed as the potential threat against the whole humanity. Pertinently, it becomes essential to adopt techniques of resource creativity in terms of religious philosophy, in rectifying environmental challenges to curb unscientific nature of social resource utilization made for industrial productivity. Thus, it requires to mention here that subverting elements operating in administrative system should be eliminated[51] for increasing resource utility, with the approach of sensitivity analysis process, so as to guide human organizations for the sake of social transparency in bringing human efficiency as well as organizational effectiveness; and

(7) Optimality in utilizing resources can further be made through recycling environmental resources, which go to strengthen organizational sustainability for increasing output by means of religious guidance in leadership strategies, to accumulate scientific productivity relationship in growing nature of population increasing throughout the world environment. Hence, it is emergently needed that religious slogans which are voiced in the name of human welfare, for propagating chauvinistic tendencies and creating restlessness situations in society, are all to be eradicated through scientific order of resource match policies as well as philosophic order of administration by organizational agencies, in making people to believe that foundation of religious ethics can only save the whole humanity from catastrophic destruction[52]. Again, it will help in revitalizing social transformation in increasing human consciousness for balancing creative thoughts on resource potentials, on the foundation of religious policies which are required to be remodelled to unify all kinds of human socio-economic activities through organizations; and which are also treated to be the positive social changing instruments in order to orient social pyramid in relativity approach.

From the above policy resolutions, we may now think on dynamic and radical consistencies of religious policies for effectuating resources match in sustaining our environment, to eliminate organizational imbalances and social distrusts from the traditional aspects of managing thoughts that have many deficiencies, from the viewpoint of environmental subsistence, global transformation for empowering people, and world level role model of religious ethical humanitarian foundation[53], to rejuvenate the picture of social change process in dynamic nature of human personality development traits. Implementing religious ideologies through trusteeship principles can be thus; fruitful for initiating organizational effective communication base, where lies the importance of human interaction in increasing resource creativity for enlarging goal of integrated human development perspective. So, it is said reasonably that irrelevant philosophical foundation of religious policies can never attain the goal of human progress in society. What is highly important in employing the techniques of resource match, is the demographic structure, on which depends psychological analysis in regard to human empowerment conditional framework as well as adaptability of religious norms, and human freedom of thinking for encouraging people to cooperate in work relationships, to establish primary grounds for the choice of spiritual policies in rebuilding social order of mankind, by means of universal human development process. Specific policy in this regard could be formulated in applying organizational objective function, to stress for utilizing resources' alternative sources in diversified means and ways, where the mission of managing organizational activities and performances has to correlate issues of human love, equity and fraternity-related subjective concept, to optimize techniques of resource utility to the fullest possible level; so that information sharing in organizational structure could be made a broad spectrum of human understanding towards unification of organizational performances for optimum level of human growth, contained in the objective leadership strategies with a view to enhance human competence building, capabilities, and credibility. Therefore, it is expected to enlarge policies of scientific guidance in ruminating developmental criterion, for the purpose of effectiveness of organizational network of management, the root of which is entrusted to religious base to percolate the core idea of human progress in holistic manner. To this philosophy, again, we are to concentrate on human excellence building norms[54] and perfection principles, for making policies stringent to help deprived people; who are not getting adequately the regular facilities needed for civic survival. Hence, Preksha meditation, as prescribed in the Jaina philosophy in their religious rites, could be assessed for utilization of resources in organizational work culture, with the assimilation of the Vedanta thought – equanimity concept of human living parameters, along with the philosophy of the equipoise nature of resource optimality, for bringing universal level organizational diversity in channelizing resource outlets, to produce goods at a lower cost, which can help in healthy way to preserve for the whole humanity; and in the long-run the techniques of input-output maximization could reduce environmental pressures. As a whole, the right strategy employed thus, in utilizing resources for efficient productive goal of the organization, would stimulate humankind to nurture environmental sustainability in creating effective system of project management utilization; so that religious value analysis are made to have justice on the administrative pattern of dealing with the particular kind of resource outlets.

In a nutshell, religious policies are taken into consideration for managing with the resource potentiality because of overall environmental sustainability[55] on the one hand, and human integrity on the other side of judgment in justifying with the reasons for standing on such a goal. Viewing from the Vedanta aspect of human democratic nature of participation, organizational work culture has to be given quite freedom of choice in making use of the particular kind of resource base with relevant nature of organizational effectiveness, in initiating human performances toward optimum level social development, in which all classes of human beings are to be provided with ample opportunities to grow in unified nature of dealing with the religious value judgment conditionality. Here, enormous problems might crop-up to deal with every kind of religious issue, but only the scientific guidelines are to be made as the framework of organizational policy resolutions, in resurgent development thought to enlighten human performances, with a view to understanding organizational cohesive forces, as and when resources are utilized for organizational productivity with the objective of increasing human welfare. Thus, it goes to say that the techniques of operative as well as functional relationship are to be made more human oriented, in relating things with that of organizational work cultural pluralism, to believe that spirituality is the foundation of social cause for human existence – to prescribe this principle in work ethics, religious values are to be chosen on the basis of human core idea of peaceful living; otherwise, the objectivity of taking into account for increasing resource potential utility would not perform to deliver result in equanimity principle of human growth perspectives. Hence, all the tools and techniques unifying organizational objective function for utilizing resource match in profitable manner could be disturbed in creating value towards human development. Where there is efficiency in projecting right policies taken from the inherent scientific principles of religious base, by means of proper investigation, it would be possible to utilize resources in balancing phase, so as to increase human welfare by means of resource diversification as well as managerial guidelines, to optimize utilizing of resource behavioural prudence. In concluding about the techniques for resource match through religious foundation of human integrity[56], it is highly important to think on organizational sustainability for the greater advantage of human beings; so that environmental balance is established in creating rules regarding the order of religious ethical guidelines for effective resource match, in bringing unified nature of human development, along with maintaining existential freedom of human race. It is thus, to be made universal, while thinking on innovative techniques of balancing resource match for organizational integrity in systematizing things and activities.

Application of Religion for Scientific Human Development

Human development is the challenging subject over the 'world at large, in these days of scientific order of societal transformation, that has been observed from the stage of growing knowledge on the discoveries and inventions of science and technology, related to the field of socio-economic empirical studies, and to those which go to record on human various problems of life as well as environmental conditions of living parameters. However, it is here pertinent to say that religion is one of the important areas of socio-parametric human behavioural science, where lies political administration in most of the developing as well as underdeveloped countries of the world; for it is essential to mention in permeable nature of human psychological findings on the study of religious fear psychosis, particularly, in case of India, Bangladesh, Pakistan, etc. in Asiatic zone in one hand; and also on the other side of the global social environment countries like in Africa, Latin America, etc. are all not free from such kind of socially alarming dehumanized tendencies, in which religion as the element of society plays vital role in making aware of the fact that development of human beings are, now becoming a more permanent nature than casually treated subject of social orientation process. In question of religion thus, the application of its fundamental truths are, therefore, related to human development process; because, due to lack of an understanding based on scientific parlance[57] in considering facts of real nature of secular thought, human development has been interrupted by means of irrelevant growth potentials, not being contained for measurement in scientific strategy through real socio-economic behavioural models formulation; but to resort by the politicized nature of communalizing tendencies in level playing role model in the techniques of vote banking system, where it has been further observed that the deprivation of human beings are increasing day-by-day in society.

It looks therefore, optimizing application reasons of religion in the field of human development parameters of study, depending on scientific investigation of facts, for which people are trying at their level best in connecting issues concerning human upliftment consciousness in developing backward areas as well as deprived people, who are politicized in administering to ameliorate the process of human sufferings from different ground realities. This is the glaring reason, for which study on religion becomes fundamental to focus on the screen of the social picture the real situational tendencies of human survival stages, to which development dimensions are yet to pave the way for human nature of participation in the process of real democratic involvement; so that holistic nature of human development perspective idea can be strengthened through strategic human behavioural prudence on religion, as the goal of social advancement, irrespective of religious discrimination that has been prevailing throughout the world environmental peripheral areas. Nevertheless, it is true that religion is the real nature of human life, where there is no justification of politicizing the system of management, at the cost of human growth and development. But still, it has been continuing for long in the historical perspective of social journey, during the course of making a process in organizing all human activities, due to some kind of vested interest of some political groups, or even certain classes of fanatic people who claim to be religious leaders, and from time-to-time; either directly, or indirectly participate in the process of political voting system to corrupt people who are actually innocent, and feels in mind to their speeches and activities. Hence, it is observed that unscientific religious policies of certain categories or groups of vested interest in question of religion, permeably disturbing the overall system of social management process of human organizational participatory role, in terms of politicizing their own cause for the interest of taking some kind of vested advantage, so as to prevail social unrest and thus, inhuman tendencies are growing day-after-day in societal environment, where these leaders are blaming themselves to one another, to concentrate on the particular pattern on vote banking enlargement process, to gain out of it, and to continue this system as a matter of fact in their disingenuous process to disinherit those of illiterate as well as innocent human beings, who are actually depending on themselves and suffering permanently, due to lack of proper education on religious beliefs and practices.

The implication of application of religion for scientific human development process is such that, once religious truths are really understandable to development issues, there would be immediate requirement of human behavioural modification, for which religious leaders, along with political parties and their leaders are to be made responsible to educate people for involving themselves to participate in the democratic nature of human activities, in augmenting people to educate for the cause of human sufferings, in which judicious reformation of the voting system can be made to change the future of the deprived masses, who have been otherwise; remaining in inhuman living conditions due to lack of adequate reach of all the facilities for civic survival in society. To this process, again, scientific behavioural traits are to be adjusted by means of imparting learning environment, which helps in eliminating blind and unscientific faiths on religion, for which people are made to live in the stage of slavery years-after-years. It is therefore essential that training on religion should be made on the basis of human reasons, for lack of which people are living in backwardness. Then and then only, people are to be enlightened, illustrating anywhere and everywhere to search for real developmental opportunities, without blaming the system which has been created by human beings, and the creation of such conditions are interrelated to ruin the social superstructure, in the down-line of bringing social environment; either to a static nature, or even unscientific nature of human growth potentials toward inadequate socialization in the process of making religious faiths, a scientific instrument of human development mechanism to change the social structure. Nevertheless, it is the scientific temper of thought necessarily to be imparted in realizing the concepts of religion, where we should take into account the fundamental truths of all religions prevailing in this world; because of making human development a subject of world thought in all spheres of socio-economic activities and scientific investigations, by means of informing people about the value system of making resources for potential development of the social environment. It is needlessly to be assumed that human religion is the foundation of socio-economic challenges of change[58], in motivating people to uproot value of love, affection and sympathy for underlying issues of fundamental growth, which has to be people-oriented as well as inclusive towards finding conclusion regarding aspects of human survival dynamicity, with the relativity of scientific human psychological background confining psychological analysis, ignoring all types of self or group interest vested reasons shown unnecessarily, to safeguard justifications in the context of presenting 'untruth as truth' or 'truth as untruth', to hold over a position in administrative system of managing concept of human growth perspectives, to the realization of political gain out of such outcome of self analysis in creating feeling in mind of illiterate human beings.

Under the above circumstances, it is essential that religious approach should be based on Preksha meditational concept of universal understanding, for unifying with the goal of human developmental strategies; where there should be logical representation of facts and cases, to figure out real nature and causes of human backwardness throughout the world order, which has been understood scientifically as the pathetic picture from all counts of statistical analysis, and presentations of various kind of government reports at national as well as international level. Understanding thus all basic parameters of growth initiatives necessary to confine things and activities, for the project management system of human upliftment conditions; there should be appropriate correlation between religion and development[59], for the sake of human advancement in life related happiness to betterment of the situations in reflecting various fundamental truths, requiring for effective management of social resources in question of efficient channelization as well as diversification of funds, for scientific order of human development in various ladders of socio-metric graphs to incorporate some important guidelines, for confining human religious philosophy in different parts of the world societies; so that international cooperation would be widespread in relating elemental ideation of religious truths for unifying human development paradigms shift, in nature of human existential scientific diversity in the midst of organizational opportunities that are undertaken, for solving burning problems of human misery, distress and hungriness. In this way, application of religion can be made healthy practices for equity of living, in order to measure concept of justice – how far issues pertaining to human development are poignantly observed to be immature in the structural adjustment of things and ideas, which go to suggest some relevant measures through religion regarding establishment of work culture, as the dharma of human administrative guidelines, to attain the goal of scientific socialization in terms of holistic welfare, which can be impressively incorporated in the corporate planning activities, for an urgent necessity of the present periods in historical perspective. Now, the jurisprudence of human justice for equanimity thought in guiding social system could be assimilated, to the religious backgrounds of human living tendencies so as to unify process of human development strategy, for the purposive orientation of integral base of human foundation, with all essential ingredients of universal religion of mankind, to which science and technology can further be made accountable to run the system in realistic tendencies of employing human upliftment programmes; which are highly important to rejuvenate social pyramid in question of development, as the instrument of scientific social change mechanism process, in cohesive nature of human participation[60], to the level playing role of religious models and statistical simulation of things in emergent manner.

In substituting the above viewpoints, organizational innovative nature of work has to be managed effectively in supplying all the facilities to backward people, who are for long days observed as remaining as the tool of vote banking issue in the name of, either secularism, or communalism in countries like – India, Pakistan, Bangladesh, and also many other underdeveloped regions of the world, in hands of corrupt politicians as well as bureaucrats and religious leaders, who claim to perform for the amelioration of poverty from the grass-root levels of the society, in terms of implementing various schemes and managing projects inefficiently, and thus; rampant loot of public resources are being made from the public exchequers in vested interest of themselves, the repercussion of the situation has now become such that people are day-by-day coming to a level of living condition, where character of animalistic tendency is found to prevail in their societal existence. Hence, it is permeably said that scientific application of work ethics and techniques of developing the onslaught of the suffered population, can only be said to enhance human religion in practices of socio-economic pattern of fund management efficiency, to reduce social conflicts and increase human efficiency for the purpose of effective management of organizational resources. So, it is further declared unequivocally and suggested herein, when realistic attitude formation would be strengthened to motivate people in understanding scientific reasons of religious backgrounds, for creating consciousness in human beings[61] that it is the dharma (work) can only guide people to the path of salvation, where humanity should come first, and all other practices in the name of religion should be interrelated to the elements of social building norms, in aiding for harmonious as well as coherent relationships between various classes of human beings, who would be able to profess any type of morally justified things in the religious behaviour of their own kind. This is to be reflected in organizational work culture to rationalize industrial productivity, and for bringing balanced nature of human development perspective in realizing human religion as the social changing instrument, where integrity and human dedication towards serving distressed people would be enlarged in incorporating the human face to the corporate mission, to objectify functions of religion as the bridge in socializing all human activities, with a view to unify organizational consistency of managing things and activities for the sake of increasing human entrepreneurial abilities as well as professional application of religious capabilities, in regard to lifting corporate veil through humanization of different socially oriented programmes and projects implementation in right direction from time-to-time.

From the illustrative discussions as made above on the applications of religion, some more important suggestive measures are also enumerated under the following guidelines to show – how scientific human development is made possible through inculcation of religious truths to the foundational concept of human pious basis of existential freedom of life:

(1) It is expected that dharma (religion) should be confined to *artha* (meaningful life), for which human action (*karma*) has to be guided for the salvation (*moksha*) of life. Hence, the four elements of human life bringing concept for harmonious nature of survival principles are to be accumulated in equanimity concept, for which, equipoise nature of thinking[62] is necessary in managing human activities; so that all-round development of whole mankind is being made possible through Vedic managerial guidelines, have already been reflected in Chapter 1;

(2) Human religion (dharma) should be abided for the principles of unifying concept of integral humanity, which is possible only when there is one religion, first of all obeyed in nature of performing all types of organizational activities of human beings in this world – scientific development of mass people who are living in malnourished conditions, due to lack of adequate housing facilities, fresh or clean drinking water supply, educational facilities, medical and health-care facilities, social infrastructural facilities required for agricultural activities, industrial activities, etc. Besides, many other means of civic living like, road transport, railway coordination system, and communicational means required for speedy development of human life;

(3) Application of religion should be made to encourage people to work in cooperative organizational relationship, to participate in the process of decision-making approach for the purpose of democratic service orientation in societal environment, in correlating issues of human backwardness, so as to solve problems of regional disparities, international conflicts of living. Hence, scientific nature of interrelationship between religion (dharma) and action (karma) can help to change fate of mankind in healthy way, to reduce social restlessness tendencies, for making human organizations cohesive towards initiating social welfare through maximum social advantage[63] for the unprivileged as well as underprivileged classes of human beings;

(4) Religious philosophy should be applied in the field of scientific human development process, by means of curbing all elements of anti-social activities, politicization of human activities for underlying principles of universal human upliftment, to which, it is to be taken care of that gaps between haves and have-nots are reduced, while uttering the causes of inefficient system of management. Here, the concept of integral humanity should be superimposed for applying with core ideas of religion on performance based issues, in developing social system, so as to eliminate corrupt practices from the administrative as well as political system to accelerate human betterment through all-round effectiveness in managing organizational activities;

(5) Dharma (religion) of work should be considered as the real worship principle, which helps in social building activities, in terms of eradicating any kind of discriminating behaviour between people, and thus; the principles of management for scientific human development should be propagated for the observance of the greatest mantra (thought), or ethics of work as – universal nature of good governance practice for whole mankind, where it is possible for the rolling of the entire human civilization in diversified ways, to reach at the same goal of human organizational system of managerial existentialism – universal peace; and

(6) Application of the principles of religion should be dedicated to bring in social harmony, in participating activities through international cooperation building between man and man, to objectify various grounds of scientific tools and techniques necessary for optimal order of human development, which is the demand of the present scientific reformation strategy, in the context of global harmony, universal peace and social tranquility all throughout the world order.

In a nutshell, it is religion, the core idea of which should be viewed from scientific angle, to eradicate social backwardness of distressed human beings; who are at this age of scientific and technological development living in stages of slavery with pitiable inhuman conditions[64]. Hence, universal system of human development should be the order of human religious foundation, where optimum love for the entire humanity should emanate in organizational work culture, to nurture a system of innovative creativity towards applying religious truths in sensitivity analysis. It is required to be inculcated in principles of good governance mantra as the key-note of managerial success, for bringing universal nature of human development with the scientific temper of management thought, for organizational consistency of doing things in equipoise order of human interrelationships.

Religious Path for Global Human Excellence Building

Human excellence building is the most important and glorious part of study of human development process throughout the world system of management. Consequently, there are enough opportunities for the development of social structure depending on human work efficiency, necessary for increasing organizational productivity as well as delivery mechanism concerned with human upliftment programmes, to which; channelization of social resources becomes more effective towards bringing mankind for providing efficient services in course of dealing with financial derivatives. Hence, it is highly important to note that competencies building are essential to find-out solution of the problems of social backwardness of human beings, where maximization of utility in terms of resource delivery system could be well balanced to meet-out problems of human sufferings and deprivation. Taking into account this point in mind of managers, it is expected that religious paths are required to be implemented for reducing social imbalances, in which, norms of increasing human efficiency as the way of life bringing process could well be adjusted to balance regional economies over the world at large. It is thus, scientific temper of thought should be confined to religious path-findings for enormous level of human potential development, so that the strategies framed for adequate level of human development purposes have certain kind of relationships, in which organizational leadership authorities are provided with efficient system of decision-making[65] criterion for empowering people to reach at the goal of global unification, concerning growth potentials in social building process, with all means of managerial communication system in regard to optimization of opportunities in all fields of human activities, towards an endeavour of humanization of the different productive means to attain the goal of universal development.

It is thus strategically asserted that religious guidelines are necessary attributes of enhancing human excellence at work environment, for which, organizational planning must be redrafted on the basis of training skills development for increasing interpersonal as well as intergroup relationships, so as to bind people with the work culture atmosphere, without politicizing power and authority related structural relationships. Thus, innovations in practice of religious truths are to be included with organizational functional relationships, to prevail justice in the nature of performing jobs; which go to lead people in equanimity concept of managing all resources of the organizations. Increasing amount of delivery is therefore possible to be attained, as and when religious basis are found on scientific forecasting regarding human inefficiency towards guiding people, where the role model of leadership pertaining to encouragement of people for increasing cooperation at work would be stimulated, to provide human motivational incentives in strengthening every element of coordination function[66]. It is therefore undoubtedly noted here, that functional relationships are influenced by creative thinking on fundamental values of religious ideologies, due to lack of which people are guided by principles of injustice that has no impact on productive system. As a result of this, dehumanization is being widespread throughout organizational structure, which has further negative impact on work relationships. So, religious truths are to be tested not by means of political biasness, but by means of practical business approach that is preponderated by assumptions of human growth imperatives. For all these reasons, there is proper justification for undertaking corporate mission directed objectives on functional delivery system of effective managerial guidelines, where essentials of training are to be fulfilled by means of scientific religious ideologies, governing humanization philosophy of work in each and every policy resolution of corporate visionary goal in leading people towards salvation of life, in terms of supplying with the minimum needs requirement necessary for civic living objectives, in actualizing things at organizational work relationships. Thus, various strategies concerning optimum development of all classes of human beings are synchronized for flexible structural relationships[67] at various levels of management, which have adequate correlation towards confining people for forward looking tendencies in societal advancement norms, with the perfect motivational guidelines from leadership point of view in balancing social structure in equipoise nature of performances. In this way, empowerment of people can be made to establish cooperative human relationship in bringing industrial democracy, for the purpose of efficient utilization of social resources to increase productivity, which can also be applied for supplying market potentials in reducing imbalances in the distribution system. As a whole, religious paths are connoting – how to meet with deficiencies to challenge for social building norms of managerial effective guidelines, to uproot social value system in terms of organizational counseling and innovative leadership practices. We should therefore, be cautious that religious ideologies are not taken at hand for utilizing resources for some personal gain, or with some kind of vested group interest in politicizing administrative affairs, which have already ruined social system for adequate level of human development perspective. It is therefore essential that religious paths are fundamentally adjusted to organizational planning functions with a view to good governance objectives, where each type of dogmatism that goes against public policy of development should be rectified with great care and good courage. This type of attitude should be involved while training manpower resources in organizations, so that politicizing terms like secularism as well as communalism tendencies which empowered our leaders to take advantage out of all these elements of anti-social slogans can be eradicated by means of scientific forecasting of training necessities, for increasing human motivational relationship to employ self for the common good of mass people. This is the technique of optimum level of excellence can be exposed in performance based entrepreneurial productivity in corporate undertaking, by shouldering adequate amount of responsibility to every kind of work, necessitated by leadership approach[68] of scientific coordination for human relationship.

Today, everywhere in the world there is enormous crises felt for human advancement, to which, relativity between religious path and organizational goal of human development has been made responsible towards initiating certain kind of perfection in human beings. As a result of this, all kinds of organized system have been observed to become failure in delivering output needed to solve problems of human numerous sufferings, due to maladjustment between planning and implementing activities. As a prescription to this problem, the solution can be suggested by saying that religious paths are to be strategically adopted in restructuring organizational innovative system of work related policies, to emulate things for the reformation of social pyramid, where every individual being should be treated with utmost care, so as to empower people for optimum level of development. Hence, organizational competencies building has to be remodeled for the purpose of enormous responsibility initiatives, which should be considered to change the onslaught of the deprived population, who are ill-fed and ill-clad due to mismatch of resources which do not reach at their door step, due to defective bureaucratic system as well as corruptive political administration. Thus, religion (dharma) as the principle of work has to be applied in the field of deficiencies for empowering people by means of decentralization of activities, not by means of fallacy in the name of secularism practices that we follow in countries like India, Pakistan, Bangladesh and many other countries of the world. Again, communal agenda and castes politics are to be nipped in the bud from religious paths and administrative system of governance. To the contrary, integral humanism should be infused in mind of people[69], to motivate them to excel in working out the dormant potentialities by way of team building approach, which will go to reform backward societies for timely delivery of different products needed for civic living conditions. Thus, religion should be seen from the angle of human development mantra in equanimity thought, for which, it will be possible to bring in holistic nature of social development of all classes of human beings, ignoring any other anti-social norms of mismanagement as well as ill governance. It is therefore responsibility of religious leaders to come forward in question of development as the common slogan of humanity; otherwise, this world of ours would become in future a battleground of destruction. All these affairs have already polluted the social environment throughout the world atmosphere of living by means of national arms race in different countries as well as international terrorism in the name of development and religion. So, it is now high time that religious agenda should confirm principles of equity, justice and fraternity in regard to development in holistic perspective for ultimate solution of human backwardness, and eradication of regional imbalances in different zones of the world environment.

Accordingly, business cooperation should be strengthened in between countries, for increasing human efficiency, work potentiality and for reconstructing transparent social order. Creating religion as the bridge of human movement for forward journey in question of making life happy[70], towards the process of universal realization requires managing human activities for the integrated development goal of global social building norms. To this positive role model, organizations are to relate things of urgency which call attention towards confining people for motivated leadership approach and thereby, spiritual ideals consisting value driven practice of work have to be enlarged in enriching the goal of human development, with the strategic functional relationship of managerial counter-part in considering innovation with training needs of manpower resources in industrial set-up. However, human excellence could well be enhanced through transformational leadership in religious undertaking, who would be mainly accustomed to discuss issues concerning human backwardness problems with that of government authorities as well as public servants, by way of establishment of consortium relationship between among business, governance and polity. In this central point, assumptions of religious thoughts for valuation of projects, guided by the philosophy of good governance practice and legal guidelines for initiating infrastructural project management system, to eradicate problems of human communication orientation should form part of the administrative and religious institutional policy. Here, specific issues concerning top priority for backward region's development should be placed at the focal point of decentralizing norms of corporate policy resolutions; so that people feel enthusiastic regarding their active involvement with the system of work environment. Thus, proper guidelines that are given by spiritual thoughts of management could pave the way for managing human activities in directive paths, required by level of structural adjustment[71] between religious goal and government policy framework adopted for human efficiency building norms. So, it is correct to say that human motivational values are required to be strengthened through religious paths of business directives, where scientific leadership approach for considering cases of human sufferings and their timely solution would be streamlined towards the means of productive resources, that go to empower people in advancing the path of socialization process through humanization of organizational activities, in integrating all sources of training methodologies for imparting human value system with all good governance practice tools and techniques. As a result of such philosophical guidance, religion should be converted into upliftment of social pyramid to a stage of international human understanding, coherence as well as harmonious intergroup relationships for confidence building norms, with a view to encourage people for producing goods to solve problems of human backwardness, inter-regional imbalances and social diversity between all classes of people in living harmonious atmosphere throughout the world environment.

From the above analysis, it is clear that religious path is the strategic line of increasing human efficiency in industrial and commercial activities, which enlightens people about the realities of human socio-economic performances, to advance society with the effective guidance of organizational management system. Thus, it is also true to mention here that fundamental principles of human religious activities are guided by the philosophy of work culture as well as participative system of management, to uproot social value orientation process towards all kinds of human endeavours, that go to reduce human conflicts in interpersonal as well as group relationships. Hence, we would like to deal with the following points for the purpose of coming at conclusion about the various managerial policies, required in implementing training modules based on the truths of religion (dharma) for work behaviour at organizational directive[72] functions, in confining people towards bringing universal level of development, concerned with leadership approach of transformational dynamicity, social consistency and global cohesiveness for encouraging people to participate more in industrial productivity:

(1) It is the justice for human advancement, who is still suffering from many kinds of social problems concerning civic living elements of optimizing human potential development. In this area of thinking, religious path is the guidance giving people opportunities for self-development, in nurturing their dormant potentials to uproot social value system in identifying various sorts of organizational structural adjustments toward fullest utilization of human resource qualities, along with other resources of organizations;

(2) It is possible to increase human acumen through scientific religious philosophy of work-related elements, narrating human empowerment concept to the plan of action of organizational policies, to humanize the system in industrial undertaking in modern days technological assumptions of information resources, to optimize organizational

productivity through innovative research techniques and creative motivational programmes, that gives importance on human upliftment schemes for the purpose of sensitizing people with the common guidelines of rapid development, in socializing goals of organization throughout the system of management innovations required for effective entrepreneurial development[73];

(3) Religious truths can be tested for enrichment of job potential in terms of training packages, where decision-making approach requires alternative ideas in good governance criterion to administer things and activities, for the greater interest of all mankind, so as to bring people in cooperative work relationship by strengthening the principles of human empowerment as well as social mobility in diversified paths, to attain the performance goal for establishment of integral humanity, in leading people towards organizational unification by means of justice and equity for developing mass people, in terms of universalizing the concept of decentralized system of modern management ideologies;

(4) Religious path has a role model value in initiating organizational team-building approach towards reaching at the goal of welfare principles, to emulate reasons for dignity of labour and strategic confidentiality in augmenting people towards orienting society on the foot-prints of civic norms of human living justification, to that of existential freedom for the choice of individual's democratic relationships with group goals, towards the process of social advancement system. Thus, regional imbalances would be reduced for establishment of universal development philosophy with the correct path of religious undertaking, in cementing policies of human excellence building norms for the purpose of integrated restructuring of the work ethics by means of good governance conditionality, in reducing social poverty, increasing human efficiency at the work place and balancing resources by effective system of management; and

(5) Increasing human potential with the challenging work behaviour can only be possible through spiritual guidelines, where people are well trained for understanding values of equanimity performance as well as scientific human development for social orientation purposes; so that 'path-goal' relationship in organized system of management can be fundamentally matched by eradicating problems of mismanagement, due to vested interest groups and politicization of organizational administrative performances, in the name of secular agenda and communal slogans. Thus, establishment of religious philosophy would help in streamlining human cooperation at work

atmosphere. It will ultimately strengthen human motivation for rationalization of industrial activities[74], and considering human backwardness as the most urgent policy of organizational planning system. In correlating issues of global level human sufferings, religious ideologies are strong guiding instruments to eradicate problems of human justified living, in an environment of peace and harmony. Thus, religious science should be made work related tools for developing deprived people, by means of training through all sources of human efficient leadership approach, to innovate the democratic path of human guidance and counselling.

Religious Mode of Organizational Work Behaviour

Human organizational activities are important for human development. It is therefore, essential that work behaviours in different types of social and business organizations are concentrated on objective assessment of human relationships, where religious mode of interacting with the people in environment will highlight on the progress of various nature of socio-economic activities, performed towards attainment of group goal as well as organizational goal. It is expected that correct idea of religious mode on the behavioural postulates will strengthen administrative functions, which would be devoted to optimize human welfare in general, and global development in particular. So, we should keep in mind that sympathy for common people, who are not getting adequate facilities for civic living will be measured from philosophical perspective of human developmental needs, concerning all classes of social beings, irrespective of any kind of distinction being made on the basis of unscientific thought on religious slogans that we follow now-a-days, in most of the underdeveloped and developing countries of the world. Hence, our organizational policies are to be guided by the philosophy of work for the common welfare of mass people. In the context of welfare view, there should be no amount of lapses on religious jurisprudence[75], in the name of exploitation of human population, which has resulted for their long-run deprivation clearly found on social structure of the present day worldwide backwardness of global masses. Thus, it requires the highest level of services in framing organizational policies for safeguarding interest of backward people. This is the real religious mode of work with the people in organizational setting, so far as the developmental issues are concerned with the societal rolling in dynamic order.

In incorporating such notion in organizational work will focus on the human face of entrepreneurial relationships, for enlightening on various issues of work related problems. Thus, it is possible to advance human society by means of international understanding on the true concept of human potentials that requires proper environment to workout qualities in work life. In this centre-point development philosophy has to be ensured, correlating universal ideas of religious behavioural mode of expressing organizational dimensions of cohesiveness in group relationships, so as to attain human dignity of labour, organizational consistency of getting things done for attaining holistic development and global level emancipation of human beings for structural readjustment of the world society. Here, discipline, dedication and delivery should be the religion (dharma) of work culture, in which organizational mission for entertaining environmental issues of human improper balancing stage of living would be stimulated, towards focussing hopes for living with the destiny of life[76] bringing possibilities; so that social ills for maladjustments in administrative constituent parts are relatively matched with that of human interpersonal as well as intergroup relationships, to encourage people in believing the fact that only development of people should be the mode of organizational work religion, in establishing social peace as well as global tranquil order to eliminate all kinds of ills of mismanagement. From all these assumptions, we may note that organizational working relationships are guided by the motives of truth, bliss and absolute idea of human development related concepts of social transformation, where core of human beings are to be realized in practice of scientific religious assumptions regarding universal development of all kinds and classes of social beings. From this ground realities, we may assume the fact that religious mode of behaviour concerning human skill building as well as organizational work culture could help in cementing human relationships, based on organizational transparency, leadership radicalism for initiating social change in positive direction and worldwide human existentialism for actualization of social rolling in diversified directions, to reach at the goal of human perfectionism through team building approach, for unifying religious objectivity towards the establishment of social movement in right direction.

All these potentials are encompassing organizational sound coordination as well as administrative skills for enumerating human behavioural postulates, to motivate people on the objective functions of human welfare maximization[77], social balance restoration for eliminating human sufferings and global peaceful environmental transcendental order of human advancement, towards unifying organizational various working relationships in rejuvenating social diversities, human living excellence for civilities and world level cultural integration. Thus, it is expected that the philosophy of work – "Vasudhaiva Kutumbakam", which we have already discussed in Chapter 1, should be further emulated through compounding principles of work religion of organizations, for development as the mantra of human integral approach of living, universal integrity for social reformations in positive directions, and global transitional order for environmental adjustments through business potentials. In this way, scientific analysis on religious mode of business transactions for interplaying resources of developmental projects, in enthusing people to emulate social sufferings of all classes of human beings would be central idea of organizational work behaviour, in managing socio-economic activities with a view to match resources in balancing order, and creating adequate diversification for fund management system in valuation of assets legally, to embrace the goal of optimum human development; wherein, punctuality, regularity, honesty, reality, and besides, elements of risks are to be attributed to the causes of human up-gradation, in unifying principles of living justice with dignity of labour and opportunity of employing self ideas of different types of social beings, to restructure organizational working model based on such philosophy of human development paradigms shift in nature. It is therefore, the development model concerning human empowerment for an endeavour towards excelling self initiated responsibility and leadership approach of integral humanity, to understand actual idea of work religion in mode of operational behavioural pursuits, to amplify 'cause-effect' relationships in poverty and social gaps could help in enlarging the process of managerial entrepreneurial abilities, to overcome problems of organizational disabilities due to prevailing political interference and involvement of administrative vested interest of certain groups, which play dominant role in propagating falsehoods towards religious behavioural assumptions should be overthrown, by means of encouraging people for development realities as the formula plan of organizational policy implications, confining all the tasks that are to be performed for holistic nature of human development issues in environmental changing situations[78]. This is the real nature of religious mode of organizational work behaviour, requires to be interpreted in connection with organizational restructuring as well as managerial models of honest behavioural prudence for human development purposes; otherwise, financial safeguard against corruptive human behaviour made to suppress things and incorporate ideas of mismanagement in the name of secular thoughts, and looting public exchequers years-after-years would be a continuity in vote-banking system to many countries of the world, has yet to be remedied through scientific model of human development strategies, as expected to deal with eliminating problems of poverty and social unrest which are observed in the present system of the world order. So, correct analysis of religious mode of operations – truth, beauty and goodness of managerial undertaking for advancing social people in diversified paths[79] should be necessary conditions of social growth and organizational dynamicity, which could hopefully change onslaught of backward people, have enough grounds of social justification for enlarging religious strategies in business practices, to the domain of human core idea of universal development initiatives an organizational transparent system of resource management creativity, with the sensitivity of managerial level playing role model practices and leadership approach of confining tasks for speedy development through optimum level of honesty and integrity.

From these standpoints, it can be asserted that religious mode regarding organizational work behaviour should be confined to human opportunities of civic living, for the purpose of understanding the realities of integral concept of justified norms of living through humanitarian perspective, and therefore, amenities of leading life with the minimum facilities, like – two handful of meals a day with minimum calories for living for all kinds of social beings, electricity facilities for domestic services as well as industrial and agricultural and business activities, transportation facilities in backward areas with the network of rail-road connectivity, housing, sanitation and healthcare facilities for all poor people, etc. are basic scientific backgrounds to be resolved in policy documents of organizational activities, both in public and private sectors; along with government body corporate as the religion (dharma) of human development. Thus, only human beings and no other things should be concentrated for uplifting masses from the long periods of slavery[80], as found in historical perspective in these days of technocrat economy. Again, relativity in social living pattern in between rich and poor should be matched with the work philosophy of organizational active interface between planning and implementation of the different programmes as chalked out for eradication of poverty alleviation, with different means of work culture. This is to be taken into account as the responsible mode of organization's dharma or religion for human development policy resolutions, irrespective of caste, creed, colour, sex, race, nationalities and religious differences throughout the world environment. Hence, sustainable concept of development should also take care about the environmental scanning for resource exploitation and utilization purposes, because of making adequate balances throughout the spectrum of the global socio-economy. Harmonious balance should also be stressed on protecting animal as well as botanical kingdom for preservation of rare species and medicinal plants. Accordingly, we should also concentrate our mind to restore a harmonious balance among man, animal and forest life; so that global warming as predicted by eminent scientists could be taken care of, with all the organizational activities for enriching our environment, and to overcome problems of natural destruction. In this way, mode of organizational operating system can be rectified through cybernetic system of human behavioural prudence, so as to bind people in the mantra of steady-state development concept. Consequently, it is very much essential that social gaps should be reduced by elimination of corruptive services, in terms of planning criterion in the field of information services as well as juristic analysis on the postulates of human efficient behavioural expediency, to inculcate mechanism for national as well as international level audit services in making concept of development effective towards providing all-round services, for speedy development of the backward areas and accelerating rate of human growth. Here, all-round human development for personality and excellence in qualities of work requires as the norm of organizational delivery system and managerial service giving norms of efficient human behaviour. From all these ideas, accountability can be built-up for long-run development of the global society, which should be the yardstick of measurement for socialization of religious mode of human organizational work behavioural system[81] and management perfection. Assessing all the factors of social growth potentials, developmental mode of working behaviour could be achieved through honesty and integrity, with the dedicated system of managerial guidance; where organizations are to be instrumental for catalytic change in social transparent behaviour as well as human challenging motive of working pursuits for development of the entire humanity. Therefore, holistic mode of religious thought as development formula plan should be made congruent to the concept of global level human excellence making mechanism. For encouraging young people, adequate training system should be made from research oriented concept of operational ideas in organizational setting; so that universality of human rolling with all diversities can be adjusted with scientific method of working models as the plan of action for making optimum level of human advancement, in all-round areas of the social environment, where humanity should be given as the only priority for feeling good with the good governance norms of religious mode of working behaviour in organizational culture of global dynamicity. In this way, consistency in establishing priority for human optimum level of growth with the fullest personality development can be made to achieve the goal of global integration[82]. This would be the real secular concept of religion, should be fundamentally adjusted with the work culture of organizational existential supremacy as well as human optimum level of freedom, for decision-making process of socio-economic activities in developing all-round spheres of world social pyramid.

Considering human religious motive for such kind of organizational authoritative functional relationship, to work-out different areas of human development deficiencies, there should be clear-cut understanding in building up leadership models respecting religious institutional philosophy of human work ethics, to uproot social value system in permeable nature of social advancement through global sustainable norms of peaceful human living environment; so that human beings are given adequate opportunities for their spurt of personality, in blooming towards social enlightenment process, to enrich organizational work culture elements in an approach of integral humanity concept, to find-out human nature of competencies level with all the aspects of credibility and empowerment potentials, in confining tasks for progressing the world society with the fundamental principles of legal justice[83], in making choice for attaining the highest order of social growth in never-ending process and uninterrupted manner. However, as and when organizational information system is based on scientific monitoring of the problems of human sufferings, there would come social balance in reducing gaps between haves and have-nots to rectify mismatch among all types of resources, for bringing adequate level of human creativity with the sensitivity analysis of the grievous problems of human malnutrition, stages of ill-fed and ill-clad condition, drain of resources due to red-tapes and corruptive administrative system of management, in bringing public policies for attaining social sustainable norms of human efficient behavioural prudence for enlarging global peaceful atmosphere, taking into account all factors of man-made system of inefficiency in dealing with implementing norms of packages for reducing social poverty. This is the real line of thinking in regard to perspective light of human development agenda and religious behavioural postulates of human dignity of living, which has a relevancy in correcting order of politicized administrative pattern of delivery mechanism towards focussing organization's decentralized pattern of decision-making approach for empowering social people. Thus, the system of management should be made more and more effective for making people accountable to rejuvenate social transparency, for encouraging themselves thinking freely in regard to development issues, to nurture organizational work culture in scientific pattern of leadership goal for motivating people to strengthen group behaviour, with a view to ascertain policies of objective assessment of organizational activities and strategic norms of human development conditionality. So, there should be universal criteria for enlarging religious goal of human advancement[84], where to principles of honesty, integrity and sincerity are to be assimilated with working philosophy to optimize human competencies, credibility and capabilities. In this system of working with the nature of environmental synchronizing mechanism, social restlessness can further be reduced to a level of naturalistic order in accelerating human growth potentials, and so, religious mode of operating with behavioural foundation should also be adjustable towards confining optimum level of human growth in all-round spheres of the world society, for encompassing all the problems of human sufferings[85] in result-oriented approach of good governance principles as well as administrative justice in human dignity of living, with all civilized norms in scientific temper of social rolling for holistic unification in mankind. In a nutshell, essentials of religious mode of organizational work behaviour should be made contemporary ideals toward all practicalities of realizing human upliftment programmes with the necessary provisions of dignified living modules; based on the practice of 'Preksha meditation' ideals to uproot social value system and providing for peaceful human living atmosphere throughout the world environment.

Human Empowerment through Religious Ideology

Human empowerment is the root of human development strategies, where people are required to be made free for understanding goal of social rejuvenation from the stage of sufferings, to a stage of existential dynamicity. It is therefore, religious ideology making a common belief for establishment of peaceful society, based on principles of absolute truth in civic living relationships, connoting specialty on the empirical research approach of human behavioural postulates, concerning development potentials of the administrative set-up of a sovereign nation. Thus, nation building activities are to be emphasized on principles of doing business activities as well as managing for good governance philosophy of human development pyramid, causing thereby social transformation[86] in terms of common development like – food, clothing, shelter, education and healthcare activities; pertaining to the process of cohesive growth of the overall pillars of social engineering to uproot human value system, in codifying religious values of truth, bliss and absolute beliefs concerning human up-gradation from the stage of slavery, towards manifestations of social pluralistic transparent managerial behavioural goal as well as leadership approaches of unified concept of living freedom. Considering all such elements inherent in work behaviour in organizational entrepreneurial abilities, empowerment of people is a must in modern days technological society, in which, religious values are required to be molded with all criterion of free opportunities for human development potentials, guaranteed through increasing scope of democratic leadership to emancipation of people from the vicious level of social grass-root conditions of living with peripheral severity[87], in trying for accelerating qualities; but complementing with all problems of society, to emanate for making visionary journey with all skills and acumen in establishing a coherence relationship between factors of development and social diversity, for encouraging people to think for the global humankind. It is thus, a challenge of change where empowerment should be found with corruption less administrative principles, in managing things for both public and private enterprises. In this regard, we should take note of the present problems of the world atmosphere, wherein; poverty has been taken as the challenge, among others like – terrorism, legal set-up and global peace in making people to realize the concept of integral humanity, which we have already explained in Chapter 1. So, empowerment of all human beings are to be made as the religious agenda for people's welfare through unified nature of development model, creating human skills for increasing production objectives to solve problems of numerous sufferings of all mankind in this world.

The destiny of such vision is therefore uprooted through religious ideology, to which every organization, be it private body corporate or government agencies should confine things for managerial effectiveness, in terms of delivery system and transparent economic behaviour for serving with the dedicated goal of – 'work for man as worship for the Almighty'. Hence, empowerment should be in the 'centre-stage' of human development process[88], where all types and classes of people are to be given optimum opportunities for decision making towards rebuilding social set-up on value-based principles of religious truths and beliefs. Here, dharma of human development should be seen as the working ideology of all organizational dynamicity, considering entrepreneurship abilities building as the tool for empowerment conditions, in which, organizational leadership should frame rules of managing with the antiquity of trusteeship principles and universal rolling of human civilization, in testifying religious ideologies which are helping for harmonious development of mankind. The rule of law as the scope of development should be applied in regard to human empowerment principles of matching with scarce resources of the environment. For this reason, religious values of unity and integrity should focus for making people in realizing principles of cooperation, as it is enormously important to understand for clarity of thought regarding human existentialism, in organizational transformation towards binding people in diversity of empowering potentials for the sake of human up-gradation, with all types of potentialities for social emancipation of mankind in managing things and activities, by means of various decision variables justifying human capacity building norms requiring for modern civilization[89], with the hope of advancing business perspectives for unifying people towards the concept of integral humanity. Redesigning organizational structure is a must for developing social gamut of human congruency towards optimization of resources, bring for absolute necessity of human problems of poverty, fighting which, modern organizations can be able to best fit for making global dynamicity with the all-embracing qualitative norms of empowerment principalities, to which humankind should find answers out of the experience of global conformity towards matching with the realistic philosophy of development mantra, as the principle of religious guidance to excel organizational qualities for the audacity of human faith and belief, towards considering development as weapon of modern technocrat society. In this way of thinking capitalistic tendencies can help to cope up with socialistic pattern of social development, as it were; in relation to social history, in which people should be expounded to make empirical research on empowerment from spiritualizing managerial challenges of change, in proactive nature of administrative thought provoking elements of effective management goal as well as social transcendental order of transformation, to rejuvenate human cooperation in all fields of human excellence building services[90].

From the above view points, it is worthwhile to note that religious ideology should be counteracted for increasing people's participation in decision-making approaches of modern organizational activities, which should further confine things to cooperate with the deprived masses for their speedy development in all-round spheres of socio-economic parameters of social building goal. In this aspect of development ideology, infrastructural means are to be developed to empower people, by planning organizational activities based on human face criterion with the norms of ancient Vedic values and moral guidelines, to motivate people for undertaking primary concept of grass-root developmental elements; wherein, all should be represented in making correct journey to the path of attaining organizational goal of civic administrative productive base – this is again, required free atmosphere, in reengineering asset management policy for encompassing human growth with the help of team[91] building approach, to which, every man should be given adequate opportunities for fuller personality development, a free chance to interplay with the administrative system, for the purposive social transformational result orientation. It is thereby helpful for strengthening national as well as global consciousness, so as to attain result for solving all types of social problems, considering managerial efficiency in nurturing people to uproot social value system, with the productive means of effective communication as well as transparent skill building through organizational competencies, leadership role models and human free existentialism, in confining tasks through latest technological and scientific research initiatives, with a view to adopt quality circle concept. However, religious ideologies regarding scientific empowerment of people should take into consideration all the aspects of human potentiality spurt through collaborative mechanism, in which management of resources are necessarily to be optimized with the effective planning and implementation[92] of programmes from time-to-time, for increasing human welfare and protecting the world societies from all such anti-social elements which go to ruin human civilization. Therefore, responsive leadership ideologies are to be merged with responsibility for social accounting, in so far as the administrative problems are concerned for eliminating ills of management. Such type of ideology, as depicted in the Vedic philosophy – 'Vasudhaiva Kutumbakam' requiring organizational guidance for counselling people, to advance goal of social transformation, in every aspect of managerial foundation for undertaking entrepreneurial spirit in utilizing resources for common good of common people. This is the realistic nature of administrative set-up required adequate attention, as and when planning of both public and private sectors are made for empowering people. So, the 'Preksha' meditational concept expounding all such causes to create optimum hope for humankind should be convergent to assessed for encouraging people, to work in group relationships and to excel for the larger benefit of organizations, to which; enterprising norms are to be made flexible in understanding the nature of maximum social welfare for all classes of social people. Here is the hidden treasure of religious ideology[93]; we have attempted so far, in connection with human development strategies for encompassing diversified nature of social growth with the innovative techniques of religious foundation.

The above analysis giving scientific guidelines for human empowerment in social building approach should be empirically researched for enlarging goal of integral humanity, for; it is impossible to rectify the present system of global management without religious background[94]. Hence, scientific temper of thought in making religious ideologies for increasing empowerment conditions are to be discussed with educational training system, in which, institutionalization of leadership model should embrace the goal of honest management practices, in sensitizing people to think for world environment. So, technology in rebuilding the world society should be incorporated for maximum social advantage, taking into account the objective function of social emancipation of people from the severe stages of long-term sufferings.

To this policy, dynamic organizational behaviour in encountering all anti-social elements causing disturbance for holistic nature of human development should enumerate principles of social sustainability, global diversity and human environmental adaptability towards the process of scientific empowerment goal. Narrating thus all such social problems with the management functionaries, to address for changing human onslaught from the grievous causes of sufferings, would be interpreted to forecast organizational planning activities; so that management of environmental scarce resources are made effective through correlating issues of environmental balance as well as human peace and social stability. Under all such circumstances, technological 'Ombudsman' should be made free in analyzing reports concerning human backwardness in various segments of the world society. Thus, appropriate strategies are required to be made stringent towards confining tasks, in achieving goal of human perfection for greater interest of mankind through entrepreneurial leadership approach, where every man should find enough hope for developing the self[95], along with organizational visionary journey in making people to realize optimum social peace, in terms of living sovereignty, establishing social fraternity, and motivated nature of sensibility approach for increasing human acumen, adding value to resources utilization capacity and at last; developing innovative creativity for managing things in regard to social excellence process[96], with enormous public responsibility as well as self and group accountability, to increase organizational effectiveness from all-round areas of social transformation. In this way of thinking, human empowerment barriers could be resolved to assimilate organizational coordination function with the urgent necessity of human development goal; for, this is the present demand of the political system reorientation for enumerating principles of good governance, as narrated in different social science backgrounds seeking human upliftment; otherwise, the world societies are to be observed as going to decay in coming years. In a nutshell, political leadership and business management has resemblance to shape the society, with reference to spiritualization of human life through practice of good governance principles, inherent to the objective function of human empowerment as well as decentralization of modern organizational and administrative activities, based on human face and social transparency.

The aforesaid facts and figures are realistically assessed for enlarging organizational objective function towards binding people to the path of human welfare, world peace and environmental sustainability. Human competencies are therefore required special attention in organizational social change mechanism, for initiating adequate level of creativity with perfect nature of training skills, where religious foundation gives adequate counselling through effective potentiality measurement of all human beings, ignoring negative social elements which go to degrade the world society day-by-day. To emulate the goal of humanity[97], organizational leadership should be cautious about every aspect of safety and security related norms of honest administrative guidelines, for creating balance between peace and human upliftment from the stage of slavery to a new dimensional path, concerning decentralization of all important social services which go to build-up the superstructure of modern societies. Hence, empowering people through strategic decision variables could achieve this goal, in establishment of cooperative work relationships toward the areas of social urgency, in which suffered classes of population should be covered through practice of coordinated approach of training methodologies; so that integrated human development in terms of productive nature of socio-economic activities would serve the purpose of organizational delivery system in effective manner. This is enlightened through sparkling analysis made in Chapter 1, where we have already observed how global empowerment of people could be enriched for effective human development process, containing religious mode in technological perspective. Thus, special attention is now further made to this Chapter for understanding various religious strategies as well as managerial challenges in front of the world system of administrative bodies, and also required level of respective national policies in entertaining human beings for managerial perfectionism, with proactive nature of spiritual guidelines[98] that go to solve most of the present problems of human civilization. In short, skill building activities and entrepreneurship development programmes by means of team building approach, with the joint coordination of multifaceted activities of sovereign nations in international spheres could reach at the goal of attaining social peace, through development of the entire global mankind in holistic nature of doing business and trading activities, for common welfare of human civilization dynamicity as well as long-run progress of the global societies.

Religion as Scientific Temper for Global Sustainability

Today, global sustainability has become crucial point of discussion in interdisciplinary subjects in social science studies, because; development of human beings over the world at large is concerned with peripheral aspects of global environmental conservative norms and human peaceful atmosphere of civic living potentialities. It is therefore paramount important idea of analyzing business criterion, based on the foundation of scientific administrative pattern of managing resources for correlating different paths of human societal journey, concerning religion as the foundation stone of global sustainable principle[99] of human development parameters, growth related initiatives and human civic living existential transcendentalism. Hence, it is remarkably said that global sustainability is required religious base, creating human beings for encountering problems of the society in scientific temper of management thought. From this standpoint, business strategies are to be remodeled for strategically taking things in relation to human backwardness, to that of environmental crises of various resources that modern industrialization has to utilize in rationalistic concept of input-output relationship. Barring under such conditionality, there would be great danger for the civil society throughout the world atmosphere, in which business decisions are required correct strategy – how to utilize natural resources for global balance restoration, in an approach of equanimity thought. The Vedas have given many important guidelines, which are immensely helpful for the modern multinational corporate bodies, along with government sector institutional entities. Thus, it is essential that policy decisions of administrative authorities are to be made flexible for enlarging ideas of integrated development base, nurturing equipoise idea of resource sustainability and taking adequate care for the protective measures, required for the safeguard of our environment as well as dynamic movement of human civilization. Science and technology should be employed from the background of empirical and investigative research references, for discovery and invention of many issues pertaining to human endeavour towards global emancipation of deprived masses. Here, it is very important to remember that the present system of capitalistic tendencies, and monopolistic attitude of different types of entrepreneurs throughout the world environment should be harnessed with balancing nature of social good, for; it is highly conducive to harmonize scientific balance between social welfare in holistic nature of human development perspective and global sustainability in terms of strategic analysis[100] of religious value-based ideologies, in so far as the present environmental crises and global warming is concerned, that all scientists and environmentalists are providing from time-to-time, as an alert to keep our environment free from the clutches of severe unscientific exploitation of natural resources.

In recapitulating about the scientific temper of religious thought, it is essential to note that in ancient times, Vedic Rishis and Sages propounded for exhibition of human knowledge regarding utilization of natural resources, taking into account sustainable conservative thought in one side, for human welfare and dynamic social journey through human excellence building, in efficient system of producing goods for the common welfare of mass people; and on the other aspect of global sustainability view – they advocated for harmonious interrelationships amongst all sentient and insentient beings and things, and so, it is easily remarkable to say that human endeavours are always nothing but the relativity of scientific rationality and artistic play of things, for making a striking balance between dynamics of social mobility and correlations of all the diversified elements of social rolling for unified agenda of human development perspective. In this way of thinking, the present idea of scientific management thought should be matched with the ecstasy of religious universal truth for strategically analyzing human development related issues of social reconstruction, merged with the principles of equity[101], justice and fraternity for civic core of living in nationalistic manner; so that effectiveness of organizational delivery system can be brought forth for general welfare of world population, who have been otherwise, remaining in deprived stage of living due to lack of all those facilities required for civil living justification. Accordingly, it is suggested herein that world religions are to be made more and more strategic for encompassing relation-based set-up, whereto, the committee of scientific society, business houses – both, at national and international levels, government authorities, along with the UNO and international financial as well as banking institutions are all to be counter-active parts of human development parameters of study, regarding peace initiative elements and social changing mechanism, so as to bring in harmonious balance between convergent philosophy of human rolling towards forward looking tendencies, and global consistency to provide for an atmosphere of world peace – it is the relative nature of development agenda for entire humanity, where the system of management could be reconciled for bringing organizational effectiveness, to reach at the goal of human upliftment, from the present problems of human sufferings.

Thus, incorporating ideas of religious values for human services could enrich pillars of societal foundation, and so, modern organizations are required to be guided from the value initiative perspective, which help in strengthening human motivational qualities for increasing organizational effectiveness, in terms of providing judicious services to backward zones of the world economy. We are, therefore, trying at level best to emulate the process of social rejuvenation based on the philosophy of integral humanity – this is prescribed in the ancient Vedic philosophy, as the guideline for human cooperation in establishing worldwide unity through equanimity principle, which we have already attempted to explain in Chapter 1. For global sustainable environment, this is now, once again, required policy resolution in organizational planning for right services that are to be performed for backward classes of citizens from time-to-time. Hence, team building approach confining things in public administration, taking into account adequate care for all segments of social population could reap at the path of social advancement, in terms of effective system of organizational delivery mechanism, meant for the neediest section of the deprived as well as unprivileged human beings[102]. Thus, the core of development policy should be made clean towards covering backward regions of the societal segment, and for this purpose, investible funds should also be deployed in measuring needs of suffered people; so that their life style can be developed by providing adequate facilities required for civic living tendencies, by means of communicating service potentials to the areas of need in time. From the above analysis, it goes to say undoubtedly that scientific exposition of religious value which are highly related to human development means, are realistically rediscovered for encouraging people to eliminate from the mind all evils of religious thought; but rather, to impose value-driven ideals of work ethics in universal nature adopting human quality assuring elements of motivational schemes and packages, that go to solve many problems of the present world. This is the relative norms of establishment of 'path-goal' relationship in organizational group activities as well as administrative role model, necessarily compatible to encounter social problems in changing world situations. Accordingly, management policies of modern organizations are to be guided by means of cooperative work culture; wherein, human face should be structurally evolved for balanced nature of development of the societal pyramid, which helps in strengthening the process of global sustainable means and ways. In this way, redefining managerial perspective[103] from the strong background of religious truths can interplay with the interface between science and philosophy of human work potentialities, organizational dynamic movement towards human capability increase, and enlarging ideas of increasing opportunities and scope for empowering people to their problems, in realistic nature of decision making approach for initiating result-oriented qualities of social growth potentials. To nurture all these ideas, religion as the social changing mechanism should be given due importance to reengineer social innovative ideas for strengthening human values, increasing organizational delivery system and reducing gaps between haves and have-nots. So, factors of scientific rationality in industrial productivity have to be judged from team building approach of management. If, it is observed that particular team working in positive relationship with the organizational policy resolutions meant for human development strategies, there is the necessity of adopting such policies for diversified nature of services requiring human side of the enterprise mechanism, to which, every organization should be placed in priority for initiative analysis, to percolate measures and techniques in project management goal for encompassing real growth, in holistic nature of dealing with the resources to bring in organizational effectiveness. Thus, religion as scientific temper of thought should be narrated for organizational performance criterion, where all groups are required to be given free atmosphere to communicate in flexible manner in relating things for the greater interest of human sufferings, and to find-out measures to solve their problems in sustainable way, as and when, resources are aimed at utilizing in dynamic organizational journey, to cope up with various inter-group activities for organizational consistency in dealing effectively, to attain the goal of universal forward looking tendencies in integrated approach of changing social fabric for human welfare attitude[104].

Organizational work behaviour should thus be framed in incorporating issues of people's participation, where the Vedanta thought of disinterested nature of work must relate people with the sort of human development strategy in sustainable social reformation process, for narrating goals of human perfection through managerial challenges in interdisciplinary way of dealing with the things for encouraging people to reinvent measures to solve poverty in multi-level aspects of human services, meant for eradicating problems of social sufferings, human propounding nature of deprivation and regional disparities through convergent philosophy of social advancement in multi-dimensional paths. So, the kind of religious superiority in planning framework expected for common good of mass people should commensurate with the scientific analysis of social crises, resource crunch and financial scarcity – this is the way, organization will be able to cope up with the nature of ultimate change, merged with the philosophy of work and code of human conduct; in so far as 'input-output' relationship is required to be established in management effectiveness of the organized nature of job as well as coordinating phase of human motivational incentives, transformed for the purposeful social order in making people realize the objective function in relation to developmental paradigms shift in nature, towards covering all sections of social beings. Hence, it is expected that religion, when considered from scientific value analysis for efficient resource management goal would enlarge human creativity[105], organizational subsistence to advance people in dynamic path and social transformation for the sake of existential freedom. Therefore, all types of anti-humanity ideals are required to be curbed, as and when organizational management in public body corporate frame human oriented policy resolutions, for initiating packages in producing things for the betterment of people on the one hand; and, to the other side of coin, for developing social structure requires efficient system of administrative notion, meant for human advancement from the pathetic conditions of sufferings, to which justice, equity and trust-worthiship principles are to be adopted in government authoritative responsibility for strengthening social pyramid. Thus, scientific reformations are the underlying philosophy of human religious transparency for undertaking responding nature of challenge, to raise social curtain from veils of dogmatic ills and miscommunication regarding religious foundation of thought, inherent in human development creativity as well as social sensitivity to match environmental resources for good governance criterion. In relating religion to human development programmes, there should be scientific forecasting on environmental scanning, so as to balance the world economy from dehumanization aspect of unscientific religious as well as anti-social slogans made in the name of human development. Thus, all types of jihad related issues and gun culture of human separatism tendencies could be immediately resolved, when government bodies and authorities in respective national levels come up with international understanding, for development of their respective nations in equanimity thought, and this would have growing positive impact on social order for furnishing things in relation to human excellence building, social mobility in transparent manner and worldwide peace to create human civilization on the path of enlightenment, through matching of the environmental resources in matchless way[106].

Covering all such elements of truth, contained in developmental spectrum of social thought provoking ideals, strategies of religious background in the field of administrative system of management are essentially to be resolved from scientific socialism and its root, towards human emancipation in holistic approach for universal experience of religious values, human motivational paths in directive leadership aspects and global level congruency in balancing order of integrated development as well as dignified nature of human living, with all potentials of organizational services incorporated in behavioural science approach as well as managerial effectiveness, for scientific skill building with innovation of human creativity for global dynamicity[107], social transformational goal and human free existentialism. It is thus predicted that scientific temper of thought in relating religion to human work culture will be good instrumental idea for confidence building measures, in organizational working atmosphere to produce goods for the greater interest of all communities of human beings, who are needed to supply quality goods for their survival needs on regularity basis. Hence, it is suggested that behavioural science approach in reengineering social structure, based on equilibrium principles of econometric studies would supplement result in solving social problems with dynamics of technological movement; whereto, fundamentals of balanced human development strategies are enormously commendable for inclusive human growth, along with social mobility in dynamic nature. So, science of work and religion of life has to be intermingled with all imperatives of social transformational ideas, increasing human productivity and industrial rationality, from the ground realities of human severe nature of sufferings observed throughout the world environment. From such assessment, it becomes now highly important to reflect on religious philosophy for creating scientific responsibility, in changing social demography and moving the world order from the present crisis to a new dimensional path, where every human being will find scope for personality development, and also human organizations would be stimulated to deliver goods in reducing social imbalances[108]. Last but not least, it is further reflected that when religion is made a pure science with the neutrality of partiality, there would come social peace, as management should be measured from visionary leadership ideologies, concerning people to involve in the decision-making process by way of decentralizing organizational activities. In this way, learning through experience of work can be transformed from one generation to another generation. As a whole, organizational management will benefit from such cultural transformation in work abilities of new entrepreneurs; because, it will strengthen the base of democratic social reformations and supply future trained leaders who are motivated to produce things for the greater interest of humankind, and longer philosophy of attributing resources to regenerate all forces of development, to the making of human civilization for greater perfection of global mankind. In brief, it is concluded that religious science in behavioural prudence of organizational consistency in doing things will be immensely helpful for global business activities. Hence, managerial effectiveness commensurate with the goal of integral humanity will result in bringing world peace through such action-oriented principle of organized management system. It is further to be consistent for rationalizing industrial activities[109], in terms of scientific motivational tools and techniques provided by means of true religious guidelines, for strengthening the pyramid of global society in cyclical order, so as to compound human experience of work ethics for the larger interest and benefit of world population. International understanding, in the field of human supremacy for adjustment with the global problems would be enumerated by all means as explained, for considering managerial diversity in bringing organizational unity of command in functional relationships, for establishment of global peace through sustainable process noted so far, in accelerating salvation of human life in unified nature.

Religious Mechanism for Global Peace

Human development is the corner-stone of global peace, as it binds people in unitary aspect of leading life process for understanding core ideas of religious truths, based on principles of social survival as well as global journey towards all endeavors that mankind have been making in historical perspective. It is therefore managing social change in positive direction, for creating peace related environment that modern civilizations have been trying, in terms of socialization of human economic activities and business pursuits for enrichment of civil society, in this age of scientific investigations and technological development. From this background, it is accustomed to be mentioned here, that the present societies worldwide are suffering from problems of social mobility in positive direction, due to lack of understanding on principles of realizing religious perspective – as to how it is required to be taken into consideration for good governance philosophy of human organizational pattern of administering things, for the betterment of modern civilization's calls, as beckoned by urgency of establishing global peace. Without developing deprived classes of the society, it is useless to think about judicious management for restoring social peace. Human hunger and poverty is fundamental crime of modern civil society, which is still a matter of shame in front of social thinkers and good administrators. Hence, our study is devoted to pious road-map, in instrumental process of social growth through human development paradigm shift in nature, where fundamental truths of religious philosophy are only alternative to produce goods, for efficient management of human sufferings with the well planned techniques of adequate delivery system, to meet-out problems of pathetic social living conditions. It thus, takes into consideration religious strategy as mechanism for undertaking social responsibility[110], by means of organizational entities and administrative pattern of effective bureaucratic model, which go to give guidelines, as to the measures for solving social crises and bringing humankind in peaceful atmosphere; so that global balance restoration, by means of scientific value analysis on religious paths can be entertained for measuring growth related potentials, and thereby, regional disparities created due to social gaps between haves and have-nots could be smoothly managed by playing effective role towards organizational leadership practices. From all such consequences, it becomes now mandatory to think for religious mechanism which go to analyze things for better results, in regard to initiate peace process through managing human socio-economic activities and guiding people for responding behavioural pursuit, in covering areas of human deficiencies where we have yet to become world leader through enrichment of the goal of global peace, and human survival in civilized nature of living with adequate level of dignities in this age of scientific discoveries and technological inventions.

As an alternative to management, it is carefully observed that modern world has been running in transitional approach of realizing between neutrality of science and religion, for advancing people towards the ecstasy of universal integrity[111], where mankind as a whole should be considered for social changing agent in positive direction. So, religious value has its origin towards social assimilation and coordination for associating attributes of development, in correct strategies and guidelines which are immensely reciprocal to establish social peace, in so far as human beings are guided for realizing common understanding of those principles of religious truths and justice for making optimum nature of sacrifice for the whole mankind, in regard to their existential freedom for living in peaceful atmosphere with all means of survival benefits. This is very important in visionary managerial communication process, because human beings are at the central place of all decision-making approach, concerning their scientific display of things for efficient management of social resources, in converting inputs into value-added type of outputs which are of fundamental controlling mechanism for effective delivery of goods, in regard to match resources and solve problems of human sufferings, social environmental balance and worldwide human cooperation. It is expected that diplomatic ties between countries of the world will uproot human value system to strengthen peace, as a result of which international cooperation will be encouraged for considering religious synthesis to accumulate business potentials, in nurturing common agenda of human growing diversity in convergent policy resolution techniques, for the sake of harmonious atmosphere on human living environment and global cohesiveness to the pluralistic tendencies of value assessment, to all frontiers of scientific religious assumptions reinforcing human capabilities, social transformation and global tranquility. To advance people for group relationships, religious organizations should adopt a framework of policy[112] initiatives, which go to enrich team building concept of work ethics in organizational pattern of management, and also 'quality circle' mechanism should be adaptable towards confining tasks for embracing entire humanity, by means of various diplomatic relationships, bilateral as well as multilateral business zones through bureaucratic convergence, in dealing with global mankind and initiate social harmony for the purpose of objective assessment of peace measures. In the long-run, international understanding on peace through spiritualizing business perspective will commensurate for human up-gradation, global integrity, and environmental challenges in reducing social gaps between people from alround spheres of integrated managerial guidance. As and when, there is global level concern for increasing human capabilities, based on scientific religious mechanism for enlightening people to receive all value-added impacts of information in positive assumptions, there would come automatically a good consciousness in mind of people for enlarging ideals of human growth, forgetting any kind of unjustified misconception regarding religious dogmatic policies that have not yet been able to serve any nation of the world; but rather ruined the entire humanity in paralyzing the economic foundation. It is therefore religion and its spiritualizing temper of scientific notion can help in the way of cementing relationships, by means of organizational active leadership, political interactive programmes and business combinations in international level; to reformulate schemes and packages for human advancement with marketing potentials and communication services, meant for the purpose of human challenges in incorporating religious values and models of human cooperation in changing onslaught of deprived people living in pathetic conditions throughout the world environment[113]. Nevertheless, all fundamental assumptions of religious truths that have repercussions for enriching social transformation, could well be experienced with the nature of integrated management approach for establishment of global peace, in terms of serving all sections to harness their problems of living in civic manner, and thus; group relationships in organizational system orientation could also be developed through exchange of views and ideas, to mechanize models for relative development structure in congruent policy resolutions and human coordination, to the process of betterment of global mankind in general, and to upgrade the respective national economy in particular.

It is vital to note that religious strategy of global peace should be made as the mechanism for human development, as it is true that conflicting nations can never attain any successful result in making their economy vibrant towards developing social structure. So, it is suggested without doubt in mind that regional disparities among the nations could be reduced by means of foreign diplomatic pragmatic relationships, in encouraging people to realize about the highest truths of fundamental elements of world religious unity, which are ingrained into human peaceful living pursuits and coherence harmonious interrelationships between nations. Thus, business regularity in dealing with cooperative environment to solve problems of human struggle against poverty, and for civic living norms of societal development are all concerned with the process of global leadership challenges[114] for undertaking issues of different sovereign alignment; and, therefore, it is imperative to be situational where religious bodies and professional entities are to set free, for setting aside problems of human secondary conflicts like religious supremacy, but rather, there should be supreme policy adopted in making things for the betterment of whole mankind. In this way, administrative behavioural science has to confine things to workout common grounds for religious truths, which would be able to complement results in communicating organizational activities to accelerate social welfare as well as speedy development of the global economy. To nurture therefore, fundamental beliefs of religious policies in mechanistic way of dealing with international trading activities and commercial relationships, there is the requirement of visionary leadership approach and political will force, which could help in prospering nations concentrating on human oriented principles of global level excellence thoughts; so that humankind would be able to live in society in secured atmosphere, ignoring any fear psychosis of their mind for lack of security in leading peaceful life. Accordingly, cost of military expenditure will be reduced when religious mechanism could bring in social restful atmosphere, through international peace and fellow-feeling nature of carrying with all types of administrative protocol, legal justice and business relationships. This way, major expenditure otherwise incurred in maintenance of world peace would be profitably employed in social building activities in different means and ways. Ultimately, global society will be enriched through religious values and thoughts for understanding importance of integral humanity, by which, world business establishments and organizational entities would be given better scope[115] for implementing schemes of human welfare, and packages for people's development in faithful and trustworthy human diplomatic relationships for the purpose of effective environmental as well as social balance. Here, we are to keep watch on issues like dogmatic religious propaganda and antisocial elements playing from time-to-time dominant role in ruining the world atmosphere. The only alternative course of action is the human development, corruption-free business intercourse and justice-related programmes to be chalked out as the plan of action, for managing things with administrative effectiveness, which will enlarge religious values and beliefs in diversity of living parameters, situational with the public relationship as well as international understanding for conformity with the goal of participatory managerial approach of democratic as well as scientific religious mechanism, to be employed for solving problems of worldwide human sufferings, social unrest and global warfare activities. As a result of all these impact and incidences, there would be restored a striking balance between peace and war by means of negotiations and collective bargaining process, and mutual trust amongst all nations would be enhanced for strengthening societal structure. In the long-run, mutual collaboration in multi-level socio-economic activities will expand, to enlighten religious motives for human cohesive nature of diversified living norms, in which, all types of activities performed so far for dehumanization[116] of social structure should get optimum opportunities, to interplay of the combined joint effort of mankind in pursuit of a regenerating force, which could be found in making the world society based on principles of international understanding, for objectifying the goal of universal integrity, human brotherhood and global tranquility.

The above discussions reflect on accumulative nature of human welfare through mechanism of religious ideologies of truths, binding people of the world for carrying out effectively coordinated approach of human fraternity in utilizing dormant qualities remaining unutilized in masses, which go to add value in production function activities with a view to represent universal involvement of people's participation in development-related competencies, by all means of credibility of organizational leadership guidance and managerial quality assurance schemes, for incorporating human talents and capabilities in developing working skills, and thus; transforming the world society in the path of radical transitional change where our future generations would be placed in way that would rejuvenate the global society for sustaining world peace, on the basis of religious unity and scientific social reformations, conjoining all elements of good governance thought for advancing mankind in attaining the goal of human rolling, towards optimal order of harmonious interrelationships among religious counterparts. In this prospective idea, vibrant management in channelizing financial resources for increasing industrial productivity and employing people to solve their problems of civic livelihood, should find-out means and ways to reduce conflicts between people regarding religious debates on points of their misfortunes, and try to assess things out of coagulation from the good ethics of religious sermons propounded in time and space; so that humanity, if ever found any good things in religious models of 'truth, beauty and goodness' could be employed in mechanistic way for encouraging people to take benefits out of those, by means of matching philosophy[117] to make codes of such religious mantra as the scientific norms of developing the societal pyramid. Herein lies, importance of universal growing of mankind through religious yardstick of measurement for survival sovereignty, administrative justice and legal acceptability, so as to bring people under the vehicle of developed social spectrum for carrying themselves towards managerial perfection, in utilizing human enormous potentialities for the optimum order of social growth, human integrity and institutionalization process in transforming global society towards the path of establishing universal peace, for harmonious human interactions in producing things for the highest good of all mankind, through maximization of social welfare[118] and minimization of human conflicts. It is the road-map of human development strategy has been attempted to find-out social transformation, for the sake of social dynamicity, human integrity and worldwide prosperity in terms of managerial practices.

As and when, organizational system is interpreted by means of such sustainable mechanism of religious endeavour for people's up-gradation, all evils of social backwardness should be overthrown from the part of mismanagement of administrative process, and corruption from the world societies will go automatically forever in bringing people to realize values of ethical religious reformative sermons, in interrelationships of organizational coordinated efforts for involving people in the decision-making approach of development strategies. This is the reason; 'management of love' has a vital role in rebuilding vista of new order of global society through peaceful mechanism[119], business entrepreneurship development and worldwide balance between haves and have-nots. When organizational leadership is inventing policies of human core living in free existentialism, as required by value-based religious discussions for social advancement, and delivery of goods towards solving social problems; there would be human motivational urges for taking things in challenging attitude for serving social people, to the utmost possibilities of honesty, dignity and sobriety. Hence, the path of religious mechanism for eliminating social ills and misfortunes, due to all types of letches could be rejoiced for happiest survival of all human beings[120]. In regard to confidentiality building between nations, such type of religious ideology will be counted and accounted as the supreme path for managing in effectiveness. Organizational initiative for changing phase of society, from human sufferings and conflicting nature of leading life in uncivilized way should be curbed, and therefore, the 'theory of unity' in diversity will be scientifically propagated by means of such democratic leadership approach; where all should find optimum scope for maximum development with the free opportunities of living atmosphere, in balancing social resources for global tranquility and human objective functional diversity, in reinventing mechanism for organizational instrument of social change[121] tools and techniques. It is therefore suggested that religious strategy as the most essential counterpart of peaceful management should be involved with human development strategy, in reorienting the present as well as future civil society towards human effective communication base, for strengthening coordinated efforts of human endeavours for establishing global peace through human dignity of living, by working together in a manner where all mankind should feel unity, in their action oriented approach of solving numerous problems of global society in general, and the humanity[122] in particular. Thus, there will be human perfection through such type of managerial guidance to change life-style of suffered people throughout the world environment.

Notes and References

1. It is a concept which is in its essence a dynamic and which in practice involves a radical transformation of society in all its aspects – economic, social, political and cultural. – Singh, Parminder: "Regional Aspects of Industrialization in India", Deep & Deep Publications, New Delhi, 1994. So, human living elements are required scientific temper of thought in understanding – how to bind people together for the sake of balanced economic development. It is further related to balanced regional development. Thus, it is helpful for planned approach of

development which is to be achieved through reducing regional disparities and increasing the rate of regional industrial growth. In my opinion, the present Prime Minister of India, Narendrabhai Damodardas Modi, generally called as Narendra Modi has taken the philosophical idea of human development above petty religious sentiments, and he remarks like – "Sabka Sath, Sabka Vikas", "Mera Eksha Pachish Koti Desh Basi", "Vasudhaiva Kutumbakam" in different platforms, both within the country and outside the country in his various speeches. His message could be for inclusive growth and against all types of cheap politics. He also considers international brotherhood philosophy which he accounts 'development' as the slogan – "Vasudhaiva Kutumbakam" and advocates for the 'Yoga' as the mantra of human peace and good health; which has further been recognized by the UNO. Thus, the core concept of human living elements has to be an enquiry into an attempt and human endeavour for all-encompassing perspective and also all-comprehensive idea of the totality of social reality. – Also see, for example, Durkheim, Emile: 1858-1917: A Collection of Essays, with Translations and a Bibliography (translated and edited by Wolff, Kurt H.), Columbus: Ohio State University Press, 1960. Thus, the social science studies and approaches may also include 'the religious perspective of human development' for human upliftment from severe social sufferings which is caused mainly due to petty human policies, in this world of living.

2.   We have the free outpouring of an unselfish spirit which does not calculate the rewards of action or the penalties of omission. Till the spiritual life is won, the law of morality appears to be an external command which man has to obey with effort and pain. But when the light is obtained it becomes the internal life of the spirit ... ... But for those who have risen above heir selfish egos, morality becomes the very condition of their being, and law is fulfilled in love. – Radhakrishnan, S.: "Indian Philosophy", Vol. 1, Oxford University Press, Delhi, 1996, pp. 228-29. But, it is pitiably to be noted that this central truth of religious life is not sufficiently understood by even some good students of Indian thought due to inherent selfish motive, which requires total sacrifice for doing services in regard to public good overcoming problems of our selfish attitude. What Hume calls "the possession of some meta physical knowledge" is possible only for the pure in heart. Laws and regulations are necessary for those men who do not naturally conform to the dictates of conscience. The law of karma is the counter-part in the moral world of the physical law of uniformity. – *Op. cit.,* p. 244. It may have been of Zarathustra too, would have acquired a more or less exact knowledge of the religious speculations of the East. – Greek Thinkers, Vol. 1, p. 127. For a different view, see Keith on Pythagoras and Transmigration, J.R.A.S., 1909. Again, the western world has now been in a position to grasp and recognize the idea that consciousness is only one aspect of mental life, and is a profound truth. All these contentions are clearly objectifying the concept of integral humanity and the eternality of human self, on which human development rests in scientific grounds of realizing the truth for original religious ideas for the mankind and their correct order of development.

3.   The reality of religion neither stands on racialism, nor on castism, separatism; but is concerned with intergroup relations, and through accommodative principles and adjustments in between races and also ethical relations. – Rose, Peter I.: "The Subject is Race", Oxford University Press, New York, 1968, Chapter 1,

pp. 5-10. For further understanding also refer to Barth, Ernest A. T. and Folta, Jeannette R.: "Teaching in the Field of Race and Ethinic Relations", University of Washington, Seattle, Mimeographed, 1959. Of course, there have been numerous studies published on the topic of race and race relations, but we are to understand all these from development perspective. Again, this reality can be judged from our indebtedness for performing services amongst the tribals, which is still today, one of the manifestations of their poverty, despite there are many government measures adopted for their protection. – Aggarwal, P. K.: "Tribal Development Planning in India", Mahaveer & Sons, New Delhi, 2007, p. 51. In reality, it is observed that various religious institutions have been playing dominant role for tribal development. But it is suggested that anything we do, must be done with pure sacrificial motive and without any intention in mind for the conversion of human religiosity, which is the fundamental core of human development can lead to the path of salvation. It is the scientific reality of all religions of the world. Again, it is observed: "In both caste and race theories, there is an attitude of the so-called higher or superior groups that their culture is superior to all other cultures and all the other beings should be judged according to their culture". – Panigrahi, S. K.: "Castism Politics in India: Issues and Regulations", Cyber Tech Publications, New Delhi, 2008, p. 77. This kind of notion has no place in understanding religion for actual human development purposes; but rather, it is detrimental to the social reformation processes which should be curbed in the greater interest of humanity. Politics should be made free from all such elements; so that scientific nature of human development has been made possible through equanimity as well as equipoise thought, has already been explained in foregoing Chapters.

4. For the welfare of mass people, we must nurture ideals of cultural humanism. S. K. George believed in the possibility of a wider fellowship of religions, comprehending all diverse human apprehensions of the Divine, none seeking to destroy the other, but each helping its neighbour to fulfill itself, by being faithful to its own inner light. – Thomas, T. K.: "The Witness of S. K. George", CLS, Madras, 1970. Also, it is better to consult George, S. K.: "Gandhi's Challenge to Christianity", George Allen & Unwin Ltd., London, 1939. Again, P. Chenchiah discovered the supreme value of Christ, not in spite of Hinduism but because Hinduism had taught him to discern spiritual greatness. – Job, G. V., Chenchiah, P. and Chakkarai, V.: "Rethinking Christianity in India", cited in Sundarisanam, A. N.: 1938, Madras. Also see, Thangasamy, D. A.: "The Theology of Chenchiah with Selections from his Writings", CISRS, Bangalore, 1966. Cultural humanism in organizational perspective will include all for understanding development by way of realizing the fact that the Vedantist gives no other attributes to God except these three – that, He is Infinite Existence, Infinite Knowledge, and Infinite Bliss, and he regards these three as one. – Chetanananda, Swami (Ed.): "Swami Vivekananda Vedanta: Voice of Freedom", Advaita Ashrama, Kolkata, 2011, p. 111. Thus, cultural humanism can help to safeguard the present decaying nature of the world order. It takes into consideration, the service to man as the service to God, and it's the real development mantra inherent in cultural humanism. It believes in the integral concept of beings and performing services for the becoming of all in all-inclusive thought for managing organizational activities.

5. Leadership criterion based on honesty and truth assumes, in religion lies the vitality of India, and so long as the Hindu race do not forget the great inheritance of their forefathers, there is no power on earth to destroy them. – Sharma, Benishanker: "Swami Vivekananda: A Forgotten Chapter of His Life", Towards Freedom, Kolkata, 2013, p. 93. According to Swami Vivekananda, so long as they forgot the past, the Hindu nation remained in a state of stupor, and as soon as they have began to look into their past, there is on every side a fresh manifestation of life. – *Op. cit.*, p. 94. So, leadership should believe in the philosophy of the past of the Hindu, because it is out of this past that the future has to be molded, this past will become the future. – *Ibid.*, p. 94. Here, it is also worthwhile to refer Martin Luther King, Jr. whose effective leadership of the civil rights struggle in the US, a struggle for democratic justice, was inextricably linked to his religious rhetoric. – Bhargava, Rajeev (Ed.): "Secularism and Its Critics", Oxford University Press, New Delhi, 1998, p. 141. Religious works meant for development of human beings must have universal leadership qualities, which should include 'knowledge of the self' and its 'immortality'. So, it is said: "If one has realized here, then there is truth; if he has not realized here, then there is great destruction". – Gambhirananda, Swami: "Eight Upaniṣads with the Commentary of Śaṅkarācārya", Advaita Ashrama, Kolkata, 2012, p. 71. A leader while performing activities should be concerned with each state of his consciousness, and thus, it will lead to the path of attaining immortality, because; the knowledge of the Self, is acquired through the self along and not through anything else. Hence, a leader must understand the basic values of the 'strength'. In the Upaniṣad of the Atharva Veda it is said: "This Self is not attained by one who has no strength (resulting from steadfastness in the Self)". – Mu. III. ii. 4. All activities concerned with man-power development should excel therefore strength in human beings, which modern leaders are to follow while guiding people.

6. Religious values teach that through pure actions and thoughts you should accumulate enough merit to counter the demerits you have acquired. – Yatiswarananda Swami: "Meditation and Spiritual Life", Advaita Ashrama, Kolkata, 2011, p. 173. It means there should be no craving or fresh worldly company and worldly talk and amusements. The whole spiritual life lies in this fearless adjustment. Religious values are to be the philosophy of purity. It is the purity stressed in all spiritual paths. This purity can change entire society in positive direction. Hence, religious values must sider this fact with utmost belief. What is important as a karma-yogī you have to work for the purification of your mind, there the matter ends. – *Op. cit.*, p. 175. Purified nature of work enshrined in religious values can help to progress in life, and therefore, our all work should be done with this type of greater faith and enthusiasm. It is here, suggested that the fruits of your efforts should concern you in the least. – *Ibid.*, p. 175. It is the core idea of human living for the realization of life order.

7. Instead of regarding a religion as one culture's expression of the creative urge (for that is what the different religions ought to represent) it gets busy counting the number of its believers. The ideas of priestly functions, propagation and conversion began to occupy the core of such a religion. – Miri, Sujata: "Religion and Society of North-East India", Vikas Publishing House Pvt. Ltd., New Delhi,

1980, p. 26. According to Nietzsche, it is this degeneration of the religious spirit which in the case of Europe has failed to create a God (almost two millennia and not a single new God) and ended up in a fanatic clinging to a particular formulation of the religions. – *Op. cit.*, p. 27. In its social dimension, dharma is defined as what sustains society, as law (such as the Varna-law) governing the social order. Thus, every gap in society should find freedom in preaching and practicing religious ideals, which could enhance democratic interrelationships between people. To the contrary, religion (dharma) becomes irrational (mithyā/māyā), but actually the concept of religion implies that the real is rational (satya).

8. The door of harmonious living is related to eternal principles of life. In this context, it is worthwhile to note that the guiding principle concerned with human eternal practices of life is the choice about the "Eternal" means that which is without beginning or end. – Chennakesavan, Sarasvati: "A Critical Study of Hinduism", Motilal Banarsidass, Delhi, 1974, p. 5. Thus, harmonious way of leading life deals with eternal or everlasting. Hence, the word 'sanatana' is the concept can only lead people towards the binding principle of social harmony. Accordingly, we have referred to 'Sanātana Dharma' as the way searching for social peace and human developmental parameters of living goal. It has a relevancy to the thoughts of the Vedas, and therefore, orthodox Hindus would call Hinduism as Sanâtana Dharma — the ancient and eternal duty. So, it said that the truths embodied in the Vedas are nitya (eternal) and it should be followed for scientific development of human beings, as well as the holistic welfare of the world society.

9. Optimum development can be possible through 'unity'. It is the primary goal of services being required to be provided for industrial harmony and increasing human productivity through unionism. So, Ramanujam states: "We find today that the number of trade unions is ever increasing, resulting in multiplicity of unions in industries and services. And most of these trade unions are busy fighting each other ... ... This has to be corrected". – Ramanujam, G.: "The Honey Bee: Towards a New Culture in Industrial Relations", Sterling Publishers Private Limited, New Delhi, 1984, p. 23. Unless we master the first and elementary lesson of unionism – 'unity', there is very little hope of orderly progress for workers, industry and the country. Backwardness of people will be eradicated from the society, when we promise to follow the first lesson of the Acharya of the Mahabharata, who taught his disciples to this effect: Satyam Vada, Dharmam Chara (Speak the Truth, Do your Duty). Hence, Ramanujam further remarks: "Workers must understand that unless they master their first lesson of unity and put into actual practice, the trade union movement will be built only on sand and will not, therefore, produce either abiding or satisfactory results. It will lack a firm foundation. – *Op. cit.*, p. 24. This is the cause behind all types of human backwardness, and it should be followed as the dharma or mantra of human development process.

10. For good governance, Bhagavan Das eulogized the scheme of Manu as propounded in the Manusmriti: "Manu has given us such a technique in his permanent (and not merely five-year or ten-year or twenty-five-year) plan of the Individual Life and the Social Life in combination, for the whole of the Human race – the only systematic and complete plan ... ... that was known to history

until Russian Communism is in the stage of experiment as yet. In that plan are included the fundamental Principles of Planned Education, Planned Family-life, Planned Economy, Planned Defence – Sanitation – Judication, and Planned Religion – Recreation – Art." – Das, Bhagavan: "Ancient Versus Modern Scientific Socialism", Adyar, Madras, pp. 6-7. Thus, good governance policies of Das can be summarized as: "India's slogans should be – not the merely materialist interpretation of History, since the Universe is obviously compounded of both Spirit or Mind and Matter, Purusha and Prakriti; not Class war, ... but 'Class cooperation' through class-balance and class-reconciliation, not a classless society, nor a dichotomized Rich-and Poor Society, nor an infinitely sub-divided fissiparous Casteful Society, but a 'Society of Temperamental-Vocational Classes' justly coordinated; not an utterly homogenous literal Equality in all respects, nor an utterly heterogenous and grossly iniquitous Inequality, but an 'Equitability' in the partition of different kinds of Work ... ... not the placing of the necks of whole Peoples under the heels of single or a few despotic Individuals ... ... nor the crushing of all Individualities under the steam-roller Wheels of Machine-like Communism or Fascism ... ..., not a sudden and complete National Genius',... ... not a blind imitation of the latest experiments going on in any other country, nor a blind clinging to all of our past without discrimination between its good and its bad ... ... but a far-sighted and judicious 'Combination of the Old and the New', 'Respect for old Tradition as well as new Exploration', not abolition of Religion and Property and Family, nor perpetuation of the conditions in which they now are, but 'Purification of Religion, Property, Family', ... not unchecked Capitalism, nor Fascism, nor Bolshevism, but the indigenous and genuinely philosophical, psychological, 'Ancient time tested Scientific Socialism' of the best Indian Tradition". – *Ibid.*, pp. vii-ix.

11. For this, all nation-states must follow the rulings of the Preamble of the 'league of Nations', which has committed for the promotion of international cooperation and peace and security, and to the acceptance of the obligations by the nation-states not to resort to war. – Melkote, Rama S. and Rao, A. Narasimha: "International Relations", Sterling Publishers Pvt. Ltd., New Delhi, 1986, p. 21. Thus, international understanding requires the prescription of open, just and honorable relations between nations, the firm establishment of understanding of international law as the actual rule of conduct among Governments and the maintenance of justice and a scrupulous respect for all treaty obligations in the dealings of organized peoples with one another. Again, international understanding will bring in cooperation between peoples of the 'Third World' countries, to uproot their whole populations in useful way in the practices of modernization and development of their countries. Technical cooperation can also be strengthened for human skill building operations by way of educational facilities in terms of international understanding for technological collaboration as well as cultural assimilation ... ... Hence, the inequalities that are at the root of the agricultural problem, political instability between the boundaries of the sovereign nations, poverty alleviation programmes, illiteracy problems, problems of infrastructure and housing, sanitation and sewerage, transport and communication means, service sector reforms, market reorientation to overcome problems of modern complexities, financial prudence behaviour for bringing

strength in both money and capital market requires, among others, can be attributed to motivate people in between nations for underlying reasons of regional disparities; where international understanding can take place to the well establishment of countries like – developed, underdeveloped and developing nations. Melkote says that in addition to these problems, the third world has to come to grips with the problems of neo-colonialism ... ... domination of the multi-nationals have all made the third world countries increasingly dependent on the rich countries without leading to any real, development and equitable redistribution of wealth. – *Op. cit.,* p. 138. All such problems could be solved when there is international understanding between nations.

12. In regard to social development, a proactive HRD staff has to anticipate educational needs and therefore, it should develop the links between the organization's strategic plan and its training plans. – Pattanaya, Biswajeet: "Human Resource Training", S. Chand & Company Ltd., New Delhi, 2003, p. 21. However, a 360-degree circle of feedback from management, peers, staff, and internal and external customers would show precisely who needs what changes to occur. As such, quantitative techniques may be required to give priority in providing decision maker with a systematic and powerful means of analysis and help, in exploring policies for achieving predetermined goals. Communication networks in the organization at a given point of time can strengthen managerial effectiveness to boost up human morale, and thus, a firm gains competitive advantage by performing all activities strategically (Bowman, Cliff: "The Essence of Strategic Management", Prentice-Hall of India Private Limited, New Delhi, 1998, p. 62) by which management of things can made distinct from politicizing activities that a modern firm performs. Hence, it helps in giving a scope to divide value activities into two broad types: primary activities and support activities. – *Op. cit.,* p. 63. Pure service should be the motto of social development which curbs against vote banking politics by making an organization with 'distinctive competence'. The entrepreneurship principles are to be followed by means of 'economies of scale' which can be beneficial for production, purchasing and distribution in giving us an adequate edge. To install justice in governance qualities, we need to improve response time. For this purpose, cooperation and communication across the organizational level needs to be encouraged for perpetuating people to enhance work responsibility, and to overcome problems of politics and power concept in organization's structure. It will pave the way for pluralistic idea in considering human development paradigms, so as to realize God in service giving concept to bind people in one united brotherhood principle – universality in living. In teaching the harmony of all religions Swami Vivekananda can thus be considered as a follower of the school of Pluralism. – Aleaz, K. P.: "Harmony of Religions: The Relevance of Swami Vivekananda", Punthi-Pustak, Calcutta, 1993, p. 211. Pluralism believes in liberal business concept, as it reflects on 'truth-claims' in complementary nature of belief, and not of a conflicting nature, according to the principle of this school of the theology of religions. Here, social understanding is initiated through human mutual participation and team building approach in making society vibrant towards developmental paths.

13. Here, it is worth noting that dharma envisages autonomy of each human group to seek its social self-fulfillment through its own unique paradigm, and

psychological integration of all such groups in a common framework of harmonious and mutually complementary, interrelationships of One World (Vasudhaiva Kutumbakam), - each group enriching the common, human understanding by making its own characteristic contribution to the collective wisdom of humanity. – Thengadi, Dattopant: "Third Way", compiled by Bhanu Pratap Shukla, Janaki Prakashan for Bharatiya Mazdoor Sangh, New Delhi, 1995, p. 33. In congruency of our living supremacy, it would be realistic to envisage: 'Global Economic System for a Peaceful World' which is to operate within the framework of an ideal Global Order. It is an integrated view – and not a compartmentalized or a fractional one. – *Op. cit.,* p. 36.

14. Our duty to others means helping others; doing well to the world. Why should we do well to world? Apparently to help the world, but really to help ourselves...... Do not stand on a high pedestal and take five cents in your hand and say, 'Here, my poor man', but be grateful that the poor man is there, so that by making a gift to him, you are able to help yourself. Be thankful that you are allowed to exercise your power of benevolence and mercy in the world, and thus become pure and perfect. – Mumukshananda, Swami: "Vivekananda His Call to the Nation", Advaita Ashrama, Kolkata, 29th Impression, May 2005, p. 59. This is the social nurturing philosophy can help people to build up social infrastructure on the pillars of service – it is the service for man as God.

15. It is in the moment of silence that we hear the voice of the Infinite. When our ears are listening to the loud voices of the world, we cannot know that another voice is speaking in our heart. Therefore, those who have obtained direct vision of Truth are not inclined to make their own voice heard. – Paramananda, Swami: "Silence as Yoga", Sri Ramakrishna Math, Chennai, 2000, p. 29. To solve human problems of living in perfect order, it is to be said that there is the need of understanding human spirituality in work order. All spiritual vision and deeper understanding are unfolded in the hours of silent reflection. We should therefore work in silence to rectify social problems, but not with our emotional speeches which go to perform nothing more than wasting time in wonderings.

16. When we prefer to make a religious background in organizational point of view, our idea must resemble to the thoughts of Vivekananda, who utterly says: "Here naturally comes the difficult and the vexed question of caste and of social reformation, which has been uppermost for centuries in the minds of our people. I must frankly tell you that I am neither a caste-breaker nor a mere social reformer. I have nothing to do directly with your castes or with your social reformation. Live in any case you like, but that is no reason why you should hate another man or another caste. It is love and love alone that I preach, and I base my teaching on the great Vedanta truth of the sameness and omnipresence of the Soul of the Universe". – Vivekananda, Swami: "To the Youth of India", Advaita Ashrama, Kolkata, 2002, p. 45. Our poor people, these downtrodden masses of India, therefore, require to hear and to know what they really are. Thus, there is a great opening for the Vedanta to do beneficent work both here and elsewhere. This wonderful idea of the sameness and omnipresence of the Supreme Soul has to be preached for the amelioration and elevation of the human race, here as elsewhere.

17. The ultimate truth has been explained in the Gita by Sri Krishna's teaching which goes like: "He who sees the Supreme Lord dwelling alike in all beings, the Imperishable in things that perish, he sees indeed. For seeing the Lord as the same, everywhere present he does not destroy the Self by the self, and thus he goes to the highest goal". – Gita, xiii. 27-28. Hence, Swami Vivekananda said in the Complete Works: "Do all work, but without attachment; work for work's sake, never for yourself". – Complete Works, Vol. VII, p. 19. The ultimate truth of life is that according to our Indian system, there are two existences: nature on the one side and the Self, the Atman, on the other. – Vivekananda, Swami: "Thoughts on the Gita", Advaita Ashrama, Calcutta, 2000, pp. 61-62. The holistic concept of social rejuvenation has been propagated through teachings of Jesus, and therefore it is uttered by Jesus: "Any country that divides itself into groups that fight each other will not last very long. And any town or family that divides itself into groups that fight each other will fall apart". – Rice, Ken: "The Man You Cannot Ignore", United Bible Societies, Singapore, 1973, pp. 64-65. It is therefore suggested that unanimity in religious philosophy which blends to the ultimate truth of God and is expressed through work philosophy in upliftment of human beings, can no longer safeguard this world, as and when people live together with notion of sacrifice and unity.

18. In this context, we may refer to Swami Vivekananda, who had the conviction that the nations of the West are coming to India for spiritual help. – Complete Works of Swami Vivekananda, Vol. III, p. 139. Hence, the idea of God was nowhere else ever so fully developed as in India. – *Ibid.,* p. 154. However, it is better to know that in the super conscious state of religious experience, if one is not a trained Yogi, can become a victim of hallucinations and Mohammad was such a victim. That is why if one reads the Koran one finds the most wonderful truths mixed with superstitions and fanaticism. – Complete Works of Swami Vivekananda, Vol. I, p. 184. About Islam the Swamiji further says: "(Mohammedanism) came as message for the masses ... ... The first message was equality ... ... There is one religion – love. No more questions race, color, (or) anything else. Join it ... ..." – Aleaz, K. P.: "Harmony of Religions: The Relevance of Swami Vivekananda", Punthi-Pustak, Calcutta, 1993, p. 126. All these are reflected to show that religion was the first and foremost importance in the East in ancient time, for which travelers came to this direction to satisfy their quest for spiritual thoughts.

19. The truths of religious ideologies are to be backed by the principles of the Hinduism. So, it is believed that Hinduism is not merely a set of beliefs and articles of faith. It is a way of life. – Chennakesavan, Sarasvati: "A Critical Study of Hinduism", Motilal Banarsidass, Delhi, 1980, p. 104. So, this world can be saved from catastrophic destruction, when we all together come to realize that the basic tenets of religion is used to mean law, justice, virtue, duty, innate nature, morality, social obligations and also the acts which result from all these. Our dharma (duty) includes both the self-regarding as well as other-regarding duties. – *Ibid.,* p. 105.

20. About participation, it is well to remember that participation in recruitment and such other functions involve a lot of administrative work. Like participation in promotion decisions, rewards, transfers, placement and such other personnel

administration functions can be very rewarding as such activities do satisfy the personal power needs of HRD staff. And that is the surest way of killing HRD as the HRD manager will not have any time left for spiritual work in HRD. – Rao, T. V.: "The HRD Missionary", Oxford & IBH Publishing Co. Pvt. Ltd., New Delhi, 1990, p. 40. The spirit should be sacrificed for systems and the HRD manager should be willing to discontinue some of the HRD mechanisms and systems if they are not serving the purpose. – *Op. cit.*, p. 38. He should differentiate HRD means/techniques/systems from HRD goals and spirit and should be able to focus on goals and spirit constantly. – *Ibid.*, p. 38. The concept of Quality of Work Life (QWL) should be viewed as a set of objective of organizational conditions and practices such as workers' participation/ involvement in management, democratic style of functioning, innovative and equitable reward system, safe and healthy working conditions, job restructuring, job security, job enrichment, team-work, opportunity for continued growth and development, open communications, etc. or equated with employees' perceptions for meeting the full range of human needs and aspirations. – Chandra, Shyam: "Studies in Corporate HRD", Varanasi Law Agency, Varanasi, 2000, pp. 108-109. Hence, organizational responsibilities are to be shouldered for human participative norms of democratic management by way of strategic managerial techniques to deal with problems of human resource management and organizational development as the bench-mark for business process reengineering (BPR). It can help to match somewhat with the MNCs/World-class industrial and commercial organizations; to enhance effectiveness for the overall development of staffs, for customer care services and at last, for the holistic concept of social development. In this way, religious organizations are expected to deliver in society in today's professionalism of human enterprising attitude.

21. For doing this, planning at the national level should be done by the Centre in consultation with the states and should cover all sectors crucial for national development ... ...-Education and National Development", Report of the Education Commission 1964-66, National Council of Educational Research and Training, Ministry of Education, New Delhi, 1970, p. 196. Thus, a flexible educational structure would be helpful for human existential freedom of living, in making choice for democratic participation to alleviate social problems. Another programme which can bring education into closer relationship with productivity is to give a strong vocational bias to secondary education and to increase the emphasis on agricultural and technological education at the university stage. – Ibid., p. 15. The land reforms, it may be added, are not just a matter of enacting laws or administration of these laws. These reforms involve radical changes in the long-established patterns of tenure relations as also of ownership and distribution of the most precious productive asset of the rural economy. To realize the objectives of land reforms peacefully, it is necessary that people interested in them are associated with their implementation. The non-governmental voluntary organizations, if brought into the picture, can do a lot in the smooth application of land reforms. They can see that the administration does its job in the proper way. They can also get the grievances of the farmers rectified by the government agencies. Their association can be very helpful in pursuing the court cases on behalf of the poor farmers. The beneficiaries of the land reforms, namely, the small farmers, being illiterate and resource-poor, can

do nothing on their own. If organized into a body, they can do a lot to ensure that the land reforms are put into practice as per the laws. Their position can be further strengthened, if they are encouraged to form their own cooperatives. This will enable them also to pool their resources of labor and land to strengthen their position as also derives the gains of economies of scale. – Agrawal, A. N.: "Indian Economy: Problems of Development and Planning", Wishwa Prakashan, New Delhi, 1997, p. 246. Above all, a strong political support is needed to ensure that the principles underlying the land reforms are rightly embodied into the legislative acts and that these laws are speedily put into practice. This requires that all the political parties commit themselves to this revolutionary change in an unambiguous language. This alone can ensure the right reformation of the agrarian system of the country. – *Ibid.,* p. 246. Besides, social foundation can be created through overcoming problems of monetary policies. In this context, Vaish remarks: "The effectiveness of monetary policy in achieving its objective depends upon the absence of time lag – no time should be lost between the need for action and action taken". – Vaish, M. C.: "Monetary Theory", Wishwa Prakashan, New Delhi, 1995, p. 253. To illuminate the picture of social development, it is necessary that the monetary policy should be framed in such a way, as it can work smoothly without hampering productivity, and also creating no problem in employment generation throughout the economy. – *Op. cit.,* p. 255.

22. In religious context, Kṛṣṇa (Krishna) indicates that the very striving for yoga perfection is a most auspicious attempt. – Prabhupāda, A. C. Bhaktivedanta Swami: "The Perfection of Yoga", The Bhaktivedanta Book Trust, Bombay. Although we may try to live peacefully, there is always a great conflagration. Hence, religious responsibility is to serve men as God. Our real business is to get out and enter into the Kingdom of God. This can be done through meditative nature of performing job with the system of yoga or by the empirical philosophical method. – *Op. cit.,* p. 15. In this way, peace can be attained and transcendental order of life can further be established, regardless of the process of work in material life. Hence, there should be a common understanding in human beings for the realization of religious truths, which have been propounded by the Vedic philosophy of work order.

23. Through the cultivation of devotion to God by taking shelter under any of these incarnations (various incarnations of God) one may, through His grace, easily gain strong attachment to God's feet and thereby attain salvation. – Goyandka, Jayadayal: "The Secret of Premayoga", Govind Bhawan Karyalaya, Gita Press, Gorakhpur, 1993, p. 34. This is the supreme goal of human existence.

24. People have been suffering for long due to unsatisfactory performances of the economy, in Indian administrative set-up, particularly, during the regime of the UPA Government. A part of explanation lies in the inefficient use of capacity due to such factors as mismanagement, delays in the completion of projects, etc. – Agrawal, A. N.: "Indian Economy: Problems of Development and Planning", Wishwa Prakashan, New Delhi, 1997, p. 163. People have been found to be depressed due to deficiency in investment potentials, low agricultural and industrial growth rates, frustration in cultivators and their case of suicides due to loss of agricultural output, adverse impact of government policies on human beings, among others. As measures to improve all such situations, rationalizing production structure, capacity creation, maintenance and utilization, improving

productivity and human efficiency, increasing workers' cooperation, fostering competition, reducing population growth, and raising capital-intensity can be attributed to the growth of national income, as the alternative approach of raising standard of human living parameters. To enhance stability among the masses, religious institutions can play dominant role as the catalytic agency functional model; so that coordination between people and the government, in the long-run has been maintained to the process of human excellence building operations, through skills, initiatives and performances.

25. As a social change mechanism in situations of adjustment, here, organizational entities are suggested to follow the 'Meditative Path' as the best prescription. Cianciosi has noted down: "The meditative path offers us a way, through the systematic trainings for inner peace that are found in the great monasteries of Asia … … It offers guidance on how to work with difficult emotions and thoughts. It shows how pain and conflict can be met with a wise and compassionate heart. It teaches us mindfulness in daily life". – Cianciosi, John: "The Meditative Path: A Gentle Way to Awareness, Concentration, and Serenity", B. Jain Publishers (P) Ltd., New Delhi, 2004, p. xii. Thus, we can overcome problems in a challenging manner to change our life, along with changing the societal dimensions of human living conditions. This path will help us in utilizing social resources efficiently for greater effectiveness of modern organizational activities.

26. Conflicts are created due to fear psychosis. As for example, one man fears that, perhaps, he will not have enough money, and that fear causes him to injure others and rob them. But, we should realize that 'I' is the only one existence rests in all beings equally. But Vivekananda had said long back: As soon as we have realized that "I am He, I am the Self of the universe, I am eternally blessed, eternally free".– then will come real love, fear will vanish, and all misery cease. – Vivekananda, Swami: "Realization and Its Methods", Advaita Ashrama, Calcutta, 1995, p. 47. So, religious doctrine has to be followed in beings, and the Vedanta therefore, propounds the concept of 'equanimity' as well as 'equipoise' thoughts; which are pivotal to lead a peaceful life.

27. In restructuring society, we are to strive for realizing the fact that our life is established in the sentient division. It is the natural phenomena of human life. Swami Ramsukhdas says: "It means that when a striver realizes that he is naturally established in the sentient division, he is freed from all evils and sins and is liberated from the shackles of birth and death". – Ramsukhadas, Swami: "For Salvation of Mankind", Gita Press, Gorakhpur, 2003, p. 91. The pyramid of the society should be thus, established on principles of human desire less action for pleasure or the surrendering attitude towards gaining fruits of action. This will lead people in an understanding to realize the dharma (religion) of work in regard to social building notions.

28. Each soul is potentially divine. The goal is to manifest this Divinity within, by controlling nature, external and internal. Do this either by work, or worship, or psychic control, or philosophy – by one or more or all of these – and be free. This is the whole of religion, suggests thus Swami Vivekananda. – Bodharasananda, Swami: "Vivekananda: His Call to the Nation", Advaita Ashrama, Kolkata, 2012, p. 56. He further says that doctrines, or dogmas, or rituals, or books, or temples, or forms, are but secondary details. He comments therefore on religion in such

language: Go and preach to all, "Arise, awake, sleep no more; within each of you there is the power to remove all wants and all miseries. Believe this and that power will be manifested ... ... ". – *Op. cit.,* p. 57. So, human rationality regarding holistic nature of development is contained in religious beliefs and faiths, without which religion can never be realized in the crying needs of human miseries, hunger and distressful conditions of leading life like – stage of slavery. Religion must have to break all such situations of human survival.

29. In this context Tilak wrote: "Dadabhai Naoroji is a new preacher of political religion who has taught us that India is our motherland and our goddess, that we are dwellers of India tied through the common bond of brotherhood and that our religion is to strive selflessly to ameliorate the political and social sufferings of our country". Pradhan, G. P.: "Lokamanya Tilak", National Book Trust, New Delhi, 2008 (Reprint), p. 25. Tilak's untiring efforts – both combative and constructive to provide relief to the people – evoke great respect for him among the people. Thus, modern organizations are required to practice liberal role in shouldering responsibility for eliminating problems of human social sufferings as their main religion. It is necessarily to be performed in line with the broad concept of our freedom fighters, like Bal Gangadhar Tilak, Dadabhai Naoroji, and others who fought against the British government which was mainly responsible for India's poverty. – *Ibid.,* p. 25.

30. In society, we have observed that rampant corruption has been decaying the national character day-by-day and years-after-years, for which morality of people has gone to such a place that even if some people in society are seen to be suffering for two handful of meals a day, we are not shocked or hurt by this scene. We are still today, after so long years of independence of the country leading life like our forefathers, who had suffered in anti-colonial and anti-imperialist struggle, and for whom, Subhas Chandra Bose had been preaching that: "The ultimate objective of our anti-colonial and anti-imperialism struggle was the establishment of a socialist order of truly Indian conception and Indian making". – Bose, Sisir Kumar: "Netaji Subhas Chandra Bose", National Book Trust, New Delhi, 2013, p. 56. Today, social building notions are to include such principles envisaged in periods of Indian struggle for independence as the ultimate objective and the means leading to that goal. So, he (Subhas) declared that the "socio-economic" structure and body politic of the future must help "to foster manhood and develop character and the will to translate into reality the highest ideals of collective humanity" ... ... "the principles which should form the basis of our collective life are: justice, equality, freedom, discipline and love ... ... in order to ensure the equality we must get rid of bondage of every kind – social, economic and political ... ..." – *Ibid.,* p. 56.

31. In doing this, we may consider the idea of the Advaitists. This idea is to generalize the whole universe into one – that something which is really the whole of this universe. And they (Advaitists) claim: "This whole universe is one, that it is one Being manifesting itself in all these various forms. They admit that what the Sankhya calls nature Exists, but say that nature is God. It is this Being, the Sat, which has become converted into all this – the universe, man, soul, and everything that exists". – Vivekananda, Swami: "Vedanta Philosophy", Advaita Ashrama, Kolkata, 2013, p. 21. Hence, according to Advaitists and some of the dualists

who believe that the whole of this universe is evolved from God, which is illustrated by the famous example of "rope and the snake" – we therefore, in spiritualizing human performances should work in equanimity, so as to consider all in making journey towards the path of perfection in life, forgetting all types of illusion or maya in this world of living. This can rebuild the superstructure of the society based on human foundation for increasing social peace and living through human happy stages of life in terms of betterment condition.

32. Common religious beliefs are to be founded on the concept of freedom. According to our philosophers, freedom is the goal. Knowledge cannot be the goal, because knowledge is a compound. It is a compound of power and freedom. So, religious beliefs must agree with the principles of law – this is law, in which nature of human eternal concept of life has to be followed by means of certain uniformity called – holistic development concept, required for human growth perspective idea of integrated living formula. If you are bound by laws, you will be a lump of clay; but the thought that we are beyond law – upon that is based the whole history of humanity. – Vivekananda, Swami: "Vedanta Philosophy", Advaita Ashrama, Kolkata, 2013, p. 68. So, people will be trained to learn about the concept of freedom, not only on the law which has limitation. But, the freedom can only guide people to open the door of liberation. It is the liberal business practices, in which work philosophy has to be founded for human integrated nature of development. Real understanding of freedom will reduce human social conflicts, and when we will realize it, the consciousness that we are free should be inculcated in organizational dynamics of social change with positivistic nature of human development paradigms. For instance, a scientist can send an electric shock to a distance of some miles; but nature can send it to an unlimited distance. This example of Vivekananda holds well, when he comments: "Nature with its infinite power is only a machine; freedom alone constitutes sentient life. – *Ibid.,* p. 68.

33. The order of thinking about religion should be directed towards God realization. This is possible through 'karma yoga' (devotion of work), confined in the process of selfless activity dedicated towards human beings from social sufferings. Thus, sacrificial nature of work done to serve society can lead to the path of God realization, even without going to churches, or mosques, or temple, etc. Vivekananda therefore, remarks rightly: "There is that beyond all books, beyond all creeds, beyond the vanities of this world, and it is the realization of God within you. Many may believe in all the churches in the world, he may carry in his head all the sacred books ever written, he may baptize himself in all the rivers of the earth, still, if he has no perception of God, I would class him with the rankest atheist. And a man may have never entered a church or a mosque, nor performed any ceremony, but if he feels God within himself and is thereby lifted above the vanities of the world, that man is a holy man, a saint, call him what you will". – The Complete Works of Swami Vivekananda, Advaita Ashrama, Kolkata, 2013, pp. 1.334-35.

34. Due to such animalism inherent in men, there are two major threats to spirituality in our interesting and ever-changing world – Jihad and McWorld derived from McDonald's, the famous international fast-food chain. In Barber's thinking, jihad stood for tribalism – specifically, religious fundamentalist tribalism, and is

wrongly understood by some terrorist groups – represents extreme religious fundamentalism: militant, aggressive dogmatism run amok – fanatical, intolerant, vicious campaign bent on converting the entire world to a narrow and savage ideology, determined to crush anything and anybody that stands in its way." – See also, Barber, Benjamin: "Jihad vs McWorld", Ballantine, New York, 1996. In this way, jihad is the destructive element in society. It should be escaped by all moral grounds and human tolerance, where religious leaders are to play dominant role for changing mind of people towards humanity by their speeches, works and social relationships.

35. To overcome problems of irreligious thoughts the power of parenting and family cannot be exaggerated, because parents and family members can have the most powerful impact of a behaviour, attitude and life. – Datta, Shyamolima: "Psychological Problems of Indian Youth", cited in Prabuddha Bharata, Advaita Ashrama, Kolkata, Vol. 120, No. 1, January 2015, p. 174. In such way, good parenting system can work as a tool to reform human beings, for accumulating social good with the truths of religious beliefs, values and customs, which are all having relevance to efficient cause of social building norms.

36. Redefining the concept of integral humanity needs understanding of the problems narrated by Bipan Chandra: "From the dungeons of prisons, from the stores of starvation consuming millions upon millions of human beings in slums and huts, from the exploited laborers, patiently or say apathetically watching the procedure of their blood being sucked by the Capitalist vampires, and the wastage of human energy that will make a man with the least common sense shiver with horror, and from the preference of throwing the surplus of production in oceans than to distribute amongst the needy producers – to the palaces of kings built upon the foundation laid with human bones … …" . – Chandra, Bipan: "Why I am an Atheist", National Book Trust, New Delhi, 2013, p. 14. Integral concept requires addressing all such fundamental questions, where lies the misfortune. So, we must try to find out solution to all these mysterious problems, and stand in the way of human progress through our considerable reasoning on the belief, theory and philosophy of human poverty driven aspects of life elements. Integral humanity is therefore, backed by the scientific temper of religious faith like universal development of mankind – here, discrimination in human beings has to be broken in terms of imposing core idea of human liberal existentialism.

37. Buddha is the only prophet who said: "I do not care to know your various theories about God. What is the use of discussing all the subtle doctrines about the soul? Do well and be good. And this will take you to freedom and to whatever truth there is". – Mumukshananda, Swami: "Vivekananda: His Call to the Nation", Advaita Ashrama, Kolkata, 29th Impression, May 2005 (Compiled), p. 61. It seems that religious philosophy requires truthfulness for doing well to others, and by selfless services performed with the dedication of human advancement will lead one to the goal of salvation in life. About transformation in organizational work life, Swami Vivekananda's suggestion is that we should work without any motive in mind, neither for money, nor for fame, nor for anything else. He remarks thus: "When a man can do that, he will be a Buddha, and out of him will come the power to work in such a manner as will transform the world". – The Complete Works of Swami Vivekananda, Vol. I, Advaita

Ashrama, Kolkata, pp. 117-18. So, we must work calmly and in a manly fashion, instead of dissipating our energy in unnecessary fretting and fuming. Hence, Swami Vivekananda was hopeful about social reconstruction, for which he uttered like: "The past was great no doubt, but I sincerely believe that the future will be more glorious still". – The Complete Works of Swami Vivekananda, Vol. IV, Ninth Edition, 1966, p. 366.

38. For such beliefs, devotion, prayer, meditation, philosophic discrimination – all help us towards our spiritual upliftment that we may have direct perception of our Ideal. Such type of belief can help people for growth and development, and so, empowerment of people at organizational work relationship should be directed to accomplish that (Ideal); otherwise, all our efforts are vain. For this reason, Swami Paramananda advised: "If we lose sight of the fundamental fact that realization must be our aim and goal, we go on adding one superficial effort to another, but they will bring very small results". – Paramananda, Swami: "Silence as Yoga", Sri Ramakrishna Math, Madras, p. 81. The spirit of Reality must be kept alive in us. We must hold fast to the sense of the Eternal Presence ... ... If we fail in this, we are failing in the fundamental principle of life, as well as in the first duty towards ourselves and towards our fellowmen. – *Ibid.,* p. 81.

39. Service to man, service to God should be our religious foundation of truth. Vivekananda truly remarks: "After so much austerity, I have understood this as the real truth – God is present in every jiva; there is no other God besides that". – Mumukshananda, Swami (Compiled): "Vivekananda: His Call to the Nation", Advaita Ashrama, Kolkata, 2005, p. 62. In this way, principles of good governance should be followed for universal human development process. Swamiji (Swami Vivekananda – the highest order of Monk) therefore with great conviction uttered: "Who serves jîva, serves God indeed". – The Complete Works of Swami Vivekananda, Vol. VII, p. 247. This is the core idea of living in this world with the great mission of human welfare, which will guide people in establishment of the world peace.

40. Attachment is the cause of all miseries and it hampers in human real growth. So, in the Gita, Sri Krishna advocated for non-attachment, which is the central idea of our life bringing possibilities. If we can perform our duties without attachment, it is enough; there is nothing more needed in this life. About all human deficiencies, the Gita prescribes for doing our activities with this (non-attachment) all-rounded and wonderful activity and combination of brain and heart, which we observe in the overall teachings of the Gita, and is still, today, a universal truth backed by the philosophy of Newtonian Science. Hence, we must leave all affairs which go to reflect artificial impressions on our mind; but rather, our policy should be to discover the absolute truths of the Vedas – perfect sanity with the chastity in bringing people to the path of self realization, along with doing well to others for universal welfare. Swami Vivekananda wonders while saying – Five thousand years have passed and He (Krishna) has influenced millions and millions. Just think what an influence Krishna has over the whole world, whether you know it or not! It is therefore suggested that religious perspectives to find out the realities of human growth should be propounded through non-attachment and sacrifice.

41. The optimum necessity of mankind is the realization of God. I mean the knowledge that is given in Prabhupâda's books – the Vedic stuff – that is the world's oldest scriptures. They say that man can become purified, and with divine vision he can see God. – Edited Works: "Chant and Be Happy", International Society for Krishna Consciousness (ISCON), Botany, NSW 2019, 1983, p. 30, If there is God, we must see Him, and I don't believe in the idea you find in the most churches, where they say, "No you're not going to see Him. He's way up above you. Just believe what we tell you and shut up". – This is expressed by George in book "Chant and Be Happy", p. 34. This is cited here, because by this we might conclude that absolute belief in human welfare and performing accordingly can lead one to the path of salvation. It should be the religious guidelines for human brotherhood principle of living and developing society with the curtain raising role model level playing part, in the system of organizational work philosophy, which brings human eternal peace to the destiny of leading life in the midst of happiness.

42. When one is in ignorance, he sees the phenomenon and does not see God. When he sees God, this universe vanishes entirely for him. Ignorance or Maya, as it is called, is the cause of this entire phenomenon – the Absolute, the Unchangeable, being taken as this manifested universe. This Maya is not absolute zero, nor non-existence. It is defined as neither existence nor non-existence. It is not existence, because that can be said only of the Absolute, the Unchangeable, and in this sense, Maya is non-existence. Again, it cannot be said it is non-existence; for if it were, it could never produce the phenomenon. So it is something which is neither; and in the Vedanta philosophy it is called Anirvachaniya or inexpressible. Maya, then, is the real cause of this universe. Maya gives the name and form to what Brahman or God gives the material; and the latter seems to have been transformed into all this. The Advaitists, then, have no place for the individual soul. They say individual souls are created by Maya. Vivekananda rightly asserts: "Even so this whole universe as it exists is that Being. It is unchanged, and all the changes we see in it are only apparent. These changes are caused by Desha, Kala and Nimitta (space, time and cauzation), or, according to a higher psychological generalization, by Nama and Rupa (name and form). It is by name and form that one thing is differentiated from another". – Vivekananda, Swami: "Vedanta Philosophy", Advaita Ashrama, Kolkata, Sixteenth Reprint, August 2013, pp. 21-22. So, in reality they cannot exist. If there were only one existence throughout, how could it be that I am one, and you are one, and so forth? – *Op. cit.,* p. 23. We are all one, and the cause of evil is the perception of duality. Swamiji therefore says to make this point clear: "As soon as I begin to feel that I am separate from this universe, then first comes fear, and then comes misery. Where one hears another, one sees another that is small. Where one does not see another, where one does not hear another, that is the greatest, that is God". – Vivekananda, Swami: "Vedanta Philosophy", p. 23. In that greatest is perfect happiness. In small things there is no happiness.

43. Each work has to pass through these stages – ridicule, opposition, and then acceptance. Each man who thinks ahead of his time is sure to be misunderstood. So opposition and persecution are welcome, only I have to be steady and pure and must have immense faith in God, and all these will vanish. – The Complete Works of Swami Vivekananda, Vol. V, 8th Edn., 1964, p. 91. Here, we can take

the example of Galelio Galilei who suffered due to his conviction for saying the truth – "The Earth moves round the Sun". It can follow this practice in reality, all kinds of miseries and distress of human beings will vanish from the world.

44. In this context, it is better to quote Swami Vivekananda again, by means of realization of his words which go like: "My hope and faith rest in men like you. Understand my words in their true spirit, and apply yourselves to work in their light. ... ... I have given you advice enough; now put at least something in practice. Let the world see that your listening to me has been a success". – The Complete Works of Swami Vivekananda, Vol. VII, 6th Edn., 1964, p. 175. Hence, the strategy for the reconstruction of the social pyramid requires scientific nature of religious thought as propounded by the ideas of Swamiji, in eradicating all types of human evil and de-motivating tendencies widespread throughout the world environment in the name of religious beliefs; which go to detriment the world society and bring down people to a stage of barbarism. The safeguard of the present world requires applying fundamental truths of religion which are universally accepted.

45. To substantiate this (dangers of social unrest), it is worth-noting that during 1938 and particularly since the beginning of 1939 when a bitter controversy was ranging between the Congress right wing and Subhas Chandra, Rabindranath Tagore stood close to him both personally and ideologically. He gave Subhas a reception at Santiniketan in January 1939. Despite the controversy that was ranging at the time, Tagore wanted to make his position absolutely clear by himself giving a public reception to Subhas in Calcutta. He wrote out an address to Subhas Chandra entitled "Deshnayak or Leader of the Nation". – Bose, Sisir Kumar: "Netaji Subhas Chandra Bose", National Book Trust, New Delhi, 1986, pp. 102-03. It is clear that all patriots in India in the past advocated for freedom, and similarly, Tagore also accepted the fight of Netaji Subhas Chandra Bose, whom he called as the 'leader of the nation' in bringing freedom and therefore, he said: "I may not join him in the fight that is to come. I can only bless him and take my leave, knowing that he has made his country's burden of sorrow his own, that his final reward is fast coming as his country's freedom". – *Ibid.*, p. 103.

46. Thus, we find that management and spirituality are not poles apart, but interdependent. In the field of management we need spirituality and meditation for obtaining concentration and overcoming stress, and for practical spirituality we need management techniques. – Nikhileswarananda, Swami: "Spirituality and Management", Prabuddha Bharata or Awakened India, A Monthly Journal of the Ramakrishna Order started by Swami Vivekananda in 1896, Vol. 120, No. 1, January 2015, p. 47. At present, some companies are integrating prayer, meditation, and worship into their work routine. This leads to the employees having a peaceful mind and consequently increased productivity. So, efficient diversification of fund management will also be possible when organizational policies are reformulated through scientific religious practice.

47. The points noted below are important, perhaps the wisest thing that the Lebanese poet Kahlil Gibran even wrote in his book 'The Prophet' was: "Life, and all that lives, is conceived in the mist and not in the crystal. And who knows but a crystal is mist in decay? – Gibran, Kahlil: "The Prophet", Wordsworth,

Hertfordshire, 1997, p. 57. Regional imbalances can be reduced with the help of adopting policies guided by – for the protection of the righteous, for the destruction of the wicked. This is the scientific base of all religions for which in the Bhagavadgita, Sri Krishna famously declares that he would be around when irreligion raises its head: "Whenever there is a decline of religion and a rise of irreligion, I manifest myself. For the protection of the righteous, for the destruction of the wicked, and for the establishment of religion, I come into being from age to age". – Bhagavadgita, 4.7-8. Sri Ramakrishna, too, promised: "Two hundred years later I shall have to go there [indicating somewhere to the northwest of Kolkata]". – Nikhilananda, Swami: "Life of Sri Ramakrishna", Advaita Ashrama, Kolkata, 2008, p. 211. See also, "Unpublished Letters of Swami Saradananda: Letter to Sara Bull dated 17 July 1902", Vedanta Kesari, Vol. 101, No. 3, March 2014, p. 100. All these can therefore be justified into taking as the guidelines for reducing imbalances in living parameters of human beings between haves and have-nots classes.

48. A headlong rush towards the promised 'Technotopia', a golden future of technology's paradise, if we fail to learn from the past, might bring us to a similar sudden shock at the lack of meaning of our electronic tools. The irony of the tale is that continuing the search one step further, West until it became East, might have saved the lives of the suicides. Instead of finding an empty void at the end of the geographical search for wealth, many regions of Asia turn the direction of the search for meaning and happiness around and look inside, seeking the fullness of the Middle Way. When brought to search inside the mind, the horizon is limitless. The true gold is the Golden Mean, the unerring Middle Way, beyond both extremes. In infusing thus, human integrated understanding for empowering people in coming to judgment for social advancement, it is therefore essential to note the comment of the language of Rev. Heng Sure: "As Internet communications shrinks our global village, Eastern spirituality has come face to face with Western technology. This interaction has allowed engineer and academics in Taiwan to hear the opinion of an American Buddhist monk on spiritual values in the hi-tech world". – Sure, Rev. Heng: "Meeting Spiritual Challenges in a Technological Age", Prabuddha Bharata, Advaita Ashrama, Kolkata, Vol. 120, No. 1, January 2015, p. 189.

49. The human body and mind remains the ultimate laboratory for looking into questions of lasting value. Only when we employ tools of traditional and ancient technology: meditation, prayer, selfless service, and generosity, will we find the right door to begin our search for the source of meaning. Only a liberal arts education in the humanities can prepare a generation of students with the skills in critical thinking to be able to distinguish means from ends. – Sure, Rev. Heng: "Meeting Spiritual Challenges in a Technological Age", Prabuddha Bharata, Vol. 120, No. 1, January 2015, p. 188. Christianity has an inner life and an external life. … … to the example of Jesus as justifying a purely spiritual path, free from the taints of the world, we need to be cautious in this regard. Certainly, Jesus certainly did speak harshly of those who cling to externals, and distanced himself from religion as a set of rules: "Woe to you, scribes and Pharisees, hypocrites! For you tithe mint, dill, and cumin, and have neglected the weightier matters of law: justice and mercy and faith. It is these you ought to have practiced without neglecting the others. You blind guides! You strain out a gnat but swallow

a camel! Woe to you, scribes and Pharisees, hypocrites! For you clean the outside of the cup and of the plate, but inside they are full of greed and self-indulgence......So you also on the outside look righteous to others, but inside you are full of hypocrisy and lawlessness". – Matthew 23: 23-5. The truth that first found its voice in the Rig Veda: "Truth is one, sages call it variously". – Rig Veda, 1.164.46. Sri Ramakrishna accepted the uniqueness and authenticity of each religion, and he proclaimed: "As many faiths, so many paths". Hence, religions can only add to – never subtract from – universal truth, as adherents progress from truth to higher truth. Patanjali states in the Yoga Sutra: "To counteract obstacles to yoga, (one should take up) the practice of one principle", which is called nishta. – Patanjali, Yoga Sutra, 1.32. About religions, Vivekananda stated, "This Rishi-state is not limited by time or place, by sex or race". – The Complete Works of Swami Vivekananda, 3.253. Indeed, it was the belief of Vivekananda that the Vedic Rishi Ideal would be the future ideal for humankind.

50. One of the early reform movements to do this was the Brahmo Samaj, established in Calcutta by Ram Mohan Roy in 1828. The Brahmo Samaj initiated a strong articulation of Vedantic monotheism among educated Hindus, such that the idea of Brahman was asserted to be akin to Western monotheism. The synthetic ideas of this movement reflect the early stages of neo-Vedanta, whereby Hindus were reacting to Western criticism of indigenous practices. There were also possible influences of Freemasonry at this time: He [Ray] was chiefly inspired by eighteenth-century Deism (rational belief in a transcendent creator god) and Unitarianism (belief in God's essential oneness), but some of his writing suggests that he was aware of the religious ideas of the Freemasons (a secret fraternity that espouses some deistic concepts). Several of his [European] friends were members of the active Masonic Lodge in Calcutta. – Basham, A. L.: "History of Hinduism", in Encyclopedia Britannica 28 Vols, 15th Edition, Encyclopedia Britannica, Chicago, 1974, 8.918. In regard to international cooperation, it can be said that the foundational beliefs of the Brahmo Samaj, published in an official statement, can uproot social value system, which prescribes: "There is only one God, who is the Creator, Preserver and Saviour of this world. He is spirit; He is infinite in power, wisdom, love, justice and holiness; He is omnipresent, eternal, and blissful......The human soul is immortal, and capable of infinite progress, and is responsible to God for its doings". – The Quest for Meaning of Swami Vivekananda, 12.

51. This has resulted for an overall dissatisfaction in mind of people. The repercussion of this type of misguided goal of humanity has converted things into dehumanization of the overall quality related issues confronting towards particular type of growth of the social pyramid. – Deb, Samar: "Global Principles on Management", Dominant Publishers & Distributors Pvt. Ltd., New Delhi, 2014, p. 149. Thus, the quality aspects are becoming now, merely a symbolic one – the dignity of labour is concealed in reality to a vested interest in business of a few to the rich class of people, at the cost of the de-controlled techniques of organizational management system, and to the multinational character of the productive management system confined to the partial development, to increase surplus capital for the dominated class of the rich people, where all other activities of human society have been defeated to overcome the problems of human poverty. – *Ibid.*, p. 149.

52. The most horrible thing about competition is that one may conquer the environments, but that where one may conquer, thousands are crowded out. So it is evil at best. That cannot be good which helps only one and hinders the majority. Patanjali says that these struggles remain only through our ignorance, and are not necessary, and are not necessary, and are not part of the evolution of man. It is just our impatience which creates them. We have not the patience to go and work the way out. For instance, there is a fire in a theatre, and only a few escapes. The rest in trying to rush out crush one another down. That crush was not necessary for the salvation neither of the building nor of the two or three who escaped. If all had gone out slowly, not one would have been hurt. That is the case in life. The doors are open for us, and we can all get out without the competition and struggle; and yet we struggle. The struggle we create through our own ignorance, through impatience; we are in too great a hurry. The highest manifestation of strength is to keep ourselves calm and on our own feet. – The Complete Works of Swami Vivekananda, Vol. 5, p. 277.

53. To cite an example, it can be said that Virchand described as a faith: "Older than Buddhism, similar to it in its ethics, but different from it in its psychology". – Neely's History of the Parliament of Religions and Religious Congress at the World's Columbian Exposition, Ed. Walter R. Houghton (Chicago and New York: F. Tennyson Neely, 1894), 62. The Tirthankaras recognize the essence of all substances, "conscious as well as unconscious, which becomes an eternal cause of all modifications and is termed God". – *Ibid.* The humanitarian foundation of religion is to improve our moral standards, and therefore, we are needed to raise position of women and the masses. It can therefore be argued that 'dogmatic aggressiveness' cannot be treated to be the essential norms of human advancement in society. Preaching of an insular creed, and spread of 'a false theology', 'not only false but positively injurious to the best interests of mankind' cannot be considered as the real truth of human's religious ethics, which hampers society to ruin day-by-day. Again, the example of emperor Akbar (1542-1605) who showed the utmost respect to the Bible when a ship of Christian traders was captured with the copies of their holy book ... ... who showered rich encomiums on the Hindus for their high character, truthfulness, and honesty. – Desai, Kumarpal (Ed.): "The Jain Philosophy", World Jain Confederation, 2009, III, pp. 94-5. All these reflect about the guideline for the restoration of religious beliefs and faiths to overcome problems of human organizational deficiencies, and to empower people through truthfulness ideology and tolerance motive for the purpose of social assimilation in regard to world level religious model.

54. We may go to refer the 'Satya Yuga' to this context. At the advent of Satya Yuga there were neither kings nor kingdoms as mentioned in the Shanti Parva of the Mahabharata in which Bhishma on his death bed is giving lessons on administrative acumen to Yudhishthira. – Pathak, Pramod: "Administrative Wisdom in the Ramayana", Prabuddha Bharata, Vol. 120, No. 4, April 2015, p. 18. Yet there was order in those stateless societies. Those were the times when societies were self-managed units working on principles of self-organized critically of natural system. The basic rule was righteous conduct based on dharma. Again, it is widely accepted that Ramarajya, the state of Sri Ramachandra, is an epitome of good governance even outside India. All these constitute human excellence building philosophy, which should be propagated in these days of

technological upheavals, if we want to build up society on principles of human perfection as well as work ethics.

55. Here, human delusion has been given due importance to the reinventing policy of meditation for managerial reengineering purposes, so that people by doing action can attain the 'Brahmic Bliss' which is the 'Absolute Order' of human life, can be experimented in business environment with the philosophic redraft of the organizational mission, and the demonstration by practice in business and human economic activities with the theory of relativity between science of getting things done on the one hand as the cause; and the art of human skill development in real philosophic order as the effective change in business practices. – Deb, Samar: "Unified Thought on Management", Kalpaz Publications, Delhi, 2004, p. 203. In bringing environmental sustainability it can be suggested the method of meditational goal, if adopted in modern organizations quite scientifically will come in the way of solving all business problems and human sufferings in this global order of business activities. – *Ibid.,* p. 203.

56. The techniques for effective resource match should follow the scientific rules of guiding human organizations as to the service of God, in doing activities for the welfare of mankind. In the darkness of the night you may speculate that there will not come any day at all. But when the Sun comes out you can never think that there is darkness in the world. – Pavitrananda, Swami: "The Practice of Devotion", Prabuddha Bharata, Vol. 119, No. 11, November 2014, p. 37. Hence, the foundation of religion based on such scientific truth can integrate social activities for the envisagement of human functional relationship to guide people in the way of unified nature of human development.

57. This kind of faith is useful, and is effective, not only in spiritual life, but in ordinary life also. It has been found that many scientists who have made profound discoveries had to struggle against difficulties. But, in spite of all difficulties, there was something within them which knew that some solution should be found, that there was no problem without a solution. They would struggle that way. – Pavitrananda, Swami: "The Power of Faith", Prabuddha Bharata, Vol. 120, No. 4, April 2015, p. 25. Real faith is an inner urge, an inner conviction, an intuition, that the goal is there, and that you can achieve it. Such was Spinoza. Throughout his life he suffered, physically and mentally, but he stuck to his faith. If you do, through the sheer power of faith you will realize the highest goal of human life. What is more important, and is perhaps less recognized, is that as a whole, Asia is different from the West. Western thinking is characterized by analysis, division, and a contrast between the pairs of opposites. Asian thinking is characterized by synthesis, unification, and harmony. – Durgananda, Swami: "A Monk's Journeys in China", Prabuddha Bharata, Vol. 120, No. 3, March 2015, p. 257. Emotion and intuition often act as an engine for growth. China is the best example, which has dramatically modernized itself. China has not only been observed to have developed its infrastructure enormously; but also, it is famous for religious and spiritual history in the world today. – *Op. cit.,* p. 16. No religion is the home of any person. An individual's true home is only one's true personality, free from all boundaries, all limiting adjuncts, free from ignorance.

58. The real challenge of human life is to live in harmony, which further means to live in peace, but it also means to be aware of all the forces in action within and

without. Both in worldly and spiritual life, our aim is to make our mind receptive. We need both brain-based and heart-based knowledge. – Bhar, Gopal C.: "The Brain and Holistic Living", Prabuddha Bharata, Vol. 120, No. 2, February 2015, p. 34. The human being is not merely a living organism but the bearer of the universal message of goodness, wisdom, beauty, and human worthiness. Birth does not automatically make a person human. Every human offspring needs to consciously become human. This is the great challenge in human life which requires potential development in social environment.

59. Correlation between religion and development can be reflected through development of human faculty of knowledge for the purpose of realizing the truth of the spirituality, which is the root of human life. Hence, Swami Vivekananda illuminates the idea thus: "The artistic faculty was highly developed in our Lord, Shri Ramakrishna, and he used to say that without this faculty none can be truly spiritual". – The Complete Works of Swami Vivekananda, Vol. 5, p. 259. To quote again from the Encyclopaedia Britannica: "The arts were cultivated in South Asia not only as a noble pastime but also in a spirit of dedication, as an offering to a god". - <http: // www. Britannica. Com / E B checked / topic 556016/South-Asian – arts> accessed 18 October 2014. Through an intense, deep, authentic bhava in the arts we can approach the Truth, we can realize God, which is the goal of human life … … If this process is followed, and we achieve harmony not only within us but also with other cultures and their ways of producing art. In the end, through art we find harmony with the whole creation. – Madhurananda, Swami: "Harmony through the Fine Arts", Prabuddha Bharata, Vol. 119, No. 12, December 2014, p. 43. Swami Vivekananda predicts: "Every science must end where it finds a unity, because we cannot go any further. When a perfect unity is reached, that science has nothing more of principles to tell us … … What will remain for us is to discover every day new combinations of that one material and the application of those combinations for all the purposes of life". – The Complete Works of Swami Vivekananda, 9 Vols. (Calcutta: Advaita Ashrama, 1-8, 1989; 9, 1997), 6-10. Thus, human upliftment requires appropriate correlation between religion, art, culture, etc. for the all-round development of human beings, to the betterment of life bringing processes and realization of happiness.

60. Thus, sensitivity training is recommended as a method of Organizational Development (O.D.) along with Industrial Democracy (I.D.). – Campbell and Dunnette: "Effectiveness of T-group Experience in Managerial Training and Development", Psychological Bulletin, 1968, referred by Abraham K. Korman. Goals of sensitivity training as given by Campbell are: (i) to increase self-insight concerning one's behaviour in a social context, to learn how others see and interpret one's own behaviour, and to gain insight into why one acts the way one does in different interpersonal situations; (ii) to increase sensitivity to the behaviour of others (reciprocal to goal one), i.e. to increase awareness of the stimuli emitted by other persons and the emotional basis for interpersonal communications; (iii) to increase diagnostic and action-oriented skills in social, interpersonal, and intergroup situations, among others. Again, Korman has observed, "The assumptions of the sensitivity training procedure are that, if these goals are achieved, one will become defensive about himself, less fearful of the intensions of others, more responsive to others and their needs, and lees likely

to misinterpret others' behaviours in a negative fashion". – Korman, A. K.: "Organizational Behaviour", Op. cit., p. 306. Thus, results expected under this training are: (1) greater creativity, (2) less hostility toward others, and (3) greater sensitivity to social psychological influences on work behaviour, etc. Thus, human participative nature of dealing requires development agenda in bringing people towards the path of salvation in life through religious sensitivity, organizational dynamic managerial behavioural prudence and people-oriented task of confining things for elimination of social poverty.

61. In understanding scientific reasons for knowing exactly religious backgrounds, we are needed to evolve with the process of human consciousness in coming to the path of integrated concept of life. Here, Sri Aurobindo describes evolution in the Sufi manner, as a rediscovery of consciousness in its ascending order till it finally becomes pure consciousness and reaches again the stage of Satchidananda. The question arises: How best can man help the evolutionary process already in progress? For this he shows the path of 'Integral Yoga'. According to Sri Aurobindo, existence is a mystery and a problem only for humanity. Therefore, only humanity has to solve it. – Raghupathi, K. V.: "Evolution: Darwin, Sufism, and Sri Aurobindo", Prabuddha Bharata, Vol. 119, No. 10, October 2014, p. 29. By freeing oneself from lower nature a human being achieves integration within oneself, and then harmony and peace. This is scientific logic for which religion should be intermingled with the kind of truth, especially for going to the path of salvation in life.

62. As soon as we react, we become slaves. We have to be curious about the freedom of life. The four principles are important, because we have no other alternative in our life for pious living but to sort-out the possibilities of searching God in man, animal and all other living beings. In this life, we have to find-out the way – for a firm stand upon these principles; so that in reality, we would be in position to realize all the purities leading to divinity in human. As such, every individual might become a living God through such kind of equality as experienced through dharma of life – confining which all other elementary principles should be embraced for working with the philosophy of Indian Vedic thought. Thus, God is pure, the same to all. Therefore such a sage would be a living God. – Bhagavad-Gita, 5: 18. The man who wants money is striving for freedom – to get rid of the bondage of poverty. Every action of man is worship, because the idea is to attain to freedom, and all action, directly or indirectly, tends to that. – Vedanta Philosophy, p. 70. Good management requires the concept of real happiness. The system of management is said to be good, when it relates to the process of disinterested way of working by sacrificing the self, which is never searching anything more than perfection. – Deb, Samar: "Unified Thought on Management", Kalpaz Publications, Delhi, 2004, p. 46. Assuming thus, we should judge results, not by statistics or the amount of money spent on work only, but by the quality of human character that is involved with the said work. – Elwin, V.: "A Philosophy for NEFA", North East Frontier Agency, Shillong, 1955.

63. If the natural resources are used in balanced manner, there would be effective result in balancing the ecological environment; and thus, many of the social problems of human beings will be solved in effective manner. Hence, the productive functions are to be carried out by modern organizations in a goal

oriented manner, so that organizational balance is maintained in converting the social, financial, natural, and other material resources into effective productive resource that go to increase human welfare in terms of solving most of the burning problems and issues of the society ... ... which is the challenging need in the present system of the growing world order. – Deb, Samar: "Global Principles on Management", Dominant Publishers & Distributors Pvt. Ltd., New Delhi, 2014, p. 277. For maximum social advantage, the principles of equanimity aspect of the development are to be corroborated with the principles of economy in doing things. In this context, 'input-output' notion has to be analyzed for bringing effectiveness in organizational productive behaviour towards producing good results in relativistic manner. So, dynamic, sustainable, creative and conservative issues are to be addressed under the subject of human welfare to reflect holistic development for a common formula of integrated human development process in a nurturing philosophy. To nurture human beings in integrated way, it requires the virtue of detachment that has a great deal to contribute towards making India economically prosperous. – Paul, Anthony J. (Ed.): "Hind Swaraj and Other Writings", Cambridge University Press, UK, 1997, p. 97. Social welfare through maximum social advantage philosophy denotes the concept of humanization process through socialization of human organizational effective delivery system. – For further understanding, also refer to Balfour, A. L.: "Green's Metaphysics of Knowledge", Mind, Vol. IX, 1884.

64. Lokamanya Tilak also wanted the world to know how India was being exploited economically by the English, such that poverty had engulfed the Indian masses, reducing them to a sub-human level. – Pradhan, G. P.: "Lokamanya Tilak", National Book Trust, New Delhi, 1994, p. 124. Tilak anticipated emergence of the Labour Party as an important force in England's political life and made sustained efforts at establishing close contacts with its leaders. – *Op. cit.,* p. 126.

65. According to Subhas, what was needed most of all was the will to be one nation and to hold together as one nation. – Bose, Sisir Kumar: "Netaji Subhas Chandra Bose", National Book Trust, New Delhi, 2001, p. 89. Thus, to him, the problem of unity was largely a mass psychological problem. Again, for promoting national unity and solidarity, he said, many things were needed, viz. a lingua franca, common dress, common diet, etc. – *Ibid.,* p. 89. In making for a decision put forward for national planning, among the principles advocated by Subhas, one such idea was – India must aim at national autonomy with respect to her principal needs and requirements from the industrial point of view. He emphasized for taking decisions in making policies for the growth and development of mother industries like – power supply, metal production, machine and tools manufacture, manufacture of essential chemicals, transport and communication industries.

66. It is needed for this purpose that there should be right policy resolution be framed for the global mankind, which is in line with the "Technical Ombudsman", and is in consonance with the parameters of human development index (HDI). The coordination thus requires 'Operational Controls' to provide for a desired direction to investment, production and distribution, etc. in various segments of an uncontrolled economy. – Gupta, A. N. and Maheshwari, R. P.: "Business, Government and Society: A Study of Business Environment", Vani Educational Books, New Delhi, 1985, p. 69. Good coordination will prevail in society, when

we will be able to try to let all nationalities (jati) of India, for example, follow their own path. The Brahmaputra, the Ganga, the Yamuna, the Kaveri, the Sind – let all of them go on and flow along their respective courses. Let there be no attempts to merge one with the other. – Cited in Guha, Amalendu: "Little Nationalism Turns Chauvinist", in Economic and Political Weekly, Vol. XV, Nos. 41, 42 and 43, October 1980, pp. 1701-1720. Hence, we should place importance on human work culture, on which depends success of organizational life of people in social living conditions. This is the criteria for bringing coordination in real life to motivate people for producing in efficient manner, to strengthen the will force of human relationships at organizational level of working with the goal of human emancipation.

67. It means that the things we are concerned in realities of management will require global level approach and reformation policy implications, so that material resources are not mismanaged that causes all types of social crises and brings in a disharmonic social atmosphere. ... ...-Deb, Samar: "Global Principles on Management", Dominant Publishers & Distributors Pvt. Ltd., New Delhi, 2014, pp. 267-68. The world today has been observed to have a silver-line between haves and have-nots kind of people. This kind of mismatch between living parameters can be eradicated when there is flexibility in implementing schemes, and therefore, organizational practices as well as governmental planned processes of different activities will require adequate relationship in confining people to shoulder responsibility, in terms of reducing poverty from each country. – *Op. cit.,* p. 320. However, the dynamicity of work in organization is dependent on the concept of empowerment of people which further requires self-concept or a good self-image. In this regard, Uma Sekaran's idea illuminates the picture of flexibility thus: "Self-concept or a good self-image, at least partly, a function of how successfully we accomplish the things we attempt to do ... ... ". – Sekaran, Uma: "Organizational Behaviour: Text and cases", Tata McGraw-Hill Publishing Company Limited, New Delhi, 1997, p. 51.

68. The approach of leadership must have to strengthen organizational climate (OC). It (OC) is internal environment of an organization which has to be made more and more productive with human efficiency of work, and so, every leader – be it religious, political, business, or otherwise, should be concerned with the essential part of preserving organizational climate, because a healthy and conducive climate in organization is helpful for augmenting mutually as well as collaborating development between the line and staff, besides harmonious relationship between group and individuals (inter and intra) in operational areas of the entire organization structure. In short, leadership must have qualities of human perceptions which are broadened by enthusing values, needs, attitudes, expectations and so on. – See also, the foot-note reference provided in Deb, Samar: "Contemporary Issues on Management", Atlantic Publishers and Distributors, New Delhi, 2001, p. 80. Today's leader should be like Gaurishankar, who was a combination of thinker, doer, meditative, and an active person. He was born in a Brahmin family from Ghogha, also known as Gogo, a seaport town about ten miles from Bhavnagar. His full name is Gaurishankar Udayashankar Oza, whom Max Müller called 'Gaurisamkara' because of their friendly relationship. – See 'A Prime Minister and a Child Wife' in F. Max Müller, Auld Lang Syne – Second Series: My Indian Friends (London: Longmans and

Green, 1899), 232, 237. Before the partition of India in 1947, there existed 565 princely states. He (Gaurishankar) was the Dewan of Bhavnagar State in Kathiawar, Gujarat, India from 1857 to 1879. If we go in detail about the life history of Gaurishankar, our vision of leadership will change, and it will help in the process of nation-building activities.

69. Integral humanism is concerned with such kind of creativity in human beings which equates with life itself by virtue of its organizing pattern, forming and questing quality (Sinnot: 1959). It also relates to the process of the product initiated for the purpose of human unity in action and so, Murray (1957) calls it productive creativity. Again, Rogers (1957) thinks that creativity is essentially known as a process, and therefore, integral approach in human creativity has to be found with the qualities of overall process making mankind erect towards cementing relationships for social foundation. It is thus, a novel relational product, growing out of the uniqueness of the individual on the one hand, and the materials, events, people or circumstances of his life on the other. – Deb, Samar: "Unified Thought on Management", Kalpaz Publications, Delhi, 2004, p. 111. Thus, integral humanism is the concept which takes into consideration the world view on human development perspective, and so, it is having the purpose of attaining the goal of individual, group, and organization at a destined way of life. – Also see, Maslow, A. H.: "Self-actualizing People: A Study of Psychological Health", in 'The Self: Explorations in Personal Growth', C. E. Moustakas (Ed.), Harper, New York, 1956, pp. 325-32.

70. While acknowledging this option, I do not intend to pursue it here as this would lead us into the vast realm of religious change … ..... – Sander, Ake: "Perceiving Other Religions", Prabuddha Bharata, Vol. 119, No. 9, September 2014, p. 38. It is observed by him that the importance of distinguishing between intra- and inter-religious differences has the relevance to the fact that the focus of what follows will be exclusively trained upon the latter. However, most of the points that will be made are applicable to intra-religious differences as well. Both can give, and have given, rise to serious problems. In the Muslim world, for example, it is likely that more blood has been spilled over intra-religious conflicts than over inter-religious ones. – *Op. cit.,* p. 40. So, religion should find its place in bringing societal peace and human happiness through inter-connected values of religious truths and beliefs, which go to expand human oriental vision for world class citizenship, and thus, "How large a difference must there be, and in what dimension of religion – belief system, mythology, ritual, and so forth – before we can claim that the tradition we are encountering is factually different, and not merely a variation of our own?" – See also, Smart, N.: "The Religious Experience of Mankind", Collins, Glasgow, 1977. An obvious question in this regard is how one religious tradition can be considered right or true, or more right and true than any other. Happiness through religious path will be possible only when mankind have their vision on the truth of religion – it needs fundamental truths, value system, beliefs, etc. and all have been clearly explained in previous Chapters with the scientific temper of religious thought. The primary aim of religion should therefore be universal realization in terms of forward looking tendencies.

71. In planning for such structural adjustment, Subhas Chandra made it clear that while advocating industrialization he was not ruling out cottage industries.

In fact, he stood for their revival and strengthening with the aid of science as in Germany, Japan and other advanced countries. – Bose, Sisir Kumar: "Netaji Subhas Chandra Bose", National Book Trust, New Delhi, 2013 (Reprint), p. 89. Now East and West must work hand in hand for the good of each other, without destroying the special characteristics of each. The West has much to learn from the East, and the East has much to learn from the West; in fact, the future has to be shaped by a proper fusion of the two ideals. – Bodhaswrananda, Swami: "Vivekananda: His Call to the Nation", Advaita Ashrama, Kolkata, 2012, pp. 30-31. Thus, structural adjustment between religious work and government policy initiatives are to be made for human efficiency building norms.

72. To give an example, it can be said that banks and post offices in China resemble those in the West in appearance, neatness, and technology. These government services offer one stop clearance – you don't have to go from window to window. – Durgananda, Swami: "A Monk's Journeys in China", Prabuddha Bharata, Vol. 120, No. 3, March 2015, pp. 20-21. Again, countries other than China that have bullet trains now are Spain 3,100 km., Japan 2,664 km., France 2,036 km., Germany 1,334 km., Italy 923 km. and also others like Russia, Turkey, South Korea, and Taiwan. These are all examples of organizational work behaviour, which India and other Asian countries are required to be adopted by learning from their directive functions which go to reflect on the dharma of work in initiating human efficiency.

73. Effectiveness in doing so, will also require environmental conservation which is the need of the hour. It requires systematic process to protect our environment, and hence, it includes the whole system of environment comprising trees, human beings, animals, and every other living being on earth. This is the real entrepreneurial ability should be well-trained for creative living goal. The aim of entrepreneurship should therefore be to maintain a right balance in the environment and to protect certain species of living beings from total extinct. Entrepreneurial abilities should be made responsible to the protection of biodiversity as the ultimate aims of conservation. This is possible with the help of science and technology. – Hazra, Dwaita: "Women and Environment Conservation", Prabuddha Bharata, Vol. 119, No. 11, November 2014, p. 20. Also see, Duffy, Rosaleen: "Nature Crime: How we are Getting Conservation Wrong", Yale University, London, 2010. Effective entrepreneurial development guidelines are also provided in the Vedas, Upanishads, Vedangas, Puranas, and Itihasas. It requires scientific institutionalization, so that humanity could be saved from destructive events.

74. It requires innovativeness of human mental stage of working with the things. The creative zeal should be empowered in people working in organizations, so that they apply sensitivity to analyze things that they practice at organizational level. – Deb, Samar: "Global Principles of Management", Dominant, New Delhi, 2014, p. 87. It is observed that a best system in managing well human activities can be placed through pure consciousness. In this way, the world heritage can be preserved. The imbalanced thought creating crisis in society and increasing poverty can be balanced when we will try to stress on value-based management (VBM). It gives idea to rethink how management can better apply the principles and practices of VBM to help deliver superior value creation on a sustained

basis. – Kumar, Sandeep: "Business Process Management: Creating the Value Managed Enterprise", A. K. Publications, Delhi, 2009, pp. 51-52.

75. It predicts that man is the builder of his future, and it lies within his power to determine what that future will be. If a man has devoted all his energies to the pleasures of life, he cannot hope to be reborn into a higher world. – Setty, E. D.: "Man in Search of God", Akansha Publishing House, New Delhi, 2006, p. 96. Life gives him glimpses of joy, knowledge, power, but in his true self (Atman) he has these without measure, since the self is essentially one with God. Man wants infinite being, infinite knowledge, infinite joy, but his highest aspiration is for multi-release from the wheel of rebirth and from the power of karma – and for freedom from the limitations that imprison him within his present existence. – *Op. cit.,* p. 97. Thus, exploitation makes man slave and so, it should be discarded for the attainment of liberation in life.

76. About the destiny of life, it is said that religion functions as soil, energy, resource as an instrument, as a motivator, stabilizer, tranquilizer, a leading light, pacifier, uplifter, satisfier, a liberator, and as a source of enlightenment. If we think of the sequence of religious, the following is the order: Vedic religion, Hinduism, Judaism, Zoroastrianism, Jainism, Buddhism, Christianity and the last born in the beginning of the seventh century is Islam. – Setty, E. D.: "Man in Search of God", 2006, pp. 3-4. So, environmental issues dictate – how religions have been possible factors for human development in confining great work culture towards the societal pyramid, which eliminates human craving for the thrust of knowledge; but all those attributes contributing to religious that requiring human development should be inculcated through knowledge of the science of religion, based on the various facets of human life bringing processes. Hence, social ills are to be eradicated through religious policies which are enumerated to strengthen human mental phenomenon, craving for the destiny of life. In every aspect of religious belief, there lies the highest truth – liberation, and it is possible through human foundation. Wilfred C. Smith: a society, that, grasping firmly the injunctions which are there revealed, dedicates itself to living according to them, and thereby sets forth on the reconstruction of human life on earth. So, comparative religions in the 19th century have started applying the scientific method and the social science armamentarium to discover the history and significance of religion. It thus, expedites the process of human development in holistic perspective with reference to social advancement and world peace. In this way, we can hope for living to reach at the liberating destiny of life in managing various things and activities at organizational system of human performances.

77. Objective function of welfare maximization should be concentrated to Prājña, sitting ākāśe ca hṛdi, in the space within the heart, becomes from the diversity (of objects and their perceiving subject) and continues to be a mere mass of consciousness, for then there is no functioning of the mind. This is how Prājña is met with the waking state. When the mind ceases to act, the same entity assumes the characteristics of Prājña.—Gambhīrānanda, Swāmī (Translated): "Eight Upaniṣads with the Commentary of Śaṅkarācārya", Advaita Ashrama, Kolkata, 2012 (Reprint), p. 187. This is the order can help in social balance restoration for eliminating human sufferings and it is considered to be the process of welfare

maximization for transcendental order of human living towards global peaceful environment.

78. As a reference to the holistic process of human development, we quote: "Socrates approached sophists with insinuating gentleness and ignorance, as though he were an ignorant man, desirous of learning. His eyes shone with benevolent intelligence. Then, from question to question he forced them to say the contrary of what they had first affirmed, and actually to confess that they did not even know that of which they spoke. Then he demonstrated that the sophists knew the cause and origin of nothing, though they pretended to be in possession of universal knowledge. After silencing them in this way, he did not triumph in his victory, but smilingly thanked his opponents for the information he had obtained from their replies, adding that the beginning of true wisdom consists in knowing that one knows nothing. – Rothwell, Fred: "The Secret History of World Religions", Mittal Publications, Delhi, 1986 (Translated), p. 193. This is the glaring example of adapting with the changing nature of situations.

79. Religion, spirituality, prayer, and meditation are intertwined. The reputed French sociologist Émile Durkheim observed that the exuberance of religious imagery and activity associated with rites and rituals such as prayer is a form of collective symbolic representation of values and ideals in social life. The function of prayer is to strengthen social bonds raising the social vitality necessary for the well working of our moral life. Durkheim perceived prayer as the divinization of the community composed of a set of beliefs, sentiments, and practices. – See Lukes, Steven: "Émile Durkheim: His Life and Work – A Historical and Critical Study", Penguin, London, 1973, pp. 242, 471, 475. It reflects thus, in saying that all types of religious activities are concerned with human growth in terms of truth, beauty and goodness to substantiate the idea of social reconstruction through organizational activities, where religious institutions should be guided through principles of human unity in action in that line of thinking to enhance human skill and creativity for advancing life towards liberating tendencies by processes of organizational activities.

80. We may thus, refer to the work of Max Weber who points out that salvation is sought, not from prayer alone, but also from the wheel of karma, causality. Rewards and punishments for every good and evil deed are automatically established by the karma, causality of the cosmic mechanism of compenzation. – See Weber, Max: "The Sociology of Religion", Translated by E. Fischoff, Beacon, Boston, 1968, pp. 25-26, 266. In this context, it is worthwhile to note that human beings are to be well trained for knowing the reasons to come out successfully from bondage and slavery; otherwise, the cycle of karma is quite impossible to be understood which gives man both the alternatives in life – bondage and slavery and also liberation, in doing tasks backed by either unscientific way of dealing with the things, or scientific way of dealing with the things. In an age of techno-economy, people are required to preserve, conserve and sustain. These principles are further enumerated in the Vedic literatures, have already been cited in previous Chapters in different explanations, to analytically interpret the holistic process of development to substantiate the scientific backgrounds of human religiosity as well as poverty eradication programmes.

81. In socializing human religious mode to the path of organizational work behaviour, it is said by Dan A. Chekki: "The gods to whom one turns for protection are regarded as subject to some social and moral order". – Chekki, Dan A.: "The Power and Mystery of Prayer and Meditation", Prabuddha Bharata, Vol. 120, No. 6, June, 2015. However, the British anthropologist Raymond Firth argues that it is not possible for human society to exist without some form of symbolic solutions which rest on non-empirical foundations. Thus, religion embodies a conceptualization and projection of the most fundamental human needs and problems. Under this system, a solution to human problems, the act of prayer, provides tension-release through verbal and other physical action. Hence, when reason of human beings fails, then the supra-rational is called to aid. In this way, prayer, worship, revelation, miracle, or other supra-normal process is claimed. – See Firth, Raymond: "Elements of Social organization", Beacon, Boston, 1961, pp. 248-49. Again, according to the German philosopher Kant, the purpose of prayer can be to induce in us a moral disposition, not seeking the satisfaction of our wants. It is therefore, managerial service giving qualities can work as the remedy for overcoming problems of human sufferings, and so, organization's policy towards human side of enterprising skill not should confront with the ideas of human emancipation from slavery, poverty and uncivilized way of societal living conditions. And all these are to be reflected in religious mode of socializing organizational work behaviour.

82. Achievement of the goal of global integration could be made possible through the process of tending towards the path of the belief that our good deeds will be rewarded and regarded. Wayne Dyer, a noted author predicts thus: "The daily practice of meditation is the single thing in my life that gives me a greater sense of well-being, increased energy, and higher productivity at a more conscious level, more satisfying relationships and a closer connection to God". – Dyer, W. W.: "Wisdom of the Ages", Harper Collins, New York, 1998, p. 26. This is the case of personality development experience through religious path, which we can follow as the secular idea of human development mantra as the way of meditative prescription, and therefore, we attempted to cite the example of 'preksha meditation' in realizing the concept of global integration as the existential supremacy for optimum level of human foundational thought for fundamental growth initiatives.

83. All principles of legal justice are guided by the reasoning of the fact which has helped in the process of making life of mankind founded on fundamental issues of science. In religion also, there are backgrounds of reasoning guided by scientific principles, to enlarge human belief towards the path of scientific spirit for human development. Accordingly, it is asserted by eminent thinkers that Swamiji's reasoning power was sharp, so he could speak boldly. Swami Vivekananda's writings are full of reasoning, and therefore, he can withstand the challenge of reason. – Pavitrananda, Swami: "Reason, Faith, and Religion", Prabuddha Bharata, Vol. 120, No. 5, May 2015, p. 19. It is thus, suggested that when our life is built up by reason, it will be possible to get everything; provided that we can direct our life in a proper way. So, the prerequisite qualification for legal justice is to judge things based on reason, and it can guide human life to the path of reaching at the goal of balanced development.

84. Advancement of human life should be made through realization of the concept of 'Existence'. Acharya Shankara believes that Existence (sat) implies to a subtle, all-pervasive thing, which is without distinctions, singular, without parts, and is Consciousness. This word, sat, he states, is known from all the Upanishads. – See Acharya Shankara's commentary on Chhandogya Upanishad, 6.2.1. In this way, religious goal should confine human activities to lead people to the path of immortality. It is the ultimate goal of human life. It is the end. So, identification with Consciousness indeed means that one is finally identified with Brahman itself. It should be the working philosophy; because, it is the unchanging, eternal Reality, and is freed from the suffering of limitation. This immortality, or identification with Brahman, gives rise to fearlessness and bliss. – See Taittiriya Upanishad, 2.9.1: "The enlightened man is not afraid of anything after realizing that Bliss of Brahman". It is translation from Eight Upanic ads, 1.386. See also, Brihadaranyaka Upanishad, 4.3.33, for the description of the bliss of one who knows the Veda and is desire less. Hence, it can be predicted doubtlessly that strategic norms of human development conditions are to be guided by the philosophical assumptions of the Vedas and Upanishads, to illustrate human honesty and integrity in work place; which modern organizations are required to follow in their policy making issues for increasing human competencies level, enhancing organizational capabilities in utilizing manpower resources and to deliver with the norms of accountability.

85. In India, while some regions such as the desert and semi-desert areas of Rajasthan and the hilly or mountainous regions of some states might remain backward, because of agro-climatic or physiographic reasons, there is no reason why large areas in well watered plains, which are well endowed to be highly productive, should remain economically and/or socially depressed. – Nath, V.: "Economic Development and Planning in India", Concept Publishing Company Pvt. Ltd., New Delhi, 2010, p. 83. Differences in levels of social development as indicated by the values of social indicators are also sharp and will increase unless vigorous steps are taken to reduce them by the State Governments where they are low. Religious mode of human behavioural foundation is the depicting nature of what determines the nature of man's next birth, what causes his soul to enter a higher or lower state of existence, is the law of karma which means that one's thoughts, words, and deeds fix one's lot in future existences. – Setty, E. D.: "Man in Search of God", Akansha Publishing House, New Delhi, 2006, p. 96. Man is the builder of his future, and it lies within his power to determine what that future will be. So, it is believed that a man reaps what he sows; his deeds shape his character and his soul. – *Ibid.,* p. 96. This philosophy of work should guide people in organizations for operating with the optimum level of human growth.

86. For this, we wish our leaders pursue an ethical code in their private and public lives. But society's progress in the economic sphere is very much a function of right policies and the efficiency of their implementation. – Mishra, Jagannath (Ed.): "India's Economic Development", Vikas Publishing House Pvt. Ltd., New Delhi, 1984, pp. 62-63. It is economic policies that have led us to this crisis, we observe today in all-round spheres of social structure. In the short-run policies dominates; in the long-run economies takes over. Transformation will come when all countries, advanced and backward, are in search of appropriate values that will be compatible to changes in society.

87. Poverty is one of the most difficult problems that policymakers face. Poor families are more likely than the overall population to experience homelessness, drag dependence, health problems, teenage pregnancy, illiteracy, unemployment, and low-educational attainment. – Mankiw, N. Gregory: "Principles of Microeconomics", Cengage Learning, New Delhi, 2006, p. 442. However, in grass-root it is observed that although it is hard to separate the causes of poverty from the effects, there is no doubt that poverty is associated with various economic and social ills, among which, blind beliefs on religious activities widespread by politicians and some religious leaders also increase the severity of the problems in society.

88. For this again, the national government should keep in mind strict vigil to develop its citizens with the value-based principles governance guided by the fact of religious truths. It is true, because the nation is conceived to be the foundation of political authority and the success or strength of the nation is the major objective of policy. – MacIver, R.M.: "The Web of Government", The Free Press, New York, 1965, pp. 120-21. The fact of slavery encouraged the tendency to regard all who engaged in menial toil or in the humbler forms of economic enterprise as an inferior order of human beings unworthy of civil rights. This is still, prevailing in many part of the world, instead of scientific revolution and technological reformations. Thus, we need to think now, as the world citizenship to deliver for ameliorating the severe causes of human sufferings from this world; so that the principle of representation, the only method by which a country could be democratically governed should be followed in recourse to reshape the dharma of human development. It will help in a way such as: "The Lord of Bhootha hordes, when the life breath is coursed upward through single Sushumna channel. And Sankara of matted locks appears before you mounted on the sacred bull". – Eraianban, H. H. Swamiji: "Vedas: An Extract of the Universal Values", Gyan Publishing House, New Delhi, 2001, p. 126. Similarly, Sushumna of the nation will be raised through adequate decision-making towards working for the holistic development of the masses.

89. In this connection, Swami Vivekananda thinks that the combination of the Greek mind represented by the external European energy added to the Hindu spirituality would be an ideal society for India … … He predicts therefore, until this absence of jealousy and obedience to leaders are learnt by the Hindu, there will be no power of organization. – Mumukshananda, Swami: "The Complete Works of Swami Vivekananda", Vol. V, Advaita Ashrama, Calcutta, 1999 (Eighth Reprint), p. 216. Again, Swamiji said, "India has to learn from Europe the conquest of external nature, and Europe has to learn from India the concept of internal nature. Then there will be neither Hindus nor Europeans – there will be the ideal humanity which has conquered both of the natures, the external and internal. We have developed one phase of humanity, and they another. It is the union of the two that is wanted". – *Ibid.,* p. 216. In this way, human capacity building will be enhanced for strengthening modern civilization through all means of developmental activities, forgetting jealousy and performing organizational activities for the greater interest of mankind. Optimization of resources will be made to bring organizational effectiveness in terms of human face of enterprising attitude, to overcome problems of human poverty, hunger and distressful situations. At last, global dynamism will prevail to embrace the qualitative norms

of human functional responsibility in rectifying social backwardness through such kind of combination being met by means of integral approach of humanity. It will bring in human dignity and empower people for participative nature of delivery mechanism towards the path of social emancipation of mankind.

90. Human cooperation is necessary element for realizing oneness to rejuvenate the picture of transcendental order in living goal. Swami Vivekananda asserts: "It was neither the philologist nor the scalar that I saw, but a soul that is every day realizing it oneness with the Brahman, a heart that is every moment expanding to reach oneness with the Universal. Where others lose themselves in the desert of day details, he has struck the well-spring of life. Indeed his heartbeats have caught the rhythm of the Upanishads – "know the Atman alone, and leave of all other talk". – The Complete Works of Swami Vivekananda, Vol. IV, pp. 280-81. The practical demonstration of this ancient principle, the embodiment of India that is past, and a foreshadowing of the India that is to be, the bearer of spiritual light unto nations. – *Op. cit.,* p. 281. In lifting corporate veil by managerial challenges, it goes to say that human excellence building services in all fields of social development is necessarily to be cooperated in terms of such social transformational goal which confines people to the process of universal thinking in realizing for the core of human beings (Atman), and it should be reflected through religious role model in expanding the path of social empowerment of people in living pursuits. Transparent idea will give us freedom to decide, so as to work-out human potentialities to the optimum level possible.

91. Training techniques can be chosen for individual level training or for training that is conducted for work teams. With the increasing popularity of teams in organizations, it is common for employers to send their teams to training sessions. – See also, Russell, J. E. A., and DeMatteo, J. S. (2002a): "Group Dynamics, Processes, and Teamwork" in Cadotte, E. J. & Bruce, H. J. (Eds.): "The Management of Strategy in the Marketplace", Chapter 2, Southwest Publishing; Russell, J. E. A., and DeMatto, J. S. (2002b): "Managing the Team to Excellence" in Cadotte, E. J. and Bruce, H. J. (Eds.): "The Management of Strategy in the Marketplace", Chapter 12, Southwest Publishing. For example, Hewlett-Packard started its team members on a two-week training and orientation programme to familiarize everyone with the existing processes and the needs of the business. – Sherman, S.: "Secrets of H P's Muddled Team", Fortune, March 18, 1996, pp. 116-118, 120. Often teams are formed with individuals from various functional areas (e.g., marketing, finance, sales, and production). These cross-functional teams may require training in other disciplines to help them understood what is involved in other functional areas (called multi-skilling or cross-training). This has been used in the military. – Cannon-Bowers, J. A., Salas, E., Blickensderfer, E., and Bowers, C. A.: "The Impact of Cross-training and Workload in Team Functioning: A Replication and Extension of Initial Findings", Human Factors, 40 (1), 1998, pp. 92-101. This technique can also be used in high-technology firms. – For detail information readers are suggested to go through Hottenstein, M. P. and Bowman, S. A.: "Cross-training and Worker Flexibility: A Review of DRC System Research", Journal of High Technology Management Research, 9 (2), 1998, p. 157. It is further observed that this technique is applicable in assembling plants. – Cottrill, M.: "Give Your Work Teams Time and Training", Academy of Management Executive, 11 (3), 1997, p. 87.

92. As one expert puts it, "The financial measures of performance have great educational value in spurring employee understanding of business fundamentals......financial measures tend to closely parallel overall firm performance". – Schuster, M.: "Gain-sharing: Do It Right the First Time", Sloan Management Review, winter, 1987, p. 23. See also Bullock, R. J. and Lawler, E. E.: "Gain-sharing: A Few Questions and Fewer Answers", Human Resource Management, 23 (1), 1984, pp. 23-40; Hatcher, L. and Ross, T. L.: "From Individual Incentives to an Organization-wide Gain-sharing Plan: Effects on Teamwork and Product Quality", Journal of Organizational Behavior, 12, 1991, pp. 169-183; Rollins, T.: "Productivity-based Group Incentive Plans: Powerful, but Use with Caution", Compenzation and Benefits Review, 1989, pp. 39-56.

93. About this, says the great Buddha: "Do not believe in what you have heard". – The Complete Works of Swami Vivekananda, Vol. IV, p. 216. Again, Swami Vivekananda remarks: "Stand up and reason out, having no blind faith". – *Ibid.,* p. 216. He asserted: "Religion is a question of being and becoming, not of believing. This is religion, and when you have attained to that you have religion". – The Complete Works of Swami Vivekananda, Vol. IV, p. 216. The hidden treasure of religion is that there is unity among us all. The unity within us should be worked out and therefore, our knowledge should be applied to find-out the unity in various means. It can strengthen group relationships to excel for the larger interest of the society, and so; enterprising norms are to be made flexible for understanding such kind of variety needed to apply in maximizing output which will commensurate social growth, human progress and national development in the long-run. It should thus, be the ideology of all religions of the world which will guide people in maximizing benefit to achieve result for the sake of maximum social advantage.

94. Empirical research findings on the Vedanta philosophy have been depicted through analysis of the good and bad. Accordingly, the wise man performs the good. But fool chooses the pleasant. These two have been equated with knowledge and ignorance. – Bhandari, M. C.: "Para Vidya: Science of the Beyond", Para Vidya Sansthan, Calcutta, 1985, p. 114. It is therefore true to mention that social building approach is concerned with the system of human empowerment, where the goal of integral humanity is inherent with the concept of global management through religious background, which embraces the idea of human dignity of living, organizational transparency for performance and delivery mechanism, and dealing with the problems of human emancipation.

95. When strategy is carried as far as this, accurately gauged necessity can be equated with wisdom and realism with high-mindedness ... ... the opportunities for economic and technical development which France could offer the new Republic......to come forward with help. – Wiles, Peter (Translated): "Jean Lacouture Ho Chi Minh, The Penguin Press, London, 1968, pp. 92-93. Organizational vision will be thus reflected for the past, present and future – all will be pulling in different ways for the scales tipped back and forth between idealistic passions and hard realities, between old grudges and new longings. In this way, a choice has to be made for leadership approach in developing the self, with the connotation of human problems in entrepreneurial activities.

96. Under this process two contemporary things are important, which Swami Vivekananda preached – (a) the elimination of one's lower self; and (b) one's increasing self-reliance, making one stand on one's own feet and struggle towards raising or developing oneself and eventually attain fulfillment in Self-realization. – Shuddhidananda, Swami (Ed.): "Vivekananda as the Turning Point – The Rise of a New Spiritual Wave", Advaita Ashrama, Kolkata, 2013, p. 220. Sensibility approach should therefore be made by bringing about changes in India's attitude to life through these two contemporary aspects of his (Swami Vivekananda) Vedanta and Manliness approaches. – *Ibid.,* p. 220. Swamiji hoped that Indians could make "men" of them and do much towards "raising India on her feet again". – The Complete Works, Vol. 4, p. 363. He therefore asserts: "Every nation, everyman, and every woman work out their own salvation. Give them ideas – that is the only help they require, and then the rest must follow as the effect. Ours is to put the chemicals together, the crystallization comes in the law of nature. Our duty is to put ideas into their heads, they will do the rest". – *Ibid.* The rational soul is subdivided into the potential or passive intellect, i.e., capable of being acted upon or of receiving action, and the active or agent intellect, which is not so much "active" as that which actually is rather than that which potentially could be. – Plott, John C.: "Global History of Philosophy", Vol. I, Motilal Banarsidass, Delhi, 1987, pp. 128-29. In relation to social excellence, philosophically, perhaps the most dominating view is that time is simply understood in relation to events. So, the past and future have their own functions and nothing can be said to stop breathing. – *Ibid.,* Vol. V, p. 192. About sensibility, Swami Vivekananda felt: "The Chinese child is quite a philosopher and calmly goes to work at an age when your Indian boy can hardly crawl on all fours. He has learnt the philosophy of necessity too well". – Sharma, Suresh K. (Ed.): "Swami Vivekananda – The Patriot-saint of Modern India", Vol. 2, Vista International Publishing House, Delhi, 2008, p. 192. The process of increasing dedication towards work which brings in human creativity should be guided through foundation of sympathy, which Swamiji did towards the miseries of the children of China in the old society.

97. This world has a good many of these demoniac natures, but there are some gods too. If one proposes to teach why science to increase the power of sense-enjoyment, one finds multitudes ready for it. If one undertakes to show the supreme goal, one finds few to listen to him. – Bodhasarananda, Swami: "The Complete Works of Swami Vivekananda", Vol. I, Advaita Ashrama, Kolkata, 1986, pp. 141-42. In Mahâbhârata it is clearly given: "To one who is devoted to the Vedanta, who is gifted with great learning, who has been filled with wisdom, who has a complete mastery over his senses, who observes the restraints laid down in the scriptures, who has a Brahmana, should a man, possessed of similar conduct and having children and wives, assign the means of livelihood". – Dutt, M. M. (Translated): "Mahâbhârata: Sanskrit Text and English Translation", Vol. IX, Parimal Publications, Delhi, 2008, p. 290. Our administrative guides are as such needed such kind of scriptural order, so as to find-out the goal of Brahmanhood in men.

98. This is reflected in the Hindu theology and philosophy which accounts for their variety and numerousness by endeavouring to evolve them as representative powers out of fundamental philosophical principles. – Rao, T. A. Gopinath:

"Elements of Hindu Iconography", Vol. I, Part II, Motilal Banarsidass, Delhi, 1985, p. 400. Freedom of trade was now more necessary than ever; questions of distribution became acute with the growth of the business unit......Consequently, greater stress has been laid upon the fact that the increase of aggregate wealth is not the same thing as the increase of material well-being. – Hastings, James (Ed.): "Encyclopaedia of Religion and Ethics", Vol. V, Charles Scribner's Sons, New York, 1960, pp. 148-49. In regard to spiritual guidelines, Swami Vivekananda has given the proactive ideas thus: "Our goal is the loftiest. We have said big words to ourselves – absolute realization and all that. Let us measure up to the words. Let us worship the spirit in spirit, standing on spirit. Let the foundation be spirit, the middle spirit, the culmination spirit". – Bodhasarananda, Swami: "The Complete Works of Swami Vivekananda", Vol. VIII, 2012, p. 120. Thus, all problems of human civilization will be solved through manifested spirit in work place in terms of reaching out the goal of common welfare and the concept of integral humanity by means of religious foundation in scientific application.

99. The sustainable principle gives the idea that not only do markets in a country that is growing rapidly make it profitable to produce more cars, but the government is led to produce more highways and to provide more recreational areas for its newly affluent (and mobile) citizens. At yet a later stage, a concern about litter, population, and ugliness may become important, and their correction may then begin to account for a significant fraction of GNP. Such "amenities" usually become matters of social concern only when growth has assured the provision of the basic requirements for food, clothing, and housing of a substantial majority of the population. – Lipsey, Richard G. and Steiner, Peter O.: "Economics", Sixth Edition, Harper & Row, Publishers, Inc., New York, 1981, p. 807. In a sustainable concept value is given more importance to nurture human life. Kautilya, while being elaborate in enlisting the punishments against various financial crimes, keeps up his human profile intact. – Jha, V. N. (Ed.): "Kautilya's Arthasāstra and Social Welfare", Sahitya Akademi, New Delhi, 1999, p. 113. On the basis of sustainability, he stresses for the necessity of employment, envisages some sort of provident fund, pension and family pension too, suggests various rewards to the efficient officers, and recommends for strong and efficient surveillance and so on. Thus, in his Arthasâstra we find that there is amazing details of fiscal management as recommended by him, are also strikingly similar to the cannons of modern fiscal management. Hence, it is true that religion as the foundation of global level sustainability has been reflected in his treatise.

100. Thus, capital movement in the form of foreign investment is advantageous to the economies of both the lending and borrowing nations. – Krause, W.: "International Economics", pp. 459-462. When the level of income is affected changes in the level of imports and exports of the countries concerned may also be caused due to their being the functions of income. – Leighton, Richard I.: "Economics of International Trade", p. 102. The market cannot be the be all and end all of all of state policy in the newly emerging global economic order of more openness and liberalization. – Mithani, D. M.: "International Economics", Himalaya Publishing House, New Delhi, 2007, p. 524. Again, globalization has its virtues and vices well. For country, when nation building is a first thing, maximization of national product need not be the sole objective of its politician

regime (Dasgupta, 1998). Liberalization, privatization and globalization (the LPG Model) just cannot ensure developmental success and sustainability of growth to a developing country. Hence, the government in a developing economy should evolve an appropriate "mix" of the LPG Model suitable of the country's socio-economic political environment. Its macro-economic policy should reconcile both demand and supply management under the adjustments and globalization programmes and establish a socio-economic sustainability net.

101. In connection with the 'principles of equity' workers' participation in management is laudable. The workers belong to the organization and their present and future state is completely dependent on the state of affairs of the organization. Thus, success or failure of the organization is largely determined by the quantitative and qualitative contributors of the workers. They also take risks and sometimes they stake their lives. Accordingly, the principle related to equity in management should be guided by philosophy of the right of workers to take part in decision-making process at least to a certain extent. – Bose, J. P.: "An Outline of Business Organization and Management", Central Educational Enterprises, Calcutta, 1991 (Reprinted), pp. 504-523. Further, there should be co-partnership in organization for prevailing justice and fraternity in living to naturalistic work environment. By co-partnership, workers' participation in management can become complete when they are taken as partners or shares in the company are purchased by them. This is a popular method can be followed to Indian industries for motivating people more and more to involve them in the decision-making process for the purpose of increase in general welfare.

102. To understand this view, we must go to reasons why breakers plunge calls for a somewhat more scientific approach. Accordingly, it is good to say that the wave must retain most of energy right up to the moment of breaking. That is why; Bascom predicts there should be nothing, such as a rough bottom, a strong wind, or substantial currents, to make the wave prematurely unstable. Any of these conditions will degrade a wave's energy by slowing it down and warping its orbits so that it breaks gradually rather than abruptly. – Bascom, Willard: "Waves and Beaches: The Dynamics of the Ocean Surface", Anchor Books Doubleday & Company, Inc., New York, 1964, pp. 162-63. In this way, organizational delivery mechanism should be rectified for eradicating social poverty in regard to human upliftment from severe sufferings.

103. In the 1970s and 1980s, the convergence of a number of economic forces led some scholars to reexamine the notion of corporate social responsibility. – Stoner, James A. F., Freeman, R. Edward and Gilbert, Jr. Daniel R.: "Management", Pearson, 2009, p. 128. Thus, business was reeling from the one-two punch of rising energy costs and the expense of complying with legislation designed to reduce pollution, protect consumers, and ensure equal opportunity. Friedman's views represent one extreme on a continuum that recognizes some division of social responsibility among the various segments of society, including government and the business community. According to him, "There is one and only one social responsibility of business – to use its resources and energy in activities designed to increase its profits so long as it stays within the rules of the game......[and] engages in open and free competition, without deception and fraud". – Also see, Friedman, Milton: "Capitalism and Freedom", University of Chicago Press, Chicago, 1963, p. 133 and Friedman, Milton and Friedman,

Rose: "Free to Choose", Harcourt Brace Jovanovich, New York, 1980. Perception and recollection are merely vibrations of the mind; in the absence of these, in the heart, in identification with the vital force, as is said in the Vedic text, "It is the vital force indeed that engulfs all these" (Ch. IV. iii. 3). This is how; redefining the managerial perspective is assimilated with the context of organizational Prājna which is met with in the waking stage. When the mind ceases to act, the same entity assumes the characteristics of Prājna. – Seefoot note, Gambhīrānanda, Swami (Translated): "Eight Upaniṣads", p. 187. In this way, the strong backgrounds of religious truths can be applied to managerial performances in making organizations dynamic and creative oriented for the attainment of highest goal in life – human salvation through realistic nature of decision-making approach.

104. To change the societal fabric, our religions are to be made universal, and so, our own religious traditions give us ethical values and offer us a vision of peaceful co-existence. Only that we have to be conscious of it, promote it and go beyond narrow political, national, economic or military objectives. – SVD, K. Jose, Bera, Gautam K., Medhi, Birinchi K. and Athparia, R. P. (Eds.): "Concept of God and Religion: Traditional Thought and Contemporary Society", Abhijeet Publications, New Delhi, 2012, p. 160. This way, inter-group activities are to be strengthened for organizational effectiveness in bringing people to the path of forward journey in life.

105. It requires a network operated and managed by professional system of institution building, as for example, by the Institute for Development and Research in Banking Technology (IDRBT) which is poised to be used for connectivity options available in the form of virtual private networks (VPNs) over public network. – Bhalla, V. K.: "Management of Financial Services", Anmol Publications Pvt. Ltd., New Delhi, 2008, p. 295. As we know that Greeks are used by professional traders for trading and managing the risk of large positions in options, for which 'Delta' is the method that measures the sensitivity of an option's premium/price to a change in the value of the underlying asset. – Pathak, Bharati V.: "The Indian Financial System: Markets, Institutions and Services", Pearson, 2009, Chapter 12, p. 351. Similarly, human creativity can be scientifically analyzed for efficient resource management techniques, to enlarge idea of objective function dealt with the process of purposeful social order with the paradigms of organizational entity concept.

106. We can match environmental resources by means of policy initiatives in structural adjustment and the process of modernization is thus, expected to be achieved through a more rational and selective investment policy. – Thakur, Devendra (Ed.): "World Economy Today: Recent Trends", Deep & Deep Publications, New Delhi, 1993, p. 199. Human excellence building requires to be improved for the purpose of technological structural adjustment in bringing overall effectiveness in investment potentials, for accelerating the development of social infrastructure. – *Op. cit.,* p. 203. Hence, we propose to eliminate wastes through making more emphasis on wider application of various economic and financial stimuli for optimizing as well as increasing the efficiency of investment. In religious path, it is the equity in movement of human civilization should be meant to be common for all the strata of the people. Here, all human beings are

to be treated equally and this is the beginning in the right direction. – Laliwala, Jaferhusein I.: "Islamic Philosophy of Religion: Synthesis of Science, Religion and Philosophy", Sarup & Sons, New Delhi, 2005, p. 149. Human civilization will be rolling, when dogmatism, intolerance, authoritarianism will go from society, and instead, there should prevail spiritual assumptions which can protect the environment of ours for peaceful co-existence.

107. Behavioral science approach speaks in terms of human creative endeavors toward the path of global excellence through dynamic business environment. It is therefore predicted by Noel Tichy thus: "The two greatest corporate leaders of this century are Alfred Sloan of General Motors and Jack Welch of GE". – Tichy, Noel: "Leadership Power Plays", Tata McGraw-Hill Publishing Company Limited, New Delhi, 2007, p. 3. Noel is a longtime GE observer and University of Michigan management professor. Ellis (cf. Corey, 1996) outlined a seven step intervention strategy to deal with the irrational beliefs so that individual resistance to organizational change may be reduced. Thus, among his steps, one important point is that people need to accept that they are largely responsible for their own emotion and behaviour. What is necessary for increasing human innovative creativity is to acknowledge and accept the fact that they (people) possess ability to significantly alter their own emotion and behaviour. – Sharma, Radha R.: "Change Management: Concepts and Applications", Tata McGraw-Hill Publishing Company Limited, New Delhi, 2007, p. 103. Global dynamicity will come when there is accountability. Hence, Etzioni recommends: "There is a constant need to provide mechanisms of control to check on fulfillment of orders and adherence to regulation from quality specification to safety rules". – Etzioni, Amitai: "Modern Organizations", Prentice-Hall of India Private Limited, New Delhi, 1964, p. 25. Accountability is likely to increase human efficiency level, and it draws on organizational reality and helps to improve it.

108. By reducing social imbalances national economy can be developed. It is fact that economic development implies capital formation and skill formation. Thus, balance between human capital and material capital is the *sine qua none* for balanced growth of the overall economy. Taneja and Myer in their combined work have assessed thus: "The doctrine of balanced growth not only implies balance between agriculture and industry, but also a balance between human capital and material capital". – Myer, R. M. and Taneja, M. L.: "Economics of Development and Planning", Vishal Publishing Co., Delhi, 2013, p. 146. In this way, investment in human capital (i.e., expansion of education, technical knowledge, managerial skill, public health, etc.) improves the quality of manpower and increases the flow of goods and services.

109. In this regard, we may say that a prolonged period of rapid world economic growth began in 1945. The period 1945 to 1973 was a golden age for the world economy characterized by rapid increases in output and especially international trade. – Sawyer, W. Charles and Sprinkle, Richard L.: "International Economics", PHI Learning Private Limited, New Delhi, 2010, p. 14. Rationalizing industrial activities in this age of competition and globalization requires that there should be adequate balance between international economics and economic development, which can help to reduce poverty, increase industrial productivity and earn foreign exchange for the rapid growth of national economies.

The empirical research findings depict that all these results in openness and, consequently it is associated with higher levels of economic growth. – Frankel, Jeffrey A. and Romer, David: "Does Trade Cause Growth?" American Economic Review, 89 (3), June 1999, pp. 379-99. For Smith, the metaphor of the invisible hand calls attention to the paradoxical simultaneity of diversity (conflict) and community in individual interests. It seems likely that understanding of the development of economic institutions, thought, and policy will be clarified by more systematic application of the paradigm of metaphor. Robert A. Nisbet has employed the development metaphor of "genesis and decay" as the basis for understanding the essentials of social change [33]. Such applications stem from recognition that there may be a sense in which "every perspective requires a metaphor to organize it. Metaphors lie at the base of inquiry and animate it" [10, p. 119]. Thus, it reflects the view that like Hume, Adam Smith's concept of man is regarded to the dominant human end as the interests or 'welfare' of society. – Ghosh, B. N. and Ghosh, Rama: "Five Great Economists", Deep & Deep Publications, New Delhi, 1994, p. 125. Hence, rationalization requires socially motivated factors to use significantly human potentials, and religion is thus – guiding force strengthens the truth of living. Industrial activities are concerned with human upliftment, and so, religious guidelines with ethical code of conduct can preserve the greater interest of mankind.

110. Religious strategy as a mechanism for human developed pattern of understanding has yet to be tested with scientific temper of thought. The development of Muslim fundamentalism over the same period (the modern period) has produced a major confrontation between tradition and modernity......Modernity, in the sense of a knowing commitment to personal autonomy, the primacy of individual conscience, democratic politics, and an essentially secular worldview dominated by physical science, has yet to shape the majority of the world's Muslims. – Adhlakha, S. K.: "Religious Mysticism: Hinduism and Islam", Mittal Publications, New Delhi, 2005, pp. 191-92. Shankara assumes, with much (perhaps the mainstream) of higher Hindu culture, that reality is ideal, spiritual, and best understood by concentrating the spirit, mind, and heart on the pure being that grounds all beings. – *Ibid.,* p. 83. Thus, religious strategy can be innovative things for taking responsibility to rebuild social segment with the Vedanta sutra (Shankara's greatest work). The Hindu culture is famous for human development as it amplifies the goal of social beings in the midst of karma (work philosophy) in spiritualizing life order – being and knowledge that are spiritual and not bound by karma. – *Op. cit.,* p. 77. The Upanishads are famous in the sense that the most sacred word of the Hindus, occurring first in the Upanishads. There is strategy for universal issues, and accordingly, social responsibility mechanism can be founded through the Sanatana practices, as depicted earlier.

111. The developmental strategy of India should be framed in such a way that it can integrate all elements of progress in unified nature. Accordingly, after independence, India evolved a strategy to become a self-reliant and self-sustaining economy. – Gupta, Sanju: "India's Foreign Policy", Pearson, Delhi, 2012, p. 169. Here, it is important to note that our castes and creed problems, and problems of religious biasness have made barriers in ideological, political and economical frontiers, for which state intervention from time to time in a country

like India where there is large area, vast population, natural resources and the like, have created enormous problems for steady development.

112. A deed, if we conceive it broadly enough, may be a beckoning hand to progress rather than a dead hand on development. – Barker, Sir Ernest: "Essays on Government", Oxford University Press, London, 1951 (Second Edition), p. 119. So, organizational policies are to be framed to maintain civil liberty, which leave the subject entire master of his own conduct, except in those points where in the public good requires some direction or restraint. – *Ibid.,* p. 139. It is to be noted that Blackstone, true to the genius of English law, makes no distinction between 'the constitution or framework of government' and 'the system of laws'. In America, beginning with the colonial constitution of 1776, that distinction is always drawn. However, on policy initiatives it is essential to the preservation of liberty and the maintenance of rights. Emotions, loyalties, feelings, chivalries – these are things that count, and count profoundly.

113. Amnesty International and other non-governmental organizations have been calling on the United Nations (UN) to investigate and report on complaints of torture for many years. – Bogohain, Bani: "Human Rights: Social Justice and Political Challenge", Kanishka Publishers, Distributors, New Delhi, 2007, p. 226. This philosophic basis has led to something of a paradox when it is applied to questions of foreign policy. When Lincoln described the United Nations as the "last best hope of earth", he was asserting that the United States was the model for the development of other countries but that it could have an effect on them only by the power of its exchange. – *Op. cit.,* p. 47. The UN agency is not primarily concerned with economic issues. Rather, it is concerned with the effects of economic growth on some of the noneconomic aspects of economic development. – Sawyer, W. Charles and Sprinkle Richard L.: "International Economics", PHI Learning Private Limited, New Delhi, 2010, p. 270. For further information, see the discussion in Eltis (1997). The end of French power is this area was not related to trade or production misfortunes, but rather to a successful uprising of the slave population in 1791 in what was to become Haiti, leading to independence in 1804 … … A prime example of the ways in which institutions may have contributed to the persistence of inequality over the long run is land policy. See Gates (1968) for a comprehensive overview of U. S. land policy. Discussions of Canadian land policy include Solberg (1987); Pomfret (1981, pp. 111-19); Adelman (1994, Chap. 2). As human, we find it relatively difficult to identify the areas where we are weak. – Deb, Tapomoy: "Human Resource Development: Theory & Practice", Ane Books Pvt. Ltd., New Delhi, 2012, (Reprinted), p. 225. The integrative framework offered by Yeung and Berman (1997) identifies three paths through which human resource development practices can contribute to business performance: (i) by building organizational capabilities; (ii) by improving employee satisfaction; and (iii) by shaping customer and shareholder's satisfaction. Thus, pathetic conditions by which people have been living in the world environment can be remedied through effective human resource development policy.

114. In this context, another very important change that has come about in recent times in the case of both the East and the West is in regard to their attitude of investment in human beings or what T. W. Shultz has called "human capital". It was long back realized in the United States, the most representative country of

the capitalist world, on the basis of the empirical enquires by M. Abramovitz and T. W. Schultz that the greater part of the product was due to the "investment in human capital rather than in physical capital". – Mishra, Jagannath (Ed.): "India's Economic Development", Vikas Publishing House Pvt. Ltd., New Delhi, 1984, p. 126. It is therefore essential that leadership role should be concerned with the issues of human emancipation for global level dynamicity.

115. A recent survey shows that even poverty-focused programmes with a "commitment" to achieving financial sustainability cover only about 70 per cent of their full costs (Micro Banking Bulletin, 1998). Again, it is observed that fixed costs represent more than 80 per cent of water service costs in the United Kingdom (Armstrong et. al., 1994). Now-a-days, excessive primary strains the whole urban system, absorbing resources that might go to other cities to improve the general quality of life. – Meier, Gerald M. and Rauch, James E.: "Leading Issues in Economic Development", Oxford University Press, New Delhi, 2006, p. 342. To assess organizational activities readers are suggested to go through Bates, Robert H.: "Governments and Agricultural Markets in Africa", 1983, in D. Gale Johnson and G. Edward Schuh (Eds.): "The Role of Markets in the World Food Economy", Boulder, Co.: Westview. From the study of public investment scenario in our countries, it reflects that there is overall lost in public investment at least five per cent of investment. That figure was multiplied by the average annual public investment in the Third Five Year Plan. – The Santhanam Committee, pp. 11-12. Again, Jones and Sakong also express doubt about the relationship between authoritarianism and autonomy in the case of Korea: "Until the early 1970s, the Pak regime was both hard and reasonably democratic" (1980, p. 140). All these pictures relate to the view that organizational entities and world business establishments are required to be given better scope to reduce social inequalities, for the purpose of global balance restoration in terms of employment, poverty eradication, and all other social building activities.

116. Due to human conflicting affairs, there has been dehumanization. There are various ways in which the conflict in man can be represented. – Mason, Philip: "Race Relations", Oxford University Press, London, 1970, p. 55. Inner conflict arises due to life in society. The child is observed born in selfish today. The child may, of course, take as his own a system identical with that of the parents, and this is what is likely to happen in a closely knit and static form of society. – *Op. cit.,* pp. 54-55. The conflict and sense of inadequacy are extreme where the antagonism is crudely violent. But if, they are expressed more politely, they are either less strong or more under control. For further detail, we may refer to Freud's teaching, his account of the structure of the personality ... ... Also see, Barnicot, N. A.: "Biology and Human Variation", in Race, May 1960; Dunn, L. C.: "Race and Biology", Paris, UNESCO, 1951; Fanon, F.: "The Wretched of the Earth", MacGibbon and Kee, London, 1965. All these reflect how dehumanization is created in modern societies due to lack of control mechanism through human personality studies in scientific temper of thought, and to use religious truths for bringing fundamental change in society.

117. To match this kind of idea, it is necessary that even costal living populations are required special attention. As for example, it can be said that the Nicobarese villages in the Great Nicobar Island are situated lineally on the western coast along the sea-shore; where, it is found that the landscape of the tribal villages is

not provided with any road. The adjacent villages are connected with irregular and indistinct foot tracks either through the dense forest or by the sea-coast. – Prokashnanda, Anshu: "The Nicobarese of Great Nicobar: An Ethnography", Gyan Publishing House, New Delhi, 1993, p. 14. Thus, it is clear that religious models rather being used for conflicting situations could well be implemented for matching life-style of such population for adequate development.

118. "Periods of rapid social change", observes Lewis, "are often associated with religious ferment – whether we think of the rise of capitalism in Europe or of Contemporary events in Africa and if we are assessing the role of religion we must take into account of the reforming zeal of the new religion just as much as of the resistance offered by the old". – Lewis, W. Arthur: Op. cit., p. 104. Caste-stratification prevents that close correspondence between in born capacity and economic activity which is so fundamental an element in economic progress and welfare. – Sinha, M. R. (Ed.): "Modernising Indian Economy", Asian Studies Press, Bombay, 1967, p. 89. "We do not know", rightly observes Ketkar, "how much harm is being done to the economic activity of the people, by putting man in the wrong places, denying as it does equal opportunities to all". – Ketkar, S. V.: "Indian Economics", Chapter on 'Social Institutes'. "As long as the village predominates", rightly observes Kingsley, Davis, "caste will be hard to eradicate, especially since it is now deeply rooted in the religion and morals of the Hindus". – Davis, Kingsley: *Op. cit.,* p. 175. Even land-ownership exists frequently on caste lines. It has shaped the culture-pattern and the psychology of various social groups. The system has developed "such minutely graded levels of social distance and superior-inferior relationships that the social structure looks like a gigantic hierarchic pyramid with a mass of untouchables as its base and a small stratum of elite, the Brahmins, almost equally unapproachable, as its apex". – Desai, A. R.: "Rural Sociology in India", p. 40. There is a direct relation between functions and property ownership and the type of the caste. The poor countries have to achieve, on the one hand, the economic standards of the advanced countries, and, on the other, many of them have to cope with their increasing populations. Thus, the process of economic transformation may be held up for a long time by the static nature of religion. It is thus, worthwhile to analyze the relations between religion and economic growth, in so far as we are concerned with social welfare problems. If religious attitudes and institutions encourage discipline, hardwork, efficiency, honesty and thrift among its followers, the social climate will impel people to apply their minds to increasing productivity, to acquire wealth and to improve their social prestige and power.

119. Here, it is also important to note that the present trend of population growth in India is not desirable and while formulating any economic policy, particular emphasis on the question of food must be given. – Agrawal, Naresh Chandra: "The Food Problem of India", Vora & Co. Publishers Private Ltd., Bombay, 1961, p. 150. Rebuilding global society on balanced situation of human living parameters can strengthen the peaceful business and economic environment. Hence, universality of scientific theories, including economic theories, therefore, does not mean "as it was in the beginning, is now and ever shall be, world without end". – Kurien, C. T.: "A Theoretical Approach to the Indian Economy", Asia Publishing House, New Delhi, 1970, p. 24. In decision-making approach, it is to be felt that technological progress is the major source of economic growth.–

Weil, David N.: "Economic Growth", Dorling Kindersley India Pvt. Ltd., New Delhi, 2009, p. 299.

120. In eliminating social ills and mismatches, we are needed to meet our targets of full utilization, and thus; we need also expansionary measures that are large in relation to excess unemployment. – Okun, Arthur M. (Ed.): "The Battle against Unemployment", W. W. Norton & Company, Inc., New York, 1965, p. 22. Letches can be overcome, "considering the numerous interests involved ... ... (also) its bearing on the relations of the U. K. with India and on British commerce as well as Indian trade". – See "Chapman's Note in Selections etc.", *Op. cit.*, p. 325. In the advanced countries of the West, however, the rise in per capita income continued long enough to bring subsequent drops in fertility rates and to permit economic growth to be sustained.–Higgins, Benjamin: "Economic Development: Problems, Principles, and Policies", Universal Book Stall, New Delhi, 1996 (Reprint), pp. 296-97. So, value-based idea of guiding economic activities can be implemented through religious philosophy; so that people are educated for civic living pursuits in terms of confidence building measures, to overcome problems of social ills and blind ideas. Corruption is severe disease in modern days. The craving for materialism and status, the greed for money and power, combined with low moral values are all signs of inferiority complexes and are fertile breeding grounds for corruption. – Khera, Shiv: "Freedom is not Free: Every Generation Needs to Earn Its Own Freedom", Macmillan India Ltd., Delhi, 2008, p. 105. Thus, a wholly corrupted system affects every area of a citizen's life. But, it can be curbed, as for examples nations like England, Hong Kong, Singapore and Sweden are such countries have beaten it and created enlightened environments. There is, however, a common thread that makes people work in harmony and cooperation. It is honesty, unity and patience in the midst of diversity. Religious tolerance is among the best alternatives, untouchables is the another principle of winning in the game of life.

121. In many a 'Third World' society, the life cycle distinction between a child and adult self is cut brutally short. Heeding children's voices justifying their self-exploitation. In the early histories of colonialism that emerge as a form of mercantilist domination by chartered joint stock companies, the relationship among European mercenaries and missionaries were deeply conflicted. – Baxi, Upendra: "The Future of Human Rights", Third Edition, Oxford University Press, New Delhi, 2006. The transition from horticultural to agricultural society was made possible largely through the invention of the plow (Lenski and Lenski, 1978: 177-179). The industrial society is based primarily on the application of science and technology to the production of goods and services. – Shepard, Jon M.: "Sociology", West Publishing Company, New York, 1981, p. 89. The agricultural economy developed two basic sections – a rural agricultural sector and an urban commercial and handicraft sector. Institutional specialization was also reflected in the increasing separation of political and religious elites. – *Ibid.*, p. 89. All these are attributed to the case of democratic leadership guided by philosophy of changing social trends, for determining as how initiatives are to be taken for people's development. Religious strategies are to be reformed in line with participative system for maximum delivery and hence, the modern tools and techniques of social changing norms are required to be resolved in organizational guiding philosophy.

122. To safeguard the humanity the United Nations Development Program (UNDP) has also taken measures for annual evaluation of matters relating to human development. – Mazumder, A., Datta, D., Biswas, S. (Eds.): "Human Development: Perspectives and Dimensions", Research Publication Cell, Women's College, Silchar, 2013, pp. 151-52. The concepts of social justice, equality, extended periphery of human rights etc., has made the problem of human resource development face a complex and tangled question. Lack of educated workers has been observed as an obstacle to the continued rapid economic growth in many countries. – Meier, Gerald M. and Rauch, James E.: "Leading Issues in Economic Development", Oxford University Press, New York, 2004, p. 216. Everybody should be having an independent chance of coming up with an idea that will benefit the rest of the human race (Ray, Debraj: 1998, p. 335), and therefore, we must combine technical progress to a diverse population; so that human civilization has been rolling in right direction with initiatives of human development process. Modern organizational managers should know the art of working in bringing positive and abrupt social change, for which human basic needs are to be satisfied with timeframe schedule. Social thinkers, leaders are to act as an innovator in the line of social inclusion of people to benefit marginal sections, in making on the foundation of existential freedom for peaceful social living environment.

Index